T0339890

Smart Economic Decision-Making in a Complex World

Smart Economic Decision-Making in a Complex World

Morris Altman
University of Dundee, School of Business, Nethergate,
Dundee, Scotland, United Kingdom

ACADEMIC PRESS

An imprint of Elsevier

Academic Press is an imprint of Elsevier
125 London Wall, London EC2Y 5AS, United Kingdom
525 B Street, Suite 1650, San Diego, CA 92101, United States
50 Hampshire Street, 5th Floor, Cambridge, MA 02139, United States
The Boulevard, Langford Lane, Kidlington, Oxford OX5 1GB, United Kingdom

Notices
Knowledge and best practice in this field are constantly changing. As new research and
experience broaden our understanding, changes in research methods, professional practices, or
medical treatment may become necessary.

Practitioners and researchers must always rely on their own experience and knowledge in
evaluating and using any information, methods, compounds, or experiments described herein.
In using such information or methods they should be mindful of their own safety and the safety
of others, including parties for whom they have a professional responsibility.

To the fullest extent of the law, neither the Publisher nor the authors, contributors, or editors,
assume any liability for any injury and/or damage to persons or property as a matter of products
liability, negligence or otherwise, or from any use or operation of any methods, products,
instructions, or ideas contained in the material herein.

Library of Congress Cataloging-in-Publication Data
A catalog record for this book is available from the Library of Congress

British Library Cataloguing-in-Publication Data
A catalogue record for this book is available from the British Library

ISBN 978-0-12-811461-2

For information on all Academic Press publications
visit our website at https://www.elsevier.com/books-and-journals

Publisher: Candice Janco
Acquisitions Editor: Brain Romer
Editorial Project Manager: Susan Ikeda
Production Project Manager: Vignesh Tamil
Cover Designer: Mark Rogers

Typeset by SPi Global, India

Dedication

This book is dedicated to the memory of the late John Tomer, who passed in late 2019, a dear friend and colleague for over a quarter of a century, with whom I shared a dream of building a behavioural economics community that was broad based, open-minded, and critical. John devoted his life to his family (his wife Doris and his sons Russell and Jeffrey and their families) and to building a more human-centred, reality-based economics.

Endorsements

"Contemporary behavioral economics often downplays the founding work of Nobel Laureate Herbert Simon and the Carnegie School. Morris Altman shows that Simon's original behavioral economics can still offer much insight, particularly in highly complex contexts. Going beyond the focus on 'errors and biases' in much of current behavioral economics, Altman develops a rich, dynamic analysis, stressing the role of institutional and environmental factors in decision-making. This is an extremely important book."
—Geoff Hodgson, Professor in Management,
Loughborough University London

"Morris Altman's understanding of behavioral economics is broad and far-reaching. In this book he has drawn on the history of economic thought, economics and ethics, and the methodology of economics to explain how behavioral economics has changed the goals and trajectory of recent economics. Especially valuable is his attention to Herbert Simon's early contribution and those of Gerd Gigerenzer and his colleagues to an ecological economics. Altman's assessment of Daniel Kahneman and Amos Tversky's influential work is perceptive and fresh. This book will be very useful to scholars and students looking for a full understanding of this important development in contemporary economic thinking, and is strongly recommended."
—John Davis, Professor Emeritus of Economics,
Marquette University

"Altman has written an excellent evolution of behavioral economics, and how it is similar and different from neoclassical theory. Anyone interested in behavioral economics will find this book interesting and informative."
—Roger Frantz, Professor Emeritus of Economics,
San Diego State University

Contents

Acknowledgements   xiii

1. **Introduction: Smart thinking in the real world of complexity**

   What this book is all about   10
   Appendix: Background sources for, smart economic decision-
       making in a complex world   14
   References   15

2. **The evolution of decision-making: Why institutions and capabilities matters**

   Introduction   17
   Assumptions matter and behavioural economics   19
   The conventional wisdom and the different faces of
       behavioural economics   20
   The bounded rationality approach in context   22
   Satisficing and procedural rationality in context   29
   X-efficiency theory and external benchmarks for
       optimal behaviour   31
   Nudging versus constraints change and redesign   32
   Conclusion   33
   References   35

3. **How complexity affects decision-making**

   Introduction   39
   Key points of overlap: Hayek and behavioural economics   40
   Assumptions matter   42
   Revisiting complexity and the expert   48
   Contemporary views on bottom-up decision making and
       individualized norms for rationality   51
   Ecological rationality and the spontaneous order   58
   Opening the door to intelligent design   60
   Opening the door to multiple equilibria: Casting shadows on the
       spontaneous order and ecological rationality   63
   Conclusion: Hayek's Golden nugget in decision-making theory   68
   References   71

4. Freedom of choice in a complex world
    Introduction   75
    Multiple equilibria in consumption   79
    Multiple equilibria in production: An introduction   80
    Multiple equilibria in production: X-inefficiency and
        managerial slack   82
    Multiple equilibria in production: X-inefficiency and agency   84
    Multiple equilibria in production: Some related scenarios   86
    Historical and logical time   87
    Rent seeking and x-efficiency   87
    Conclusion   88
    References   90

5. Understanding rational inefficiency: A scientific
    basis for economic failure and success
    Introduction   93
    Introducing rationality and rational inefficiency   94
    Institutions, efficiency, and rationality   99
    Different types of rationality   102
    Production inefficiency   107
    Consumption inefficiencies   115
    Macroeconomic choices and rational behaviour   120
    Conclusion   125
    References   127

6. How consumers can achieve freedom of choice:
    When consumers are truly sovereign
    Introduction   131
    An alternative model of preference formation   132
    Conventional perspectives and critiques   134
    Constructing an alternative theory of welfare maximization   136
    Choice x-inefficiency and x-inefficiency in production   142
    Conclusion   142
    References   144

7. Inside the black box of the firm: Why choice,
    power and preferences matter for productivity
    and efficiency
    Introduction   147
    Origins of efficiency wage theory   150
    Real wages, effort variability, and efficiency wages   151
    Efficiency wage theory revised   156
    Foundations of x-efficiency theory   163
    Linking x-efficiency and efficiency theories   178

Conclusion   183
References   185

8. How smart people can be involuntarily employment
    when misguided policy dominates decision-making
    Introduction   189
    Keynes and the real wage rate   191
    Keynes and the demand side   195
    The behavioural model and employment   198
    Conclusion   206
    References   207

9. Why financial literacy matters for socio-economic
    wellbeing
    Introduction   211
    The conventional wisdom   215
    Fast and frugal decision-making and smart heuristics   216
    Institutions matter   218
    Errors and biases and 'irrational' heuristics   219
    Financial education and literacy and the different faces of
        behavioural economics   222
    Linkages between financial issues, financial education, and
        financial literacy   224
    Pensions and saving   224
    Investing in financial assets   227
    Bubbles and busts: Animal spirits and decision-making   228
    Informational problems and errors in decision making   232
    The trust heuristic   233
    Ponzi schemes and the trust heuristic   234
    Conclusion: Economic theory, financial literacy and public
        policy   236
    References   242

10. How labour markets really work
    Introduction   245
    What is behavioural labour economics   246
    Modelling labour supply: A standard rendering   247
    A behavioural model of labour supply: A target approach   250
    Non-labour market income and labour supply   255
    Unemployment insurance and labour supply   257
    Non-economic variables and errors or biases in labour market
        decision-making   258
    Demand for labour and the supply of effort   262
    Efficiency wage and x-efficiency theory   265

**Some labour market implications of generalized x-efficiency
theory**   269
Population growth with real women   272
Conclusion   274
References   275

Index   281

Acknowledgements

Thanks to my research assistant, Daisy Jarrett, who was completing her undergraduate degree in economics at the University of Newcastle, Australia.

Many thanks to Louise Lamontagne, my wife and partner of over 40 years, for her many insightful comments on this manuscript. I also thank our daughter, Hannah Altman, now working on her PhD in economics, for her many excellent and thoughtful comments on this book manuscript.

Thanks to the Elsevier team for their excellent work on this book. Special thanks to Susan Ikeda and also to Graham Nisbet who supported getting this project off the ground. I also thank Vignesh Tamilselvvan for the copyediting of this book.

Chapter 1

Introduction: Smart thinking in the real world of complexity

Chapter outline

What this book is all about	10	References	15
Appendix: Background sources for, smart economic decision-making in a complex world	14		

A fundamental point that I make in this book is that individuals tend to be smart and are capable of making decisions that are in their own best interest.[a] But their decisions are impacted by their decision-making environment and their decision-making capabilities (which include bargaining power and human and gender rights). Gaps in this environment and their capabilities, which should be expected in the real world of complexity and differential power relationships, can result in decisions that are not best or 'optimal' from the point of view of the individual. But this has more to do with circumstances that are exogenous; largely beyond the control of the individual. Ultimately, people end up making smart decisions, doing the best they can (or satisficing) given their particular circumstances.[b] But these smart individuals can make poor or error-prone decisions given the constraints and opportunities (or lack thereof) which they face. And, these sub-optimal decisions can be improved upon by changing their decision-making environment and their decision-making capabilities (Altman, 2017a, 2017b).

This does not mean that smart decision-makers (concerned with their own wellbeing or even that of their families or close friends) will be intent on doing the best for their communities, firms, or even households. Their smart, intelligent, or rational behaviour can be harmful to others. As economists would put it, individual behaviour can have negative externalities. This problem can be fixed by repairing the decision-making environment so that individuals bear the cost of their socially pernicious behaviour (Thaler & Sunstein, 2008).

---

a. The concept of smart decision-making is introduced and elaborated up in Altman (2017).

b. Satisficing is a term coined by Simon to refer to behaviour that is not optimizing (as would be the case in standard or conventional economics). Rather, individuals are doing the best they can given their decision-making environments and capabilities.

Smart Economic Decision-Making in a Complex World. https://doi.org/10.1016/B978-0-12-811461-2.00001-8
1

Overall, I argue, one should respect the preferences of individuals. Individuals, however, require the environment and capabilities to construct informed preferences and make choices that improve their wellbeing without causing harm to others. One should not be bent on forcing and manipulating individuals to make choices that experts prefer, unless free choice causes harm to others.

This book builds upon the research of Herbert Simon and, more generally, the Carnegie-Mellon school of behavioural economics. I refer to this approach to behavioural economics as the bounded rationality methodological approach to behavioural economics (Altman, 1999, 2005, 2015, 2017a, 2017b).[c] In this perspective, the prior assumption is that decision-makers are relatively rational, intelligent and smart (satisficing, boundedly rational and evolutionarily rational). As one of the intellectual leaders of the Carnegie-Mellon school, James March (1978, p. 589) stated, it is of primary importance to determine if we can explain human behaviour in terms of rationality, broadly defined, even if at first glance such behaviour does not appear rational and might even appear to be error-prone or 'biased'. More generally, I refer to this methodological approach as smart decision-making (Altman, 2017a, 2017b), which encompasses bounded rationality, procedural rationality, fast and frugal heuristics, slow and fast thinking, the brain as a scarce resource (following the insights of Freidrich Hayek) and the institutional, sociological and psychological-neurological determinants of decision-making. This is counter-posed to the world view of conventional or neoclassical rationality as well as the heuristics and biases perspective on behavioural economics, pioneered by Kahneman and Tversky (Kahneman, 2003, 2011), that now dominates contemporary behavioural economics. This perspective is closely tied to the nudging approach to public policy wherein one serious point of focus is assuming that experts can drive welfare enhancing decisions on behalf of highly biased and, moreover, persistently biased individuals.

Smart decision-making encompasses intelligent or smart decision-makers or agents, who develop or adopt decision-making processes and make decisions given their cognitive limitations, the decision-making mechanism of the brain, individuals (or economic agents) decision-making capabilities, decision-making experience, environmental factors, which include institutional and legal parameters, culture and norms, relative power in the decision-making process and related sociological factors. It is also recognized that cognitive limitations are affected by technology (computers and calculators, for example), the capabilities to effectively use new or improved technologies and the learning processes that affect how the brain is hardwired (neuroplasticity). Smart decision-makers or agents do the best they can, given the pertinent circumstances that affect the decision-making process and related outcomes. Herbert Simon refers to the act of doing the best we can as satisficing behaviour. Satisficing, however, need not

---

c. My research is also influenced, for example, by the contributions of Harvey Leibenstein (x-efficiency theory), George Akerlof (asymmetric information), Douglass North (the importance of institutions), and Martha Nussbaum and Amartya Sen (the significance of capabilities to decision-making).

result in the best possible or optimal outcomes for the firm, household, society or individual; but it can, depending on circumstances.

Deviations from optimality do not imply that decision-makers are not smart and in this sense irrational. Nor does establishing that decision-makers are smart imply that decision-making outcomes are optimal. Here rationality, broadly defined, relates to the choices people make and the decision-making processes adopted by individuals given their various constraints and opportunities as well as their decision-making environment. Optimality in production and consumption at an individual, firm, household or social level need not necessarily flow from smart decision-making. Smart decision-making, however, would often be a necessary but not a sufficient condition for optimality to be obtained. What these sufficient conditions might be are critically important to research that stems from the smart agent or smart decision-making perspective.

Inadequate decision-making environments, for example, would preclude smart agents from achieving optimal results from their own and from society's perspective (where externalities exist). For example, you might wish to increase your savings for retirement, but you invest in high-risk high-return financial paper because of the false or misleading financial information provided to you, resulting in you losing much of your savings. You might employ a low wage strategy for your firm because you are adopting (with good intent) a false mental model (theoretical framework) on the impact of higher wages of firm competitiveness. Women might want to have one child, but they end up giving birth to four or five, because they are not empowered to realize their preferences. A firm's productivity might not be maximized because decision-makers are maximizing a complex utility function that includes managerial slack and short-term returns. None of the above is a product of irrationality. They are a product of preferences, misleading information, false mental models, decision-making capabilities, experience and the overarching decision-making environment.

Conventional theory's point of focus is on very generalized concepts related to how humans should behave and are expected to behave to generate optimal outcomes. As long as the analytical prediction is correct, all is well. This is effectively the correlation-based analysis promoted by Friedman (1953). If you get the prediction correct, you can assume for reasons of simplicity that humans behave as if they are maximizing profits, minimizing costs and maximizing utility (which is often assumed to be identical wealth maximization, controlling for risk). The realism of the simplifying assumptions we make about decision-makers, the decision-making processes and the decision-making environment are not of importance from this perspective. We can simply assume that individuals behave as if they are maximizing profits or utility, as long as the analytical prediction is the correct prediction (Berg & Gigerenzer, 2010). The assumption here is that individuals ideally should behave 'neoclassically', if they are rational, which they are assumed to be. Rationality is defined in terms of neoclassical rationality. Apart from this, what transpires in the decision-making process is not of substantive interest. We simply abide methodologically with neoclassical simplifying assumptions of how individuals behave within the firm and in the household. Moreover, it is further assumed that the decision-making environment allows for the realization of optimal outcomes, given neoclassical rationality, for the individual, the household and the firm.

The analytical focus, therefore, is on correlation as opposed to true causation, where the latter relates to determining what particular behaviours and decision-making environments generate particular outcomes. Modelling true causation would address issues of spurious correlation, omitted variables and the possibility of alternative behaviours, yielding similar sustainable outcomes. What is key is the determination of what specific behaviours, decision-making processes and institutional and sociological variables yield specific outcomes. This deeper modelling agenda is part of the bounded rationality approach to behavioural economics.

The bounded rationality tradition in behavioural economics plays particular attention to identifying the actual decision-making process that generates particular outcomes. It ventures into the black box of the firm, the household and the individual. Only by understanding how individuals actually behave, how they make decisions, can we determine if these decisions are smart and in this broad sense rational. Hence, rationality here is contextualized. Benchmarks for what is rational are, therefore, not constructed by some imagined ideal unrelated to the decision-making capabilities and environments of the individual, household or firm.

For this reason, a core attribute of the approach taken in this book is, following from Simon, the overall importance of reasonable, reality-based, simplifying modelling assumptions for robust economic analysis. Related to this is the significance of situating our definition of rationality and smart decision-making in context. Simon writes (1986, p. s209):

> *The judgment that certain behavior is 'rational' or 'reasonable' can be reached only by viewing the behavior in the context of a set of premises or 'givens.' These givens include the situation in which the behavior takes place, the goals it is aimed at realizing, and the computational means available for determining how the goals can be attained. In the course of this conference, many participants referred to the context of behavior as its 'frame,' a label that I will also use from time to time. Notice that the frame must be comprehensive enough to encompass goals, the definition of the situation, and computational resources.*

The smart agent, smart decision-making approach to decision-making and behavioural economics not only stands in contrast to what we find in much of conventional economics, it also stands in contrast, as mentioned above, to a theme running through much of contemporary behavioural economics where much of the typical individual's behaviour is deemed irrational and error-prone (Altman, 2017a, 2017b). This is the heuristics and biases approach pioneered by Kahneman and Tversky (Kahneman, 2003, 2011). A common thread running through this approach and conventional economics is adopting neoclassical benchmarks for rationality and, flowing from this, benchmarks for optimal outcomes in the domain of consumption and production (although the latter is not a point of focus in the heuristics and biases approach). In the heuristics and biases approach, as in conventional economics, these various benchmarks are not empirically derived. Rather they are taken for granted. As in the conventional approach, causal analysis is not the point of focus, and it appears that analytical prediction (correlation analysis) is of greatest significance. However, in the heuristics and biases approach psychological factors are introduced into the modelling framework to supplement or replace economic variables. Typically, such new variables are said to generate deviations from neoclassical optimality and, therefore, errors in decision-making. This is often derived from assumed, but not proven, hardwired biases in the human decision-maker. However, in terms of the derivation and introduction of psychological variables, these are often *not* predicated upon an assessment of how individuals behave within the household and the firm. Rather, they are generalized descriptors of human behaviour introduced into the modelling framework to produce improved analytical predictions or predictions that are as robust as those generated in conventional models, but now contain more 'realistic' behavioural assumptions. To reiterate, the realism of these new assumptions is typically not tested against how individuals actually behave in the real world of decision-making.

A point of commonality between the bounded rationality approach, the broader smart agent approach and the heuristics and biases approach is recognizing that real-world decision-makers typically do not behave like the individuals in the traditional economic models. We should note that Becker (1996), for example, makes a similar point with regard to neoclassical models ignoring sociological variables to their analytical and scientific peril. He argues that neoclassical predictions are often wrong because they systematically ignore how social context impacts the decisions of rational agents. North (1971) makes a similar point with respect to neoclassical economics systematically ignoring the importance of institutional variables to decision-making by rational agents. Both sociological and institutional parameters affecting decision-making are crucial to the smart agent approach to decision-making.

Especially with respect to the heuristic and biases approach, a large scholarly industry has developed documenting the extent to which actual human behaviour deviates from predicted neoclassical behaviour. More generally, experimental economics, often done in classroom settings, has documented significant deviations from neoclassical norms. The fact that individuals tend not to behave neoclassically is no big surprise, even to many neoclassical economists. The latter simply assume that individuals behave as if they make decisions and choices based on neoclassical norms, not that they actually behave in this fantastical manner.

Still this research remains important as it disabuses economists (theoretical and applied), model users and various types of practitioners, including policymakers, from the notion that humans behave neoclassically. The big question is what does this actually means for analysis and policy? Experiments suggest that, on average, individuals engage in wide array of behaviours that are contrary to what conventional economics assumes. For example:

- Individuals weigh losses more than gains.
- Emotions and intuition drive much of decision-making.
- Individuals are willing to self-sacrifice to punish those who they deem are treating them unfairly.
- Individuals are willing to punish or hurt those they don't like.
- Individuals are willing self-sacrifice for those who they feel sympathy towards.
- Ethical concerns play a role in economics decision-making.
- Wealth maximization, even when controlled for risk, finds many exceptions.
- Framing affects choices.
- Relative positioning often matters more than absolute levels of income or wealth.
- Sentiment or animal spirits often matter more to decision-making than 'real' economic variables.
- Individuals often follow the leader when making decisions (herding).

Are these 'average' human traits a sign of hardwired cognitive biases, yielding suboptimal choices, as the heuristics and biases approach intimates? Or, are these characteristics of smart agents given their capabilities, experience and decision-making environment, even when some of their decisions are wrong, at least in the first instance (a one-shot game)?

This is where the smart agent or smart decision-making approach and bounded rationality approach part company with the heuristics and biases approach. From the smart agent approach, deviations from neoclassical norms typically implies that rational decision-makers do not abide by these norms for good rational reasons that need to be identified and understood to better engage in robust causal analysis. From the heuristics and biases approach, deviations from the neoclassical norms implies systemic biases and errors in decision-making, typically a function of how the brain is hardwired. Human do not and typically cannot behave the way they should behave to obtain optimal outcomes. Freewill in decision-making can result in perverse socio-economic outcomes that can sometimes be corrected by experts nudging individuals to behave in the appropriate fashion as defined and articulated by the expert (referred to in the literature as the choice architect) (Thaler & Sunstein, 2008).

From the smart decision-making perspective, errors in decision-making can and do occur. There can be biases in decision-making, individuals can make decisions that are not in their own self-interest or they can make decisions in their self-interest but not in the interest of their group, organization or society, and preferences can be inconsistent across individuals and within an individual across historical time. All such non-traditional behaviours can be consistent with the hypothesis that economic agents are smart and, broadly speaking, rational. Moreover, these smart agents need not generate choices that are in any sense efficient. This is in stark contrast to the conventional approach wherein being 'rational' implies efficient outcomes. However, rationality need not imply efficiency or optimality in either consumption or production.

Not conforming to neoclassical behavioural norms need not be symptomatic of irrationality, and free will in choice behaviour in and of itself need not result, therefore, in perverse socio-economic outcomes. Errors and biases and suboptimal socio-economic outcomes, for example, can be the product of inadequacies in decision-making capabilities, suboptimal decision-making environments and lack of experience. In this sense rationality does not mean perfection in actual behaviour or outcomes. Of critical importance is the determination of the conditions under which decisions and the decision-making processes can be improved upon; under what circumstances can rational or smart decision-making result in efficiency or optimality in either consumption or production? Identifying these circumstances is a critically important research agenda.

Also, non-neoclassical behaviours can generate superior outcomes to those that flow from traditional neoclassical norms, such as narrowly maximizing behaviour. In other words, conforming to neoclassical behavioural norms can generate suboptimal outcomes and might therefore even signal irrationality in behaviour or at least serious biases and errors in decision-making. Gigerenzer (2007) and his colleagues have articulated this perspective in their fast and frugal heuristics narrative. Heuristics (decision-making short cuts), often considered to be biased and error-prone in the heuristics and biases narrative, is argued to exemplify superior decision-making processes in the fast and frugal modelling of decision-making. From this perspective individuals have evolved decision-making processes that are partially derived from the fact that the brain is a scarce resource, has a particular processing capability and processes information within a particular decision-making environment. A prior assumption here is that individuals are broadly speaking rational. Hence, it is important to investigate whether, and the extent to which, non-neoclassical behavioural norms (such as fast and frugal heuristics) yield superior outcomes, and under what circumstances.

At one extreme it could be argued that not only are individuals always rational, but their decision-making processes and decisions are always optimal as well. This perspective is derived from Hayek and his notion of ecological rationality (Gigerenzer, 2007; Hayek, 1948; Smith, 2003). But it is critical to determine benchmarks for smart or broadly rational behaviour and, moreover, contextualized benchmarks for efficiency and optimality in decision-making outcomes. In other words, fast and frugal heuristics, need not generate superior or, more broadly speaking, optimal outcomes. Using a particular heuristic does not imply optimality simply because the decision-maker is smart. Smart decision-making is not a necessary and sufficient condition for efficiency and optimality.

Kahneman (2011) has articulated a categorization of different types of decision-making, which he refers to as slow and fast thinking. He is basically looking at when particular thought processes yield better outcomes. Sometimes these might be fast thinking (fast and frugal); very often these would be slow thinking. Some would argue that individuals do not know which type of thinking best serves their own self-interest and that of their organization and, all too often, individuals make the wrong choices as to which thinking decision-making platform to use. This would be contrary to the fast and frugal approach that maintains that typically individuals make the right choices with regard to decision-making platforms. From the smart decision-making perspective, it is a testable hypothesis as to which thinking platform would be best. This hypothesis needs to be contextualized by the capabilities and experience of individuals and their decision-making environment. Therefore, it is possible that individuals will adopt heuristics and make choices that are sub-optimal and that these heuristics can persist over time. But from the smart decision-making perspective this can be a product of the capabilities and experience of individuals and their decision-making environment.

A critical point here is that the thinking platform the individual should adopt is not determined a priori by the expert or by theory. It is context dependent. Moreover, although such decision-making can be expert informed, it is a bottom-up approach, informed by individuals involved and affected by the decision-making process and the decisions made. But given the decision-making environment and the preferences of decision-makers, choices made by individuals can be sub-optimal. And individuals' decision-making can be improved by improvements to the decision-making environment and expert advice. As an example, it is important to understand when the slow thinking platform works best as opposed to the fast thinking platform. And, this is very much contingent upon the context of decision-making.

The smart decision-making approach has differential implications for policy and approaches for structuring decision-making. The conventional wisdom is, in its extreme, very 'hands off' on policy, both in terms of government and even on suggestions of what can be done inside the firm and household to improve decision-making processes and decision-making outcomes. The prior assumption is that 'free' markets plus rational agents will generate optimal results. So, government could intervene to make markets 'freer' and perhaps to better secure property rights. If individuals are hardwired to be error-prone and biased (the heuristics and biases approach) then intervention must be much more proactive, nudging or more forcefully driving individuals to make what are deemed optimal or at least better decisions.

With the smart decision-making or smart agent approach, it is assumed, at least as an analytical starting-point, that individuals are rational. Hence, we need to address issues of capabilities, decision-making environments, experience and externalities, to determine what is required to facilitate best practice, but also context informed, decision-making processes. Barring externalities, it becomes critically important to construct decision-making capabilities and environments to facilitate and nurture informed decisions, based on the free choice of decision-makers. Therefore, it also becomes important to understand the circumstances under which individuals lose the capacity (or this capacity is severely reduced) to make informed choices, such as possibly severe addictions and mental illness, and perhaps even more importantly the power and even the legal rights to make informed choices.

These methodological differences between the smart agent–smart decision-making approach to behavioural economics (related to the concept of bounded rationality), the heuristics and biases approach to behavioural economics and conventional economics are illustrated in Fig. 1.1. The smart decision-making approach incorporates and is informed by bounded rationality, process rationality and institutional design. These are informed by a variety of variables, inclusive of human capital, mental models, preferences, information, power and learning. Smart decision-making can result in either optimal or suboptimal outcomes depending on the above economic, sociological and institutional variables. Both these outcomes can be 'rational' from the perspective of the individual, but they can generate socially inefficient outcomes. We can have what I refer to as rational inefficiency, but this can be corrected (more often than not) by changing some of the key variables mentioned above. However, benchmarks for what yields optimal outcomes is largely unrelated to neoclassical behavioural norms, which also tend to be very general such as maximizing or minimizing behaviours. Rather, these benchmarks need to be reality based and context specific.

In contrast, the heuristics and biases approach predicts that what is often hardwired behaviour yields deviations from conventional norms for optimal behaviour, that is, from neoclassical rationality. The latter is retained as the gold standard for achieving optimality for the individual, the household, the firm and society. Deviations from the neoclassical rationality yield persistent errors in

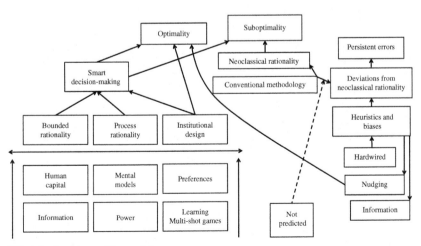

FIG. 1.1   Decision-making models.

decision-making, hence suboptimal outcomes. This can be corrected by nudging (which can involve varying degrees of paternalism) and, sometimes, by correcting for failures in institutional design. The latter includes improvements to information. Also, the latter as well as institutional design are critically important to the smart decision-maker approach to behavioural economics. Neoclassical models predict neoclassical rationality and optimal outcomes. They do not predict persistent deviations from neoclassical rationality, which have been well documented in the literature.

The alternative, smart agent or smart decision-making approach to behavioural economics, central to this book, rooted in the tradition established through the research of Herbert Simon and his colleagues, holds much promise to better understand and inform real world decision-making. This is so because the smart agent approach incorporates learning from the bounded rationality approach, the heuristics and biases approach, the slow and fast learning narrative, institutional economics as well as important insights from other disciplines, such as sociological and psychological analyses and neuroscience. The smart agent approach to decision-making, because it is multi-faceted and reality based, enriches any discourse on the determinants of decision-making and what makes for effective decision-making from both an individual and social perspective that takes place in the real world of complexity and bounded rationality.

What this book is all about

The second chapter of this book, 'The Evolution of Decision-making: Why Institutions and Capabilities Matters' different approaches to how decision-making evolves over time. I explore the evolution of behavioural economics from a multidisciplinary rational agent approach to the errors and biases or errors and heuristics narrative that currently dominates the field. I argue that although the errors and biases approach pioneered by Kahneman and Tversky has made significant contributions to the field, the bounded rationality approach holds most promise, with its focus on methodology and related causal analysis and modelling, smart decision makers, capabilities, and institutional design. The errors and biases approach is more focused documenting deviations from the neoclassical behavioural norm, where the latter is considered to be the normative ideal. It also pays considerable attention to how heuristic-based biased behaviour better describes and explains a good deal of economic behaviour and outcomes. The approach discussed in this chapter contributes to an explanation of why heuristics, given appropriate decision-making capabilities and institutional settings (largely non-neoclassical or conventional economic), can generate best possible decision-making outcomes and also why both optimal and sub-optimal outcomes can persist over historical time.

In Chapter 3, *How complexity affects decision-making*, I discuss the evolution of decision-making and best practice decision-making from an evolutionary, bottom-up perspective articulated by Hayek who argues that individuals can't know everything, nor can any one individual know and plan what is in the best interest of another individual. The world is just too complex. Aspects of Hayek's analytical framework is very much consistent with the decision-making analytical frame developed by Herbert Simon, that individuals do not behave as predicted or proscribed by conventional economic theory. But such non-conventional behaviour is arguably the most rational or intelligent approach to decision making. However, the Hayek perspective is contrary to the more dominant approach to behavioural economics advanced by Daniel Kahneman and Amos Tversky wherein it is argued that the non-conventional heuristics that characterize average human behaviour is often biased and error-prone, yielding choice and economic inefficiencies. It is also assumed in the Kahneman–Tversky tradition that ideal preferences are similar across individuals. Deviations from the ideal can best be fixed and welfare maximized by inducing individuals to behave neoclassically (based on the expert's set of definitions). Hayek also recognizes the importance of stable and transparent institutional frame (rules of the game) as a necessary condition for effective decision-making to take place. Also, institutions play a vital role in inducing bad people to do good things in their decision-making, something that does not come naturally.

In Chapter 4, *Freedom of choice in a complex world*, I discuss the importance of the notion of multiple equilibrium for better understand decision-making and the freedom afforded to individuals with respect to choices made given the real world of complexity and bounded rationality. In the conventional economic wisdom, the notion of unique equilibria that are efficient and Pareto optimal dominates the modelling discourse. Hebert Simon proposed an alternative analytical framework where the notion of multiple and sustainable equilibria is critical. Multiple equilibrium is the crucial stylized fact of economic life that requires better understanding and modelling. Of particular significance, Simon touched on the importance of institutions and differential power relationships in affecting economic outcomes. But this modelling approach was not well developed by Simon. Following from his contributions, further develop the notion of multiple equilibria especially in the realm of production with an emphasis on x-efficiency theory. I bring to bear the importance of institutional parameters (including power relationships), culture, norms, ethics, and moral sentiments to the determination of economic outcomes. In the model developed here, boundedly rational decision-makers' choices are contextualized and constrained by complex environmental factors. No one choice is either inevitable or economically efficient. A multiplicity of outcomes is possible and sustainable inclusive of those that are suboptimal. Much depends on individual preferences and institutional design. This has significant implication for institutional design and policy.

The following chapter, Chapter 5, *Understanding rational inefficiency: A scientific basis for economic failure and success*, presents a modelling narrative on rational choice or smart behaviour from a bounded rationality perspective, building in part on the pioneering work of Herbert Simon and Harvey

Leibenstein. I argue that smart or rational individuals can behave inefficiently at both the micro or macro (social) level in both the realm of production and consumption. Smart people can be efficient or inefficient. Hence it is possible to have rational inefficiency. It is shown that such inefficiency can persist over time irrespective of the competitive environment. Also, one cannot necessary derive choices and related outcomes that will be efficient from the smartness or rationality assumption. Additionally, what is rational from the individual's perspective might very well be irrational from the social perspective. Private rationality is not the same thing as social rationality. It is also important to differentiate rational individual choice behaviour from behaviour that is error-free or decisions that aren't subject to regret. Making mistakes can be consistent with rational or smart behaviour. Much depends on the decision-making capabilities of the individuals and the relevant decision-making environment. It is these capabilities and environments that critically determine the extent which outcomes are either privately or socially efficient.

In Chapter 6, *How consumers can achieve freedom of choice*, in contrast with the conventional perspective on choice behaviour, a model of preference formation is developed of rational or intelligent utility maximizing agents wherein they can possess preferences that are objectively suboptimal from both an individual and social perspective. In other words, one should not assume consumer sovereignty as a given. In addition, the revealed preferences of agents might be optimal from the perspective of the individual agents, but might conflict with the preferences of other agents. With optimal but heterogeneous preferences, based on issues of gender or class, for example, moral and political dilemmas might arise with respect to resolving such optimal but conflicting preferences. Thus, the revealed preferences of agents cannot be deemed, necessarily, as an indicator of what is in the best interest of the agent and of society at large. For optimal preferences to be constructed and chosen requires an appropriate institutional setting. Moreover, the extent to which preferences are optimal affects the relative efficiency of the economy. Understanding how optimal preferences are constructed and realized is thus critically important from an analytical and from both an individual and social welfare perspective.

Chapter 7, *Inside the black box of the firm: Why choice, power, and preferences matter*, challenges the simplistic behavioural and institutional models of the firm. Critical facets of the behavioural model of the firm and of economic agency within the workplace was developed by Harvey Leibenstein through his articulation of efficiency wage and x-efficiency theory. In these theories it is assumed that effort is a discretionary variable and that output need be maximized at some ideal level. If effort is discretionary, then individuals can choose how smart and hard they work. The assumption of effort discretion differs fundamentally from what has been traditionally assumed in the conventional economic wisdom and has had an important effect on economic theory and, related to this, on public policy. The basics of Leibenstein's theories are critically assessed and then extended. It is shown that rational individuals in competitive markets can generate the same type of economic inefficiencies as Leibenstein's irrational economic agents in a monopolistic environment. It is also shown, in contrast to Leibenstein, that in a world of effort discretion, there is no reason to expect market forces to drive out inefficient players from the market place nor should one expect that high rates of employment to be an enduring effect of the existence of effort discretion. Efficiency is largely a product of work environments and institutional setting within which the work environment is embedded, not necessarily or only a product of market forces. Thus, the introduction of effort discretion into the modelling of the economic agent allows for the construction of analytical frameworks which, in effect, generates more accurate predictive and causal analyses than the conventional models and for improved policy with regards to enhancing firm productivity and thereby the material wellbeing of the population.

Chapter 8, *How smart people can be involuntarily employment when misguided policy dominates decision-making*, examines the modelling of decision making in the ever so critical macro side of the economy. The perspective of modern macroeconomic theory, be it new classical or old and new Keynesian, is that unemployment can be reduced only if real wages are cut. The modern Keynesians, basing themselves upon the microfoundations of efficiency wage theory, argue that real wages cannot and will not be cut by firms for efficiency wage reasons. This generates involuntary unemployment based on a market coordination problem. A behavioural model that contrasts with efficiency wage theory is presented here which suggests that reducing real wages need not affect the marginal cost of labour and, therefore, the number of individuals employed. This relates to how employees and employers respond to changes in labour benefits. In the behavioural model, wherein there exists some linearity in the relationship between real wages and working conditions and labour productivity, a lower real wage rate is not a necessary condition for reducing the unemployment rate nor is a higher real wage an obstacle to reducing it. In this scenario, unemployment, to the extent that it is demand-side induced, is not related to movements in real wages. Therefore, restoring full employment after a negative demand shock becomes a matter for demand management, not demand management that must be coordinated with measures designed to reduce real wages.

Chapter 9, *Why financial literacy matters for socio-economic wellbeing*, summarizes different methodological approaches to financial literacy with implications for better understanding decision making in this domain and with implications for public policy. Conventional economics predicts no substantive improvement to financial literacy flowing from improvements to financial literacy. The errors and biases approach to behavioural economics suggests limited improvements to decision making from financial education as errors and biases are largely hardwired in the brain. Government and expert intervention affecting individual choice behaviour is recommended. The evidence suggests that the bounded rationality approach to behavioural economics, with its focus on smart decision makers and the importance institutional and environmental constraints on decision making, is the most promising lens through which to analyse financial decision making. From this perspective, financial decision making can be improved by providing decision makers with better quality information presented in a non-complex fashion, an institutional environment conducive to good decisions, an incentive structure that internalizes externalities involved in financial decision making, and financial education (financial literacy human capital) that facilitates making the best use of the information at hand within a specific decision-making context and environment.

In Chapter 10, *How labour markets really work*, I discuss some key issues raised by behavioural economics for better understanding the working of the labour market through the decisions made by employees and employers. Amongst the key points addressed in this chapter are: (i) a revised modelling of the labour supply curve, with a specific focus on the target income approach, (ii) elaborating on the importance of effort variability for understanding labour supply and demand, (iii) discussing some of the cognitive/informational/institutional factors affecting decision-making, including modelling the role of errors or biases in labour market decisions, and (iv) the importance of recognizing power relationships within the household and women's rights for better understanding the determinants of population growth. This chapter also compares the conventional to the errors and biases and the bounded rationality approaches to labour markets, their different underlying assumptions, and analytical predictions, with implications for public policy and institutional design. As with all of the above chapters, introducing more realistic and reasonable behavioural and institutional assumptions allows to better understand choice behaviour in the real world of complexity and bounded rationality.

Appendix: Background sources for, smart economic decision-making in a complex world

Chapters from this book are derived from and built upon the following publications: Chapter 1, Morris Altman (2017) 'Introduction to Smart Decision-Making', in Morris Altman (Ed.), *Handbook of Behavioural Economics and Smart Decision-Making: Rational Decision-Making Within the Bounds of Reason*. Cheltenham, England: Edward Elgar, pp. 1–10; Chapter 3, Morris Altman (2017) 'A Bounded Rationality Assessment of the New Behavioral Economics', in Roger Frantz, Shu-Heng Chen, Kurt Dopfer, Floris Heukelom and Shabnam Mousavi (Eds.), *Routledge Handbook of Behavioral Economics*. Routledge: London and New York, pp. 179–193; Chapter 4, Morris Altman (2017) 'Policy Consequences of Multiple Equilibria and the Indeterminacy of Economic Outcomes in a Boundedly Rational World: Closing the System with Non-Economic Variables', *Forum for Social Economics* 64: 234–251; Chapter 5, Morris Altman (2017) 'Rational Inefficiency: Smart Thinking, Bounded Rationality, and Scientific Basis for Economic Failure and Success', in Morris Altman (Ed.), *Handbook of Behavioural Economics and Smart*

Decision-Making: Rational Decision-Making Within the Bounds of Reason. Cheltenham, England: Edward Elgar, pp. 11–42; Chapter 6, Morris Altman (2010) 'A Behavioral and Institutional Foundation of Preference and Choice Behavior: Freedom to Choose and Choice X-inefficiencies', *Review of Social Economy* 69, 395–411; Chapter 7, Morris Altman (2007) 'Effort Discretion and Economic Agency and Behavioral Economics: Transforming Economic Theory and Public Policy', in Roger Frantz (Ed.), *Renaissance in Behavioural Economics Harvey Leibenstein's Impact of Contemporary Economic Analysis.* New York: Routledge, pp. 105–145; Chapter 8, Morris Altman (2006) 'Involuntary Unemployment, Macroeconomic Policy, and a Behavioral Model of the Firm: Why High Real Wages Need Not Cause High Unemployment', *Research in Economics* 60: 97–111; Chapter 9, Morris Altman (2012) 'Implications of Behavioural Economics for Financial Literacy and Public Policy', *Journal of Socio-Economics* 41: 677–690 and Morris Altman (2013) 'What Behavioural Economics Has to Say About Financial Literacy', *Applied Finance Letters* (Special Issue on Financial Literacy) 2: 12–17; Chapter 10, most of the this chapter has not been published. The part related to population growth is based on Morris Altman (1999) 'A Theory of Population Growth When Women Really Count', *Kyklos* 52: 27–43.

References

Altman, M. (1999). The methodology of economics and the survivor principle revisited and revised: Some welfare and public policy implications of modeling the economic agent. *Review of Social Economics, 57*(4), 427–449.

Altman, M. (2005). Behavioral economics, power, rational inefficiencies, fuzzy sets, and public policy. *Journal of Economic Issues, 39*(3), 683–706.

Altman, M. (2015). Introduction. In M. Altman (Ed.), *Real-world decision making: An Encyclopedia of Behavioral economics.* Santa Barbara, CA: Greenwood, ABC-CLIO.

Altman, M. (2017a). A bounded rationality assessment of the new behavioral economics. In R. Frantz, S.-H. Chen, K. Dopfer, F. Heukelom, & S. Mousavi (Eds.), *Routledge handbook of behavioral economics* (pp. 179–194). New York: Routledge.

Altman, M. (Ed.), (2017b). *Handbook of behavioural economics and smart decision-making: Rational decision-making within the bounds of reason.* Cheltenham, England: Edward Elgar.

Becker, G. S. (1996). *Accounting for tastes.* Cambridge, MA: Harvard University Press.

Berg, N., & Gigerenzer, G. (2010). As-if behavioral economics: Neoclassical economics in disguise? *History of Economic Ideas, 18*(1), 133–166.

Friedman, M. (1953). The methodology of positive economics. In M. Friedman (Ed.), *Essays in positive economics* (pp. 3–43). Chicago, IL: University of Chicago Press.

Gigerenzer, G. (2007). *Gut feelings: The Intelligence of the Unconscious.* New York: Viking.

Hayek, F. A. (1948). *Individualism and the economic order.* Chicago, IL: University of Chicago Press.

Kahneman, D. (2003). Maps of bounded rationality: Psychology for behavioral economics. *American Economic Review, 93*(5), 1449–1475.

Kahneman, D. (2011). *Thinking, fast and slow.* New York: Farrar, Straus and Giroux.

March, J. G. (1978). Bounded rationality, ambiguity, and the engineering of choice. *Bell Journal of Economics, 9*(2), 587–608.

North, D. C. (1971). Institutional change and economic growth. *Journal of Economic History*, *31*(1), 118–125.

Simon, H. A. (1986). Rationality in psychology and economics. *Journal of Business*, *59*(4), S209–S224.

Smith, V. L. (2003). Constructivist and ecological rationality in economics. *American Economic Review*, *93*(3), 465–508.

Thaler, R. H., & Sunstein, C. (2008). *Nudge: Improving decisions about health, wealth, and happiness*. New Haven, CT/London: Yale University Press.

Chapter 2

The evolution of decision-making: Why institutions and capabilities matters

Chapter outline

Introduction   17
Assumptions matter and
   behavioural economics   19
The conventional wisdom and the
   different faces of behavioural
   economics   20
The bounded rationality
   approach in context   22
Satisficing and procedural
   rationality in context   29

X-efficiency theory and external
   benchmarks for optimal
   behaviour   31
Nudging versus constraints
   change and redesign   32
Conclusion   33
References   35

Introduction

Initially, at least, behavioural economics was a response to the very simplistic approaches to decision-making entrenched in conventional economics, given the world within which decisions are made is actually made is complex and decision-makers are vested with different levels of decision-making power. Complexity is typically assumed away, as not being of analytical importance in the conventional economic model. And, power relationships are of marginal importance. Hence, this simplifying assumption should be of no consequence with regards to generating robust causal analyses and predictions. However, I argue that complexity and power relationships as well should be foundational to models of decision-making. And, this brings to the fore the significance of the decision-making environment and individuals' decision-making capabilities.

I explore the evolution of behavioural economics, from a multidisciplinary rational agent or bounded rationality approach that was pioneered and championed by Simon (1959, 1978, 1987) from the 1950s, to heuristics and biases approach that currently dominates the field. I argue that although the heuristics and biases approach pioneered, by Kahneman and Tversky (1979), Kahneman (2003, 2011), and Tversky and Kahneman (1981), has made significant

Smart Economic Decision-Making in a Complex World. https://doi.org/10.1016/B978-0-12-811461-2.00002-X

contributions to the field, the bounded rationality approach holds most promise, with its focus on methodology and related causal analyses and modelling, smart (rational) decision makers, capabilities, and institutional design (see Chapter 1 and Altman, 2017).

The heuristics and biases approach, where heuristics refers to decision-making shortcuts, is more focused documenting deviations from the neoclassical or conventional behavioural norms (typically non-heuristic in orientation), where the latter is considered to be the normative ideal and fundamentally reflective of rational behaviour. It is important to note that this normative ideal, largely accepted in the heuristics and biases approach, is typically rejected in the bounded rationality approach as it falsely predicts that following this norm typically leads to optimal choices and outcomes even in a world of complexity, differential power relationships, and differential decision-making capabilities. The heuristics and biases approach also pays considerable attention to how modelling behaviour as being heuristic-based and, therefore, biased behaviour better describes and explains a good deal of economic behaviour and outcomes than the conventional economic wisdom. But from the heuristics and biases perspective, recognizing the reality that humans persistently violate conventional economic behavioural norms, is consistent with accepting these norms as ideal for achieving optimal choices and outcomes or biased decision-making. People just don't behave as conventional economics suggests they do and should behave.

This heuristics and biases descriptive narrative raises questions about the analytical relevance of conventional economics, in many domains, and remains vitally important not only to the behavioural economics narrative, but also to economics in general. For all perspectives in economics the dynamic interaction, the passionate tango, between facts and theory, is supposed to be a linchpin of scientific analysis.

A common thread running through behavioural economics is that many economic outcomes are inconsistent with the predictions of conventional economic theory.

Documenting this inconsistency represents key contributions of Herbert Simon, but especially that of Daniel Kahneman and Amos Tversky, all of whom are considered to be amongst the core founding fathers of contemporary behavioural economics. Significant efforts to document these inconsistencies of behaviour with conventional theory have also been made by Smith (2003), one the founding fathers of contemporary experimental economics, and by Gigerenzer (2007), a pioneer in developing the notion of rational decision-making heuristics (decision-making shortcuts). This documented inconsistency opens the door wide open to various alternative models of human decision-making and their determinants. This is particularly true if one concludes that these inconsistencies are persistent and represent an important subset of choice outcomes; not just some interesting outlier anomalies.

Behavioural economics sometimes affords us with quite different and opposing perspectives on what the deviations from the conventional or neoclassical economic norms mean for our understanding of human behaviour, the causes of such deviations, and for the development of robust economic theory and policy. These points of difference are a central theme of this chapter.

Assumptions matter and behavioural economics

In the contemporary literature on behavioural economics (the heuristics and biases approach), attention is drawn to behavioural economics as better describing economic reality than conventional theory in terms of both choice behaviour and the outcomes of these choices, which tend to deviate from what's predicted by conventional economics. And these outcomes are interpreted as being all too often a product of error-prone and biased decision-making processes, where decisions are often driven by 'irrational' emotional considerations as opposed careful and considered calculating behaviour. Apart from this interpretation of choice outcomes, an objective of documenting deviations from predicted conventional outcomes (a point of commonality with the bounded rationality approach) is to demonstrate that conventional theory too often fails to predict choice behaviours and choice outcomes. It is important to note the research on emotions which suggest that emotions and intuition (based on experience) often plays an important and positive role in decision-making (Damasio, 1996). But too much emotion can result sub-optimal decisions.

But this worldview is completely contrary to methodological perspective of conventional economics, one that permeates other approaches to economic analysis as well. This outlook stems from the classic 1953 methodological paper by Friedman (1953), where he argued that the realism of simplifying modelling assumptions are not of any significance in building robust economic models or theories. Getting the description right with regards choice behaviour is not of importance—all that counts is predicting the outcomes of choice behaviour correctly. Of course, behavioural economists have additionally found that all too many of the predictions of the conventional model are incorrect. Related to this, a critical point made by Simon (1987) and in the bounded rationality approach, is that the realism of the simplifying assumptions of models is vitally important to achieve rigorous analytical predictions and causal analyses (Altman, 2005a, 2005b, 2012, 2015).

Friedman (1953) argues that trying to be more accurate in the realism of ones assumptions 'only confuses the issue, promotes misunderstanding about the significance of empirical evidence for economic theory ... [and] ... wildly inaccurate descriptive representations of reality, and, in general the more significant the theory, the more unrealistic the assumption (in this sense)'. A realistic modelling of assumptions is, therefore, of no consequence. The ultimate test of whether modelling assumptions are 'good enough' or appropriate is the model's predictive power, even if the assumptions are markedly inaccurate. In other words, inaccurate and, even more extremely, assumptions that have no bearing on how decision-makers actually behave are quite acceptable when they generate reasonably robust predictions. From this methodological perspective, causally, cause and effect, as opposed to correlation, is difficult to determine. And, correlation can be misinterpreted as causation (Altman, 2006).

A critical facet of the bounded rationality approach is that causality can only be determined with reference to simplifying assumptions that are empirically derived. Only in this manner can one test whether a model's analytical predictions are robust and impute causation to the independent variables of the model and more specifically to the particular behaviours of decision-makers and their decision-making environment. This also reduces the probability of generating omitted variable problems. It also changes the analytical rules of the game away from necessarily assuming that individuals make decisions in optimally yielding optimal results (an analytical default option in the conventional wisdom) towards determining how decision-makers actually behave and their decision-making constraints. Because Friedman assumes that individuals behave in manner consistent with 'optimal' economic behaviour it is also often assumed that outcomes are optimal even if, on the surface, they appear not to be so. This too runs contrary to the behavioural economics narrative where what appear to be sub-optimal outcomes are interrogated and tested for sub-optimality and then related to the choice behaviour of decision-makers.

In addition, this bounded rationality approach is not consistent with the modelling by some behavioural economists who introduce various psychological or sociological assumptions, as replacements for the conventional neoclassical ones, that yield robust predictions but which are not derived empirically. Although this approach to model building might appear reasonable, derived from the decision-making literature, the model's underlying assumptions are not derived from the actual decision-making process. For example, this approach would *not* assume that individuals behave as if they compute simultaneously hundreds of equations to optimize their results—which is the Milton Freidman approach modelling. But it would allow for assumptions that don't appear 'absurd' but are equally as unreasonable as are Friedman's deliberately wildly unrealistic assumptions. The common core here is that assumptions are not being empirically derived and what matters is the predictions are robust (Altman, 2015; Berg & Gigerenzer, 2010). In the bounded rationality approach, behavioural and context-related assumptions need to be sensible and realistic given the context of decision-making, the hypothesis being tested, and the outcomes being explained. This assumptions matter perspective also allows for testing the reasonableness and the implications of different sets of plausible behavioural assumptions for causality, prediction, and for improved decision-making outcomes.

The conventional wisdom and the different faces of behavioural economics

According to Simon (1987), bounded rationality refers to rational choice behaviour. But bounded rationality refers to the type of rational choice behaviour that one finds in the real world. Such choice is bounded by a variety of factors, such as the cognitive limitations of decision makers, including limitations to their knowledge of pertinent information (and their ability to acquire such knowledge) and to their computational capabilities and capacities (see Akerlof, 1970, on information asymmetries; see also Altman, 2020). Also important are institutional factors that can hinder or improve the decision-making process and outcomes. More recently, behavioural economists and others have increasingly introduced psychological (Kahneman, 2003, 2011; Kahneman & Tversky, 1979; Lewis, Webley, & Furnham, 1995; Tversky & Kahneman, 1981) and sociological factors in models of decision-making (Akerlof & Kranton, 2010). One can also refer to Becker (1996), although very much immersed in price theory, he argues that sociological variables are vital to understand decision-making and choice behaviour.

But what are the conventional economic or neoclassical norms for optimal behaviour? Not everyone would completely agree. However, there are certain core assumptions that are often made reference to by both neoclassical economic and behavioural economists:

1. Individuals can and do make consistent choices across all possible bundles of goods and services and through time.
2. It is assumed that all individuals have thorough knowledge of all relevant available options at any given point in time and they all have the means to process and understand this information in a timely manner—the brain is assumed not to be scarce resource and individuals' computational ability is unlimited.
3. Individuals can forecast the implications of their decisions through time and hence calculate at least in a measurable probabilistic sense the consequences of their choices.
4. Individuals are assumed to make choices across alternatives that maximize utility or wellbeing. It is typically assumed either explicitly or implicitly that, controlling for risk, utility maximization is consistent with wealth or income maximization.
5. It is assumed that individuals are effective and efficient calculating machines or at least they behave as if they are, irrespective of age, experience, or education.
6. It is assumed that all individuals independent of context should behave in the same calculating manner (following conventional behavioural norms) to maximize utility or efficiency.

The 'new' behavioural economics, emanating from the initial research outcomes and initiatives of Kahneman and Tversky, sets out to develop theories that are better able to describe human behaviour, where often such behaviour is related to economic issues. In this vein, for example, they developed Prospect Theory as an alternative to Subjective Expected Utility Theory. Certainly, Kahneman and Tversky view their scientific project as bearing down on better describing choice behaviour than conventional economic theory. In the Kahneman and Tversky approach, such descriptive theories are typically related to the behaviour of the average individual. The focus on the average has also been a mainstay of conventional economics. This implicitly assumes that the average is the most appropriate point of reference for descriptive and analytical purposes. But a fundamental point in the Kahneman and Tversky narrative is that their average individual does not behave neoclassically—their average decision-maker is fundamentally different that her or his neoclassical counterpart.

This 'new' behavioural economics also interprets the 'average' individual's deviations from the conventional economic norms for optimal decision making to be error-prone and biased, and typically persistently so. On the one hand, this perspective on behavioural economics maintains and adheres to a fundamental premise of conventional economics, that there is particular way of behaving in the economic realm resulting in a particular set of choices and therefore outcomes that are optimal (most, effective, efficient, unbiased). But it represents a big break with conventional economics in that individuals tend not to behave optimally in a large array of choice scenarios. It is argued that individuals tend to engage in biased and error-prone behaviours. And they do so because they do not conform to conventional or neoclassical behavioural norms.

The bounded rationality approach in context

The bounded rationality approach breaks with conventional economics by recognizing that individuals and organizations all too often behave in a manner that deviates from the conventional economic norms for optimal and even rational behaviour. But unlike with the 'new' behavioural economics, in the bounded rationality approach, such deviations often signal decision-making processes and outcomes that are optimal and rational given the preferences of the decision-makers and the constraints that face. These constraints can be of a physiological, neurological, psychological, or institutional nature. Hence, the bounded rationality approach rejects, on an empirical basis, that individuals and organizations generate decisions that are typically consistent with conventional economic theory predicted outcomes, whilst also rejecting the null hypothesis that one should typically use conventional economic theory benchmarks to determine which outcomes are optimal from either an individual or social perspective. This approach does not deny the possibilities of errors and even biases in decision-making. Moreover, there is a focus here on causal analysis. Modelling is important. Identifying which particular behaviours yield particular outcomes is critical. This shifts attention from correlation-based prediction to cause-and-effect modelling. The former remains the basis of much of conventional economics.

Herbert Simon developed the key analytical concepts of bounded rationality and satisficing as an alternative to the conventional economic concepts of rationality and maximizing or minimizing behaviour. He argued that these alternative analytical tools were better able to describe and explain (causally) the behaviour of human decision makers in the real world as well as providing more reasonable normative benchmarks for rational behaviour. He accepted a basic premise of conventional economics that most individuals (the typical individual) are goal-oriented and have reasons for what they do, for the decisions they make. Being goal-oriented and having reasons behind one's actions is what Simon considered to be fundamental to any reasonable definition of rationality. But determining rationality required placing human action in the context of an individual's and an organization's decision-making environment (Simon, 1987; Todd & Gigerenzer, 2003).

One of Simon's main differences with and concerns about conventional economics throughout his career was that conventional economics decontextualized the meaning of rationality. It thereby defines rationality in terms of norms that are often dissociated from the overall decision-making environment. Conventional economics also tends to assume that individuals and organizations behave in a manner consistent with these decontextualized norms, where such behaviour is considered to be the only behaviour that is rational. In this case, if individuals are rational, which is a bread-and-butter assumption of conventional economics, one must assume that behaviour is consistent with conventional norms of rational behaviour.

But if, as Simon argues, rationality needs to be more broadly defined and defined in a contextualized manner, conventional norms should not necessarily be used as a benchmark of rational behaviour. What is rational from the perspective of conventional economics might be irrational from a bounded rationality perspective. And, what conventional economics considers to be an irrational behaviour, might very well be rational behaviour. Market forces should, according to the conventional wisdom, wipe out the former in a short enough period of time such that irrational behaviour from a conventional economic perspective should not be of analytical significance (Reder, 1982). But the bounded rationality approach would consider deviations from the conventional norm to be not uncommon and to persist over time, especially if such deviations are product of some rational decision-making process. What is sensible, smart, or rational behaviour must be placed in the context of the decision-making environment and the decision-making capabilities of individuals. And, the real world context happens to be significantly different from what is assumed in the conventional economic narrative.

One example of the bounded rationality approach is provided by March (1978, p. 589), a close associate of Simon during the golden years of the foundational period of behavioural economics in Carnegie-Mellon University. March argued that one should approach the determination of the rationality of decision-making in the context of the decision-making environment. March, therefore, concludes that in the first instance one should assume that choice behaviour is sensible and therefore rational even if this behaviour deviates from conventional economic norms, even by a significant extent:

Engineers of artificial intelligence have modified their perceptions of efficient problem solving procedures by studying the actual behavior of human problem solvers. Engineers of organizational decision making have modified their models of rationality on the basis of studies of actual organizational behavior...Modern students of human choice behavior frequently assume, at least implicitly, that actual human choice behavior in some way or other is likely to make sense. It can be understood as being the behavior of an intelligent being or group of intelligent beings...

This does not imply that all choices are rational or sensible. But one should not determine rationality, sensibility, or optimality, by the extent to which choice behaviours and outcomes deviate from conventional norms of rationality. Moreover, one should not attempt to achieve superior outcomes by inducing individuals or organizations to conform to or adhere to conventional economic behavioural norms. These norms are not context dependent and can result is serious errors in decision-making.

More recently, Vernon Smith, a pioneer of contemporary experimental economics concluded, in a similar vein, but based on evidence derived from classroom experiments. One his key finding is that behaviours that generate economic success are all too often not consistent with what contemporary economic theory considers to be rational or smart decision-making. But then this implies that there is something fundamentally wrong with the theory, in this case the assumption that profit maximizing behaviour generates economic success and optimal economic outcomes. One should not challenge the rationality of decision-making that's consistent with economic success, when economic success is the normative end-game of the theory. Moreover, in this scenario the conventional economic model's prediction is also wrong. Profit maximization would not result in firm success whereas forms of non-maximization would.

Smith finds that (2005, pp. 149–150; see also Smith, 2005):

It is shown that the investor who chooses to maximize expected profit (discounted total withdrawals) fails in finite time. Moreover, there exist a variety of nonprofit-maximizing behaviors that have a positive probability of never failing. In fact it is shown that firms that maximize profits are the least likely to be the market survivors. My point is simple: when experimental results are contrary to standard concepts of rationality, assume not just that people are irrational, but that you may not have the right model of rational behavior. Listen to what your subjects may be trying to tell you. Think of it this way. If you could choose your ancestors, would you want them to be survivalists or to be expected wealth maximizers?

Simon developed the concepts of bounded and procedural rationality, as well as satisficing as alternatives to conventional economic rationality and maximizing/minimizing/optimizing behaviour. These alternative concepts have embodied in them alternative sets of rational behaviour which differ from those embodied in conventional economic modelling. Simon provided these alternative sets of concepts to capture rational or sensible behaviour that was inconsistent with conventional economic norms. It was not enough to simply critique conventional economics as being descriptively incorrect. It was imperative to also provide conceptional vehicles to facilitate modelling human decision-making.

Bounded rationality (BR) refers to goal oriented and even deliberative and, therefore, rational behaviour. Unlike the conventional economics definition of rationality, BR is more broadly defined and is empirically derived, based on how smart people behave in the real world situations given the various parameters or constraints faced by the decision-maker and the decision-making environment.

Bounded rationality is a contextualized and operational definition of rationality. Rational decision-making is bounded by a number of factors. And these bounds generate decision-making and outcomes and processes different from what one would predict or assume from the perspective of conventional economics. Of particular importance are the cognitive limitations of decision makers, including limitations to their knowledge of pertinent information given the inherent complexity of information (and their ability to acquire such knowledge) and the limitations to their computational capabilities and capacities. The latter acknowledges the brain as a scarce—we are not endowed with unlimited cognitive capability or capacity. Our processing capacity can be potentially increased through the development of calculators and computers—a crucial point made of Simon. An additional point that needs to be made is that this potential can only be realized if individuals can afford these computational aids and know how to use them. Hence, one integrates into ones modelling framework the importance of income and education affecting the type of decisions made by rational but constrained individuals.

In this context, what appears to be a sub-optimal choice or an error or bias in decision-making from a strictly conventional economics perspective or even from the heuristics and biases approach (Kahneman, 2003, 2011; Kahneman & Tversky, 1979) is rather a product of cognitive, educational or income constraints faced by the decision-maker. So, when a decision appears to be odd or irrational, this modelling framework demands that one should determine if there are bounded rationality constraints that can explain these 'odd' decisions as rational. Here, improvements to decisions relate to improving individuals' decision-making capabilities (and, of course their decision-making environment). And, one of Simon's passions was to develop mechanical decision-making aids to improve individuals' decisions and therefore economic efficiency and also better meet the preferences of decision-makers. Overall, what might appear to be an irrational choice is quite rational within the bounds of reason—individuals are doing the best they can given their constraints, capabilities, and opportunities.

Also important are institutional factors that can hinder or improve the decision-making process and outcomes. Institutional parameters, either formal or informal rules of the game, impact on the decision-making process and rules of the game. This is a point emphasized by Simon and of importance to the bounded rationality approach to behavioural economics. Choices that appear to be irrational or suboptimal might simply be a product of perverse institutional parameters that induce suboptimal choices. On the other hand, a different set of institutional parameters might be necessary for optimal decisions to be made from either an individual or social perspective (North, 1971; Simon, 1987). Simon places considerable weight on the importance of the old institutional economics, exemplified by Commons (1931) in explaining rational but non-neoclassical choice behaviour.

Also, as mentioned above, sociological factors can impact of choice behaviour, generating choices that might also appear to be irrational or suboptimal. This is a point made by Becker (1996), one of founding fathers of contemporary or mainstream economic theory. But he breaks with his peers by arguing for integrating social variables into his modelling of human decision-making. Price theory alone can't explain choice behaviour, at least in many critical instances. Relations with others in the past and present and one's place and standing in one's community are of vital importance to explain behaviour that in the first instance might appear to be irrational. Sociological factors are typically not due given consideration in behavioural economics but can be vitally important in better explaining and predicting choice behaviour. A clear exception to this 'rule' is Akerlof and Kranton (2010) who develop identity economics, where a person's utility maximizing behaviour is driven by desire of individuals fit into their group or community. One can go back in time to the contributions of Veblen (1899) and there is also Duesenberry (1949) who developed the concept of relative positioning in income as key to a person's utility as opposed a person absolute state of wealth. The latter concept is key to the work of Kahneman and Tversky's Prospect Theory, with an emphasis how this yields suboptimal behaviour by focusing on relative as opposed to absolute states of wealth or income.

Overall, institutional and sociological factors can also be important to explain and predict both suboptimal and optimal choices, where the latter are conditional upon an appropriate institutional and sociological environment. This is apart from the state of cognitive and related variables. Introducing such non-economic variables is most consistent with the bounded rationality approach given that they help explain rational choices that appear irrational from the perspective of the conventional wisdom. It is important to note that rational choices need not generate optimal outcomes, given the constraints faced the individual. This point is not emphasized enough in either perspective of behavioural economics (Altman, 2005b, 2015). Rational or smart decision-makers can yield inefficient outcomes (Altman, 2005b, 2015). One can end up with rational inefficiencies as opposed errors and biases in decision-making, which is a focal point of the heuristics and biases approach to behavioural economics. Where constraints and capabilities can be changed, rational individuals can be expected to adjust their decisions yielding improved choices. The importance of capabilities was later refined and articulated by Sen (1985) and Nussbaum

(2011). Better education, improved access to computers (and computer literacy programs), improved institutional and sociological parameters, for example, can yield choices that can be more economically efficient and yield a higher level of utility or wellbeing to the individual.

Within the bounded rationality analytical framework one also has heuristics as possible efficient shortcuts in the decision-making process. In this case, individuals do not engage the careful and detailed calculating behavioural assumed by and considered to be normatively ideal in conventional economics. Heuristics are considered to an effective means to make decisions in a cost effective manner given by the various constraints and limitations faced by individuals in the decision-making process. Hence, Simon and those adhering to and developing the bounded rationality approach to decision-making, begin their analysis with the assumption that heuristics are used because they are the smart or rational means of engaging in the decision-making process.

This analytical approach has been further refined by Gigerenzer (2007) and colleagues who have advanced what is referred to as the fast and frugal heuristics toolbox. Evidence suggests that heuristics typically outperform conventional economic behavioural norms. It is important to note, however, that it is not assumed here that heuristics necessarily refer to simplistic notions of gut reactions to challenges and opportunities. This is particularly the case in this book. Gut reactions are often based on prior learning and experience and generate efficient boundedly rational outcomes. For this very reason, it is important to appreciate that a particular fast and frugal heuristic is often a product of a process of past learning and experience either by one's self or by others, whose learnings and experiences allow for the making efficient and fast decisions. Actually, this is a type of human capital formation related to the development of fast and frugal heuristics. Simply going with one's gut, where one's gut has not been well nourished by appropriate learnings and experiences can result in serious errors in decision-making. This very significant point is all too often ignored in the fast and frugal literature. Also, heuristics or decision-making shortcuts can be a product of careful deliberation where and when time permits. Some short-cuts might be longer than others. This point is also not given enough attention in the literature, but it is critical to a bounded rationality approach to decision-making. In a word, following neoclassical norms can result in errors in decision-making, but so can inappropriate heuristics.

Inappropriate heuristics can be chosen given the decision-makers constraints, capabilities, and information available to the decision-makers. The latter can result in smart decision-makers having a false mental model or understanding as to what is the best heuristic given the decision-making context.

In the bound rationality approach, the norms for optimal behaviour should be empirically derived from the circumstances surrounded real world decision-making as opposed to being imposed exogenously without any connection to the empirics underlying decision-making. But the assumption that non-conventional behavioural norms (aka heurstics) typically outperform conventional behavioural norms in terms of outcomes, is another key distinction between the conventional wisdom and the bounded rationality approach to behavioural economics and between the bounded rationality and the heuristics and biases analytical frameworks. But, once again, which heuristic works best must be empirically derived. The evidence simply points to the fact that non-neoclassical norms have outperformed neoclassical forms in many critical domains.

To reiterate what we've discussed above, in the conventional model a core assumption is that rational individuals must behave in a rigorously calculating manner and this will yield optimal outcomes. And, because we all behave in this manner, outcomes should be optimal. The bounded rationality perspective stands in stark contrast to this conventional scenario and to the heuristics and biases approach to behavioural economics. The latter typically starts with the hypothesis that heuristics are biased and error prone because they deviate from the conventional economic norms for optimal decision-making behaviour.

More recently, Kahneman (2011; Altman, 2015) himself, has presented a more nuanced argument whereby heuristics can represent a relatively effective decision-making tool, under certain circumstances. Kahneman argues that individuals use or should use different types of mental processes to engage in decision-making, broadly categorized as System 1 and System 2. In System 1, decision-making tends to be fast, emotionally driven, and intuitive and therefore, often based on deep-grained habits (or hardwired), and therefore, very difficult to modify and control. In System 2, decision-making tends to be thoughtful and deliberative involving much more effort and time than System 1 related decision-making. Kahneman argues that System 1 behaviour can be more efficient in certain circumstances, but is more subject to systematic errors and biases. System 2 behaviour is more efficient in other circumstances and is less subject to systematic errors and biases. So, an important aspect of this type of more nuanced categorization of decision-making behaviour is to determine which system works best and when, where, and for whom. And, System 1 errors, I would argue might be a function of decision-makers not always understanding the context within which fast and frugal heuristics (System 1 thinking) yields the best possible outcomes.

In this revisionist approach articulated by Kahneman, heuristics are error prone and predisposed to biases and are especially inefficient when decisions can and should take place over a longer period of time (providing that the time to think and analyse is available). This is an important intervention to the practical decision-making debate. It raises the important point that optimal decisions might require more time and effort than would a fast and frugal heuristic. The gut does not always yield optimal results and should not necessarily be designated as the optimal default. But the System 2 thinking need not be neoclassical in its details. Rather, it simply more deliberative and can also be more consultative. Think of this example. Take an arrogant leader (could be sociopath). He knows everything, of course. And, his gut is the source of all truth and optimal decisions. But his fast and frugal heuristic can result in disastrous decisions for the household or the firm. System 2 thinking would incorporate the leader being forced to consult and deliberate, yielding different and often superior outcomes, because typically no one knows everything. Consistent with the bounded rationality approach there are a wide array of heuristics that are possible, not all of which will be error-free, unbiased, or best-practice. However, in the real world, heuristics as opposed to conventional economics norms are almost always used to make decisions. In the bounded rationality approach, the default assumption is that heuristics are superior to conventional decision-making norms, having evolved over time and through experience. The critical question then becomes, again, under which circumstances are particular heuristics optimal and under which circumstances are they not.

Satisficing and procedural rationality in context

With regards to satisficing, there is no denying here that individuals are assumed to be purposeful and even contemplative about their decisions at least in the longer term. Nor does satisficing deny, based on the evidence, that most individuals at least most of the time attempt to do the best they can. But it does deny that rational or smart individuals typically behave in the type of calculating marginal analysis that the conventional wisdom assumes. Moreover, most successful decision makers don't behave in accordance with conventional behavioural norms, according to the evidence (Altman, 2012, 2015; Simon, 1959, 1978, 1987).

Satisficing is posited as an alternative to optimizing, foreshadowing the literature on heuristics. It is argued that individuals and organizations develop and adopt decision-making shortcuts or heuristics based on experience. When satisficing, an individual makes choices based on what meets predetermined criteria for what's good enough. There is often a form of stopping rule that's applied. The argument here is that given the constraints, capabilities, and opportunities faced by decision makers in the real world, using heuristics and, therefore, satisficing, generates superior choices in a more efficient and effective manner than engaging in what conventional economics would define as optimizing behaviour. This is especially the case when individuals update their heuristics as errors are uncovered and when better heuristics are discovered or developed. Satisficing heuristics need to evolve over time. When they don't, we can end up with errors in decision-making and suboptimal results. The key to sub-optimal decision-making is not adopting heuristics to circumstances and capabilities.

Procedural rationality relates to bounded rationality, satisficing, and the use of heuristics in decision-making. Simon sets procedural rationality in stark contrast to the rationality of conventional or neoclassical economics, where the latter is referred to substantive rationality. With substantive rationality the objective world is easily identified by the decision-maker who has unlimited computational capacity. And, one can deduce how an individual should behave to maximize efficiency or utility from the utility function of the individual. So, Simon argues that if the world is as the conventional wisdom assumes, there would be no problem with its modelling of choice behaviour. One could take this particular argument to task. But, be this as it may, a critical point made by Simon (1986, p. S211) is that:

> ...*if we accept the proposition that knowledge and the computational power of the decision maker are severely limited, then we must distinguish between the real world and the actor's perception of it and reasoning about it...we must construct a theory (and test it empirically) of the processes of decision. Our theory must include not only the reasoning processes but also the processes that generate the actor's subjective representation of the decision problem, his or her frame...The rational person of neoclassical economics always reaches the decision that is objectively, or substantively, best in terms of the given utility function. The rational person of cognitive psychology goes about making his or her decisions in a way that is procedurally reasonable in the light of the available knowledge and means of computation [it is context dependent].*

Procedural rationality is a form of bounded rationality. It relates to what are the best procedures to achieve the objectives (the utility of preference function) of an individual or an organization, given decision-making environment faced by the individual or organization and the decision-making capacities and capabilities of the individual and organization. The benchmark for what are the norms for best practice behaviour can't be given exogenously. There might also be alternative paths to achieve a given objective. Hence, what is procedural rationality can only be empirically derived, based on the capabilities and capacities of decision-makers and organizations and their preferences at any given point of real or historical time (Simon, 1986, p. S212).

> *To move from substantive to procedural rationality requires a major extension of the empirical foundations of economics. It is not enough to add theoretical postulates about the shape of the utility function, or about the way in which actors form expectations about the future, or about their attention or inattention to particular environmental variables. These are assumptions about matters of fact, and the whole ethos of science requires such assumptions to be supported by publicly repeatable observations that are obtained and analyzed objectively...The application of this procedural theory of rationality to economics requires extensive empirical research, much of it at micro-micro levels, to determine specifically how process is molded to context in actual economic environments and the consequences of this interaction for the economic outcomes of these processes.*

Satisficing, to reiterate, is a general term that relates heuristics in decision-making in contrast to maximizing or minimizing behaviour. It is part and parcel of the concept of procedural rationality. It is a conceptual term that encapsulates how goal oriented individuals tend to behave in the real world of decision-making. But what is procedurally rational—which satisficing heuristics are developed, adapted or adopted—is contingent upon goals and circumstances. Exogenously determined and imposed standards for optimality are rejected in this approach in contrast to the worldview of both the conventional economic wisdom and heuristics and biases approach.

X-efficiency theory and external benchmarks for optimal behaviour

There is another approach to procedural rationality and bounded rationality that uses rough conventional or neoclassical benchmarks for optimal performance but rejects logically derived neoclassical procedures to achieve optimal performance. Note that the heuristics and biases approach also uses neoclassical benchmarks to determine optimality but in a less nuanced and in a much more generalized manner. Leibenstein (1966, 1979; Frantz, 1997) argues that for firms to be economically efficient workers, managers, and employers, must be working as hard and as smart as they can, irrespective of their preference function. For efficiency to be achieved, certain behaviours must be realized. In the conventional model the quantity and quality of effort input per unit of time, ceteris paribus, is assumed to be constant, but it is also typically and implicitly assumed to be fixed at some maximum.

But because, in reality, individuals and organizations deviate from conventional economic norms of effort maximization, firms tend to be economically inefficient; they are not as productive as they might otherwise be. Leibenstein refers to this scenario as x-inefficiency in production. Individuals and organizations that are x-inefficient are considered to irrational or quasi-rational at best, according to Leibeinstein. Such quasi-rational behaviour is assumed to be a function of individuals maximizing their utility, where utility maximization is consistent with x-inefficiency in production. In this case, a Darwinian-survival of the fittest process that forces individuals to maximize effort inputs is not in place. The latter process is assumed in the conventional model.

In the bounded rationality approach, x-inefficient behaviour would be considered rational because the decision-makers are achieving their goals and objectives. But outcomes are suboptimal in the sense that the firm's output is less than it might otherwise be. We have rational inefficiencies (Altman, 2005b, 2006, 2015). The fact that Leibenstein refers to x-inefficient decision-makers as quasi-rational or irrational is beside the point since, he argues, that their choices are purposeful and deliberate as well as utility maximizing. But their choices derived from the decision-makers' utility maximizing preferences simply don't generate economically efficient outcomes.

For Leibenstein, the conventional economic norm of effort maximization is a reasonable one if productivity is to be maximized, but one that is typically not realized in the real world economy. A critical difference between Leibenstein and conventional economics is that he does not assume that organizations necessarily perform x-efficiently in production. Whether they do or not can't simply be assumed. It becomes an empirical question—a key methodological point amongst behavioural economists. In addition, a key point of focus for Leibenstein is the process by which an organization might achieve x-efficiency or the conditions under which sub-optimal levels of production (x-inefficiency) are realized. This is well situated in the bounded rationality approach with its focus on procedural rationality—what are the actual behaviours required to meet a set of objectives are investigated and articulated (Cyert & March, 1963). According to Leibenstein, one can identify market structures, decision-maker's preferences, and industrial relations structures that are most conducive to x-efficiency in production. This can't be done by framing ones' analysis in terms of maximizing or minimizing behaviour—this is too simplistic and not empirically based. One might argue that x-efficiency is more related co-operative forms of governance than to mechanistic maximizing–minimizing behaviour (Altman, 2005b, 2006). Leibenstein also argues that there is no natural imperative for x-efficiency in production to take place, hence the importance of garnering an understanding of how firms behave inside of the black box of the firm.

Assuming that x-efficiency always exists (as the conventional narrative would have it) generates serious missing variable problems thereby misspecifying some of the key causes of a firm's suboptimal performance. Overall, from this perspective, the conventional overarching behavioural norms might be correct (effort maximization is required to maximize productivity), but this does not imply that these norms will be achieved or that the path to achieve these norms can be reduced into a simplistic optimisation space. Akerlof (2002) presents a related model of sub-optimal effort performance through an application of efficiency wage theory, a variant of x-efficiency theory, to macroeconomic theory and policy.[a]

Nudging versus constraints change and redesign

In popular lore, behavioural economics is very much about getting the individual to do what the expert perceives to be in the best interest of the individual. This is somewhat exaggerated, but is consistent with important aspects of the heuristics and biases approach to behavioural economics. This stems from the fact that individuals' choices tend to systematically deviate from conventional economic behavioural norms, assumed to be the benchmark for rational-optimal behaviour, and that individuals are hardwired to behave in this deviant fashion. This has given rise to the nudge literature spearheaded by Thaler and Sunstein (2008). Although some of the nudge literature is oriented towards improving information stocks and flows and processing capabilities (arguably consistent with enhancing the freedom of choice afforded to decision-makers), the substance of the argument is to either softly (soft paternalism) and or to much more forcefully induce individuals to make choices which do not necessarily correspond with their preferences. The focus of the nudge narrative is in the

a. Akerlof and Shiller (2009) for a broader application of behavioural economics principles to an understanding of macroeconomic phenomenon.

domain of consumption. This is achieved through what's referred to as choice architecture.

Thaler and Sunstein (2008, p. 6) maintain that: 'Individuals make pretty bad decisions in many cases because they do not pay full attention in their decision-making (they make intuitive choices based on heuristics), they don't have self-control, they are lacking in full information, and they suffer from limited cognitive abilities'. They also argue that those who oppose choice architecture make the false assumption that individuals typically make choices that are in their own best interest or that their choices are better than those that would be made on their behalf by the expert or choice architect (Thaler & Sustein, 2008, p. 6). The essence of this approach is imposing external norms for what is deemed to be in the best of the individual on individual preferences and choices.

In the bounded rationality approach, the null hypothesis is that individuals do the best they can (satisficing) given the constraints, capabilities, and opportunities that bound their choice sets. Hence, errors in decision-making or individuals' inability to realize their preferred preferences are often viewed as being a function of the constraints, capabilities, and opportunities faced by decision-makers—their decision-making environment. The core problem is typically viewed as not being a function of the hardwiring of the individual. Hence, the focus is on improving the decision-making environment, which would include improving the capabilities of the individual to process, understand, and access relevant information sets. Also, mechanisms could be put in place to resolve social dilemmas, or to provide a more equitable environment where such dilemmas can be resolved. For example, if women have relatively weak bargaining rights and capabilities they have less ability to realize their preferences than do men. The same can be said of employees as compared to employers—this a point made well over 200 years ago by Adam Smith. There is still the possibility of individuals not having the capability of making optimal self-interested decisions because of issues psychological and physiological issues (such as addiction and mental illness). But this another matter. Hence, in the bounded rationality approach, the focus is on institutional design and improving decision-making capabilities and technology, as opposed to nudging individuals to make decisions that best fits into the experts worldview of what's in the best interest of some average individual.

Conclusion

A summary of the differences between conventional economics and the bounded rationality and heuristics and biases approaches to behavioural economics is presented in Fig. 2.1. A critical difference between the bounded rationality approach and heuristics and biases approach is that the former does not necessarily use conventional behavioural norms as the ideal for rational and optimal behaviour. Deviations from conventional norms demonstrate a critical weakness of the conventional economic wisdom but, according to the bounded rationality

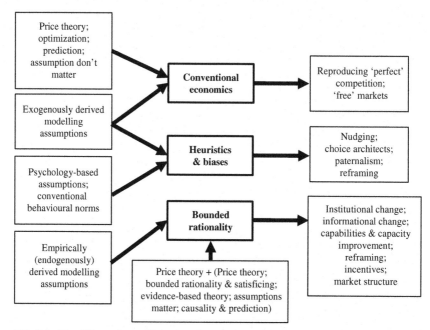

FIG. 2.1 The different faces of behavioural economics and the conventional wisdom.

approach, do not necessarily imply errors, biases, or irrationality in decision-making. On the other hand, one cannot assume that simply because individuals adopt heuristics as opposed to conventional decision-making rules, that these heuristics and related decisions are in some sense necessarily optimal. Errors and biases can exist. Needless to say, in the bounded rationality approach the typical prior assumption is that individuals do the best they can, given their decision-making capabilities and their decision-making environment. But this does not mean that such rational decisions, from the perspective of the individual, are best for the organization or society at large. As a footnote, one should point out that the individual might not achieve her objective because of flaws in the overall decision-making environment.

From the bounded rationality perspective, which behavioural and related norms should be used as optimal decision-making benchmarks must be empirically derived and contextualized by individuals' decision-making capabilities and their decision-making environment. These benchmarks should not be externally imposed as it is the conventional economic wisdom and for the most part in the heuristics and biases approach.

For this reason, in the bounded rationality approach much attention is paid to changing the capabilities and constraints that bound an individual's decision-making environment. This would include education, improvements to information availability, asymmetries, and understandings, changes to incentives, power relationships, and changes to the broader decision-making and related institutional environment. In contrast, from the heuristics and biases perspective the tendency has been to correct or fix decision-making problems from the perspective that individuals need be nudged towards choices that they might not otherwise make due to hardwired behavioural flaws. The ideal or optimal choices are prescribed exogenously. To reiterate, in the bounded rationality approach the ideal choices are derived from individual preferences and what these would be in an ideal decision-making environment (Altman, 2010, 2011).

When particular individual preferences generate negative externalities, then one has a social dilemma that needs to be resolved, going well beyond articulating a framework to facilitate the realization of the ideal choices of the individual decision-maker. Examples of these social dilemmas are:

- Firm decision-makers might prefer a low wage, even conflictual, x-inefficient firm to one that is relatively high wage, co-operative, and x-efficient even if both are equally cost competitive, in contrast to the preferences of most employees.
- Smokers might not care about the second-hand smoke they impose on others violating the preferences of non-smokers.
- Some individuals' utility is enhanced by freeriding on others which can cause common pool problems.

These conflicting preference and free rider issues and problems can't be resolved simply by addressing individualized choice problems, which have been a major point focus of behavioural economics. But behavioural economics can inform the resolution of such social dilemmas by informing the conversation about the actual preferences of individuals and their formation and how this might contribute towards resolving social dilemmas.

References

Akerlof, G. A. (1970). The market for 'lemons': Quality uncertainty and the market mechanism. *Quarterly Journal of Economics*, *84*, 488–500.

Akerlof, G. A. (2002). Behavioral macroeconomics and macroeconomic behavior. *American Economic Review*, *92*, 411–433.

Akerlof, G. A., & Kranton, R. E. (2010). *Identity economics: How our identities shape our work, wages, and well-being.* Princeton, NJ: Princeton University Press.

Akerlof, G. A., & Shiller, R. J. (2009). *Animal spirits: How human psychology drives the economy, and why it matters for global capitalism.* Princeton NJ: Princeton University Press.

Altman, M. (2017). Rational inefficiency: Smart thinking, bounded rationality, and the scientific basis for economic failure and success. In M. Altman (Ed.), *Handbook of behavioural economics and smart decision-making rational decision-making within the bounds of reason.* Cheltenham, England: Edward Elgar.

Altman, H. J. R. (2020). *The behavioural economics of organizational inefficiency: The example of the New Zealand fitness industry.* Australia: Masters of Philosophy (Research), School of Economics and Finance Faculty of Business, Queensland University of Technology.

Altman, M. (2005a). Reconciling altruistic, moralistic, and ethical behavior with the rational economic agent and competitive markets. *Journal of Economic Psychology*, *26*, 732–757.

Altman, M. (2005b). Behavioral economics, power, rational inefficiencies, fuzzy sets, and public policy. *Journal of Economic Issues, 39*, 683–706.

Altman, M. (2006). What a difference an assumption makes: Effort discretion, economic theory, and public policy. In M. Altman (Ed.), *Handbook of contemporary behavioral economics: Foundations and developments* (pp. 125–164). New York: Armonk.

Altman, M. (2010). A behavioral and institutional foundation of preference and choice behavior: Freedom to choose and choice X-inefficiencies. *Review of Social Economy, 69*, 395–411.

Altman, M. (2011). Behavioural economics, ethics, and public policy: Paving the road to freedom or serfdom? In J. Boston (Ed.), *Ethics and public policy: Contemporary issues* (pp. 23–48). Wellington: Victoria University Press.

Altman, M. (2012). *Behavioral economics for dummies*. Mississauga, ON: Wiley.

Altman, M. (2015). Introduction. In M. Altman (Ed.), *Real-world decision making: An encyclopedia of behavioral economics*. Santa Barbara: Greenwood, ABC-CLIO.

Becker, G. S. (1996). *Accounting for tastes*. Cambridge, MA: Harvard University Press.

Berg, N., & Gigerenzer, G. (2010). As-if behavioral economics: Neoclassical economics in disguise? *History of Economic Ideas, 18*(133–166), 2010.

Commons, J. R. (1931). Institutional economics. *American Economic Review, 21*, 648–657.

Cyert, R. M., & March, J. C. (1963). *A behavioral theory of the firm*. Englewood Cliffs, NJ: Prentice-Hall.

Damasio, A. R. (1996). *Descartes' error*. London: Penguin.

Duesenberry, J. S. (1949). *Income, saving, and the theory of consumption behavior*. Cambridge, MA: Harvard University Press.

Frantz, R. S. (1997). X-efficiency theory, evidence and applications. In Vol. 23. *Topics in regulatory economics and policy*. Boston/Dordrecht/London: Kluwer Academic.

Friedman, M. (1953). *The methodology of positive economics*. In *Essays in positive economics*. (pp. 3–43). Chicago: University of Chicago Press.

Gigerenzer, G. (2007). *Gut feelings: The intelligence of the unconscious*. New York: Viking.

Kahneman, D., & Tversky, A. (1979). Prospect theory: An analysis of decision under risk. *Econometrica, 47*, 263–291.

Kahneman, D. (2003). Maps of bounded rationality: Psychology for behavioral economics. *American Economic Review, 93*, 1449–1475.

Kahneman, D. (2011). *Thinking, fast and slow*. New York: Farrar, Straus and Giroux.

Leibenstein, H. (1966). Allocative efficiency vs. 'X-efficiency'. *American Economic Review, 56*, 392–415.

Leibenstein, H. (1979). A branch of economics is missing: Micro-micro theory. *Journal of Economic Literature, 17*, 477–502.

Lewis, A., Webley, P., & Furnham, A. (1995). *The new economic mind*. New York: Harvester Wheatsheaf.

March, J. G. (1978). Bounded rationality, ambiguity, and the engineering of choice. *Bell Journal of Economics, 9*, 587–608.

North, D. C. (1971). Institutional change and economic growth. *Journal of Economic History, 31*, 118–125.

Nussbaum, M. (2011). *Creating capabilities: The human development approach*. Cambridge, MA: Harvard University Press.

Reder, M. W. (1982). Chicago economics: Permanence and change. *Journal of Economic Literature, 20*, 1–38.

Sen, A. (1985). *Commodities and capabilities*. Amsterdam: North-Holland.

Simon, H. A. (1959). Theories of decision making in economics and behavioral science. *American Economic Review, 49*, 252–283.

Simon, H. A. (1978). Rationality as a process and as a product of thought. *American Economic Review*, *70*, 1–16.

Simon, H. A. (1986). Rationality in psychology and economics. *Journal of Business*, *59*, S209–S224.

Simon, H. A. (1987). Behavioral economics. In J. Eatwell, M. Millgate, & P. Newman (Eds.), *The New Palgrave: A dictionary of economics* (pp. 221–225). London: Macmillan.

Smith, V. L. (2003). Constructivist and ecological rationality in economics. *American Economic Review*, *93*, 465–508.

Smith, V. L. (2005). Behavioral economics research and the foundations of economics. *Journal of Socio-Economics*, *34*, 135–150.

Thaler, R. H., & Sunstein, C. (2008). *Nudge: Improving decisions about health, wealth, and happiness*. New Haven and London: Yale University Press.

Todd, P. M., & Gigerenzer, G. (2003). Bounding rationality to the world. *Journal of Economic Psychology*, *24*, 143–165.

Tversky, A., & Kahneman, D. (1981). The framing of decisions and the psychology of choice. *Science*, *211*, 453–458.

Veblen, T. (1899). *Theory of the leisure class: An economic study of institutions*. New York/London: Macmillan.

Chapter 3

How complexity affects decision-making

Chapter outline

Introduction 39
Key points of overlap: Hayek and
    behavioural economics 40
Assumptions matter 42
Revisiting complexity and the expert 48
Contemporary views on
    bottom-up decision making
    and individualized norms for
    rationality 51
Ecological rationality and the
    spontaneous order 58
Opening the door to intelligent
    design 60
Opening the door to multiple
    equilibria: Casting shadows
    on the spontaneous order
    and ecological rationality 63
Conclusion: Hayek's Golden
    nugget in decision-making
    theory 68
References 71

Introduction

Much of Hayek's research that relates to behavioural economics stems from his scholarship on the development of the concept of ecological efficiency and, related to this, effective real-world decision making, all which is directly pertinent to the theme of this book. This, in turn, relates to what Hayek refers to as the spontaneous order, where the most effective decisions and institutions arise 'spontaneously' from bottom-up decision making processes, often in an unplanned and non-deliberative manner. Critical to Hayek's research platform is integrating into economic theory an understanding of the limited processing capacity of the human brain, the reality of complex and costly information, and the manner in which people process such information in day-to-day decision making. These are core issues in behavioural economics. Given such a neurological and informational environment, Hayek argues that evolutionary, bottom-up derived behavioural norms are most reasonable and actually superior to norms constructed by expert design.

In contrast to this perspective, both conventional economics (inclusive of free-market economics) as well as most contemporary behavioural economists deem experts' construction of decision making norms to be rational and capable of generating optimal outcomes. Hayek does not refer to bottom-up decision

Smart Economic Decision-Making in a Complex World. https://doi.org/10.1016/B978-0-12-811461-2.00003-1
39

making as rational, because it is not necessarily planned or the product of a clear and unequivocal deliberative process. However, Hayek's understanding of the decision making process is consistent with what many behavioural economists, especially those following in the tradition of Herbert Simon, consider to be rational behaviour; rational in terms of the decision making constraints faced by individuals and their objectives. This is now referred to as ecological rationality, but it is actually closely related to the concept of bounded rationality proposed by a pioneer in behavioural economics, Simon (1955, 1978, 1979, 1987).

In this chapter, there is no effort to try to 'prove' that Hayek was a closet behavioural economist or that behavioural economics should be re-cast in a Hayekian or Austrian School mould. Rather, it is of interest to better understand the overlap between Hayek's research, which was very much influenced by his understanding and appreciation of the complexity of information and the brain as a scarce resource, and behavioural economics (Caldwell, 2004; D'Amico & Boettke, 2010). This is especially true of the stream of behavioural economics pioneered by Herbert Simon, where the same concerns and issues are identified. So, I focus on examining the overlap between Hayek's research and behavioural economics, especially as it pertains to the complexity of information, decision making heuristics, institutional design and—related to this—the rules of the game. As well, I ponder some of the insights and questions that Hayek's research platform raises for better understanding behavioural economics and, more importantly, building more robust economic theory. Of particular importance, Hayek's arguments serve to illuminate key analytical differences between different perspectives in behavioural economics as well as between behavioural economics and conventional economic theory.

Key points of overlap: Hayek and behavioural economics

Before going into any great detail on the links between Hayek's research on decision making and behavioural economics, it is useful to outline these linkages. There is considerable overlap between Hayek's research and behavioural economics. Moreover, Hayek provides valuable insights into the descriptive and analytical aspects of behavioural economics—how individuals actually behave and why they behave the way they do.

Hayek's scholarly contributions overlap and inform the notion of bounded rationality, advanced by Simon (1955, 1978, 1979, 1987). Bounded rationality refers to decision making that takes into account the limited capacity of the human brain to process all relevant information and to predict the probability of outcomes or the consequences of our choices. It also relates to how the overall decision making environment faced by the individual decision maker impacts on the decision making process and the choices individuals make. Moreover, generally, Hayek's research speaks to how individuals deal with complex information, where the brain is a scarce resource (D'Amico & Boettke, 2010; Hayek, 1944, 1945, 1952).

Hayek also deals with how the brain processes complex information and how this affects decision making. Process affects outcomes. This is a long-standing point made by scholars working in the tradition of Herbert Simon, such as Gigerenzer (2007) and Smith (2003, 2005, 2008). By contrast, conventional economics make the implicit—and often explicit—assumption that how individuals make decisions (the decision making process) has no effect on outcomes. All outcomes are assumed to be consistent with detailed cost-benefit analyses of the available options.

Behavioural economists argue that individuals don't behave, on average, in the manner prescribed and predicted by conventional economics. However, Hayek's understanding of human decision making, from a normative perspective (how individuals should engage in decision making), stands in marked contrast to much of contemporary behavioural economics where design (conventional or neoclassical calculation) is typically ranked as superior to bottom-up, relatively spontaneous, decision making. In the behavioural economics program initially configured by Kahneman and Tversky (1979, 2000; see also Kahneman, 2003, 2011; Tversky & Kahneman, 1986), neoclassical behavioural norms serve as the benchmark for rational, optimal, efficient, and often smart behaviour. This approach to behavioural economics is often referred to as the 'errors and biases' approach.

According to conventional economic wisdom—as well as in the errors and biases approach of behavioural economics—neoclassical behavioural norms, given by design, typically generate superior decision making and socio-economic outcomes to less precise, bottom-up approaches to decision making. In other words, the expert typically knows best—or better—than the average individual how to achieve efficient outcomes, or even outcomes that generate higher levels of utility, satisfaction or happiness. Conventional economics assumes that individuals, on average, behave in accordance with neoclassical norms. Individuals are doing the best they can as a consequence of following best-practice (neoclassical) behavioural norms.

Hayek's understanding of day-to-day and optimal human decision making is normally and normatively consistent with the research platforms of Herbert Simon, Vernon Smith, and Gerd Gegerenzer.[a] Their approaches to decision making are often referred to as ecological rationality. Ecological rationality defines rational or smart behaviour in terms of what individuals are capable of doing given the physiological constraints they face as decision makers as well as the constraints they face with regards to their decision making environment.

---

a. But more recently Kahneman (2011) introduced more nuanced perspective to decision making as compared to the heuristics and biases narrative. His slow and fast thinking narrative is about which approach to decision making makes more sense if one is to generate the best possible decisions— slow or fast (the latter often associated with the fast and frugal narrative of Gigerenzer, 2007). This slow and fast thinking approach, I would argue, is quite consistent with Hayek's favourable take on bottom-up decision making.

This approach is in stark contrast to the now dominant errors and biases approach in contemporary behavioural economics: conventional or neoclassical behavioural norms are rejected as a baseline for determining what's rational, efficient, effective, optimal or smart. So, it is important to reiterate that Hayek's approach is consistent with the arguments and findings across behavioural economics that individuals tend not to behave in conformity with neoclassical behavioural norms.

Assumptions matter

Underlying Hayek's approach to understanding human agency and decision making and public policy are the behavioural assumptions he makes with regards to information, information processing, human cognitive abilities, the extent of heterogeneity of evolved preferences across individuals, the meaning of 'optimal' decisions and behaviour, and how best-practice institutions evolve or develop. These assumptions differ dramatically from those of conventional economics. They also differ from those contemporary behavioural economists that follow the errors and biases research platform advanced by Daniel Kahneman and Amos Tversky. Upon the basis of a different, and more reality-based set of behavioural assumptions, Hayek builds an alternative theoretical edifice.

One important link between Hayek and behavioural economics is his understanding that realistic modelling assumptions are important in forming a better understanding of human action and, related to this, of the economy. Unlike conventional economics, Hayek argues that it is important to introduce assumptions related to human behaviour and individuals' decision making environment that are reality-based. For conventional economics what's of fundamental importance is whether a model generates good predictions about human behaviour. It is not important whether or not individuals actually behave in the manner assumed by the economist. For much of contemporary economics, how individuals actually behave is of little analytical consequence. This is exemplified by the calibration exercises that increasingly dominate empirical economics. The models simply need to fit the data, irrespective of the realism and reasonability of the models' behavioural assumptions (Freedman, 2011).

This follows in the traditional Friedman methodological pathway and his understanding of objective, positive, or scientific economics, where a model's predictive capacity is what counts, or its fit/correlation with the facts. Friedman (1953, p. 14) maintains that getting one's behavioural assumptions even reasonably correct:

> ...is fundamentally wrong and productive of much mischief. Far from providing an easier means for sifting valid from invalid hypotheses, it [testing for the realism of assumptions] only confuses the issue, promotes misunderstanding about the significance of empirical evidence for economic theory, produces a misdirection of much intellectual effort devoted to the development of positive economics, and impedes the attainment of consensus on tentative hypothesis in positive economics.

Friedman also argues (1953, p. 14) that good theory contains: '…wildly inaccurate descriptive representations of reality, and, in general the more significant the theory, the more unrealistic the assumption (in this sense)'.

Also, in conventional economics, normatively, individuals are expected to behave in a fashion that will result in optimal economic outcomes. People are expected to behave according to plan, or least as if they are behaving according to plan to produce optimal economic outcomes. The pie size should be maximized, costs should be minimized—causing material welfare to be maximized. Once again, this optimality assumption builds upon the assumption that rational or smart people will behave according to the design recommended by conventional economics.

In his research on information complexity, Hayek focuses on what he argues to be a fundamental flaw in mainstream economics: the assumption that any one individual has the capacity to know and process all information relevant to decision making. This includes information on prices and preferences. He also challenges the assumption that any one individual—a central planner, Walrasian auctioneer, or expert—can know all relevant information required to make optimal economic decisions in either a static or, more realistically, in a dynamic economic environment. At one point Hayek (1945, pp. 519–520) argues:

> *The peculiar character of the problem of a rational economic order is determined precisely by the fact that the knowledge of the circumstances of which we must make use never exists in concentrated or integrated form, but solely as the dispersed bits of incomplete and frequently contradictory knowledge which all the separate individuals possess. The economic problem of society is thus not merely a problem of how to allocate 'given' resources – if 'given' is taken to mean given to a single mind which deliberately solves the problem set by these 'data.' It is rather a problem of how to secure the best use of resources known to any of the members of society, for ends whose relative importance only these individuals know. Or, to put it briefly, it is a problem of the utilization of knowledge not given to anyone in its totality.*

Hayek (1945, p. 522) makes the related point:

> *The common idea now seems to be that all such knowledge should as a matter of course be readily at the command of everybody, and the reproach of irrationality leveled against the existing economic order is frequently based on the fact that it is not so available. This view disregards the fact that the method by which such knowledge can be made as widely available as possible is precisely the problem to which we have to find an answer.*

For Hayek, the most realistic behavioural assumption to make when modelling individual decision makers at the microeconomic level is that, in a world of complex and costly information, the individual knows best what's in her or his best interest. This information is most effectively and efficiently conveyed through the price mechanism. At a microeconomic level, effective and efficient decision making does not typically take place in the supra-calculating fashion prescribed by conventional economics. This flows from the complexity of information and the related costly information processing costs (Hayek, 1944, 1945, 1948).

Hayek's preferred bottom-up approach to decision making—which deviates, in broad strokes, from the prescribed 'rational' conventional economic behaviour—is also assumed to be best-practice decision making. Each individual might take a different, yet rational, approach to decision making (and the resulting choices) given the decision making constraints that she or he faces. Thus, if one recognizes the reality of the constraints facing individual decision makers, according to Hayek, one would expect them to behave in a manner that deviates from the best-practice calculating behaviour prescribed by conventional economics. Moreover, this bottom-up process of information processing and interpersonal communication is most consistent with individual liberties. Given the assumption he makes pertaining to decision making constraints, Hayek does not wish to dictate how individuals should behave. Rather, how people do behave, as free individuals, is typically how they should behave, for their decisions to be effective and efficient.

Also, Hayek (1944, 1945, 1948, 1952, 1981, 1989) clearly assumes that decision making processes or heuristics evolve over historical time. Hayek (1952); D'Amico & Boettke, 2010) also argues that the brain evolves in terms of memory, understanding, and instinct: we are not who we were born as. In addition, Hayek emphasizes the importance of cultural change as an evolutionary mechanism to deal with decision making challenges. The brain remembers evolved heuristics, which then underlies much of our decision making, especially intuitive decision making. Moreover, we often do not understand the heuristics we use. We tend to use heuristic or decision making processes that we believe work in particular circumstances or environments; even if they are not developed or adopted in a calculated and carefully thought-out manner, consistent with conventional norms of rationality. This is analogous to driving a car. Most of us don't have a clue how the engine works. But we know that pressing the gas pedal accelerates the vehicle and pressing on the brakes slows the car down. Most of us cross the street, first checking for traffic; or drive our car on the 'right' side of the road; or repair a computer, without much thought, intuitively. Actually, thinking about what we're going to do might cause us more harm than good, causing decisions to be inefficient and ineffective.[b]

Hayek argues (1945, p. 527):

> *The most significant fact about this system is the economy of knowledge with which it operates, or how little the individual participants need to know in order to be able to take the right action.*
> *The problem which we meet here is by no means peculiar to economics but arises in connection with nearly all truly social phenomena, with language and most of*

---

b. This assumes that individuals have developed the intuition, over time, that will yield the 'correct' decisions without thinking carefully about their decisions. This raises the question of when does it make good sense to carefully think over one's decision if one has the time to so. This slower deliberative process could also be based or informed by the evolved experience of the decision maker. This point relates to the fast and slow thinking narrative developed by Kahneman (2011).

our cultural inheritance, and constitutes really the central theoretical problem of all social science. As Alfred Whitehead has said in another connection, 'It is a profoundly erroneous truism, repeated by all copy-books and by eminent people when they are making speeches, that we should cultivate the habit of thinking what we are doing. The precise opposite is the case. Civilization advances by extending the number of important operations which we can perform without thinking about them.' This is of profound significance in the social field. We make constant use of formulas, symbols and rules whose meaning we do not understand and through the use of which we avail ourselves of the assistance of knowledge which individually we do not possess. We have developed these practices and institutions by building upon habits and institutions which have proved successful in their own sphere and which have in turn become the foundation of the civilization we have built up.

Critical to Hayek's worldview is that we learn and internalize decision making procedures. Once again, for Hayek, understanding the procedures is not of any great practical or analytical significance. It is the evolutionary learning process that is critical to effective and efficient decision making. But Hayek's argument is at a very general level, providing little insight or discussion on the most effective ways of internalizing decision making procedures or rules. Overall, Hayek appears to sympathize with a learning-by-doing approach, which is most consistent with bottom-up or decentralized decision making in a world of complex information.

Hayek (1981, p. 157) maintains that:

In other words: man has certainly more often learnt to do the right thing without comprehending why it was the right thing, and he still is often served better by custom than understanding. Other objects were primarily defined for him by the appropriate way of conduct towards them. It was a repertoire of learnt rules which told him what was the right and what was the wrong way of acting in different circumstances that gave him his increasing capacity to adapt to changing conditions – and particularly to co-operate with the other members of his group. Thus a tradition of rules of conduct, existing apart from any one individual who had learnt them, began to govern human life.

Hayek aspires to model how individuals behave, broadly speaking, in the real world. To produce such a descriptive model, behavioural and institutional assumptions matter tremendously. This is a key point, made more recently by Herbert Simon and by Daniel Kahneman and Amos Tversky. Like Simon, for Hayek more reasonable modelling assumptions yield models that not only better portray how real people make decisions, but provide insights on how effective and smart decisions are made—and can be made—in the real world. Also like Simon, Hayek rejects the conventional economic benchmark for smart, effective, and efficient behaviour. Based on Hayek's behavioural and institutional assumptions, the conventional benchmarks are not reasonable or appropriate. So, the conventional norms for smart behaviour are rejected.

But unlike Simon, Hayek pays little attention to the specifics of what best-practice or optimal decision making processes might look like given his more realistic assumptions about human decision making. Simon (1955, 1978, 1979, 1987) examines how effective decisions can be made based on an individual's specified goals and objectives and the various physiological, psychological, and institutional constraints faced by the decision maker. This is referred to as process rationality. If there is an effective or more efficient way of doing things then it is possible that there can be errors in decision making. Also, economic outcomes can be socially sub-optimal. Individual behaviour might be the best possible from the individual's point of view, but well below par from the perspective of society. So, choices might be inefficient from a broader social perspective even while these same outcomes might be consistent with the preferences of individual decision makers (see also Chapters 3 and 4).

Because Hayek argues that best-practice decision making processes are very case specific—very individualized—it is just about impossible, according to Hayek, to identify what best-practice decision making processes should look like—what optimal decisions are. The expert does not have the ability to determine what decision making processes and outcomes are reasonable or possibly optimal given the constraints and preferences of individuals or groups of individuals. Often, Hayek appears to take on a tautological judgmental approach to evaluating decision making: whatever was and is must be optimal because it took place or is taking place, as part of a bottom-up evolutionary process. This is an extremely strong form of approach to ecological rationality. From this perspective there can be no normative basis to judge if particular decisions and outcomes are flawed from the individual's or society's perspective. From a very profound methodological and policy perspective, the bottom line for Hayek reads like the bottom line in mainstream neoclassical economics of the efficient market-rational expectations variety (Fama, 1970). However, individuals behave in the real world, what counts is that individual choices tend to yield optimal results. What you see is optimal. Individuals behave as if they are optimizing: yielding choices and outcomes consistent with optimizing behaviour. But mainstream economics assumes that individuals *should* behave in a *specific* manner for outcomes to be optimal. So, although Hayek strongly rejects the latter as being farfetched, unrealistic, and unreasonable, he ends up assuming that quite diverse behaviours—simply because they are bottom-up or organically based, not driven by someone else's design (top-down)—will generate optimal or best-possible outcomes. Still, it is important to reiterate that Hayek emphasizes that assumptions about best-practice human behaviour must be based on an understanding of how real people make decisions in the real world. Otherwise, our economic theories are, at best, logically consistent fantasy plays.

Although some of Hayek's core arguments sit comfortably with the emphasis that behavioural economists tend to place on real world behaviour when modelling decision making, Hayek's assumptions about the optimality of outcomes are far removed from the arguments behavioural economics makes on the benchmarks for best-possible decisions and decision making processes. Overall, his assumptions are even further removed from much of contemporary behavioural economics, which follows upon the path set by Kahneman and Tversky's errors and biases approach.

As in the analytical perspective developed by Hayek, Kahneman and Tversky's errors and biases approach rejects mainstream economics' assumption that people behave in accordance with the dictums of conventional economic theory. However, in the Kahneman and Tversky approach, systematic errors and biases in decision making are identified, arising from typical and expected human behaviour: people tend not to behave in accordance with conventional economic norms. The latter typically represent the norms or benchmarks for rational and effective behaviour.

Like Hayek, behavioural economists working in the tradition of Kahneman and Tversky develop descriptive models of human behaviour—models that predict how real people behave, on average, in the real world. Hayek actually engages less in precise predictive model building and more in developing general narrative models on how individuals can be expected to behave in a world of complex information. But unlike Hayek, in the Kahneman and Tversky tradition, there is little possibility that such predicted behaviour can be smart or rational. There is little analytical space here for ecologically rational behaviour that systematically breaks from conventional economic behavioural norms. From this perspective, because individuals make decisions that are inconsistent with conventional behavioural norms, their decision processes and choices tend to be ineffective, inefficient, and laden with errors and biases. Evolved (through some evolutionary process) decision making processes and choices can very well be error-prone and biased. The decision making constraints faced by decision makers often result in errors and biases in decision making. This is not to say that actual choices must always be error-prone and biased because they deviate from conventional decision making norms. But this approach tends to lean towards persistent errors and biases in decision making as pervasive in the real world of decision making.

Moreover, unlike Hayek, emotions and intuition are introduced by Kahneman (2003) as an important cause for errors and biases in decision making. But Kahneman also maintains that there are important exceptions to this rule. Kahneman (2003) argues that although: '…intuition was associated with poor performance [in the examples discussed by Kahneman], intuitive thinking can also be powerful and accurate. High skill is acquired by prolonged practice, and the performance of skills is rapid and effortless'. For Kahneman and those following in his and Tversky's tradition, this is of great significance, since emotion and intuition underlie much of bottom-up heuristic-based decision making.

For Hayek, emotions and intuition are key components of intelligent bottom-up decision making, given the constraints faced by real-world decision makers. However, according to Hayek, they typically yield efficient and effective choices, in spite of the fact that these choices often deviate from conventional economic behavioural norms. For Hayek, conventional norms for decision making are typically inappropriate benchmarks for best-practice behaviour.

Revisiting complexity and the expert

Hayek rejects the notion that there can be unique normative standards for optimal behavioural that can be applied to all individuals at any given point in historical time. This point stems from Hayek's assumptions relating to the complexity of information and human beings' limited processing capabilities. This is tied to: the cost of acquiring and processing information, the importance of tacit information—which only individual decision makers can effectively and efficiently access, and differential preferences across individuals that belie efforts to impose a limited number of objectives on any given population. This argues against expert design and imposition of rules for decision making, and the forcing of exogenously determined choices upon economic agents.

We are too complex in our preferences, and information is too complex for the expert to arrive at better heuristics and choices than the individual. With paternalism, there are externally determined and imposed standards or norms for optimal behaviour—individuals' revealed preferences would not be their own; they would become those of the expert and driven by his or her limited knowledge. Individual utility would not and could not be maximized in this type of scenario, according to Hayek. It is important to emphasize that this perspective is not only in stark contrast to conventional economic wisdom's assumptions about ideal decision making procedures, the costliness of information, and the human brain's decision making capabilities. It is also in stark contrast with the assumption that one can typically use some generic economic 'man' (*homo economicus*) to model human behaviour that contravenes and assumes away the reality of individuals with different—very often conflicting—preferences.

Hayek's view also stands in contradistinction to the dominant errors and biases approach of behavioural economics, which uses exogenously determined benchmarks, not only to determine optimal decision making procedures, but also to determine the preferences that individuals *would* have if their welfare or wellbeing were to be maximized. The public policy side of the errors and biases approach is now often represented by the notion of 'soft paternalism' and relates to a basic premise in the Kahneman-Tversky perspective that individuals' psychological and cognitive limitations often yield errors and biases in decision making and, related to this, produce choices that contravene the decision maker's self-interest. Thaler and Sustein are leading expositors of this worldview. They (2009, p. 6) write: 'Individuals make pretty bad decisions in many cases because they do not pay full attention in their decision making (they make intuitive choices based on heuristics), they don't have self-control, they are lacking in full information, and they suffer from limited cognitive abilities'.

They also make the point that (Thaler & Sustein, 2008, p. 6), people opposing choice architecture do so because they make the false assumption that: 'almost all people, almost all of the time, make choices that are in their best interest or at the very least are better than the choices that would be made by someone else. We claim that this assumption is false. In fact, we do not think that anyone believes this on reflection'.

Thaler and Sustein (2003) argue that people are irrational in that they do not behave in accordance with the expectations of standard economic theory:

> *People do not exhibit rational expectations, fail to make forecasts that are consistent with Bayes' rule, use heuristics that lead them to make systematic blunders, exhibit preference reversals (that is, they prefer A to B and B to A) and make different choices depending on the wording of the problem. Furthermore, in the context of inter temporal choice, people exhibit dynamic inconsistency, valuing present consumption much more than future consumption. In other words, people have self-control problems...*

Ultimately, in the biases and errors approach, people can and should be tricked (framed) into making choices the experts believe will be in their best interest. Precisely what that best interest is, it bears repeating, is very much in line with behaviours and decision making processes that are 'neoclassical', rooted in conventional economic wisdom. One need not be overly concerned at decision makers being coerced here, Thaler and Sustein (2008, p. 5) argue, since nudging-type paternalism does not involve coercion. Nudges are designed (they claim) to influence choices such that the choosers will be better off 'as judged by themselves'. Moreover, they argue that (Thaler & Sustein, 2008, p. 5):

> *The libertarian aspect of our strategies lies in the straightforward insistence that, in general, people should be free to do what they like – and to opt out of undesirable arrangements if they want to do so...We strive to design policies that maintain or increase freedom of choice...The paternalistic aspect lies in the claim that it is legitimate for choice architects to try to influence people's behavior in order to make their lives longer, healthier, and better.*

Key questions remain as to whether or not choosers are really better off post-nudging and whether or not individuals are being connived into making choices they would actually prefer not to have made.

A fundamental assumption of Hayek is that the individual knows best what's in her or his best interest. For this very reason, it is better for economic and social planning to take place at the level of the individual, family, community, or firm as opposed to being orchestrated by the central planner who does not have the ability or knowledge to even approach maximizing the economic and social wellbeing of an invariably complex set of individuals.

Hayek predicts that the imposition of expert preferences and heuristics yield sub-optimal levels of utility for most individuals and lead to a less productive economy.

Hayek (1945), pp. 520–521):

The various ways in which the knowledge on which people base their plans is communicated to them is the crucial problem for any theory explaining the economic process. And the problem of what is the best way of utilizing knowledge initially dispersed among all the people is at least one of the main problems of economic policy-or of designing an efficient economic system. The answer to this question is closely connected with that other question which arises here, that of who is to do the planning. It is about this question that all the dispute about 'economic planning' centers. This is not a dispute about whether planning is to be done or not. It is a dispute as to whether planning is to be done centrally, by one authority for the whole economic system, or is to be divided among many individuals.

The significance of tacit information in decision making is crucial to Hayek. This, to reiterate, relates to the complexity of information that the decision maker must process and interpret. But once it is recognized that the perfect information assumption is incorrect, we have to deal with the economic and social problem of how best to optimally allocate this information across agents—who is going to do the information planning? Tacit information is very task specific. It is highly idiosyncratic and can be obtained only at a very high cost by outside parties. But it is critical to decision making. Given the nature of tacit information, it is optimal for it to be managed bottom-up, rather than by experts.

However, Hayek maintains that scientific information is best managed and processed by the expert. So, there is a very important role for experts in Hayek's decision making narrative. But the expert does not do the planning or decision making. Planning and decision making is optimally achieved as a bottom-up process, which makes use of scientific advice: from doctors, engineers, architects—even, on occasions, from economists. Experts can inform an optimal decision making process and choices, but are not the ultimate decision makers. Moreover, which experts are chosen and which of the experts' advice (often conflicting) is selected should, according to Hayak, be a function of a bottom-up decision making process. Although scientific knowledge is important, it is tacit information that is most critical to day-to-day decision making. Further to the importance of tacit knowledge Hayek (1945), pp. 520–521):

But a little reflection will show that there is beyond question a body of very important but unorganized knowledge which cannot possibly be called scientific in the sense of knowledge of general rules: the knowledge of the particular circumstances of time and place. It is with respect to this that practically every individual has some advantage over all others in that he possesses unique information of which beneficial use might be made, but of which use can be made only if the decisions depending on it are left to him or are made with his active cooperation.

Contemporary views on bottom-up decision making and individualized norms for rationality

Hayek's line of reasoning sits well with some of the core arguments on intelligent decision making put forth by Vernon Smith and Gerd Gigerenzer, and by the early pioneers in behavioural economics, James March and Herb Simon. Also, of some importance is the evolutionary perspective articulated by Armen Alchian in 1950: the identification and understanding of conventional economic norms for efficiency are not necessary to garner understanding or analytically predict the behaviour or choices of economic decision makers. A major thrust of this argument is that much of human decision making behaviour—and the choices people make—are rational, even if they appear not to be so from the perspective of conventional economic wisdom.

The basic point made by Alchian is that economic entities evolve in a manner consistent with their survival. This evolution is in the context of decision makers' constraints and their changing and evolving decision making environment. Decision makers need not behave in a manner consistent with conventional economic norms of rationality, and often do not. Decision makers typically have no knowledge of what these norms are and can behave in a manner quite inconsistent with them. What counts is that decision makers behave in a manner consistent with their survival as economic (or social) entities. Firms need not be profit maximizers and households need not be utility maximizers to survive. But their actions must ultimately be consistent with survival. Such actions and decisions are rational, even if they are inconsistent with conventional economic norms of rational behaviour. At any given moment in time, however, there might be many economic entities that are engaged in inefficient and ineffective decisions. But we can predict that these decisions will result in their elimination by relatively more efficient economic concerns. Only the relatively fittest economic entities survive over historical time. Bottom-up decision making need not be efficient or effective in all economic entities. But, as in Hayek, efficient and effective decision making is what characterizes the reality of decision making at the end of the day. Although, for Hayek, there is often a strong hint of efficiency and effectiveness at any given point in time. Conventional behavioural economic norms play no role here as a benchmark for effective, efficient, or best-practice behaviour.

Simon introduces the concepts of bounded rationality and procedural rationality, which take into account the reality of everyday decision making. These concepts, therefore, define rationality in the context of what makes sense to the individual decision maker, given the constraints that he or she faces, as opposed to using some exogenously given and often unrealizable set of norms for rational behaviour. Bounded rationality is posited as an alternative to the traditional baseline for rationality—Subjective Expected Utility (SEU) theory. Subjective expected utility theory is exogenously given to us by the expert. The latter assumes that the individual can make decisions in a supra-calculating, unemotional manner, incorporating large amounts of data, and predicting the probable outcomes of alternative decisions. Moreover, it is assumed that behaviour conforming to SEU theory yields the best-possible results. Deviations from the SEU norm are both irrational and sub-optimal. For Simon subjective expected utility theory is wrong because it has no basis in the reality of the human decision maker and his or her typical decision making environment. This sits well with Hayek's celebration and focus on bottom-up decision making in the face of complex information and heterogeneous preferences (decision making objectives) across decision makers.

But Simon also pays attention to what might be ideal decision making procedures from which it is possible to deviate. Errors are possible, but they are not systemic and are correctable. More significantly, errors are not considered to be symptomatic of irrationality or of biases in decision making. Like Hayek, bottom-up, individualized, context dependent decision making is considered to be rational. And such behaviour is rational when it can be explained though a reality-based understanding of human decision making. But unlike Hayek, Simon leaves his modelling door open to possible errors in decision making. What decision makers do is not necessarily optimal, although these sub-optimal decisions can be rational.

First, with regards to his pioneering concept of bounded rationality, Simon (1987, pp. 266–267) notes that:

> The term 'bounded rationality' is used to designate rational choice that takes into account the cognitive limitations of the decision maker – limitations of both knowledge and computational capacity...Theories of bounded rationality, then, are theories of decision making and choice that assume that the decision maker wishes to attain goals, and uses his or her mind as well as possible to that end; but theories that take into account in describing the decision process the actual capacities of the human mind... What distinguishes contemporary theories of bounded rationality from these ad hoc and casual departures from the SEU [subjective expected utility] model is that the former insist that the model of human rationality must be derived from detailed and systematic empirical study of human decision making behavior in laboratory and real-world situations.

Simon emphasizes the importance of understanding deviations from SEU theory norms rooted in real life decision making. Such behaviour is certainly not irrational, given the reality of human decision making capabilities. One cannot expect rational people to behave in a manner that's inconsistent with their capabilities and their decision making environment. Simon argues (1987, p. 266):

> The particular deviations from the SEU assumptions of global maximization introduced by behaviourally oriented economists are derived from what is known, empirically, about human thought and choice processes, and especially what is known about the limits of human cognitive capacity for discovering alternatives, computing their consequences under certainty or uncertainty, and making comparisons among them.

Related to the concept of bounded rationality, Simon (1978) pays particular attention to the overlapping analytical concept of procedural rationality. Simon once again emphasizes the overriding importance for economic theory of the reality of decision making for explaining and analytically predicting economic events. Procedural rationality is all about the procedures individuals choose in order to achieve specified ends, given the multifaceted decision making constraints that they face. Critical to model building is gaining an understanding of the decision making procedures or heuristics that are appropriate, given an individual's decision making environment. Procedures that are exogenously given—but have little relationship to real world decision makers and decision making environments—should not be core to the modelling or understanding of choice theory.

However, Simon often pays heed to the notion of substantive rationality—procedures that individuals should choose if they are to achieve their objectives in an optimal manner. But, Simon appears to consider substantive rationality to be an ideal that may not be achievable, given current constraints on decision making. And, ceteris paribus, being procedurally rational can be the most that can be hoped for. However, Simon is very interested in how relaxing certain constraints—for example, introducing computer aids to decision making—can bring procedural rationality closer to substantive rationality. For example, computer technology can help decision makers become more efficient and effective in the decisions they make. Improvement to decision making aids and improvements to decision making technology (inclusive of knowledge) can contribute to increasing the wealth of nations.

Some of the ideals (optimal benchmarks) for improvements in decision making are rooted conventional economic norms of best-practice decision making. But procedural rationality informs us of what can be achieved here and now—in the real world of decision making. For Simon, it is procedural rationality that falls into the parameters of bounded rationality that defines what is rational behaviour. Simon (1978, pp. 8–9) elaborates:

> In complex situations there is likely to be a considerable gap between the real environment of a decision (the world as God or some other omniscient observer sees it) and the environment as the actors perceive it. The analysis can then address itself either to normative questions – the whole range of consequences that should enter into decisions in such situations – or descriptive questions including the question of which components of the situation are likely to be taken into account by the actors, and how the actors are likely to represent the situation as a whole. In the pre-computer era, for example, it was very difficult for managers in business organizations to pay attention to all the major variables affected by their decisions.
>
> In a world where these kinds of adjustments are prominent, a theory of rational behavior must be quite as much concerned with the characteristics of the rational actors – the means they use to cope with uncertainty and cognitive complexity – as with the characteristics of the objective environment in which they make their

decisions. In such a world, we must give an account not only of substantive rationality – the extent to which appropriate courses of action are chosen – but also procedural rationality – the effectiveness, in light of human cognitive powers and limitations of the procedures used to choose actions. As economics moves out toward situations of increasing cognitive complexity, it becomes increasingly concerned with the ability of actors to cope with the complexity and hence with the procedural aspects of rationality.

For Simon, bounded rationality and procedural rationality are the bases for modelling actual human decision making. They are also the bases for arriving at normative judgments on whether decision makers are doing the best they can, given their objects and the constraints which they face. This is in sharp contrast to the conventional economic wisdom that focuses on substantive rationality, where the normative benchmark for efficient and effective decision making is determined exogenously—outside the real world context of the decision making environment.

Hayek's focus on the superiority of bottom-up decision making sits well with Simon's pioneering approach to economic modelling. However, it is important to note that Simon sees a role for the expert—of providing the decision maker with an improved means of making more effective and efficient decisions, given the objectives of the decision maker. The expert can help improve decision making processes and outcomes by providing decision makers with better decision making tools (this point is not inconsistent with Hayek's understanding of the role of the expert in the decision making process. But, unlike Hayek, Simon does not insist that current decision making practices are necessarily the most effective and efficient. There can be errors in decision making. And, the benchmarks for these errors are not those of conventional economic wisdom. Like Hayek, Simon focuses on how real world decision makers make choices, given the decision making constraints and their objectives.

A close associate of Simon, James March, has also argued against using conventional benchmarks of rationality to determine if decision makers are behaving rationally, adopting best-practice decision making procedures, and making smart choices. March argued—way back in 1978—that our prior assumption, when examining actual decision making processes and outcomes (choices), should be that these processes and outcomes are rational, smart, and efficient. This should be the case even if individuals are behaving in a manner quite contrary to what's recommended by conventional economic wisdom. According to March, we should try to better understand how smart people behave in the real world. Individuals can be irrational, but we can't assume this from the get-go, simply because observed behaviour and choices are inconsistent with the norms for rational behaviour, as articulated by conventional economic wisdom. Models of human decision making need to be modified to incorporate alternative benchmarks of intelligent and rational decision making that are derived from the actual terrain of decision making, be it in the firm or the household.

March maintains that (1978, p. 589):

Engineers of artificial intelligence have modified their perceptions of efficient problem solving procedures by studying the actual behavior of human problem solvers. Engineers of organizational decision making have modified their models of rationality on the basis of studies of actual organizational behavior...Modern students of human choice behavior frequently assume, at least implicitly, that actual human choice behavior in some way or other is likely to make sense. It can be understood as being the behavior of an intelligent being or group of intelligent beings...

Like Hayek, for March the null hypothesis is that bottom-up decision making procedures are superior to the benchmarks that are exogenously determined in conventional economic wisdom. Decision makers, who are in the trenches of decision making, typically know what's best. This is because they best understand the constraints and context within which decision making invariably takes place.

More recently, Smith the economist and Gigerenzer (2007) the psychologist, have analysed decision making and generated results that often clash with the behavioural norms of mainstream economics. But both scholars regard much of such deviant behaviour as rational—part and parcel of a tried and tested evolutionary process. They find the good sense underlying much of what behavioural economists—adhering to the errors and biases approach—deem to be aberrant and possibly irrational behaviour. Typically less complex, more intuitive (based on past experience) decision making processes trump—in terms of survival of the organization and as benchmarks for rational and efficient decision making processes—the more complex, calculating processes celebrated by the conventional economic wisdom and by the errors and biases approach in behavioural economics. The working assumption or hypothesis of both Smith and Gigerenzer, is that bottom-up decision making processes and related choices tend to be superior, no matter how much they might deviate from conventional norms. This hypothesis is open to refutation by empirical testing. Moreover, for Smith, one can better explain and analytically predict the evolution of organizations and the behaviour of individuals by modelling decision making as a bottom-up process, where decision makers engage with their decision making environment, given the constraints they face.

Models should reflect (in simplified form) the reality of human decision making—as opposed to some ideal behavioural and institutional assumption imposed by the expert, that often has little relationship with real world decision makers and their decision making environment. Smith's (2003) perspective on decision making is explicitly tied to that of Hayek and his notion of the spontaneous order: bottom-up decision making that is often unplanned—not orchestrated in its details by the expert or central planner—yields the most effective and efficient results for both economy and society. With regards to the assumption of the superiority of bottom-up decision making, Smith finds that (2005, pp. 149–150; see also Smith, 2003):

> *It is shown that the investor who chooses to maximize expected profit (discounted total withdrawals) fails in finite time. Moreover, there exist a variety of nonprofit-maximizing behaviors that have a positive probability of never failing. In fact it is shown that firms that maximize profits are the least likely to be the market survivors. My point is simple: when experimental results are contrary to standard concepts of rationality, assume not just that people are irrational, but that you may not have the right model of rational behavior. Listen to what your subjects may be trying to tell you. Think of it this way. If you could choose your ancestors, would you want them to be survivalists or to be expected wealth maximizers?*

Gigerenzer has made similar arguments, further exploring the concept of ecological rationality. As with March and Smith, the benefit of the doubt—in terms of what is rational behaviour—is given to the actual behaviours and choices of the decision maker. Gigerenzer interprets the concept of bounded rationality, first introduced by Simon, as rationality that is contextualized by various decision making constraints which face individuals—including the neurological and environmental (such as social, cultural, and institutional)—and help mould the decision making processes adopted by individuals and the decisions they make. Rationality is not defined by benchmarks that are determined exogenously by the 'experts', where the latter is more consistent with conventional economic wisdom and the errors and biases approach to behavioural economics. In a world of bounded rationality individuals tend to choose decision making processes and tools (heuristics) that work, given the constraints they face. These bottom-up choices tend to be efficient and ecologically rational—more so than the decision making norms prescribed by experts. Gigerenzer and his colleagues argue (Todd & Gigerenzer, 2003, pp. 147–148; see also Gigerenzer, 2007):

> *... bounded rationality can be seen as emerging from the joint effect of two interlocking components: the internal limitations of the (human) mind, and the structure of the external environments in which the mind operates. This fit between the internal cognitive structure and the external information structure underlies the perspective of bounded rationality as ecological rationality – making good (enough) decisions by exploiting the structure of the environment... Heuristics that are matched to particular environments allow agents to be ecologically rational, making adaptive decisions that combine accuracy with speed and frugality.*

What Gigerenzer argues and emphasizes is that there is much evidence consistent with the hypothesis that bottom-up decision making processes tend to be more effective and efficient than top-down decision making processes—the normative benchmark of efficiency and rationality in conventional economic wisdom. What looks odd, weird, and irrational, appears smart, rational, and efficient from the perspective of ecological rationality. This bottom-up, constrained and contextualized perspective on decision making is in line with Hayek's worldview, that flows from the assumption of complex information and an overall complex decision making environment. Todd and Gigerenzer elaborate (2003, pp. 153–154):

> *In sum, by matching the structure of information in the environment with the structure implicit in their building blocks, heuristics can be accurate without being too complex. In addition, by being simple, these heuristics can avoid being too closely matched to any particular environment, and hence can escape the curse of overfitting. This marriage of structure with simplicity produces the counterintuitive situations in which there is little trade-off between being fast and frugal and being accurate...Experimental evidence is growing that humans do indeed use simple heuristics to make decisions in an ecologically rational manner, using as little information as possible and tailoring their information and option search to the structure available in the environment.*

The emphasis here, as in Hayek, is in the typical superiority of decision making processes that are bottom-up and task specific, as opposed to those driven by exogenously determined (expert) norms that are typically disconnected from relevant decision making environments and neurological and social contexts. There is little space or discourse allocated to errors and biases in decision making in this narrative.

But errors and biases are possible if individuals don't adopt the best available heuristics to achieve their individualized goals and objectives. Simply because an individual makes particular choices that are not expert-driven does not mean that such choices are the best an individual could make, given her or his preferences, goals, and objectives. But the benchmarks for best-practice decision making processes or for best-possible choices are not based on mainstream economic modelling. Rather, they should be based on what we learn from how individuals actually behave in the real world and the objectives that individuals have set for themselves; be they building a successful business, losing weight, or becoming a successful athlete (Altman, 2020).

Even given real world constraints, specific decisions made by particular individuals may not result in the best-possible outcomes, even from the perspective of individual decision makers. Errors can be made that can be identified by the expert and this information can help the individual realize their preferred objectives or outcomes. But Gigerenzer doesn't elaborate upon these points, although as with Simon his analytical framework definitely allows for errors in decision making. And little attention is paid to the implications of decision making errors and how they can be corrected. To the extent that Hayek admits to errors, they tend to be short term and are predicted to be corrected as a form of evolution—where ineffective decision making rules or processes are eliminated in a type of Darwinian process. These prospective errors are much ado about nothing. This is akin to the evolutionary process of the survival of the fittest (economic entities and decision processes) discussed by Alchain (1950).

But by paying little heed to the very real possibility of errors in decision-making one runs the risk (very much part and parcel of conventional economics) of assuming that whatever exists, exists because it is efficient and utility maximizing. In this case, we could systematically overlook serious errors in decision making, which might have nothing to do with deviating from conventional economic behavioural norms, but much to do with not developing best practice decision making rules and behaviours.

Ecological rationality and the spontaneous order

Generally speaking ecological rationality refers to a relatively spontaneous evolution of best-practice decision making heuristics and higher-level rules of the game (inclusive of behavioural norms). Such an evolution relates human decision making capabilities to the decision making environment that individuals face. The evolutionary (or spontaneous) development of heuristics and rules are deemed to be superior—especially in the long run—to heuristics and rules, or decision making heuristics given by design and fiat. However, ecological rationality does not presume that whatever has evolved is necessarily the most efficient or optimal set of heuristics or rules possible. But it is often thought that one can predict that the bottom-up approach tends to produce superior or more efficient results.

In its strong form, ecological rationality reads very much like historical determinism—societies evolve in the long run in an optimal manner. There can't be any errors and biases in decision making—especially in the long run—because sub-optimal results flowing from sub-optimal decisions cannot survive in the economic or social realm. All heuristics and rules are, by definition, optimal because they exist; and they exist because they are optimal. But they dominate even when they're not consistent with neoclassical norms. In its soft form, ecological rationality defines rationality in terms of the relationship between human decision making capabilities, the decision making environment faced by the decision maker, and how sensible a decision is in relation to these two binding decision making constraints. This does not imply that decisions—or decision making rules—need be optimal. Mistakes can be made. Decisions and rules can be improved upon. But best-practice decision making heuristics and rules of the game need not necessarily dominate. Still, the analytical prediction remains that bottom-up heuristics and rules of the game should be superior to those that are top-down (developed by design), which tend not to be informed by the specific understandings and needs of decision makers (although experts do and should inform, but not control, the decision making process).

At the end of the day, however, there is considerable ambiguity in Hayek's perspective on optimal institutional design and the rules of the game that facilitate best-practice decision making. Hayek typically goes on to specify particular institutional designs that he argues work best, based on historical experience. Only a spontaneous order that fits a particular libertarian ideal is optimal.

It appears that the expert plays a role in Hayek's thinking in determining what are possible sets of optimally designed institutions and rules of the game, helping to configure the institutions that contextualize and incentivize individual decision making. This raises issues about possible conflicts and synergies between design and the spontaneous order.

However, Hayek oft-repeats his thesis that spontaneous 'design' is best; that evolved institutions, rules of the game, heuristics yield optimal results; that whatever is in the process of becoming must be best or better than what existed in the past. If whatever evolves is optimal because it is a by-product of bottom-up decision making, the argument for ecological rationality becomes tautological. There is no analytical space for errors in decision making or multiple equilibria—where both optimal and sub-optimal results can persist simultaneously in historical time (discussed below). Only the optimal or the (Darwinian) fittest outcomes can survive the evolutionary process.

From a positive perspective this economic narrative stands in stark contrast to the errors and biases approach to behaviour economics. In this dominant approach in behavioural economics, evolved heuristics may not be optimal, and usually aren't. Errors in decision making abound even in a severely competitive environment. Actually, sub-optimal outcomes can dominate optimal ones. Here there is no such thing as the survival of the fittest. Indeed, decisions and choices characterized by errors and biases are thought to permeate—and sometimes dominate—the decision making landscape. For this reason, the errors and biases approach in behavioural economics links the state and the expert as important players facilitating and even determining optimal socio-economic decisions. There is a strong emphasis on intelligent design by experts.

The strong version of ecological efficiency is also quite in contrast to the fast, frugal and procedurally rational approach to behavioural economics, where one can identify and distinguish evolutionary heuristics that are optimal from those that are not (see Chapters 2, 3, and 4). Decision-making shortcuts or heuristics might be error-prone—in spite of their being derived from bottom-up decision making processes or through the spontaneous order. These sub-optimal decisions might be smart or rational and still wrong from the perspective of the objective function of the decision maker. Bottom-up decisions might also generate significant negative externalities and still pass the mustard of the survival test (in a world of multiple equilibria), so important to Hayek's perspective on the spontaneous order. It is also possible for rational individuals to make mistakes when information is misleading and difficult to comprehend. Also, in a world of individuals with different or heterogeneous preferences, an optimal decision from the perspective of the individual—one that is ecologically rational and thus sustainable—might be sub-optimal from the perspective of society at large. It might actually reduce the wealth of society or its level of utility or wellbeing, even whilst increasing the wealth and wellbeing of particular decision makers. Moreover, it is possible for the preferences of individuals with greater bargaining, legal, or social power to dominate the preferences of other individuals with less power. In terms of the softer approach to ecological rationality, the bottom-up approach is predicted to generate superior results to the top-down approach to decision making. But the bottom-up approach might, nevertheless, be characterized by errors in decision making and by socially sub-optimal behaviour.

Hayek is most sympathetic to the hard version of ecological efficiency, where rational individuals make choices that are optimal or the best possible, given the circumstances. Optimal decisions are made spontaneously in a decentralized manner, giving rise to outcomes that are so efficient and effective that they appear to be a product of design: of top-down, centralized decision making. Errors or mistakes, if made, are eliminated through an evolutionary process. Moreover, it is impossible to predict what will end up being decision making errors or mistakes a priori. Finally, whatever decisions are made from the bottom-up—short run errors and all—tend to be superior to those imposed from above.

Hayek (1981, p. 168) in fact argues, more often than not, that bottom-up decisions ultimately result in the best-possible choices, spontaneously:

> *I have so far carefully avoided saying that evolution is identical with progress, but when it becomes clear that it was the evolution of a tradition which made civilization possible, we may at least say that spontaneous evolution is a necessary if not a sufficient condition of progress. And though it clearly produces also much that we did not foresee and do not like when we see it, it does bring to ever-increasing numbers what they have been mainly striving for.*

Hayek (1981, p. 176) further elaborates:

> *If the Enlightenment has discovered that the role assigned to human reason in intelligent construction had been too small in the past, we are discovering that the task which our age is assigning to the rational construction of new institutions is far too big. What the age of rationalism – and modern positivism – has taught us to regard as senseless and meaningless formations due to accident or human caprice, turn out in many instances to be the foundations on which our capacity for rational thought rests. Man is not and never will be the master of his fate: his very reason always progresses by leading him into the unknown and unforeseen where he learns new things for.*

Opening the door to intelligent design

Although Hayek argues institutional design should and does evolve towards some optimal configuration, Hayek has in mind what such an optimal configuration should look like. He is very specific about certain necessary conditions for optimal institutions. In this instance, Hayek appears very much an engineer designing and recommending what optimal institutions should look like. However, it is clear that Hayek believes that institutions designed to maximize individual choice and facilitate decentralized decision making are critical to optimal institutional design. For example, Hayek (1981, p. 161) argues that what has been necessary to the development of vibrant economies and societies is largely the: '...relaxations of prohibitions: an evolution of individual freedom and a development of rules which protected the individual rather than commanded it to do particular things'. Moreover, and more generally, Hayek argues that:

- Institutions should encourage other regarding behaviour.
- Institutions should force individuals to incorporate externalities.
- Individuals should be punished for violating the rules of the game.
- Institutions should facilitate freedom of choice.
- Institutions should facilitate and encourage bottom-up decision making.
- Institutions should protect competitive markets.

It is especially true, in his earlier work, that Hayek explicitly speaks to expert, intelligent intervention with respect to the organizational change necessary to configure institutions that facilitate human liberty and economic competition so vital to bottom-up decision making. For example, Hayek argues in his 1939 pamphlet Freedom and the Economic System (Hayek as quoted in Caldwell, 2004, p. 238.):

> We can 'plan' a system of general rules, equally applicable to all people and intended to be permanent (even if subject to revision with the growth of knowledge), which provides an institutional framework within which the decisions as to what to do and how to earn a living are left up to the individuals. In other words, we can plan a system in which individual initiative is given the widest possible scope and the best opportunity to bring about effective coordination of individual effort.

This point is further elaborated upon in Hayek's, The Road to Serfdom (Hayek, 1944, p. 41):

> It is important not to confuse opposition against this kind of planning with a dogmatic laissez faire attitude. The liberal argument in favor of making the best-possible use of the forces of competition as a means of coordinating human efforts, not an argument for leaving things just as they are. It is based on the conviction that, where effective competition can be created, it is a better way of guiding individual efforts than any other. It does not deny, but even emphasizes, that, in order that competition should work beneficially a carefully thought-out legal framework is required and that neither the existing nor the past legal rules are free from grave defects. Nor does it deny that, where it is impossible to create the conditions necessary to make competition effective we must resort to other methods of guiding economic activity. Economic liberalism is opposed, however, to competition's being supplanted by inferior methods of coordinating individual efforts. And it regards competition as superior not only because it is in most circumstances the most efficient method known but even more because it is the only method by which our activities can be adjusted to each other without coercive or arbitrary intervention of authority.

This being said, Hayek's thought evolves towards a belief in a form of historical determinism where institutions—and, underlying these, human behaviour at the micro-level—evolve towards best-practice or optimal levels. This suggests that institutional forms and underlying human behaviour are almost always prone to be optimal, effective, and efficient. There is an efficient and effective Darwinian process that drives human behaviour and institutions towards optimality. If we would only stand back and leave things be, we will end up with the best of all possible worlds. Here, Hayek considers, the expert and centralization in decision making are anathema to best-practice decision making and economic prosperity. Particular types of institutions can play a time consistent role in subverting the type of economy and society that Hayek regards as optimal. We can end up being driven towards the 'road to serfdom' by experts, by top-down decision makers, who impose their preferences on society at large.

For example, Hayek (1981 p. 163) maintains that:

Man did not adopt new rules of conduct because he was intelligent. He became intelligent by submitting to new rules of conduct. The most important insight which so many rationalists still resist and are even inclined to brand as a superstition, namely that man has not only never invented his most beneficial institutions, from language to morals and law, and even today does not yet understand why he should preserve them when they satisfy neither his instincts nor his reason, still needs to be emphasized. The basic tools of civilization – language, morals, law and money – are all the result of spontaneous growth and not of design, and of the last two organized power has got hold and thoroughly corrupted them understand.

Hayek also writes (1981, pp. 172–173):

Our civilization advances by making the fullest use of the infinite variety of the individuals of the human species, apparently greater than that of any wild animal species, which had generally to adapt to one particular ecological niche. Culture has provided a great variety of cultural niches in which that great diversity of men's innate or acquired gifts can be used. And if we are to make use of the distinct factual knowledge of the individuals inhabiting different locations on this world, we must allow them to be told by the impersonal signals of the market how they had best use them in their own as well as in the general interest. It would indeed be a tragic joke of history if man, who owes his rapid advance to nothing so much as to the exceptional variety of individual gifts, were to terminate his evolution by imposing a compulsory egalitarian scheme on all understand.

For Hayek, it would be best for the evolutionary process to dominate—with all the uncertainty that this entails. But all evolutionary processes are embedded in micro- and macro-economic institutional structures: from households and firms to local and national governments. This remains a key tension in Hayek's work where, on the one hand, rational or smart behaviour is assumed to be consistent with error free choices, economic efficiency, and optimal institutional forms. But, on the other hand, Hayek either states explicitly—or implicitly assumes—that only particular institutional set-ups are consistent with his vision of the 'good society'. And Hayek sometimes admits that institutions are—at least partly, and often importantly—affected by intelligent human intervention, for better or worse. Once way or another, institutions matter.

Even in his later work, Hayek speaks to rules of social conduct and customs that need to be developed and enforced for society to progress. Individuals must be punished by society—and by their peers—if they engage in 'unacceptable' or 'bad' behaviour, for society to move forward. However, this typically requires rules and regulations, as well as educational facilities, that are constructed—not willy-nilly, but through some type of intelligent design. Hayek's views overlap with the research of behavioural economists who regard punishment as a means of encouraging and enforcing 'desired' behaviour such that it eventually becomes intuitive (Fehr & Gachter, 2000, 2002; Field, 2001). But, like Hayek, it is typically assumed that such punishment arises naturally, in an evolutionary fashion. Hayek writes (1981, pp. 171–172):

> *All morals rest on the different esteem in which different persons are held by their fellows according to their conforming to accepted moral standards. It is this which makes moral conduct a social value. Like all rules of conduct prevailing in a society, and the observance of which makes an individual a member of the society, their acceptance demands equal application to all. This involves that morals are preserved by discriminating between people who observe them and those who do not, irrespective of why particular people may infringe them. Morals presuppose a striving for excellence and the recognition that in this some succeed better than others, without inquiring for the reasons which we can never know. Those who observe the rules are regarded as better in the sense of being of superior value compared with those who do not, and whom in consequence the others may not be willing to admit into their company. Without this morals would not persist.*

But morally a person breaking the rules must be regarded as bad even if he or she knows no better. The fact that, often, people will have much to learn in order to be accepted by another group is much to the good. Even moral praise is not based on intention but on performance, and this must be so.

Opening the door to multiple equilibria: Casting shadows on the spontaneous order and ecological rationality

Critical to Hayek's methodological narrative is the superiority of bottom-up or decentralized decision making. Related to this, Hayek also emphasizes the likelihood that decentralized decision making weaves the web of the spontaneous order that yields efficient and optimal economic outcomes. This is a point also raised by Alchain (1950). This view is consistent with much of contemporary economics, especially that which is embedded in the notion of the efficient market hypothesis (Fama, 1970). Deeply rooted in this argument is a Darwinian notion of the survival of the fittest: the survival and evolution over historical time of the most efficient economic and social entities.

But an evolutionary approach to economic understanding that ends up rationalizing current behaviours, institutions, and economic outcomes as efficient, effective, or optimal is challenged by Simon. Individuals that are rational need not generate efficient outcomes. Society, populated by rational decision makers can be stuck in sub-optimal equilibria. Rational, bottom-up decision making, is not necessarily the cause of—or consistent with—optimal economic outcomes. Inefficient economic outcomes can survive the evolutionary process. Even the relatively most efficient economic and social entities need not dominate the economic and social landscape. It is well established that inefficient economies can survive for centuries, existing side-by-side with relatively efficient ones. For example, inefficient firms co-exist for generations with efficient firms (see for example Altman, 1999, 2001, 2005a; Frantz, 1997; Leibenstein, 1966, 1979). Simon (1986, p. 223) argues:

> *In the biological world at least, many organisms survive that are not maximizers but that operate at far less than the highest achievable efficiency. Their survival is not threatened as long as no other organisms have evolved that can challenge the possession of their specific niches. Analogously, since there is no reason to suppose that every business firm is challenged by an optimally efficient competitor, survival only requires meeting the competition. In a system in which there are innumerable rents, of long-term and short-term duration, even egregious suboptimality may permit survival.*

Simon (1978, p. 4) elaborates on this point:

> *The point may be stated more formally. Functional arguments are arguments about the movements of systems toward stable self-maintaining equilibria. But without further specification, there is no reason to suppose that the attained equilibria that are reached will be global maxima or minima of some function rather than local, relative maxima or minima. In fact, we know that the conditions that every local maximum of a system be a global maximum are very strong (usually some kind of 'convexity' conditions). Further, when the system is complex and its environment continually changing (that is, in the conditions under which biological and social evolution actually take place), there is no assurance that the system's momentary position will lie anywhere near a point of equilibrium, whether local or global. Hence, all that can be concluded from a functional argument is that certain characteristics (the satisfaction of certain functional requirements in a particular way) are consistent with the survival and further development of the system, not that these same requirements could not be satisfied in some other way. Thus, for example, societies can satisfy their functional needs for food by hunting or fishing activities, by agriculture, or by predatory exploitation of other societies.*

Simon also discusses organizational slack wherein different decision making procedures and different types of organization are consistent with economic survival. In this type of real world scenario, one cannot predict that, simply because a procedure or an organization survives it is efficient. Survival is consistent with a variety of procedures and organizational forms. Once again, we have the possibility—and even the high probability—of multiple equilibria. This runs contrary to Hayek's articulation of ecological efficiency and the spontaneous order. Simon's notion of multiple equilibria also contravenes the efficient market hypothesis. Economies and societies cannot be expected to converge towards some wealth and welfare maximizing optimal equilibrium—other than in a theoretical very long run. But Simon's modelling perspective is also consistent with the hypothesis that bottom-up decision making is rational and can be more effective and efficient than top-down expert driven decision making. Introducing variables, such as organizational slack, into his modelling framework helps explain and analytically predict much real world behaviour and outcomes, which tend to be highly diverse and even contain inefficient outcomes. It is possible for there to be rational inefficiency (Altman, 2005a, 2010). There is no prediction here of a movement towards some unique equilibrium that is both rational and efficient. Much depends on institutional structures, the preferences of decision makers, their state of knowledge, and the ability and power of individuals to realize their preferences. Simon argues (1979, p. 509):

> The presence of something like organizational slack in a model of the business firm introduces complexity in the firm's behavior in the short run. Since the firm may operate very far from any optimum, the slack serves as a buffer between the environment and the firm's decisions. Responses to environmental events can no longer be predicted simply by analyzing the 'requirements of the situation', but depend on the specific decision processes that the firm employs. However well this characteristic of a business firm model corresponds to reality, it reduces the attractiveness of the model for many economists, who are reluctant to give up the process-independent predictions of classical theory, and who do not feel at home with the kind of empirical investigation that is required for disclosing actual real world decision processes. But there is another side to the matter. If, in the face of identical environmental conditions, different decision mechanisms can produce different firm behaviors, this sensitivity of outcomes to process can have important consequences for analysis at the level of markets and the economy. Political economy, whether descriptive or normative, cannot remain indifferent to this source of variability in response.

The significance of multiple equilibria and their relationship to Hayek's spontaneous order are illustrated in Fig. 3.1. The case made by Simon is that there is an array of choices that are sustainable over historical (real) time in real world economic environments. I've argued that this would be the case even in highly competitive product markets (Altman, 1999, 2005b). If point A represents a sustainable outcome, such as a particular competitive unit cost or a particular consumer choice, there is an array of choices consistent with A in a world of multiple equilibria—for example, all choices up to point C. With regards

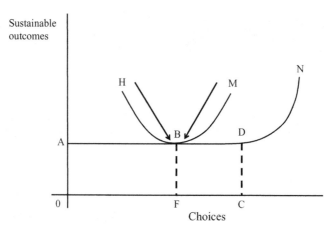

FIG. 3.1 Multiple equilibria and choice behaviour.

to the firm, these choices might represent higher wages or improved working conditions, where a range of these choices—from low to high wage rates, for example—yields the same average cost. The latter can be a function of productivity offsets—higher productivity offsetting higher labour costs (see, for example, Altman, 1999, 2001, 2005a). In this case, only one choice—given by point C—is consistent with the highest level of productivity and economic efficiency. But low productivity choices are sustainable in this multiple equilibria scenario. There is no imperative here for convergence towards some unique equilibrium. Only a movement beyond point C would be unsustainable—diminishing returns set in, associated with unsustainable outcomes, forcing movement back towards C. In a Hayekian world, there is a unique choice equilibrium given by points F and B yielding a unique sustainable outcome at point A. One can deviate from points F and B, but the evolutionary process will force convergence towards these choice points. In a world of multiple equilibria, ecological efficiency is consistent with an array of choices. Some of these choices, however rational they might be, need not be efficient or error-free. Simon's conceptualization of multiple equilibria also opens the door to a discourse on which types of institutional setting are most conducive to economic efficiency, and decision making environments in which decision making errors are minimized. Inappropriate institutional settings can result in persistent inefficiencies—even in persistent errors in decision making (see Altman, 2017, for a detailed modelling multiple equilibrium).

Related to this, Hayek pays little attention to the fact that the application of the survival principle in the realm of production can be quite different from when it's applied to that of consumption (Altman, 2005b). In production, firms must survive based on price and quality. In consumption, individuals need not pass any particular survival test. A vast array of quite different choices can persist over time, based on the preferences of individuals and their capacity to realize these preferences (Altman, 2010). These choices can be error-prone and still be sustainable. Evolutionary processes need not eliminate them. But these choices can be ecologically rational, in the sense of being reasonable choices based on the individual's decision making environment. Nevertheless, they might not be optimal—in the sense that different and better choices would be made with improvements in information and education, for example. This speaks to the significance of intelligent institutional design in a world of multiple equilibria.

These points are illustrated in Fig. 3.2. Here we have a conventional indifference curve analysis with a given price line/budget constraint given by AB. But there are three indifference curves tangential to the price line, each part of a multiple equilibria set of choices that is sustainable over time. But, from Hayek's perspective, indifference curve U0 should yield a relatively lower level of utility because the equilibrium choice is determined by the expert and by conventional economic decision processes. Indifference curve U1 should yield a higher, indeed highest, level of satisfaction since it is a product of bottom-up decision making and is the 'free will' of the decision maker. But the higher indifference curve U2 is very highly unlikely in the Hayekian universe. In Fig. 3.2, let's assume that indifference curve U1 yields choices where bottom-up decisions are based on misleading information. Individuals are informed that they are investing in safe financial assets, where this information is false. They are informed that their house is built up to safety code standards and it is not. They are told that a food item is organic, when it is not. An individual's choice here is boundedly rational, but can be improved upon by institutional changes that force and enforce the provision of accurate information. Such a choice is given by indifference curve U2 and yields the highest level of utility. Behavioural economists such as Shiller, 2010 emphasize the significance of such institutional changes that can improve the welfare of the decision maker whilst maintaining her or his freedom to choose what he or she desires (see also Altman, 2012).

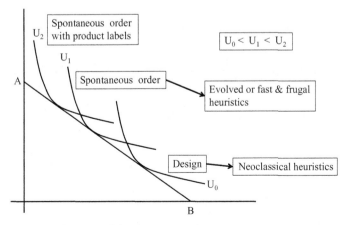

FIG. 3.2 Utility, preferences and the spontaneous order.

Conclusion: Hayek's Golden nugget in decision-making theory

A critical implication of Hayek's perspective on the economy and society is that the complexity and related costliness of acquiring and processing information, plus the limited processing capabilities of the human brain, result in bottom-up, decentralized decision making being most effective and efficient, and most consistent with the wellbeing of society at large. Moreover, such decision making is rational in the sense of being smart. It is important to reiterate that, for Hayek, smart decision making is not of the calculating, deliberative type stressed by conventional economic wisdom. Smart decisions can be a by-product of unplanned and dynamic interactions among individuals. The starting analytical assumption for Hayek is that decentralized decision making, respecting individuals' preferences and choices, makes for a better economy and society—are welfare improving. In addition, Hayek recognizes the diversity of human preferences: we can be quite different in our wants and desires. And, he argues, one should respect individuals' preferences as the benchmark for what is in the best interest of individuals and for what is smart behaviour—what can be referred to as bounded, or ecological rationality. Also, of some consequence is Hayek's emphasis on the importance of appropriate institutional parameters for efficient, effective, welfare improving decisions.

Hayek's worldview is simply illustrated in Fig. 3.3, using the Production Possibility Frontier (PPF). Given the costliness of processing and acquiring information, and the overall significance of tacit information to decision making (and therefore the significance of individualized knowledge), decentralized, bottom-up, and often unplanned decision making (spontaneous order) yields a higher PPF, AB, than what can be generated using centralized, top-down decision making—decision making by design. The latter is given by PPF, CD. This flips the conventional economics view on its head, where planning, with

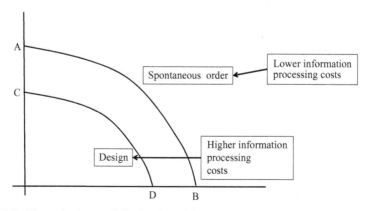

FIG. 3.3 The production possibility frontier and the spontaneous order.

a reference point to the expert's vision of best-practice behavioural norms and outcomes, yields sub-optimal results. This point is a bit tricky, since most conventional economists subscribe to the notion that a decentralized economic market (a 'free' market) works best. But, on the other hand, how one engages in decision making is determined by what the experts deem most effective and efficient. The experts generate the benchmarks for economic efficiency and rationality. Expert-led decision making is part and parcel of what Hayek considers be the centralized decision making package. And this expert-led decision making—which is often far removed from real world decision making constraints—is predicted to yield a relatively less efficient economy, as is given by PPF, BD.

One can divide Hayek's analytical prediction into two parts. In the first, the price mechanism provides the optimal vehicle for coordinated decision making and allocating resources. In part two—even given relatively free reign to the price mechanism—a necessary condition for economic efficiency is bottom-up decision making, that flows from the free interactions of decision makers, generating choices in the context of their specific decision making environment and their unique preferences. Critical to Hayek is a different benchmark for efficient and effective decision making, as compared to the benchmark of *homo economicus* adhered to by conventional economic wisdom.

This particular worldview sits well and informs the behavioural economics that flows from the research and analytical perspectives of Herbert Simon. Simon's concept of bounded rationality, and his articulation of the concept of procedural rationality, captures the reality of costly and asymmetric information cobbled with the notion of the brain as a scarce resource. This causes him to argue that modelling the decision maker differently, using more realistic behavioural assumptions from homo *economicus* (the supra-calculating, all knowing individual), generates much improved analytical predictions. But such models not only paint a more accurate picture of decision making behaviour, they suggest that much non-conventional behaviour—what conventional economics regards as irrational and sub-optimal—is often more effective and efficient than the behaviour of the conventional economic decision maker, or *homo economicus.*

Hayek predicts that decision makers will not behave as *homo economicus*, especially if not forced to by coercive superiors and institutions. Hayek's default evaluation of decision making deviations from conventional benchmarks for smart behaviour is that such deviations represent smart (boundedly or ecologically rational) and best-practice behaviour. But it is not clear from Hayek what these alternative benchmarks for best-practice behaviour should or might be. This remains an important topic of research for those who regard bottom-up decision making as superior to conventional top-down forms. It should possible to determine when and under what conditions particular bottom-up decisions will result in errors in decision making. And, it should also be possible to identify what decision rules or processes are most likely to yield 'optimal' decisions.

But optimality is unlikely to be related to conventional economic behavioural norms. This is an important point gleaned from Simon's narrative on procedural rationality.[c]

Hayek's argument that one should expect decision makers to behave differently from what conventional economics predicts, is an empirical mainstay of behavioural economists and experimental economists coming from a wide array of perspectives. A common thread across behavioural economists is that decision makers consistently deviate from conventional benchmarks of rationality. But Hayek's methodological perspective—rooted in the complexity of information, the significance of tacit information, the brain as a scarce resource, and the diversity of preferences—lends weight and analytical focus to the hypothesis that decision making that deviates from conventional norms is the most appropriate. Hayek's arguments lend support to the hypothesis that individuals tend to be ecologically rational, however much their decision making processes and choices deviate from conventional economic norms. It also focuses attention on the different approaches to behavioural economics. Behavioural economics is clearly delineated by whether one's default hypothesis is that typical choice behaviour is rational and smart, or whether it is too often characterized by errors and biases.

Hayek's research also raises important methodological questions about evolutionary and institutional approaches to economic and social development. Hayek's default hypothesis is that economy and society evolve towards optimal configurations where economies are most efficient—some maximum production possibility frontier. Another apparent default hypothesis is that smart choice behaviour—from the perspective of the individual decision maker—is synonymous with economically efficient outcomes. Hayek's approach raises important questions about whether individual rationality necessarily implies economic efficiency and whether the evolutionary process necessarily imposes economic efficiency on economic outcomes. Too often behavioural economics pays little heed to the survival test when analysing human decision making and the invariable non-conventional decision making processes and economic outcomes. Needless to say, Hayek often challenges his own inevitability hypothesis, discussing the importance of constructing institutions that facilitate optimal bottom-up driven decision processes and choices.

Issues raised by Hayek with regards to the importance of institutions for economic outcomes also serve to highlight important considerations discussed by Simon on the significance of multiple equilibria for economic analysis. For Simon, individual rational choice need not result in socially rational economic

---

c. Although Kahneman does not speak directly to this issue, most recently in his formulation of the fast and slow thinking narrative (Kahneman 2017), he makes the point that under certain conditions slow thinking yields better results than fast thinking. None of this is related to conventional economic behavioural norms. Different decision problems require different systems of thinking if one is to avoid errors in decision making.

outcomes or institutions. There are a wide variety of economic choices and outcomes that can pass the survival test and are therefore consistent with the evolutionary process. This, in turn, forces analytical attention on to the relationship between rational choice and economic efficiency and the significance of institutional change and particular institutional configurations for the decision making processes individuals adopt, the choices they make, and related economic outcomes. Although bottom-up decision making processes tend to generate superior socio-economic outcomes, these superior outcomes and economic efficiency are not inevitable. Much depends on the decision making environment and individual preferences (see also Altman, 2005b, 2008b). Moreover, bottom-up decision making might ideally generate the best-possible choices for the individual, but individuals' capacity to realize their preferred preferences might be precluded by, for example: poor or misleading information, inadequate education, weak bargaining power, and institutions that bias decision making in favour of particular groups or individuals. Such preference inefficiencies can easily persist over historical time in a world of multiple equilibria (Altman, 2010). And these important issues remain to be investigated in behavioural economics.

Overall, what is of core importance in Hayek's research into behavioural economics—his analytical golden nugget—is his foundational contribution on the raison d'être, significance, and inherent rationality (good sense) of bottom-up decision making, given the reality of the decision making environment. His focus on the decision making environment and on the significance of evolutionary processes forces attention onto the importance of macro variables in understanding choice behaviour and economic outcomes. Hayek's research questions and hypotheses encourage behavioural economists (economists more generally speaking) to further test for:

- The rationality (more broadly defined) of human decision making;
- The optimality of institutions—not only for economically efficient but also for welfare maximizing outcomes;
- Establishing benchmarks for efficient and effective decisions, given real world decision making environments;
- The role of experts in facilitating welfare maximizing decisions and outcomes.

References

Alchain, A. A. (1950). Uncertainty, evolution and economic theory. *Journal of Political Economy*, *58*, 211–221.

Altman, M. (1999). The methodology of economics and the survivor principle revisited and revised: Some welfare and public policy implications of modeling the economic agent. *Review of Social Economics*, *57*, 427–449.

Altman, M. (2001). *Worker satisfaction and economic performance: The microfoundations of economic success and failure*. Armonk, New York: M.E. Sharpe.

Altman, M. (2005a). Behavioral economics, rational inefficiencies, fuzzy sets, and public policy. *Journal of Economic Issues, 34*, 683–706.

Altman, M. (2005b). Reconciling altruistic, moralistic, and ethical behavior with the rational economic agent and competitive markets. *Journal of Economic Psychology, 26*, 732–757.

Altman, M. (2008b). Towards a theory of induced institutional change: Power, labor markets, and institutional change. In N. Mercuro & S. S. Batie (Eds.), *Alternative institutional structures* (pp. 300–329). London: Routledge.

Altman, M. (2010). A behavioral and institutional foundation of preference and choice behavior: Freedom to choose and choice X-inefficiencies. *Review of Social Economy, 69*, 395–411.

Altman, M. (2012). Implications of behavioural economics for financial literacy and public policy. *Journal of Socio-Economics, 41*, 677–690.

Altman, M. (2017). Policy consequences of multiple equilibria and the indeterminacy of economic outcomes in a boundedly rational world: Closing the system with non-economic variables. *Forum for Social Economics, 64*, 234–251.

Altman, H. J. R. (2020). *The Behavioural economics of organizational inefficiency: The example of the New Zealand fitness industry*. Australia: Masters of Philosophy (Research), School of Economics and Finance Faculty of Business, Queensland University of Technology.

Caldwell, B. (2004). *Hayek's challenge: An intellectual biography of F.A. Hayek*. Chicago: University of Chicago Press.

D'Amico, D. J., & Boettke, P. J. (2010). Making sense out of the sensory order. *Advances in Austrian Economics, 13*, 357–381.

Fama, E. (1970). Efficient capital markets: A review of theory and empirical work. *Journal of Finance, 25*, 383–417.

Fehr, E., & Gachter, S. (2000). Fairness and retaliation: The economics of reciprocity. *Journal of Economic Perspectives, 14*, 159–181.

Fehr, E., & Gachter, S. (2002). Altruistic punishment in humans. *Nature, 415*, 137–140.

Field, A. J. (2001). *Altruistically inclined: The behavioral sciences, evolutionary theory, and the origins of reciprocity*. Ann Arbor, MI: University of Michigan Press.

Frantz, R. (1997). *X-efficiency theory: Evidence and applications* (2nd ed.). Boston/Dordrecht/London: Kluwer Academic Publishers.

Freedman, D. H. (2011). Why economic models are always wrong. *Scientific American*. Available at: http://www.scientificamerican.com/article.cfm?id=finance-why-economic-models-are-always-wrong.

Friedman, M. (1953). *The methodology of positive economics', essays in positive economics.* (pp. 3–43). Chicago: University of Chicago Press.

Gigerenzer, G. (2007). *Gut feelings: The intelligence of the unconscious*. New York: Viking.

Hayek, F. A. (1944). *The road to serfdom*. Chicago: University of Chicago Press.

Hayek, F. A. (1945). The use of knowledge in society. *American Economic Review, 35*, 519–530.

Hayek, F. A. (1948). *Individualism and the economic order*. Chicago: University of Chicago Press.

Hayek, F. A. (1952). *The sensory order: An inquiry into the foundations of theoretical psychology*. Chicago: University of Chicago Press.

Hayek, F. A. (1981). *The political order of a free people, Vol. 3, law, legislation and liberty*. Chicago: University of Chicago Press.

Hayek, F. A. (1989). The Pretence of knowledge. *American Economic Review, 79*, 3–7.

Kahneman, D. (2003). Maps of bounded rationality: Psychology for behavioral economics. *American Economic Review, 93*, 1449–1475.

Kahneman, D. (2011). *Thinking fast and slow*. New York: Farrar, Strauss, Giroux.

Kahneman, D., & Tversky, A. (1979). Prospect theory: An analysis of decisions under risk. *Econometrica, 47*, 313–327.

Kahneman, D. & Tversky, A. (Eds.), (2000). *Choices, values and frames*. New York: Cambridge University Press & Russell Sage Foundation.

Leibenstein, H. (1966). Allocative efficiency vs. 'X-efficiency'. *American Economic Review, 56,* 392–415.

Leibenstein, H. (1979). A branch of economics is missing: Micro-micro theory. *Journal of Economic Literature, 17,* 477–502.

March, J. G. (1978). Bounded rationality, ambiguity, and the engineering of choice. *Bell Journal of Economics, 9,* 587–608.

Shiller, R. J. (2010). How nutritious are your investments? In *Project syndicate*. Available at: http://www.project-syndicate.org/commentary/shiller71/English.

Simon, H. A. (1955). A behavioral model of rational choice. *Quarterly Journal of Economics, 69,* 99–188.

Simon, H. A. (1978). Rationality as a process and as a product of thought. *American Economic Review, 70,* 1–16.

Simon, H. A. (1979). Rational decision making in business organizations. *American Economic Review, 69,* 493–513.

Simon, H. A. (1986). Rationality in psychology and economics. *Journal of Business, 59,* 209–224.

Simon, H. A. (1987). Behavioral economics. In J. Eatwell, M. Millgate, & P. Newman (Eds.), *The New Palgrave: A dictionary of economics* (pp. 266–267). London: Macmillan.

Smith, V. L. (2003). Constructivist and ecological rationality in economics. *American Economic Review, 93,* 465–508.

Smith, V. L. (2005). Behavioral economics research and the foundations of economics. *Journal of Socio-Economics, 34,* 135–150.

Smith, V. L. (2008). *Rationality in economics: Constructivist and ecological forms*. New York: Cambridge University Press.

Thaler, R. H., & Sustein, C. (2003). Behavioral economics, public policy, and paternalism: Libertarian paternalism. *American Economic Review, Papers and Proceedings, 93,* 175–179.

Thaler, R. H., & Sustein, C. (2008). *Nudge: Improving decisions about health, wealth, and happiness*. New Haven and London: Yale University Press.

Todd, P. M., & Gigerenzer, G. (2003). Bounding rationality to the world. *Journal of Economic Psychology, 24,* 143–165.

Tversky, A., & Kahneman, D. (1986). Rational choice and the framing of decisions. *Journal of Business, 59,* 251–278.

Chapter 4

Freedom of choice in a complex world

Chapter outline

Introduction	75	Multiple equilibria in production:	
Multiple equilibria		X-inefficiency and agency	84
in consumption	79	Multiple equilibria in production:	
Multiple equilibria in production:		Some related scenarios	86
An introduction	80	Historical and logical time	87
Multiple equilibria in production:		Rent seeking and x-efficiency	87
X-inefficiency and		Conclusion	88
managerial slack	82	References	90

Introduction

A critical point made by behavioural economists from a wide set of methodological perspectives is that individuals typically do not make decisions that are consistent with conventional economic theoretical norms of rational behaviour. These are all points raised in the Chapters 1–3. This is true of behavioural economists building on the errors and biases, or heuristics and biases, approach derived from the research of Kahneman (2003, 2011), and Thaler and Sunstein (2008), and those building upon the bounded rationality approach introduced by Simon (1978, 1979, 1987), Altman (1999), Gigerenzer (2007), and Smith (2003). Such 'irrational' behaviour from the perspective of the mainstream is considered to be inefficient or suboptimal. And suboptimal outcomes should not be able to survive; that is they should fail the test of the survival of the fittest.

However, different socioeconomic outcomes or solutions to the same specific decision problems appear to be consistent with survival in the market place. This is even true of economic outcomes, when firms are not maximizing productivity. Both low and high productivity firms can survive simultaneously in the market. Moreover, ethical or socially considerate firms, and other-giving and empathic individuals, can also survive and persist, even if such behaviour is often considered to be suboptimal and irrational from the perspective of conventional economic wisdom.

Smart Economic Decision-Making in a Complex World. https://doi.org/10.1016/B978-0-12-811461-2.00004-3
75

It was just such apparent anomalies that Herbert Simon attempted to address through the concept of multiple equilibria, set in contrast with the more mainstream focus on convergence toward some optimal and unique equilibrium (see Chapter 3). Game theorists recognize the existence of multiple equilibria and even the existence of suboptimal Nash, Prisoner's Dilemma-type, equilibria. But this is more in tune with the existence of a multiplicity of possible equilibria that are achievable where only one of the possible set is actually realized. From this perspective, both inefficient and efficient economic entities can persist over time in equilibrium. Therefore, survival and existence need not be, in any way, indicative or proof of uniqueness, optimality, or efficiency in outcomes or decision-making processes. Multiple equilibria is also indicative of the choices economic agents or decision makers have in the economic domain. They not somehow predetermined to make particular choices, be they sub-optimal or not.

It is important to note that the conventional and dominant economic methodology that deduces optimality and efficiency, and even uniqueness, from survival and existence is derived from the methodological paradigm articulated by Milton Friedman (1953) and see also, Alchian, 1950. He maintained that survival is proof of optimality and efficiency in both outcomes and decision-making processes. One can deduce from outcomes—from survival—that individuals or economic agents behave in a particular and unique fashion—optimally and efficiently.

One can also infer causality from results—the firm has survived because it currently exists—so that individuals or economic agents must have behaved in a particular and optimal fashion, and such behaviour generated the observed outcome (survival). One need not investigate, empirically, how individuals actually behaved with regard to pertinent decisions and processes. Related to this, one can construct the normative statement that the surviving firms are optimal and efficient. Surviving firms of the moment must be optimal and efficient because they exist. No empirical investigation need be made as to the actual state of the firm because of the allowed- for deductions predicated upon what is assumed, willy-nilly, about the surviving or, more precisely, current firms. The possibility of multiple equilibria is assumed away in Friedman's representation of the market economy. It is assumed that real markets function in a fashion that results in optimality and efficiency without testing this assumption (Altman, 1999).[a]

Any observed outcome A is assumed to be efficient, and it is further assumed to be caused by B. Hence, if A, then B. There can be, by assumption, no suboptimal outcome A′, A″, A‴, or An that can exist simultaneously with A. Nor can there be alternative behaviours or processes, B′, B″, B‴, or Bn that can yield some optimal outcome A0.

---

a. In Chapter 3, above, I discussed the concept of ecological rationality where, at least, from Hayek's perspective bottom-up decision-making should yield optimal results. Hence, what one sees (reality) should be optimal if these are a function of bottom-up decision making. Indeed, market forces should ensure optimal choices.

$$A \Leftrightarrow B$$
$$B \Leftrightarrow A$$

A and B are both highly correlated, with B causing A. All other possibilities are eliminated by assumption. A and B represent two stable and causally connected equlibria.

Although, thus far, emphasis has been on the firm, the unique equilibrium—optimality approach has also been applied to consumer behaviour. A strict but common interpretation of consumer sovereignty assumes that consumers make choices that are optimal and welfare maximizing not only from their own perspective, but also from the perspective of a calculating omnipotent decision-maker (see also Chapter 6).

Building on Simon, I examine and model alternative reasons for why non-conventional or non-neoclassical decision outcomes can survive in both the medium and long run, even while relatively more efficient options and entities exist (hence multiple equilibria). This is largely ignored in the conventional economics literature, which focuses on logical time as opposed to historical time when analysing various possible decision-making outcomes. Also discussed is how optimal outcomes can be achieved through alternative means—different organizational and related decision-making processes can generate the same output, with the possibility of persistent multiple process equilibria.

Overall, this chapter presents a modelling framework that captures and allows for the existence of multiple equilibria in its many dimensions, hence recognizing the importance of human agency, freedom of choice, in the decision-making process. Methodologically, this provides us with a broader theoretical lens, which incorporates the possibility that convergence toward a unique equilibrium is not necessary in the short, medium, or long run; one size does not fit all. The evolutionary process does not necessarily generate the most economically efficient and socially optimal outcomes. Hence, one should not so easily deduce optimality from the existence of a phenomenon, especially when relatively more efficient phenomena/outcomes also exist simultaneously. This has significant implication for policy and analysis (see Chapter 3).

What appears to be a unique equilibrium output might only be a point in a set of multiple equilibria. But this possibility can only be evident from a modelling framework (effectively a data search engine) that allows for and emphasizes the significance of multiple equilibria. Otherwise, this possibility and reality would be simply assumed away, with serious theoretical and policy consequences. The approach taken in this chapter is part of the behaviouralist tradition developed by Herbert Simon, wherein one's theory is synergistically and dialectically derived from one's observation of pertinent aspects of reality.

One may begin this multiple equilibria discourse, building on Simon, with two critical quotes from Simon in this domain. In the first quote, Simon focuses on the possibility of suboptimal equilibria. As long as all competitors are at least equally sub-optimal and inefficient, equilibrium can be achieved in a suboptimal state (Simon, 1997, p. 283):

> *In the biological world at least, many organisms survive that are not maximizers but that operate at far less than the highest achievable efficiency. Their survival is not threatened as long as no other organisms have evolved that can challenge the possession of their specific niches. Analogously, since there is no reason to suppose that every business firm is challenged by an optimally efficient competitor, survival only requires meeting the competition. In a system in which there are innumerable rents, of long-term and short-term duration, even egregious suboptimality may permit survival.*

Simon (1978, p. 4) elaborates on this notion of suboptimal equilibrium, moving toward the notions of multiple equilibria, and the possibility of achieving these through different means:

> *The point may be stated more formally. Functional arguments are arguments about the movements of systems toward stable self-maintaining equilibria. But without further specification, there is no reason to suppose that the attained equilibria that are reached will be global maxima or minima of some function rather than local, relative maxima or minima. In fact, we know that the conditions that every local maximum of a system be a global maximum are very strong (usually some kind of 'convexity' conditions). Further, when the system is complex and its environment is continually changing (that is, in the conditions under which biological and social evolution actually take place), there is no assurance that the system's momentary position will lie anywhere near a point of equilibrium, whether local or global. Hence, all that can be concluded from a functional argument is that certain characteristics (the satisfaction of certain functional requirements in a particular way) are consistent with the survival and further development of the system, not that these same requirements could not be satisfied in some other way. Thus, for example, societies can satisfy their functional needs for food by hunting or fishing activities, by agriculture, or by predatory exploitation of other societies.*

There is some overlap between Simon's approach, the narrative presented in this chapter and complexity theory (see Arthur, 2013; Elsner, 2015 on the latter). As you will see below, however, in my multiple equilibria narrative the prevailing equilibrium can be a determinant one given by institutional variables, power relationships, and preferences, for example.

There two important and distinct multiple equilibria scenarios that are important to consider. One relates to multiple equilibria in outcomes, and the other relates to multiple equilibria in processes. To the extent that such multiple equilibria can persist for a reasonable length of historical time, one cannot infer the simple fact that, for 'survival' and existence, that which exists is necessarily the most economically efficient outcome or process to achieve a particular outcome. One causal inference often made in conventional economics is that one can deduce economic efficiency from survival. Only the efficient (or in a softer sense, the relatively efficient) can survive. Hence, survival implies, if not proves, economic efficiency. The same can be said of the inferred causality between unique particular processes yielding economic efficiency. However, the possibility of multiple equilibria should force the analyst to think carefully about such simple causal inferences, where other possible and reasonable explanations for survival are available and are, moreover, consistent with the evidence.

This formulation of multiple equilibria is related to David Hume's is-ought problem or fallacy, articulated in the A Treatise of Human Nature (1738/2014, p. 576). This raises the problem of individuals deducing what ought to be from what is and attributing particular causes to that which exists in a particular moment in time. Moreover, it is assumed that what exists is normatively ideal because it exists. But because these deductions are not empirically based, according to Hume, they represent fallacies. At best, these propositions represent testable hypotheses. One cannot impute anything in particular from the reality of existence of a phenomenon. This is, of course, exactly what Friedman does, flowing from his assumption that markets must generate optimal and efficient outcomes. Simon rejects this form of empirically empty causal and normative analyses. The concept of multiple equilibria allows for different understandings of existing phenomena, inclusive of the conventional economic interpretation of events.

The possibility of multiple equilibria can take on different forms, largely conditional upon an organism or economic entity's ability to survive in the short to long run. When survival does not require optimality or efficiency, multiple equilibria are possible across a set of differentially efficient or inefficient economic entities. Moreover, survival is consistent with a range of behaviours (processes and decisions), none of which need generate economic efficiency, and take the form of severe calculating behaviour of *homo economicus* (economic man).

This approach opens the door to better understanding which set of processes and under what circumstances yield optimal outcomes.

Multiple equilibria in consumption

As a prelude to this discussion it is important, to note that a large array of choices are not subject to any market discipline and therefore cannot be forced, even in theory, to converge on a unique equilibrium (Altman, 2005b). For example, acts of altruism (choices which generate an immediate reduction in income or wealth with no high probability of income or wealth returns on such expenditures) need not negatively impact on the survival of the donor. The same holds true of expenditure on more expensive 'ethical' products or tipping for service, which can have an ethical component. Such acts simply reduce the income or wealth of the individual, but need not negatively impact on their current health, life expectancy, or capacity to procreate. Indeed, such acts of 'giving' are consistent with an individual realizing their preferences and, thereby, are consistent with such acts increasing their well-being or utility, as measured by the individual.

Hence, one might have a multiplicity of equilibria with regard to non-wealth or income maximizing decisions (controlling for risk), each a function of the preferences of the individual. Each individual could have multiple sustainable choices.

Also, there could be multiple sustainable choices across several individuals. These multiple equilibria could be derived simply from the differential preferences of individuals. There is a choice set that is not sustainable. This would be one where an individual's choices reduced their level of material well-being below what was required for survival—a highly unlikely scenario. Even here, the individual can survive if he or she is vested in a family or community that supports or subsidizes choices that are not sustainable on an individualized basis. So, even when those choices are made, they can represent a sustainable equilibrium, part of a wider spectrum of equilibria, when part of a sustainable group or community. Here the important question arises as to the conditions under which individuals, when vested with free choice, have the capabilities to make choices that maximize their wellbeing. This point is addressed in some detail in Chapter 6.

A possible prediction of unique equilibrium with regard to consumer choice would flow logically from the assumption that individuals are wealth or income maximizers. If one assumes that all economic agents are wealth maximizers, by backward induction, one could derive a unique equilibrium for each individual consistent with income and wealth maximizing, controlling for risk. Deviations for such benchmarks could then be identified as unstable equilibria to be dissipated through the choices of 'rational' wealth and income maximizing individuals or economic agents. However, this type of scenario is not generally consistent with the actual behaviour of individuals. Most decision-makers, in the domain of consumer choice, are not unconditional wealth or income maximizers. There is an array of individualized preferences, only some of these (a subset) are consistent with the wealth or income maximizing assumption of conventional economics. So long as preferences are not homogeneous with regard to wealth and income maximization, one should not expect or predict a unique equilibrium. For such a unique equilibrium would not be consistent with the decision-maker's utility, satisficing, or maximizing behaviour. Differences in preferences yield different equilibria across individuals (multiple equilibria). This should be one's prior hypothesis given the reality the economic agent across time and space.

Multiple equilibria in production: An introduction

At first glance, a unique equilibrium, or the convergence to a unique equilibrium, in the domain of production might appear to be a reasonable proposition, at least when modelling immediate and longer run scenarios. But this type of prediction hinges upon an array of unreasonable behavioural and institutional assumptions. As referenced above, a key point made by Simon is that multiple equilibria are pervasive and that it is crucial to explain and model this reality. A critical assumption in the conventional economic wisdom is that market forces should force all firms into being optimally efficient for reasons of survival. Alternatively, a milder assumption put forth by Alchian (1950) is that market forces would ensure that only the relatively most efficient firms survive. An even stronger hypothesis is that economic agents are hardwired to be wealth or income maximizers, such that they behave in a fashion consistent with firms being optimally efficient. All these assumptions imply a unique equilibrium in terms of economic efficiency. All surviving firms should, therefore, be either efficient or relatively efficient, or converging to this unique equilibrium. But the conditions allowing for multiple equilibria are pervasive. Hence, one might argue that the default modelling assumption should be multiple equilibria inclusive of inefficient points within a set—a distribution of economic entities that ranges from efficient to inefficient. The type of distribution would be an empirical question. In the unique equilibrium approach, all firms should be bunched together at the efficient end of the distribution. In the multiple equilibria approach, the distribution would be spread all over the efficiency–inefficiency spectrum. One could have a uniform distribution, with firms spread equally across the efficiency–inefficiency spectrum. Alternatively, firms could be normally distributed around some level of inefficiency, or one could even have two normal distributions, with one set of firms being efficient and the other being relatively inefficient.

An important starting point of this analysis is to understand that being cost competitive does not require that firms are economically efficient. This point is elaborated upon by Leibenstein (1966, 1979) in his discussion of x-efficiency theory. Moreover, product price need not be directly linked to the extent of economic efficiency—an argument advanced by Altman (1996, 2005a, 2005b, 2008). In this case, economically efficient firms need not be low-priced-product firms and low-priced-product firms need not be economically efficient. In the latter case, market forces, per se, cannot guarantee efficiency. In addition, it is sustainable to have a wide array of firms, in terms of different degrees of efficiency, in a relatively uncompetitive environment. However, as I shall argue, even a competitive environment is not sufficient to either guarantee economic efficiency or a unique equilibrium—such as when only the relatively most efficient firms survive (see also Chapter 5 and 7).

Since the extent of competitiveness and market forces are critical to conventional wisdom's assumption that economies converge toward an efficient equilibrium, it is important to appreciate the extent to which market forces can be mitigated, and often are. To the extent that economic entities can be protected from market forces, higher cost firms (inefficient firms) that charge higher prices to compensate for maintaining a 'normal' rate of return can survive over time, in the long run. The extent of protection afforded to firms can determine the extent to which relatively higher cost firms survive in the market in the long run. And differential protection across firms yields multiple equilibria in terms of firms that are characterized by higher to lower unit costs of production for the same product. Protection can take on many forms inclusive of subsidies, tariffs, protective rules, and regulations. One should note that, dynamically, subsidies and tariffs, in the short run, can contribute to the development of efficient firms and sectors (this related to the infant industries argument). Be this as it may, once one introduces protection, there need not be convergence toward one unique efficient equilibrium and one should expect differences in equilibria across firms and nations contingent upon levels of protection. Therefore, at any given point in time, surviving firms should not, necessarily, be expected to be economically efficient.

Multiple equilibria in production: X-inefficiency and managerial slack

This brings us directly to a discussion of x-efficiency theory and its pertinence to a discussion of convergence toward a unique equilibrium and multiple equilibria. A key point made by Leibenstein (1966, 1979) is that when product markets are not highly competitive, this generates not only the standard allocative inefficiencies (which are more of a macro-phenomenon), which tend to be relatively small, but also what he refers to as x-inefficiencies in production. Leibenstein breaks with the conventional wisdom, arguing that economic agents do not automatically maximize productivity, given the constraints that they face, most significant of which would be capital, labour, and technology. He argues that a key component of productivity is how hard and smart economic agents work. This translates into the assumption that effort inputs per unit of labour time are a variable in the production function and in the utility function of economic agents. Leibenstein focuses on effort discretion on the part of managers and owners—agents at the top end of the firm's decision-making hierarchy. This is unlike the conventional modelling of the firm, where it is assumed that effort inputs are fixed at a minimum, if not maximized. If decision-makers maximize their utility by reducing effort levels (quantity and quality dimensions), effort diminishes from some optimum or fixed level, thereby reducing firm productivity and increasing unit cost of production. Here, one would have an instance of managerial slack. The difference between what firm productivity is when effort is, in some sense, maximized and its actual level of productivity is a measure of x-inefficiency.

The direct relationship between productivity and average cost is illustrated below, where average cost can be given by the following equation, which assumes a very simply economy where labour is the only costed input (Altman, 2001). If labour is only one of a number of inputs, this does not affect the general direction of the argument.

$$AC = \frac{w}{(Q/L)}\ldots \tag{4.1}$$

Average cost (AC) is average cost; w is the wage rate or, more generally, the unit cost of inputs; (Q/L) is the average product of labour; Q is total output; and L is labour input measured in terms of hours worked. Anything that reduces productivity, such as managerial slack will, ceteris paribus, increase AC. This assumes that w remains constant in the face of changes to average cost.

Another way to visualize this argument is as follows:

$$\Delta e \rightarrow \Delta\left(Q/L\right) \rightarrow \Delta AC \dots \qquad (4.2)$$

Changes in effort input (e) yield changes in labour productivity (Q/L) yield changes in average costs (AC). Maximizing effort input maximizes average product and, thereby, minimizes average cost.

This takes the initial protection scenario deeper into the black box of the firm. Here, higher costs are explicitly modelled as a function of the preferences of the firm's decision-makers, where these preferences are not in sync with conventional assumptions of profit maximization. These higher costs need not be a product of diminished returns or outdated technology; they could be a product of the choices made by decision-makers. In this case, given protection, one cannot expect convergence to an efficient equilibrium. Moreover, one would predict multiple equilibria in terms of the extent of x-inefficiency and average cost, given different levels of effort inputs. These multiple equilibria are sustainable with different levels of protection afforded across firms and across countries. Changes in the level of protection can be expected to yield changes in the level of x-inefficiency across firms and countries.

Some of these points are illustrated in Fig. 4.1. In the Leibenstein narrative, managerial slack increases average cost by reducing labour productivity, and this is given by a LCM. With no managerial slack, the firm becomes x-efficient, given by point a. X-inefficient firms can survive on the market as consequence of protection, given by protection curve, PP′. The extent of protection is given by the vertical distance between line segment PP′ and LCM. Note, for example, that the protection required by the most x-inefficient firm is given by the difference in average cost between the latter and the average cost in the most x-efficient firm, Pa in this case. The smaller is the difference in average cost between a given x-inefficient firm and the most x-efficient firm, the less protection

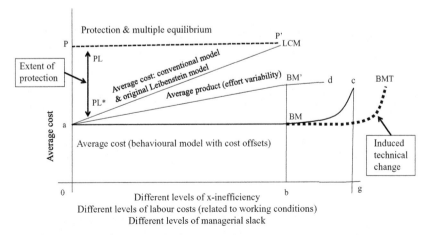

FIG. 4.1   Multiple equilibria in production.

that is required. Such protection allows for multiple equilibria across firms from the most to the least x-efficient firms.

Leibenstein maintains that such x-inefficiency is a product of quasi-rational behaviour since managerial slack deviates from neoclassical economic norms. But I would argue that, since managerial slack is utility maximizing from the perspective of the economic agents in question, it is rational (see Chapter 5). However, such choice behaviour is socially suboptimal as it reduces productivity and output from what it might otherwise be when effort is maximized. Moreover, such individually rational but socially suboptimal choice behaviour can represent a stable equilibrium. This would be a case of rational inefficiency. Rational or smart behaviour does not imply x-efficiency (see Chapter 5).

Multiple equilibria in production: X-inefficiency and agency

One can take this argument one step further (Altman, 1996, 1999, 2002, 2005a, 2005b). Evidence suggests that there is causal relationship between labour costs, inclusive of all aspects of the overall work environment, and productivity, with variations in effort input being an important intermediate variable. This relates to principle–agent issues, where a particular resolution to principle–agent problems need not yield x-efficiency in production, especially in a conflictual work environment. The empirically based prediction here would be that improvements in the work environment yield higher effort levels (quantity and quality dimensions) and this yields improvements in productivity, while a poorer work environment yields lower effort levels. Of course, changes in productivity affect average cost, ceteris paribus. Ceteris paribus is Leibenstein's original scenario, as only effort input is allowed to vary, as illustrated in Eq. (4.1). But if labour costs are allowed to vary, and these are causally connected to changes in productivity through variations in labour's effort input, average cost need not change as effort inputs, and therefore productivity, varies (se Chapters 5 and 7).

Because of this positive relationship between labour costs, effort input, and productivity, increases in labour productivity serve to offset increases in labour costs, while reductions in labour productivity serve to offset reductions in labour costs. These cost offsets can be enhanced to the extent that technological change is induced by higher labour costs, and lower labour costs impede technological change. This type of induced technological change is motivated by pressure to remain competitive in the face of rising or relatively high labour costs (Altman, 2009).

To the extent that changes in labour costs are just offset by changes in labour productivity, it is possible for average cost to remain constant along an array of labour costs—low to high. In this case, there would be an array of levels of labour productivity consistent with constant average cost. Here again, there is no unique equilibrium and multiple equilibria exist with regard to sustainable levels of productivity and therefore sustainable levels of x-inefficiency.

But, unlike in the initial Leibenstein modelling scenario, such multiple equilibria would even be consistent with no product market imperfections or protection to support the relatively inefficient economic entities. Moreover, there is no market imperative for convergence to take place toward some particular efficient equilibrium. Each point along an array of different productivity levels is sustainable since average cost is fixed across this array.

A critical point here is that even in the conventional economic ideal modelling scenario, where product markets are perfectly competitive, and even when market pressure is at its most severe, there need not be any market imperative toward a unique efficient competitive equilibrium. Therefore, competitive markets are not a sufficient condition to achieve or force convergence on a unique efficient equilibrium in the realm of production. Human agency, preferences of decision-makers, and how the firm is organized internally, become significant independent determinants of the extent to which the firm is x-efficient.

Some of these points are illustrated in Fig. 4.1. In the conventional narrative, x-efficiency is assumed, and increasing wages or labour costs drive up average costs, given by aLCM. However, given x-inefficiency and the causal relationship between labour cost and the related work environment, effort input, and productivity, changes in labour costs need not have any impact on average cost until effort input is effectively maximized, given by aBM. Past point BM, labour cost increases by more than increases in effort input and related increases in labour productivity, wherein average cost increases with increases in labour cost. This can be discerned from average productivity curve, a BM'd. Thereafter, increases in labour cost can incentivize firms to engage in technical change (Altman, 2009), shifting the average cost function to the right to a BMT, for example. But along a BM, there are multiple equilibria across firms with different levels of x-efficiency, different levels of labour cost, and different incentive environments. These various (non-unique) equilibria are sustainable in the long run, given the cost offsets, positive and negative, allowed for through effort variability and induced technical change.

In this scenario, different levels of efficiency (multiple equilibria) are contingent upon different incentive environments within the firm that induce different levels of effort inputs and therefore different levels of x-inefficiency and different levels of technical change (Altman, 2002, 2009). Related to this, different preferences among decision-makers toward their employees can affect the level of labour productivity. An array of such preferences can yield an array of levels of labour productivity. But these might all be consistent with a given level of average cost. For example, employers who favour higher wages and an improved work environment might not see an increase in average cost if this results in compensating increases in productivity. Employers who favour lower wages and a poor or even deteriorating work environment need not witness a reduction in average cost if this causes compensating decreases in labour productivity (Altman, 2002). Also, one might have a cooperative organization where higher wages and improved working conditions are part of the mission of the organization. Where labour costs, effort input, and labour productivity are highly and positively causally correlated, one cannot glean from the survival of firms, even in perfectly or highly productive product markets, that such firms are efficient. In this multiple equilibria scenario, one has to delve into the black box of the firm to determine the extent to which the firm is relatively efficient and the type of in-firm processes which give rise to the level of efficiency that characterizes a particular firm. And these in-firm processes, themselves, need not be unique (Cyert & March, 1963; see also Chapter 5 and 7).

Multiple equilibria in production: Some related scenarios

Related to the above modelling scenario, one can interrogate a number of propositions that flow from the conventional wisdom, a crucial one being that ethical behaviour by the firm should result in the firm's demise, unless it is protected from market forces. Ethical behaviour might take the form, for example, of improving working conditions within the firm or working toward making one's plant more environmentally friendly. This should increase production costs, *ceterus paribus*. Ethical firms would therefore have to be protected from the competitive threat posed by the relatively lower cost of less ethical firms. But this assumes that firms are already x-efficient, and technological change is not induced (Altman, 2001, 2002, 2005b, 2009). But in this scenario, there can be no efficient unique equilibrium since the higher cost ethical firms, through protection, could coexist with their relatively unethical counterparts. If x-efficiency cannot be taken as a prior, and protection is not sufficient, then ethical firms can be expected to find ways of improving productivity to remain competitive. This might not always meet with success. However, the appropriate prediction would be that ethical considerations can be expected to induce increased productivity by increasing the level of x-efficiency and through induced technical change.

Given the pervasiveness of multiple equilibria, one would expect that different processes would be in place across firms to achieve outcomes consistent with firm survival where some of these processes are consistent with x-efficiency and others are not. Moreover, efficient outcomes might be achievable through an array of different processes. For example, co-operative organizations (worker or consumer owned) would achieve efficiency through different means than a privately or investor-owned firm. But evidence suggests that even investor-owned firms tend to achieve efficiency through co-operative labour–management–owner processes as opposed to conflictual–non-cooperative processes (Altman, 2002). Therefore, one would predict multiple equilibria in this domain as well. There are different ownership forms that can achieve x-efficiency. There is no one-size-fits-all process by which efficiency is achieved within firms—a key point of behavioural approaches to the firm. And, this fits well with a multiple equilibria approach to modelling.

Historical and logical time

Another area of concern with regard to multiple equilibria is in the domain of historical time as opposed to the logical time in which conventional economics is largely vested. In logical time, the focus is on the determinants of equilibrium and how one moves from disequilibrium to equilibrium in particular markets, where the ceteris paribus assumption holds. The argument presented here is that when one models equilibrium scenarios, it is most probable that there will not be a unique equilibrium. Rather, there will be multiple equilibria, even when highly competitive product markets prevail. This interrogates the conventional wisdom at its core.

But this particular focus abstracts from the process by which equilibrium is achieved. In the real economy movement toward some equilibrium, including multiple equilibria, takes place over historical time and it can take considerable time to move toward an endpoint. During this process, one would expect that, taking a snapshot at a given point in time (a moment), there would be an array of firms that would be inefficient, even if the conventional hypothesis holds that in equilibrium, all economic entities need to converge toward a unique equilibrium. Existence or survival, at any given point in time does not imply, in itself, that economic efficiency prevails. This is contrary to strong interpretations of the efficient market hypothesis, that firms should always be efficient.

Rent seeking and x-efficiency

One last point is worthy of consideration. When one considers economic efficiency or x-inefficiency, one is largely investigating the extent to which firms are x-efficient. However, x-efficiency in production does not imply that such x-efficient firms are contributing positively to an economy's overall growth performance.

One example of this would be rent-seeking firms—firms whose objective is to earn income by transferring into their own coffers the income of others. This can be achieved by coercion or through rules and regulation that facilitate such rent-seeking behaviour. These are not productive or wealth-generating activities. Rather, they are ventures in income and/or wealth redistribution. And, to the extent that the macro-institutional environment encourages rent-seeking behaviour, more investors will move into this domain as opposed to productive economic activities (North, 1990, 1994).

Rent seekers can be perfectly x-efficient, but serve to reduce the wealth of nations. Even if all existing rent seeking firms converge toward a unique efficient equilibrium, one cannot deduce from this a signal that society is maximizing its real income or real growth rate. Quite the opposite might be taking place. Economic efficiency at a local level does not necessarily translate into economic efficiency at the societal level.

Conclusion

A multiple equilibria analytical framework affords an alternative and more scientifically robust modelling scenario than does the modelling assumption of convergence toward a unique equilibrium that is both economically efficient and imputes unique processes by which such a unique equilibrium is achieved. In the multiple equilibria scenario, a unique equilibrium represents but one possible outcome. A multiple equilibria framework and narrative were championed by Herbert Simon as the more realistic and scientifically appropriate modelling worldview with which to tackle real-world socioeconomic issues. From Simon's perspective and approach to behavioural economics and scientific analysis, economic theory must be related (induced) from the stylized facts of life, which is the case in multiple equilibria scenarios. The multiple equilibria analytical template forces one to go beyond superficial analyses, which starts with the assumption of a unique and efficient equilibrium in consumption and production and in the process(es) to achieve this equilibrium out- come. This is driven by market forces and the hardwiring of the economic agent or decision-maker.

The possibilities of sustainable alternative choices in consumption, production, and decision-making processes are assumed away. This falls victim to the ought-is fallacy of assuming that that which is (exists, survives) is both rational and efficient because it exists. Related to this, extreme versions of ecological efficiency (a concept pioneered by Hayek) suggest that outcomes and choices, even if they are inconsistent with conventional economic norms, are not only rational (or smart), but are also efficient. Why? Because these choices and outcomes have passed the test of survival (see Chapter 3).

The pervasive success of the unique equilibrium approach is its simplicity, and its consistency with conventional economic worldviews that market forces should generate efficient outcomes. Developing upon Simon's insights, I model the conditions whereby multiple equilibria in choices, processes, and outcomes are sustainable in consumption and production. These conditions are reasonable given the structure of real-world economics and the behavioural characteristics of human decision-makers. Therefore, the existence of particular choice sets, organizational forms, or processes should not be taken as proof of efficiency or uniqueness. One has to delve further into the black box of the firm and the household to make a determination of whether particular choices and outcomes are efficient or, in some sense, optimal.

Some of these arguments are highlighted in Figs 4.1 and 4.2. In Fig. 4.2, multiple equilibria are linked to both consumption and production outcomes and to decision- making and organizational processes. In the consumption domain causality is linked importantly to differences in preferences (this needs to be controlled for real income and relative prices). In the production domain, causality is linked to market forces, differential preferences (among economic agents), bargaining power (affects decisions, the decision-making process, and thereby outcomes), the legal environment, and customs (inclusive of norms, culture). Also of importance are multiple equilibria in human resource management

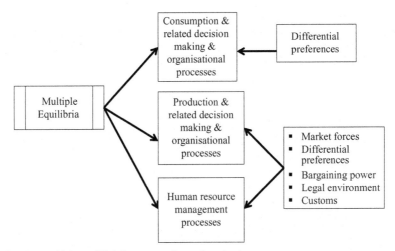

FIG. 4.2   Multiple equilibria in consumption and production.

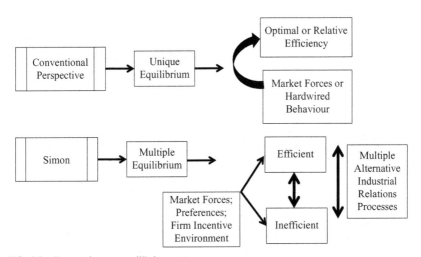

FIG. 4.3   Perspectives on equilibrium states.

processes, which are causally linked to the same causal variables as production outcomes.

Fig. 4.3 highlights some of the key differences between the conventional and Simon (multiple equilibria) modelling approaches. In the former, unique and efficient equilibria are causally related to market forces and hardwired behaviour, whereas multi equilibria are causally linked to a spectrum of sustainable outcomes and processes.

A fundamental difference between these two different analytical approaches is that, unlike the efficient unique equilibrium approach, from a multiple equilibria perspective, one does not presume uniqueness and efficiency as a given.

These are only possibilities. Any particular outcome that reveals itself in the market can no longer be taken as indicative of efficiency or representative of some unique revealed preference of decision-makers. This approach is also consistent with rationality in decision-making as no presumption is made that any particular sustainable outcome and decision-making process is irrational because it deviates from a particular conventional economic norm. A multiple equilibria approach of this type opens the door to richer, more nuanced, and causally robust analyses of economies, building upon how actual economies function and evolve through historical time.

Some very basic examples of the analytical and policy implications of the multiple equilibrium approach are:

- That low-wage firms persist and can even be dominant does not imply that higher wage firms can't thrive, yielding Pareto-superior outcomes.
- That polluting firms are profitable and can even be dominant does not imply that greener firms can't thrive, yielding Pareto-superior outcomes.
- That in some societies and communities, females have many children and also do not receive an education similar to what is obtained by males, does not imply that this is an efficient or utility-maximizing outcome for all (in particular for females). Other outcomes are possible, yielding higher levels of utility to females and even Pareto-superior outcome overall.
- Efficient and utility 'maximizing' outcomes are conditional upon institutional arrangements and the mental models used by decision-makers (agents) to drive choice. By changing these parameters, one ends with different equilibrium outcome, which can be superior in terms of efficiency and utility of wellbeing.
- There need not be one unique decision-making process yielding efficiency in production or consumption. Best practice processes are context dependent. But agency, accurate information, transparency, are critical to optimal decisions. And, in production, more co-operative forms of governance tends to yield more x-efficient outcomes.

References

Alchian, A. A. (1950). Uncertainty, evolution and economic theory. *Journal of Political Economy, 58*, 211–221.

Altman, M. (1996). *Human agency and material welfare: Revisions in microeconomics and their implications for public policy.* Boston: Kluwer Academic Publishers.

Altman, M. (1999). The methodology of economics and the survival principle revisited and revised: Some welfare and public policy implications of modeling the economic agent. *Review of Social Economy, 57*, 427–449.

Altman, M. (2001). When green isn't mean: Economic theory and the heuristics of the impact of environmental regulations on competitiveness and opportunity cost. *Ecological Economics, 36*, 31–44.

Altman, M. (2002). Economic theory and the challenge of innovative work practices. *Economic and Industrial Democracy, 23*, 271–290.

Altman, M. (2005a). Behavioral economics, power, rational inefficiencies, fuzzy sets, and public policy. *Journal of Economic Issues*, *39*, 683–706.

Altman, M. (2005b). The ethical economy and competitive markets: Reconciling altruistic, moralistic, and ethical behavior with the rational economic agent and competitive markets. *Journal of Economic Psychology*, *26*, 732–757.

Altman, M. (2008). Behavioral economics, economic theory and public policy. *Australasian Journal of Economic Education*, *5*, 1–55.

Altman, M. (2009). A behavioral-institutional model of endogenous growth and induced technical change. *Journal of Economic Issues*, *43*, 685–714.

Arthur, W. B. (2013). *Complexity economics: As (SFI working paper 13-04-012)*. Retrieved from http://www.santafe.edu/media/workingpapers/13-04-012.pdf.

Cyert, R. M., & March, J. C. (1963). *A behavioral theory of the firm*. Englewood Cliffs, NJ: Prentice-Hall.

Elsner, W. (2015). *Policy implications of economic complexity and complexity economics (MPRA paper no. 63252)*. Retrieved from http://mpra.ub.uni-muenchen.de/63252/.

Friedman, M. (1953). The methodology of positive economics. In M. Friedman (Ed.), *Essays in positive economics* (pp. 3–43). Chicago, IL: University of Chicago Press.

Gigerenzer, G. (2007). *Gut feelings: The intelligence of the unconscious*. New York, NY: Viking.

Hume, D. (1738/2014). *A treatise on human nature*. Some Good Press [Kindle file].

Kahneman, D. (2003). Maps of bounded rationality: Psychology for behavioral economics. *American Economic Review*, *93*, 1449–1475.

Kahneman, D. (2011). *Thinking fast and slow*. New York, NY: Farrar, Strauss, Giroux.

Leibenstein, H. (1966). Allocative efficiency vs. 'X-efficiency'. *American Economic Review*, *56*, 392–415.

Leibenstein, H. (1979). A branch of economics is missing: Micro-micro theory. *Journal of Economic Literature*, *17*, 477–502.

North, D. C. (1990). *Institutions, institutional change and economic performance*. New York, NY: Cambridge University Press.

North, D. C. (1994). Economic performance through time. *American Economic Review*, *84*, 359–368.

Simon, H. A. (1978). Rationality as a process and as a product of thought. *American Economic Review*, *70*, 1–16.

Simon, H. A. (1979). Rational decision making in business organizations. *American Economic Review*, *69*, 493–513.

Simon, H. A. (1987). Behavioral economics. In J. Eatwell, M. Millgate, & P. Newman (Eds.), *The New Palgrave: A dictionary of economics* (pp. 266–267). London: Macmillan.

Simon, H. A. (1997). Models of bounded rationality. In Vol. III. *Empirical grounded economic reasons*. Cambridge, MA: MIT Press.

Smith, V. L. (2003). Constructivist and ecological rationality in economics. *American Economic Review*, *93*, 465–508.

Thaler, R. H., & Sunstein, C. (2008). *Nudge: Improving decisions about health, wealth, and happiness*. New Haven, CT: Yale University Press.

Chapter 5

Understanding rational inefficiency: A scientific basis for economic failure and success

Chapter outline

Introduction	93	Production inefficiency	107
Introducing rationality and		Consumption inefficiencies	115
rational inefficiency	94	Macroeconomic choices and	
Institutions, efficiency,		rational behaviour	120
and rationality	99	Conclusion	125
Different types of rationality	102	References	127

Introduction

The core argument of this chapter is that individuals (economic agents) can behave inefficiently in a number of domains, at both the micro or macro (social) level. But this behaviour can be considered to be rational in the sense that such inefficiency can be a product of smart or considered choice behaviour. Smart people can be efficient or inefficient. From a smart-rationality assumption, one cannot necessary derive choices that will be efficient in outcomes. Moreover, what might appear to be irrational and, therefore, inefficient behaviour from the perspective of conventional economics might very well be, and often is, rational, smart, intelligent, considered, and even purposeful behaviour from a smart agent perspective.

Inefficient outcomes can be a product of the preferences of decision-makers. And, this is related to who are decision-makers, how are they chosen (within the household and firm, at least), and the decision-making process. This is affected by power relationships within the household and the firm. Or, inefficient outcomes can be a product of incorrect or incomplete information (Akerlof, 1970) about what is required to achieve efficiency and how this might affect the utility or wellbeing of decision-makers. The latter is related to the mental models individuals adopt to make choice decisions, and these models might be incorrect or misleading resulting in decisions yielding economically inefficient outcomes.

Smart Economic Decision-Making in a Complex World. https://doi.org/10.1016/B978-0-12-811461-2.00005-5

Rational or, more generally speaking, smart behaviour, should not be convoluted with socially rational behaviour. What's rational from the individual's perspective might very well be irrational from the social perspective as preferences across individuals and social groups might and typically do differ dramatically. Maximizing the preferences of a CEO need not be consistent with long term viability of the firm. Maximizing the wellbeing of the male partner in a relationship can be inconsistent with maximizing wellbeing of the female partner. In addition, it is important to differentiate rational individual choice behaviour from behaviour that is error-free or decisions that aren't subject to regret. Making mistakes and regretting these errors in decision-making can be consistent with rational or smart behaviour. Much depends on the decision-making capabilities of the individuals and the relevant decision-making environment. In a word, this chapter presents a modelling narrative on rational choice behaviour from a bounded rationality perspective. This builds on the pioneering work of Simon (1959, 1978, 1986, 1987) integrating the concepts of bounded and procedural rationality and overlaps and is informed by the research and research-orientations of Gigerenzer (2007), Hayek (1944, 1945, 1948), Leibenstein (1957, 1966, 1979), and Smith (2003, 2005) as well as my own research on the subject (Altman, 1999, 2005, 2006a, 2006b, 2010, 2011, 2012, 2015). It is also informed by the research of Kahneman and Tversky (1979), Kahneman (2003, 2011), see also Tversky & Kahneman (1981); the heuristics and biases perspective and also by Kahneman's (2011) more recent slow and fast thinking narrative where the type of decision-making processes or systems is contextionalized by the decision problem at hand. However, the smart decision-making approach generates results and orientations that contravene the heuristics and biases approach to decision-making and behavioural economics, which maintains conventional economic benchmarks for rationality and efficiency.

Introducing rationality and rational inefficiency

To proceed in this narrative one has to clarify what is meant by rationality and by efficiency and what benchmarks one has to meet to be deemed rational and efficient. This remains a gap in the literature critical of conventional economics and, indeed, of the literature critical of the heuristics and biases approach and of the nudging approach to behavioural economics. Conventional economics is relatively clear on what is meant by rationality, what rational behaviours are, and what the expectations are for rational decision-making and its relationship to choices and outcomes. Conventional economics not only has reasonably clear benchmarks for rationality (discussed below and Chapter 3, above), it also predicts rationality in human decision-making and hence in the outcomes emanating from these decisions. But one should acknowledge that market failures remain a theoretical possibility even within the domain of conventional or neoclassical rationality when negative or positive externalities are present and not internalized by the decision-maker.

Overall, conventional economics hypothesises that rational inefficiency should not occur. This is predicated on the assumption that decision-makers are neoclassically rational (related to conventional economics definitions of rationality, discussed below and in Chapter 3, above). Moreover, given the prior assumption of the neoclassical rationality of decision-makers, it is assumed or predicted that the choices made by such rational agents will be efficient (assuming for simplicity, no externalities exist). Given this overarching assumption of neoclassical rationality, one can predict that an individual's choices yield optimal or 'best' outcomes given the constraints faced by the individual. By the prior assumption of rationality and de facto optimality on the part of individual decision-makers one ends up predicting that outcomes must be efficient and optimal. That which exists is presumed to be efficient by assumption as opposed to determining the extent of efficiency by empirical analyses. In this modelling scenario, it becomes possible to presume efficiency and optimality even when they actually don't exist. This can detract scholars from actively pursuing an analysis of the actual state of affairs, be it efficient or not, and its specific determinants. Note that in this approach to rationality is defined such that rational choice behaviour yields efficient outcome. A core argument in this chapter is that smart decision-making is rational, but not necessarily neoclassically so. Rational behaviour can be inconsistent with 'neoclassical' behaviour and, moreover, rational behaviour can yield sub-optimal and efficient outcomes.

Overall, the conventional methodological approach fits nicely with what is referred to as the Humean fallacy, articulated in the *A Treatise of Human Nature* (2014 [1738], p. 576). Hume raises the problem of individuals deducing from what is, what ought to be (efficiency) and then attributing particular causes to the assumed efficiency, in this case a particular type of rationality. Since these deductions are not empirically based, they represent fallacies according to Hume. In fact, assuming that outcomes are necessarily efficient when choices are neoclassically rational is merely a testable hypothesis.

This Humean fallacy is rooted in the dominant methodology in economics best articulated by Friedman (1953, pp. 21–23; see also Reder, 1982) in his classic work on the praxis of positive economics. He argues that economically efficient outcomes are invariably the product of neoclassically rational behaviour. The derivative of this is that one does not have to investigate how actual humans behave or the process by which choices are made. It is good enough to assume that individuals behave as if they are neoclassically rational. Why? Because only efficient agents can survive on the market. If they survive, they must be efficient. This efficiency can only be a product of neoclassically rational behaviour inside the firm. 'Natural selection', additionally, forces neoclassical rationality (in this case, what Friedman refers to as maximization-of-returns consistent behaviour) to dominate the behaviour of firm members and more specifically the decision-makers inside the firm. Therefore, the evidence in favour of rationality, joined with efficiency, is revealed by the survival of existing firms. Moreover, the persistence and dominance of the maximization-of-returns cum rationality assumption in the literature, both scholarly and popular, aided and abetted by no 'credible' alternative hypothesis explaining firm survival is, according to Friedman, further evidence of the scientific validity of the maximization-of-returns assumption. Overall, Friedman makes that case that humans are neoclassically rational decision-makers; at least one can make this behavioural assumption without causing any harm to either causal (true cause and effect) or predictive analysis or public policy.

This type of argument is also developed in Alchian (1950) who argues that market forces create an environment wherein efficient choices are imposed on decision-makers, at least those with a preference for surviving on the market. There is no need that individuals attempt to explicitly or carefully maximize profit of utility. Firms that survive are relatively efficient, because they survive. Hence, the behaviour of firm decision-makers must be consistent with such outcomes. This line of argument can be situated within the analytical domain of a Humean fallacy, any behaviour consistent with survival is considered to be acceptable and appropriate. For Alchian (1950), survival of the firm is evidence of relative efficiency, but there is no theory of human choice behaviour to benchmark which type of behaviours can yield or should yield relatively efficient outcomes. Like Friedman, there is little interest in how individuals actually behave. What is of concern is that any such behaviour yields economically efficient outcomes, at least in the long run.

Alchian argues (1950, p. 213):

> *Realized positive profits, not maximum profits, are the mark of success and viability. It does not matter through what process of reasoning or motivation such success was achieved. The fact of its accomplishment is sufficient. This is the criterion by which the economic system selects survivors: those who realize positive profits are the survivors; those who suffer losses disappear. The pertinent requirement-positive profits through relative efficiency is weaker than 'maximized profits,' with which, unfortunately, it has been confused. Positive profits accrue to those who are better than their actual competitors, even if the participants are ignorant, intelligent, skillful, etc.*

The conventional worldview (and variations of this) is that individuals either behave in a fashion consistent with neoclassical rationality or they behave as if they are so doing. Ultimately it is expected that the outcomes will be economically efficient or utility maximizing either because market forces will guarantee this outcome or because individuals are hardwired to behave in this manner. The latter stronger assumption is all too often made. Typically, this is done implicitly. The end result is that a dominant prior assumption in the conventional wisdom is that outcomes will be economically efficient or utility maximizing. Moreover, it is assumed that because individual neoclassical rationality results in micro-level economic efficiency, this morphs into macro-level or social economic efficiency. It is then no longer analytically important to determine how individuals make their choices and which choices are made or even whether or not outcomes are in some identifiable sense efficient. Even institutional design and policy lose their importance if neoclassical rationality is predicted to yield economic efficiency in and off itself—appropriate institutional design and policy are assumed to naturally evolve in an accommodating manner.[a]

Mancur Olson elaborates on this point with regards to social or macro-level economic efficiency derived from assumptions pertaining to micro-level neoclassical rationality and economic efficiency. Olson (1996, pp. 4–5) writes:

> *The idea that the economies we observe are socially efficient, at least to an approximation, is not only espoused by economists who follow their logic as far as it will go, but is also a staple assumption behind much of the best-known empirical work. In the familiar aggregate production function or growth accounting empirical studies, it is assumed that economies are on the frontiers of their aggregate production functions ... If the ideas evoked here are largely true, then the rational parties in the economy and the polity ensure that the economy cannot be that far from its potential, and the policy advice of economists cannot be especially valuable.*

As evidenced above, critical to this neoclassical or conventional rational economic efficiency perspective is the assumption that the survival of economic entities is proof of economic efficiency and, correlated to this, economic efficiency as demonstrated by survival is proof of rationality. This survival principle builds upon the assumption that only efficient economic entities, which also happen to be rational, can survive on the market. To the extent that inefficient economic entities can survive in a moment in time (cross-sectionally) and over time, survival can't serve as proof of efficiency or neoclassical rationality—critical to the conventional efficiency–rationality narrative. Survival would imply neither efficiency nor rationality. Moreover, if neoclassical rationality is not necessary to economic efficiency, then economic efficiency is not proof of economic agents being neoclassically rational.

Another point that is important to note and which will be elaborated on further below is that the rationality/inefficiency/efficiency narrative can be applied to the realm of consumption or consumer behaviour. Conventional economics assumes that the revealed preferences of consumers through their choices off and on the market coincide with their true preferences—their wants and desires. In the realm of consumption this assumption represents an important aspect of consumption efficiency. Moreover, it is assumed that the process by which the choices are made are consistent with the carefully calculating and prescient behaviour of consumers assumed in conventional economics. Hence consumption efficiency presumes the identity between revealed preferences and true preferences and these preferences being actualised within the parameters of neoclassical behavioural processes.

---

a. This type of perspective on the necessary evolution of 'efficient' institutions is strongly critiqued by North (1971).

However, even if one assumes neoclassical processes, this is not sufficient to guarantee that revealed preferences are identical to the true preferences of decision makers. This prior assumes that neoclassical processes are indeed the most effective means for achieving preferred ends. This is typically not the case in the real world of complex, costly, and asymmetric information. This being said, the assumption equating revealed and true preferences builds implicitly upon very strong and unrealistic assumptions about the necessary conditions required for this equality to hold. Institutional parameters are critical in determining the extent to which revealed preferences are below optimal preferences. Moreover, unlike with respect to the reference to firm rationality and efficiency, market forces can't guarantee that individuals should adhere to neoclassical behavioural decision-making protocols. There's s no so-called survival of the fittest in the domain of consumption, even if one accepts the assumption that competitive forces can drive such neoclassical outcomes in the domain of production (Altman, 2010).

From the perspective of the heuristics and biases approach (Kahneman and Tversky, 1979), there would be such sub-optimal consumer behaviour, but this would be a product of the hardwired cognitive limitations of decision makers, not the 'inefficiency' of institutional parameters, for example. And, one expects sub-optimal behaviour to be the rule, not the exception. This is most clearly elaborated and expressed in the Nudge approach to decision-making and well-articulated in Thaler and Sunstein (2008).

The more Simon-related behavioural economists situate consumer decision making (as they do all types of decision making) in the 'environmental' space, broadly speaking, within which decision-making takes place. Given this space, outcomes are considered to be optimal even though the realization of such outcomes does not follow neoclassical decision-making processes. This is now referred to as ecological rationality. Different decision-making processes (non-neoclassical ones) are expected to generate these optimal outcomes in the realm of consumption. So what might appear to be irrational or error-prone and biased behaviour form the perspective of both the conventional wisdom and from heuristics and biases approaches could very well be both rational and optimal given the decision making environment. This particular approach championed by Gigerenzer (2007), referred to as fast and frugal heuristics and ecological rationality, has roots in the work of Herbert Simon. Still, it remains an empirical question if, when, and where particular heuristics yield optimal outcomes from the perspective of the individual or society. But, clearly, the benchmarks for what is consumer efficiency and rationality and what are the expected outcomes of the decision-making process is quite different in the conventional wisdom compared to what would be case from the various perspective in behavioural economics.

Also, of significance to the smart agent approach to decision-making is an understanding of how sociological variables impact on choice behaviour, affecting the constraints and opportunities that frame the decision-making process and the choices made by economic agents. What is rational choice behaviour must also be contextualized by sociological variables such as peers, families, social norms, and culture, for example (Akerlof & Kranton, 2010; Becker, 1996). Changing the social context of the choice environment impacts on what choices a smart individual will make.

More generally, the conventional worldview as well as most other methodological perspectives in economics, inclusive of the 'new' behavioural economics (heuristics and biases and related nudging approaches) and heterodox modelling, often also tend to rely, analytically, on the typical agent, household, and firm, where these are supposed to be the equivalent of representative agents. Where it is not assumed that all economic agents, each and every one of them, are neoclassically rational and economically efficient, it is the typical agent, household, and firm that is assumed to be so. This typical agent more often than not implicitly or explicitly refers to the average behaviour of economic agents, households, and firms. But the average cannot represent typical behaviour unless most individual behaviour is identical to the average. This assumption is unlikely to be true and can't be assumed to be true without empirical validation. A critical focus on the typical or average is clearly articulated by Alchian (1950)—attention is placed on predicting accurately average outcomes and then imputing economic efficiency from these outcomes.

But if the objective is to determine the extent of economic efficiency and its determinants (very much a function of the choices made by agents given their constraints, opportunities, and capabilities), one has to go beyond the average and analyse the various empirical slices that comprise the average. There might be slices that comprise the average or typical that are efficient and others that are not. And, there might be different means by which economic efficiency is achieved, which are smart but not neoclassically rational. Moreover, within each analytical slice agents might be facing different opportunities and constraints and might possess different capabilities. These will affect what one means by rational or smart decisions. The latter must be contextualized by the decision-makers' overarching decision-making environment.

Institutions, efficiency, and rationality

Institutional frames are vitally important to a discussion of rationality and efficiency at both the micro and macro (social) level. Whether or not decision-making is rational, and the extent to which efficiency is achieved, can only be determined if the decision-making process and the choices that flow from this process are contextualized by the institutional environment within which decisions are made. This is typically not done by conventional economists or even by economists off the mainstream. Not only must decision-making be institutionally contextualized, this framing must be empirically based. This entails that the framing must be derived from the actual institutional parameters within which the decision making process takes place. One can't assume that optimal institutional parameters are in place or will evolve willy-nilly. This is a point addressed by Simon (1987), articulating the importance of institutional parameters for decision-making processes and outcomes.

Douglas North, one of the founding 'fathers' of what is oft-referred to as the New Institutional Economics, critiques conventional economics for paying no attention to the role institutions play in affecting choice behaviour and thereby economic outcomes, especially when decision making is a dynamic process taking place through historical time. Of course, this is exactly the type of environment within which decision-making is embedded. Conventional theory is more concerned with stipulated equilibrium conditions given a particular institutional environment; often conditional upon an assumed institutional design that yields optimal economic outcomes. North (1994, p. 359) remarks:

> Neoclassical theory is simply an inappropriate tool to analyze and prescribe policies that will induce development. It is concerned with the operation of markets, not with how markets develop. How can one prescribe policies when one doesn't understand how economies develop? .... The very methods employed by neoclassical economists have dictated the subject matter and militated against such a development. In the analysis of economic performance through time it contained two erroneous assumptions: (i) that institutions do not matter and (ii) that time does not matter.

North (1991, p. 97) provides one possible definition of institutions and it would be this framework that North argues is ignored or assumed to be analytically irrelevant to cogent economic analysis: 'Institutions are the humanly devised constraints that structure political, economic and social interaction. They consist of both informal constraints (sanctions, taboos, customs, traditions, and codes of conduct), and formal rules (constitutions, laws, property rights)'.

The reason why institutions are of analytical importance, argues North, is because they affect the incentive environment within which decision are made. For example, relative prices and relative opportunity costs of various types are conditional upon institutional parameters. North writes (1991, p. 97):

> Institutions and the effectiveness of enforcement (together with the technology employed) determine the cost of transacting. Effective institutions raise the benefits of cooperative solutions or the costs of defection, to use game theoretic terms. In transaction cost terms, institutions reduce transaction and production costs per exchange so that the potential gains from trade are realizeable. Both political and economic institutions are essential parts of an effective institutional matrix.

North continues that optimality in outcomes is not inevitable even if one assumes neoclassically rational agents. The types of institutions that are constructed, monitored, and enforced determine outcomes. North remarks (1991, p. 110):

> When economies do evolve, therefore, nothing about that process assures economic growth. It has commonly been the case that the incentive structure provided

by the basic institutional framework creates opportunities for the consequent organizations to evolve, but the direction of their development has not been to promote productivity-raising activities. Rather, private profitability has been enhanced by creating monopolies, by restricting entry and factor mobility, and by political organizations that established property rights that redistributed rather than increased income.

In North's take on institutional economics, institutional design plays a pre-eminent role in determining the choices decision makers. Institutions, therefore, play a critical role in determining whether the outcomes of these institutionally affected choices are economically efficient. It is important to reiterate that North's decision makers can be neoclassically rational. But such rationally need not generate either economic efficiency at a micro level or at a social level. But given the institutional parameters imposed by a particular institutional design, such rationality would be utility maximizing, at least broadly speaking, from the perspective of the decision maker. North makes the case for utility maximizing rational inefficiency contingent on whether or not institutional design incentivises such inefficiency. And, this is the case even one makes the 'extreme' (and not empirically based) assumption of neoclassical agents or decision-makers.

Another pre-eminent economist, often associated with the conventional worldview, also makes the case for rational inefficiency, contingent upon institutional design. Mancur Olson argues that the evidence is overwhelming that there are trillions of dollars lying on the sidewalk—something that should not occur in a world of rational wealth cum utility maximizing agents (Olson, 1996, p. 19):

The evidence from the national borders that delineate different institutions and economic policies not only contradicts the view that societies produce as much as their resource endowments permit, but also directly suggests that a country's institutions and economic policies are decisive for its economic performance.

A key point made by Olsen is that even given the assumption of individual-based neoclassical rationality, societies can be socially inefficient and socially 'irrational', and they are socially irrational because they are socially inefficient. Institutional design determines the extent to which neoclassically rational agents generate socially inefficient economic outcomes. He guestimates that such rationally inefficient outcomes are more the rule than the exception. Olson writes (1996, p. 23): 'Some important trends in economic thinking, useful as they are, should not blind us to a sad and all-too-general reality: as the literature on collective action demonstrates … individual rationality is very far indeed from being sufficient for social rationality'.

At a very basic level the New Institutional Economics is incompatible with the core modelling assumptions of conventional economics. It makes the point that economic inefficiency can be rational and that economic efficiency requires particular institutional parameters to be in place. One can have billions if not trillions of dollars lying on the sidewalk even in the long term without rational or smart people picking these up. The incentive environment need not be appropriate for socially optimal behaviour to take place amongst utility maximizing individuals. Private utility maximization, which can take the form of rent seeking behaviour, for example, can be consistent with social inefficiency. An economic agent, a decision maker, might be maximizing utility, operating along her or his utility function, whilst the economy is operating in the interior of the economy's production possibility frontier. Given a person's utility function and given the institutional environment, it makes sense for the individual to maximize utility and profits through redistributing wealth as opposed to wealth creation.

North's and Olsen's efficient institutions are very much related to secure property rights and highly competitive markets; especially product markets. Taking this argument further, derivative of the 'old' institutional economics, I would argue that such sub-optimal (inefficient) outcomes could easily and predictably take place even with more appropriate (lower) transaction costs and more secure private property rights where agents are relatively secure that their legal gains from trade and that their assets will not be arbitrarily confiscated by the state or by other private agents. The capabilities of individuals, the preferences of decision-makers, and the power relationship between decision-makers and potential decision-makers can impact the efficiency of economic outcomes, even given effective property rights and competitive market structures being in place. For example, inefficiency producing preferences, which would be a consequence of a preference for managerial slack (firm inefficiencies) or rent-seeking (social inefficiencies), can dominate even across different institutional parameters (Altman, 2005). This social and power perspective to institutional economics is also absent not only from the New Institutional Economics, but also from the current and various perspective in behavioural economics.

Different types of rationality

It is important to have an understanding of what conventional economists tend to agree are the behavioural norms for optimal behaviour; that is behaviour that yields efficient economic outcomes. Not everyone would completely agree on what these norms are. However, there are certain core assumptions that are often made reference to by both neoclassical or conventional economists and by behavioural economists as well. What I outline below it not a straw 'man' that's easy to attack and shoot down. And, there are variations and modifications to this narrative. But many would agree that the following is representative of the assumptions underlying much of conventional economic modelling (this is also discussed in Chapter 2, above):

1. Individuals can and do make consistent choices across all possible bundles of goods and services and through time.
2. It is assumed that all individuals have thorough knowledge of all relevant available options at any given point in time and they all have the means to

process and understand this information in a timely manner—the brain is assumed not to be scarce resource and individuals' computational ability is assumed to be unlimited with respect to the decision-making process and problem in hand.

3. Individuals can forecast the implications of their decisions through time and hence calculate at least in a measurable probabilistic sense the consequences of their choices.
4. Individuals are assumed to make choices across alternatives that maximize utility or wellbeing, hence choices should not be subject to regret.
5. It is typically assumed either explicitly or implicitly that, controlling for risk, utility maximization is consistent with wealth or income maximization.
6. It is assumed that individuals are effective and efficient calculating machines or at least they behave as if they are, irrespective of age, experience, education, or social context.
7. It is assumed that all individuals independent of context should behave in the same calculating manner (following conventional behavioural norms) to maximize utility or efficiency.

Herbert Simon rejects this neoclassical or conventional economics definition of rationality in favour of what he refers to as bounded rationality and, related to this, satisficing. Simon considers the conventional definition to be completely unrealistic and therefore useless with respect to constructing models that can speak to causation (as opposed to correlation) and to actual normative requirements to achieve optimal decisions and choices. Bounded rationality refers to smart or considered choice behaviour in the context of the choice environment and the decision-making capabilities of the decision maker. Hence, for Simon there is no unequivocal benchmark for rationality. It is context dependent and recognizes that decision-making capabilities differ across individuals, firms, households, ethnicities, cultures, religions, regions, and nations. Satisficing is doing the best one can with what means are realistically available given the reality of bounded rationality. A key message here is that simply because decision makers aren't behaving neoclassically in their decision-making processes, this does not imply that they are irrational or inefficient. Indeed, behaving neoclassically might very well be irrational given the decision-making environment, yielding sub-optimal outcomes (Simon, 1978, 1986, 1987).

This point is clearly articulated by James March, a close colleague of Simon. Rationality can't be defined and modelled outside of the context of the decision-making environment and the decision making capabilities of decision makers (March, 1978, p. 589):

Engineers of artificial intelligence have modified their perceptions of efficient problem solving procedures by studying the actual behavior of human problem solvers. Engineers of organizational decision making have modified their models of rationality on the basis of studies of actual organizational behavior...Modern students of human choice behavior frequently assume, at least implicitly, that actual human choice behavior in some way or other is likely to make sense. It can be understood as being the behavior of an intelligent being or group of intelligent beings...

Vernon Smith, a pioneer of experimental economics, makes a related point, basing his understanding of rational behaviour and on what works in effectively generating the preferred outcomes of decision makers. Such non-neoclassical behaviour, which one might refer to as satisficing would be the most rational course of action for smart agents and should form the basis for constructing general norms for best practice behaviour or decision-making processes. Smith (2005, pp. 149–150; see also Smith 2003) writes:

It is shown that the investor who chooses to maximize expected profit (discounted total withdrawals) fails in finite time. Moreover, there exist a variety of nonprofit-maximizing behaviors that have a positive probability of never failing. In fact, it is shown that firms that maximize profits are the least likely to be the market survivors. My point is simple: when experimental results are contrary to standard concepts of rationality, assume not just that people are irrational, but that you may not have the right model of rational behavior. Listen to what your subjects may be trying to tell you. Think of it this way. If you could choose your ancestors, would you want them to be survivalists or to be expected wealth maximizers?

One can also refer to Gigerenzer (2007), who developed the concept of fast and frugal decision-making. The latter refers to decision-making processes that appear to be efficient in spite of being inconsistent with neoclassical processes. Fundamentally, the argument presented here is that decision-making must be contextualized and evaluated in terms of the decision-making environment and the decision-making capabilities of the individual (Gigerenzer refers specifically to Simon's conceptualization of bounded rationality). Todd and Gigerenzer argue (2003, pp. 147–148):

...bounded rationality can be seen as emerging from the joint effect of two interlocking components: the internal limitations of the (human) mind, and the structure of the external environments in which the mind operates. This fit between the internal cognitive structure and the external information structure underlies the perspective of bounded rationality as ecological rationality – making good (enough) decisions by exploiting the structure of the environment... Heuristics that are matched to particular environments allow agents to be ecologically rational, making adaptive decisions that combine accuracy with speed and frugality. (We call the heuristics "fast and frugal" because they process information in a relatively simple way, and they search for little information.) The study of ecological rationality thus involves analyzing the structure of environments, the structure of heuristics, and the match between them.

The foundational behavioural economists, led by Simon, made a point of emphasizing that they do not dispute that human beings acting in the economic sphere (economic agents) are rational. They do not dispute this assumption of conventional economics. But they disagree on how conventional economics defines rationality. On rationality, Simon writes (1986, p. S210):

> *I emphasize this point of agreement at the outset-that people have reasons for what they do-because it appears that economics sometimes feels called on to defend the thesis that human beings are rational. Psychology has no quarrel at all with this thesis. If there are differences in viewpoint, they must lie in conceptions of what constitutes rationality, not in the fact of rationality itself. The judgment that certain behavior is 'rational' or 'reasonable' can be reached only by viewing the behavior in the context of a set of premises or 'givens.' These givens include the situation in which the behavior takes place, the goals it is aimed at realizing, and the computational means available for determining how the goals can be attained.*

Simon further elaborates on rationality with regards to other social sciences, emphasizing that the conventional economics definition of rationality is a significant outlier in the social sciences (Simon, 1986, p. S210):

> *In its treatment of rationality, neoclassical economics differs from the other social sciences in three main respects: (a) in its silence about the content of goals and values; (b) in its postulating global consistency of behavior; and (c) in its postulating 'one world' that behavior is objectively rational in relation to its total environment, including both present and future environment as the actor moves through time.*

In defining rationality relative to decision-making Simon (1986, p. S211) point out that:

> *The rational person of neoclassical economics always reaches the decision that is objectively, or substantively, best in terms of the given utility function. The rational person of cognitive psychology goes about making his or her decisions in a way that is procedurally reasonable in the light of the available knowledge and means of computation.*

Simon elaborates on his concept of bounded rationality, making it more specific and nuanced. This brings him to a discussion of process rationality, which refers to the process of and the procedures used in arriving at a decision given the decision-making environment, the capabilities of the decision-maker, and the objectives of the decision-maker. Moreover, process rationality takes into consideration that decision-makers' understanding of what's best practice or optimal might be misconstrued or flat out wrong, but they rationally act upon such a misperception. Simon (1986, p. S211) argues that:

> *...if we accept the proposition that knowledge and the computational power of the decision maker are severely limited, then we must distinguish between the real world and the actor's perception of it and reasoning about it...we must construct a theory (and test it empirically) of the processes of decision. Our theory must include not only the reasoning processes but also the processes that generate the*

actor's subjective representation of the decision problem, his or her frame...The rational person of neoclassical economics always reaches the decision that is objectively, or substantively, best in terms of the given utility function. The rational person of cognitive psychology goes about making his or her decisions in a way that is procedurally reasonable in the light of the available knowledge and means of computation [it is context dependent].

Bounded rationality, satisficing, process rationality, all fit into a modelling paradigm that has as its core assumption that decision-makers are fundamentally smart. There can be exceptions to this rule. But of critical importance is that one needs to begin one's analysis with the premise of smart agents doing the best they can given their circumstances, their preferences, their understanding of available choices, and their understanding of the best or optimal means of achieving their objectives. Deviations from neoclassical behavioural norms should not imply irrationality or inefficiency. More nuanced context dependent norms need to be constructed for rational behaviour and what this implies for economic efficiency. This also implies a better understanding how social context, social relationships, social norms, and cultural factors, most of which can be reconfigured, impact on the rational choices that individuals make (Akerlof & Kranton, 2010; Becker, 1996).

The 'new' behavioural economics, emanating from the initial research outcomes and initiatives of Kahneman and Tversky (1979) and Kahneman (2003, 2011); see also Tversky and Kahneman (1981), sets out to develop theories that are better able to describe human behaviour, where often such behaviour is related to economic issues. This heuristics and biases approach rejects the neoclassical prediction that decision-makers will behave in a manner that will generate predicted 'optimal' choices. In this vein, for example, they developed Prospect Theory as an alternative to Subjective Expected Utility Theory. Certainly, Kahneman and Tversky view their scientific project as bearing down on better describing choice behaviour than conventional economic theory. In the Kahneman and Tversky approach, such descriptive theories are typically related to the behaviour of the average individual. The focus on the average has also been a mainstay of conventional economics. This implicitly assumes that the average is the most appropriate point of reference for descriptive and analytical purposes.

This 'new' behavioural economics also interprets the 'average' individual's deviations from the conventional economic norms for optimal decision making to be error-prone and biased, and typically persistently so. On the one hand, this perspective on behavioural economics maintains and adheres to a fundamental premise of conventional economics, that there is particular way of behaving in the economic realm resulting in a particular set of choices and therefore outcomes that are optimal (most, effective, efficient, unbiased). But it represents a big break with conventional economics in that individuals tend not to behave optimally in a large array of choice scenarios. It is argued that individuals tend to engage in biased and error-prone behaviours. But they do so because they do not conform to conventional or neoclassical behavioural norms. Hence, the heuristics and biases approach retain neoclassical normative benchmarks for efficient and rational behaviour (although little mention is made of the term rational) (Altman, 2017; Berg, 2014; Berg & Gigerenzer, 2010).

In the bounded rationality or smart agent approach to behavioural economics errors and biases are not hardwired. There are those individuals with mental disabilities who engage in hardwired-biased behaviour—but these are clearly the exception to the rule. Overall, there are rational reasons that would explain most such biased and error prone behaviour. At least this is the starting point of the smart agent perspective to economic modelling. What is meant by rational and even by efficiency (at least in the domain of consumption) would be different from that specified by the conventional wisdom and by the heuristic and biases approach to behavioural economics.

Two key points need to be made and further developed. One is that it is important to specify or to think through (or model) the conditions under which rational decision makers generate either persistent local or social inefficiencies. It is important to also specify the extent to which such rational inefficiencies are a product of preferences of decision makers, gaps in their capabilities, biases, or problems with institutional design. This is true for both the production and the household and consumer space. Of course, modelling the necessary conditions for rational inefficiencies is the mirror image of modelling the necessary conditions for rational efficiencies. The focus of most conventional and behavioural economists has been on the process of achieving efficiencies, often decontextualized from pertinent institutional parameters.

The second key point is the importance of better articulating the benchmarks for rationality and efficiency. For behavioural economists, following from the Simon or bounded rationality perspective, this is a much more nuanced and complex narrative from what one finds in conventional economics or from the heuristics and biases approach, which rely on largely on conventional benchmarks.

Production inefficiency

In production, inefficiency can be defined as *not* making the best use of resources that are available for the task at hand. Hence, one would be operating inside the production possibility frontier. Or, one would operating along a production isoquant that is further removed from the origin then it need be. In the latter case one would be using more inputs than required to generate a given level of output. This is also referred to as x-inefficiency in production (following upon the researches of Leibenstein, 1966, 1979) as opposed to allocative inefficiency. The latter is a function of a distortion to relative prices, typically caused by oligopolistic market structures and presumed government distortions of the price mechanism. This leads to the misallocation of resources and hence to lower levels of productivity below what would be the case when market prices are not distorted. But it appears that allocative inefficiency is only of marginal importance as compared to x-inefficiency (Frantz, 1997; Leibenstein, 1966).

Leibenstein considers x-inefficiency to be a product of irrational behaviour largely because decision makers deviate from the norms of rational neoclassical behaviour (see also Cyert & March, 1963). Leibenstein maintains that x-inefficient firms are a product of decision makers, such as managers, not maximizing profits or minimizing costs as they should and would if they behaved in accordance to conventional economic norms. However, Leibenstein's definition of rationality, although quite consistent with the overarching perspective of the heuristics and biases approach (using neoclassical behavioural benchmarks), it is not at all related to whether decision makers are making smart decisions given their constraints and opportunities and their preferences. Rationality is quite narrowly defined as it is in the conventional approach and in the heuristics and biases perspective. But, more importantly, Leibenstein creates an analytical space for persistent economic inefficiency by modelling x-inefficiency as a product of the preference function of decision makers, where there is a preference for leisure as opposed to maximizing profits and minimizing costs. Here we have a preference function embodying managerial slack, yielding x-inefficiency in production. Decision makers are, broadly speaking, maximizing their utility which, given their preferences, yield x-inefficiency.

An important assumption in the conventional model is that preference functions of decision makers are consistent with there being x-efficiency in production—firms using the fewest inputs possible to produce a given level of output. In reality, preferences of decision-makers are all too often not consistent with x-efficiency in production. This conventional benchmark for x-efficiency, minimizing inputs per unit of output, is a reasonable one, unlike the assumption of agents being super-calculators with prescience and perfect knowledge (in the relevant decision-making domain). I have argued that preferences inconsistent with x-efficiency (minimizing inputs per unit of output) are consistent with rational or smart behaviour. Agents can be purposeful, deliberative, and even calculating, whilst still making choices that yield economic inefficiency (Altman, 1999, 2005, 2006a, 2006b, 2015).

Leibenstein introduces the concept of effort discretion into the modelling of economic agents, something that runs contrary to conventional wisdom's typical exposé of the economic agent. Effort should be, at a minimum, constant or even constant at some maximum according to the conventional wisdom. But when managers organize the firm such that effort inputs diminish, then productivity falls and, ceteris paribus, average cost increases. The firm is better off if it is x-efficient but, in this case, x-inefficiency in production is consistent with the preferences of decision-makers and, hence, with these agents maximizing their utility. Rational or smart agents attempt to 'maximize' their utility even if this results in sub-optimal outcomes for the firm and society at large.

This point can be illustrated in the equation below, representing a simple economy with labour as the only factor input. Fundamental results do not change as one adds other factor inputs to the production function.

$$AC = \frac{w}{\left(\dfrac{Q}{L}\right)}\ldots \tag{5.1}$$

AC is average cost; w is the wage rate or, more generally, the unit cost of inputs; (Q/L) is the average product of labour; Q is total output; and L is labour input measured in terms of hours worked. Reducing productivity by, for example, increasing managerial slack will, ceteris paribus, increase average cost (AC). Leibenstein assumes that w remains constant in the face of changes to productivity and average cost.

Another way to visualize this argument is as follows:

$$\Delta e \rightarrow (Q/L) \rightarrow \Delta AC \ldots \tag{5.2}$$

Going to the basic point, changes in effort input (e) yield changes in labour productivity (Q/L) which, in turn, yield changes in average costs (AC). In this model, maximizing effort inputs, maximizes average product and, thereby, minimizes average cost. This would be consistent with x-efficiency in production. Such effort maximization is possible when the preferences of decision makers are consistent with this particular objective. I argue that effort maximization is rational or smart only under certain circumstances. Hence, economic efficiency (maximum x-efficiency), even amongst rational agents, should not be assumed as the natural state of things, given that economic inefficiency can be consistent with the preferences of decision makers. And such preferences can't be assumed to be irrational simply because they aren't consistent with effort maximization. One can't simply assume that working as hard and a s smart as one can (effort maximization) is what makes one happy.

Leibenstein maintains that given that decision makers prefer the easy way out (managerial slack), unless product markets are highly competitive, x-inefficiency will persist. Since most markets are not highly competitive, he argues, x-inefficiency should be expected to dominate at different rates in different sectors, with a predicted strong positive causal relationship between more competition and more x-efficiency. But Leibenstein argues that the political economy of market economies (which includes lobbying) would preclude product markets being competitive enough for economic efficiency to be achieved. Within the context of imperfect product markets managerial preferences play a key causal role in determining the extent of x-inefficiency. X-inefficient behaviour is protected in the context of imperfect product markets.

One can take this one step further. Smart agents and their preferences have a critical role in determining role in the extent of economic inefficiency because less than maximum levels of effort need not yield higher average costs, hence potentially threatening such firms' survival on the market. The point made in Altman (2005, 2006a, 2006b, 2010, 2011, 2012, 2015) is that managerial decisions (the extent of managerial slack for example) affect the quality and quantity of effort inputs amongst the 'community' of economic agents that comprise the firm as a unit of production. But changes to effort levels are a costly process, affecting the levels of compensation to economic agents as well as investments in the quality of the work environment. Moreover, fixed costs are incurred if the system of management is transformed to change the level of productivity. This being said, if effort levels decrease this can be accompanied by lower wages and deteriorating working conditions and one would anticipate higher wages and improvements to working conditions when effort levels increase. From Eq. (3.1), one would expect that w to be positively related to changes in productivity (Q/L). *One would anticipate cost offset changes in effort levels.* Rational or smart agents, therefore, have significant discretion as to how efficient firms end up being in long run equilibrium since even with highly competitive product markets, inefficient firms can remain competitive and efficient firms need not have a cost advantage over the less efficient firms. This is the case, when effort variability and the choice made with regards to effort input and, therefore, productivity, results in just offsetting relatively low to the relatively high input costs, represented here by w or the wage rate.

In this scenario, even competitive market forces can't enforce economic efficiency on economic agents where this is incompatible with the preferences of the firm's decision makers. Simply introducing more competitive product markets need not generate optimal economic efficiency. One can end up, as the evidence suggests we do, with firms ranging from highly inefficient to highly efficient even when the highly efficient outcomes are feasible and viable given current institutional parameters. We have multiple equilibrium in outcomes that flow from a multiple equilibrium in preferences (Altman, 2016). In this narrative the preferences of members of the firm, whose preferences dominate the decision-making process, become of primary importance.

This argument is illustrated in Fig. 5.1. In this figure, aLCM represents our cost curve for the conventional firm if wages increase and for the Leibenstein model if effort input is sub-optimal. Average cost would increase in both scenarios. And for the firm to survive, they would need protection, at a maximum of PLPL*. Leibenstein's x-inefficient firms can only survive when such firms are protected either through government policy or through imperfect product markets. But such protection is often afforded to inefficient firms. But alternatively (in the Altman model), x-inefficient firms can survive by offsetting lower productivity related higher costs, by reducing labour costs. Along aBM, x-inefficient firms at different levels of x-inefficiency all produce at the same average cost as the x-efficient firm, given at point b. Cost offsets allow for multiple equilibrium with respect to x-inefficient and x-efficient firms. Market forces need not eliminate x-inefficient firms, even in the absence of product market imperfections and government protection, and even in the long run. The other

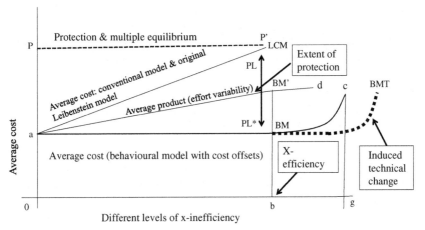

FIG. 5.1   Multiple equilibrium in production.

side of the coin is that higher wages and improved working conditions need not generate higher average costs if compensated for by higher effort inputs which, in turn, yield compensating higher levels of labour productivity, here given by aBM'. In this scenario, higher levels of x-efficiency are consistent with higher labour costs. Indeed, the latter might be the cause of the former, forcing a reduction in the level of managerial slack, for example. Such higher labour cost firms can generate further cost offsets if higher labour cost induce technological change, which is illustrated by a shift in the average cost curve from aBM to ABMT (Altman, 2009).

This modelling narrative is consistent with what is articulated in the traditional Prisoner Dilemma (PD) model wherein particular 'common knowledge' assumptions yield social outcomes that represent a worst case scenario, even given the assumption of neoclassical rationality. In the realm of production, the worst case social outcome is one where productivity or output is at some minimum—the PD solution. It occurs when each participant in the game believe (common knowledge) that the other invests the least possible amount of time and effort into the process of production; maximizes her or his gains. This is consistent with narrowly self-interested maximizing behaviour (neoclassical rationality). In this narrative, one can increase (and maximize) one's own individualized benefits by behaving in very narrowly self-interested fashion, if the other party actually contributes more than the anticipated minimum to the process of production. This is the case even though pie size is less than it might be otherwise (x-inefficiency in production). On the other hand, if one chooses to behave in a manner that increases the size of the economic pie one risks a reduction in individualized benefits if the other party acts in a narrowly self-interested fashion.

If the common knowledge is that the other party will act in a narrowly self-interested fashion, it would be rational to do the same, for only in this way can one minimize any potential losses to oneself. Only if one changes the common knowledge of the other's behaviour will it be rational to behave in a fashion consistent with the common or social good, increasing the size of the economic pie. With increased pie size, each player of the economic game could see her or his real income increase—everyone is a potential beneficiary. This would be a cooperative solution to the economic problem, in direct contrast with the Prisoner's Dilemma solution.

Non-cooperative solutions are possible, as discussed above, when non-cooperative firms are protected from market forces or when they are able to trade-off low productivity with low wages and poor working conditions. Both PD and cooperative outcomes are sustainable and rational given the preferences of decision makers and the decision-making environment within which their decisions are made.

It also needs mention that the constraints on decision making within the firm are set by members of the firm hierarchy in the traditional investor-owned firm. If joint preferences of the firm hierarchy are of the non-cooperative type wherein utility is maximized, the PD solution is inevitable. If a cooperative solution is what maximizes joint utility then a cooperative solution would follow. In cooperative (worker-owned) firms the joint preferences would veer towards the cooperative solution. Also, power dynamics within the firm can affect which solution dominates. More bargaining power in the hands of workers can, but does not guarantee, a more cooperative solution as members of the firm hierarchy must find the means to increase productivity to offset the increasing direct costs of production that often follows when the bargaining power of employees is enhanced. Also, firms where employees have more substantive say on managerial and corporate decisions (a mixed hierarchical model), a cooperative solution is more likely. The same would be the case if owners and mangers have a joint preference in favour of more cooperative outcomes (Altman, 2002).

Further related to the neoclassical assumption of what comprises rational behaviour within the firm, in behavioural-type models of the firm, simplistic formulations of profit maximization or cost minimisation, especially in its mathematical presentation, tells us little what is required for firms to be economically efficient. Being efficient is not a matter of equating marginal revenue to marginal cost. For example, even within the framework of a very simple model, assuming that firm decision makers can actually and effectively do this calculation in a dynamic fashion, one can equate marginal cost and marginal revenue without effort being maximized. For any given level of effort input one can do this calculation. Hence, the firm could be economically inefficient even when marginal equals marginal benefit. The relevant marginal cost and marginal revenue functions would simply be different from what they would be if effort input is maximized. Also, in this type of modelling, the decision makers would be maximizing their utility at different levels of effort input.

The utility maximizing level of effort input is given by the preferences of the decision makers. Hence, any model that is scientifically robust must incorporate the conditions under which effort levels inside of the firm are higher or lower since these conditions are critically important for any determination of why and how rational or smart agents generate a particular level of effort input and, therefore, a particular level of productivity. The details of what transpires inside of the 'black box' of the firm becomes critically important because it is in the black box that one can deconstruct the methods adopted by decision-makers to achieve their chosen ends.

There may also be alternative means to achieve efficiency, all of which might be consistent with the generic and often vacuous normative directive that efficiency is achieved when economic agents equate or behave as if they equate marginal costs to marginal benefits. There are those who are argue that a heavily monitored and punitive environment where labour costs are minimized (such as wages and quality of the work environment) serves to maximize labour productivity. However, there is strong evidence to suggest that a more collaborative work environment based on teamwork, trust, and reciprocity is better able to achieve economic efficiency. Here there is a more equitable (but not equal) distribution of power and income inside the firm. Both organizational structures and related processes could be rational from the perspective of the dominant decision makers (and their preferences), even though neither adheres to the behavioural processes that fit into the simplistic marginal cost equals marginal benefit narrative of conventional economics (Altman, 2002).

Related to the conventional prediction that rational behaviour should yield economic efficiency, there is the recent commentary of Richard Posner on the (2007–08) global economic crisis. Posner was a leading proponent of the efficient market hypothesis and neoclassical rationality as the best way of modelling the economy and the relationship between law and the economy. He shifted theoretical ground towards to one that the overlaps with the Simon or bounded rationality modelling perspective. His perspective also overlaps with the view that rationality should not be interpreted as neoclassical rationality. Amongst the critical points made by Posner is that decision makers' rational behaviour in terms of efforts to maximize income need not take the form of neoclassical processes (they could involve emotion, intuition, and herding). All of these rational behaviours, however, can cause long run harm to the firm, even whilst generating significant short and even long run benefits to the individuals engaging in such rational behaviours.

Posner (2009, p. 111) elaborates:

In sum, rational maximization by businessmen and consumers, all pursuing their self-interest more or less intelligently within a framework of property rights and contract rights, can set the stage for an economic catastrophe. There is not need to bring cognitive quirks, emotional forces, or character flaws into the causal analysis. This is important both in simplifying analysis and in avoiding a search, likely to be futile, for means by which government can alter the mentality or character of businessmen and consumers.

Posner argues that to prevent an economic meltdown, or least to reduce the probability of one, one should not attempt to re-wire decision-makers so that he or she behaves more neoclassically. Neither should one attempt to re-wire them so that they become less greedy or less narrowly self-interested—which Posner argues is very difficult to operationalize with substantive effect on the economy. To prevent or minimize the probability of narrowly rational income, wealth maximizing or 'greedy' individuals (those attempting to maximize their private income or wealth) causing social harm, which incorporates reducing long run firm real income, wealth and/or productivity, government must change the institutional environment. This goes beyond simplistic references to improvements to property rights and reducing transaction costs, which is often the focus of the New Institutional Economics. Also of importance would be providing decision makers with improved information sets, improved information processing and analytical capabilities, better understanding of viable organization options (low wage versus high wage, for example), and internalizing externalities to the firm and individual decision makers (hence reducing the probability of moral hazard). Shiller (2008, 2012) argues for the improvements in the legally enforceable and regulated provision of transparent, accurate, and understandable information to be important to a well functioned and socially efficient market economy.

Overall, rational inefficiency is a very reasonable outcome given the preferences of dominant decision makers and the institutional environment within which they are embedded. By acknowledging the possibility of rational inefficiency and its underlying determinants one can suggest means of achieving more efficient outcomes. Moreover, if we are able to better model the conditions underlying rational inefficiencies one can better identify when and where they exist as opposed to assuming ex ante that decision makers make choices that yield economically efficient outcomes.

Thus far, I've discussed rationality and efficiency in terms of productive sectors as opposed to rent-seeking sectors of the economy. But it is important to note that even if all agents behave in an economically efficient fashion, this does not preclude this x-efficiency in production taking place in sectors of the economy that are of a rent-seeking nature, wherein the firm's wealth is a product of transferring resources from one sector to another or from one individual to another. Here, the non-productive sectors are x-efficient, but the economy as whole is operating below its production possibility frontier. What's important to note is that criminal behaviour, lobbying, corruption, war machines that engage in income transfers to the conquering population, can be run in an economically efficient manner. Institutional parameters can make such organizational forms more attractive (profitable) to economic agents. Economic efficiency, even when agents are neoclassically rational at the organizational level, in no way necessarily translates into social efficiency. At an extreme, one can have a rent-seeking based society, run by rational agents, that is efficient at the level of the organization, but which is socially inefficient.

Rationality implies neither efficiency nor efficiency in production. Rationality also does not imply neoclassical behavioural norms in the realm of production. Smart decision-makers can deliver firm and socially efficient outcomes in production, contingent on the preferences of decision-makers, decision-making and organizational capabilities, and the overall incentive environment. But these conditions all too often do not prevail. From a smart agent perspective, it is a critically important scientific task to identify those conditions conducive to economic efficiency at both a firm and social level. Smart agents can generate x-efficiency at both the firm and social level given the appropriate circumstances.

Consumption inefficiencies

Although I've devoted considerable attention to the rationality-efficiency-inefficiency narrative in the domain of production, contemporary behavioural economics devotes considerable energies to rationality-efficiency-inefficiency in the realm of consumption-related behaviour. A fundamental prior in contemporary microeconomic theory is that the revealed preferences of individuals represent their true and, related to this, utility maximizing preferences. Moreover, it is assumed that these true preferences can be realized through the choices a person makes given her or his income and given relative prices. I've referred to this a choice x-efficiency (Altman, 2010). And conventional economics assumes that choice x-efficiency is the rule in any given society and at given point in historical time.

In brief, true preferences represent those preferences of an individual that are formed in an environment wherein he or she has excess to relatively complete and truthful information pertaining to pertinent choice decisions, has the capabilities process and understand such information, and where this person's preference formation and choices are not constrained by coercive circumstances. These assumptions are layered over the assumption that individuals are rational in their decision-making process. All these assumptions must hold for choice x-efficiency to prevail. Actually Harsanyi (1982), one of the pioneers of choice theory, makes similar points with regards to the necessary conditions for revealed preferences to equal what one might refer to as true preferences (see also, Altman, 2010).

I have argued that rational or smart choice behaviour requires the prevalence of the above preference formation and choice environment. But, to be realized, such rational choice behaviour only requires boundedly rational behaviour as opposed to the unreasonable and unobtainable prescient and super-calculating behaviour of conventional neoclassical economics. This being said, even smart decision makers can't realize choice x-efficiency unless the appropriate preference formation and choice environment prevails. Hence, one can end up, under very reasonable circumstances, with rational inefficiencies (what I refer to choice x-inefficiencies) in the realm of choice. Even if one can form 'true' preferences, rational individuals may not have the power to translate these preferences into choices or revealed preferences. In this scenario individuals are not free to choose. For example, a woman may want to have one child, but may be forced into having six or a parent might want her daughter to learn to read and write but are not empowered to do so given social norms and legal parameters.

Overall, building on a bounded rationality platform, one can model conditions wherein choice x-inefficiencies/x-efficiencies can be obtained. Only under particular institutional/environmental/social circumstances can choice x-efficiency be realized. Hence one should be able to identify the circumstances under which choice x-inefficiencies (with smart decision-makers) exist and how such circumstances need be changed for revealed preferences to converge to an individual's true preferences.

It is important to note that true preferences, these utility maximizing preferences, irrespective of how 'rational' they might be, need not be socially rational. Choices that cause harm to others can be rational and reveal the true preferences of the individual decision maker. This socially sub-optimal behaviour represents a form of market failure wherein externalities are not internalized by the individual decision-maker. Such market failures are not part of the conventional narrative even when one can legitimately assume that revealed preferences equal true preferences. This is case even though the 'forefathers' of preference theory recognized this very real possibility (Harsanyi, 1982). But market failure of this type can be easily incorporated into a modelling of preference formation and choice realization, as articulated above.

In my modelling of choice x-inefficiencies and choice x-efficiencies, like in the conventional wisdom, there is the possibility of revealed preferences being identical to true preferences (Altman, 2010). But there is also the possibility that this equality need not hold—there is an analytical space for rational choice inefficiencies, irrespective of whether or not one models agency from a neoclassical or boundedly rational perspective. Moreover, there is a possibility that individuals do not have the capabilities and are not in a decision-making environment for true preferences to be formed. There is also the possibility of market failure in the domain of choice. This modelling narrative, therefore, does not accept as a prior working assumption that choice efficiency at an individual and social level prevails everywhere and always. Its existence and prevalence is an empirical question, very much contingent upon the necessary institutional parameters (inclusive of appropriate power relationships) and individual decision-making capabilities being in place.

Freedom of choice philosophically underpins the conventional wisdom's normative preference for the revealed preference-utility maximizing modelling of decision making. The individual's preferences determine choice that, in turn, allows the individual to maximize her of his utility. Here freedom of choice is valued as core to the ability of individuals to 'maximize' their utility, their level of wellbeing. Modelling preference formation and choice from a critical and bounded rationality perspective does not obviate a normative focus on the critical importance of individual freedom for utility maximization (accept when the latter causes harm to others). This overlaps with the critical approach taken by Nussbaum (2011) and Sen (1985) on this matter applying their capabilities analytical framework. Here too freedom of choice is critically important. The problem is that this freedom only exists if the institutional and individual decision-making capabilities are present. Once these conditions are met then, in this modelling framework, as in the conventional wisdom, one would predict that individuals' choices should be 'maximizing' their utility or level of satisfaction. But in the bounded rationality-choice x-efficiency approach, public policy would be required to assure that conditions for choice efficiencies and hence for freedom of choice are met. In the conventional approach it is typically assumed, ex ante, that such conditions are present everywhere and always.

But this normative approach has been challenged by the stream of behavioural economics linked with the heuristics and biases analytical framework developed by Kahneman and Tversky. A key point made here is that individuals are hardwired to be error-prone in decision-making. The capacity to form and execute one's true preferences, therefore, will not preclude persistent errors and biases in decision-making. If anything, such freedom (even assuming that there are no choice x-inefficiencies—true preferences can be realized) can predictably cause more harm than good.

This perspective has been most forcefully and poignantly developed and articulated by Thaler and Sunstein (2008) in their nudge approach to behavioural economics and public policy. They argue that there are clear objective benchmarks for what it means for individuals to be better off or maximizing their utility. These benchmarks appear to be universal, running across individuals. But, it is argued, these universal benchmarks for utility maximizing, 'best-practice' behaviour, cannot be realized by the typical individual exercising free choice. This is in part because individuals aren't properly hardwired to do so—hence the persistent biases in choice behaviour, resulting in individuals' choices yielding sub-optimal outcomes for the individual decision-maker and society at large. An important assumption in this modelling is that preferences are the same across individuals—homogeneous preferences. Hence what is good for all individuals is based upon what is deemed to be good from the perspective of the expert. Individual preferences do not inform the content of what is 'good'. The baseline for what is good is largely based 'neoclassical' benchmarks and a depth of knowledge and emotionless understanding beyond the pail of the typical human decision-makers. But it is assumed that the expert has the capabilities, knowledge and understanding to identify the good and the means to achieve this in a most efficient and effective manner.

Thaler and Sunstein (2008, p. 176), maintain:

We intend 'better off' to be measured as objectively as possible, and we clearly do not always equate revealed preference with welfare. That is, we emphasize the possibility that in some cases individuals make inferior choices, choices that they would change if they had complete information, unlimited cognitive abilities, and no lack of willpower.

Critical to this interpretation of what is good for the individual and what is the baseline for the good is choice architecture and the choice architect. An important feature of choice architecture is reconfiguring the choice environment in a manner that induces or, in more extreme circumstances, forces the individual to make choices that the expert deems to be in the individual's best interest. Note that each individual does not have her or his own specific choice architecture. The latter is generic, as all individuals are assumed to homogeneous in preferences. Actual differences in preferences across individuals are not recognized here (a type of simplifying assumption). The choice architect is the expert who designs the choice environment nudging the individual to make choices that will make her or him better off from the perspective of the choice architect or expert. This would be the case even if the affected decision-maker did not believe that her or his nudged choices increases her or his level of satisfaction or utility—making this person better off. The expert—the choice architect—knows best.

A fundamental policy implication of the heuristics and biases approach is that people opposing choice architecture do so because they make the assumption that each individual knows what is in her or his best interest. This assumption is fundamentally flawed from the heuristics and biases approach. In other words, this approach contests a fundamental worldview of conventional neoclassical economics as well as that of the boundedly rational-smart decision-maker perspective articulated here. In the conventional perspective revealed preferences always (or almost always) reveal the true preferences of the individual, which equates with behaviour that maximizes an individual's level of utility or satisfaction or wellbeing. Smart decision-makers would do what's in their best interest if they have the capabilities to form and then to realize their true preferences. But from the heuristics and biases approach, true preferences are expected to be inconsistent with what's in the best interest of the decision-maker. Thaler and Sunstein (2008, p. 6) argue that: '...almost all people, almost all of the time, make choices that are in their best interest or at the very least are better than the choices that would be made by someone else. We claim that this assumption is false. In fact, we do not think that anyone believes this on reflection'.

It is important to recognize that the nudging perspective contains many elements, some of which are paternalist, and others which are consistent with creating the conditions for the formation and realization of true preferences. However, the focus has been on the paternalist component, inducing or forcing individuals to make choices consistent with the expert's preferences. An important component of the nudging approach is framing options such that individuals make expert-consistent choices. This could involve forcing organizations to re-frame options available to consumers so that consumers make expert-consistent choices. Of course, what the expert deems optimal, may not be consistent with the true preferences of the individual who's being framed into making the choices preferred by the expert.

A fundamental argument put forth by Thaler and Sustein is that choice options are always framed and that there is always someone who constructs the frame. Little analytical attention has been paid to framing because conventional economics assumes that framing does not affect the choices made by decision makers. The implicit assumption in the nudging approach is that different frames contain no new information pertinent to a particular decision. Hence, individuals are easily manipulated by changing the framing of a choice option even when the revised frame is not substantively different from the prior frame. A classic example given is that of the framing of pension options. If the default option is not to invest in a pension, then most employees will not invest. However, if the default is to invest, most people will invest. The frame, in this case, is the default option. Simply changing the frame appears to have a huge impact of whether or not individuals invest in a pension. The assumption is that individuals are indifferent in terms of utility between the two different frames and simply make their choices based on the different frames whilst their utility remains constant. However, it is further assumed that one of the frames yields choices that make the individual and society better off (they are both individually and socially optimal and welfare improving). Hence the positive view of interventionist role of the expert, of the choice architect.

This apparently clear-cut example appears to demonstrate the case for soft and even hard paternalism. However, at a minimum, in a world of complex, asymmetric, and even misleading information and the limited decision-making capabilities of decision-makers (partially based on learning deficiencies), defaults can represent signals to decision-makers as to which choice or choices have the highest probability of making them better off. When the default is not to invest in pensions (especially in a particular pension plan) this signals that experts deem this not to be the best idea, and the opposite if the default is to invest. Hence, the decision-maker is relying on the integrity of those setting the default to inform the decision-maker on which choice might be the best choice. By changing the default from non-investing to investing the 'expert' must assure that the investor knows what he or she is getting into, such as various opportunity costs and risks. Re-framing is not simply changing the frame from one to another wherein no substantive information is being changed. Re-framing typically involves making substantive changes to the information affording to the decision-maker. This is why it is rational for decision makers to change their behaviour when frames are changed (Altman, 2011, 2012, 2019; Gigerenzer, 2007).

How choices are framed is important because frames contain information fundamental to the determination of choice. Hence, for choices to be 'optimal' requires that the frame provides the individual with truthful, comprehensible, and accessible information so that the individual can make the best possible decision given the choice set available. This alternative, smart agent approach to framing, focuses on providing decision-makers with an environment wherein they can better form their preferred choices and exercise these choices. This approach would not apply to situations when an individual's optimal choice causes harm to others. Examples of this would be smoking in public spaces, taking heroine whilst pregnant, being abusive to one's spouse and children, closing factories and asset stripping to maximize short term gain for major shareholders, and cheating and deceiving customers.

The smart agent approach focuses on improving the preference formation and decision-making environment, whilst accounting for and incorporating negative and positive externalities in this endeavour. Although there is some overlap between this and the nudging approach, the prior working assumption of the smart agent approach is that individuals' preferences should, for the most part, be respected and that when choices are sub-optimal even for smart decision-makers, they tend to be so for reasons of institutional design, for environmental reasons, for reasons of capabilities. Hence the focus is on institutional design, capabilities development, and empowerment of decision-makers. This approach also pays attention to the enforcement of rules and regulations that can contribute towards an improved decision-making environment. From this perspective errors in decision-making can and are often made. But this is more related to environmental and capabilities issues as opposed to the hardwiring of the human brain.

The expert plays a role in this analytical construct by contributing to improvements in the decision-making environment as opposed to determining which decisions individuals should make. This bounded rationality smart agent approach is libertarian in orientation, but one that recognizes the importance of various levels of government and expert intervention to improve the overall decision-making environment and the decision-making capabilities of decision-makers as well as developing an incentive environment that accounts for negative and positive externalities.

Martha Nussbaum, the co-developer, along with Amartya Sen, of the capabilities approach, makes a similar point. She argues (1999, p. 49): 'Government is not directed to push citizens into acting in certain valued ways; instead, it is directed to make sure that all human beings have the necessary resources and conditions for acting in those ways. By making opportunities available, government enhances, and does not remove, choice'. Related to my narrative on choice x-efficiency and smart decision-making, what Nussbaum is speaking to is the creation of optimal preference formation and decision-making environments as opposed to experts determining the choices that people should make.

Macroeconomic choices and rational behaviour

As with microeconomic behaviour, in the macroeconomic domain, conventional economics makes the case that decision-makers must be neoclassically rational. The evidence suggests this is not how individuals behave and this has had some major repercussions in the construction of macroeconomic theory and the same for finance theory (Akerlof, 2002; Akerlof & Shiller, 2009). But these reconstructions are rejected outright by those who remain strict adherence to the conventional assumptions of rationality combined with assumptions related to flexible factor prices and the capacity of micro decisions having direct and immediate impact in the macroeconomic domain. The latter 'school of thought', in their pre-Keynesian incarnation has been dubbed the classical school whereas their modern equivalents have been referred to as the new classical school of macroeconomics.

Many of the underlying revisions to macroeconomic theory were made decades ago by Keynes, in his articulation of business cycle theory, more specifically his theoretical narrative on the making of deep recessions and the mechanism involved in the economy transitioning from a deep recession or depression to recovery. Keynes' narrative is largely based on the assumption of smart agents making decisions in a world of complex and asymmetric information with asymmetric power relationships across decision-makers. Keynes introduces the notion of 'animal spirits' as an important to the determination of the timing and depth of recessions and upturns. His narrative suggests that animal spirits as a determinant of decision-making are rational in the sense that decision makers are making due, doing their best, satisficing, given their decision-making environment. Hence, Keynes recognizes the importance that non-economic variables and heuristics can play in economic (macroeconomic) outcomes (Keynes, 1936).

In the conventional wisdom non-economic variables are assumed away. Keynes also recognizes the importance of sticky prices as being a possible and possibly important determinant of recession/depression, given negative demand shocks. But the relative importance of sticky prices in determining economic downturns, especially severe ones, is subject to heated debate amongst those writing in the Keynesian tradition. But there is no denying the empirical significance of sticky prices.

Most recently Akerlof (2002), in theory, and Bewley (1999), empirically, have made the case that sticky prices in the face of a negative demand shock are rationally determined. This is based on what is referred to efficiency wage theory, first modelled by Leibenstein (1957). Smart agents make local (within the firm) utility and profit maximizing decisions that have negative macroeconomic consequences, such as persistent unemployment. Firms don't cut real wages for fear that workers will retaliate by cutting effort inputs thereby reducing productivity. Here effort is a variable in the production function. Employers are also concerned that their best workers will quit, given the opportunity, for what are perceived to be fairer firms, also damaging firm productivity. But workers maximize their utility by taking such action, which is common knowledge to employers. Akerlof considers sticky-price related unemployment to be involuntary. The employed don't want to lose their jobs or keep others unemployed even though their locally rational decisions have this effect.

It is important to note that classical economists, old and new, pay no attention to this efficiency wage modelling of unemployment. But they interpret such behaviour as a reflection of labour's preference for leisure at least on the margin. And, there would be the assumption that in the face of negative aggregate demand shocks, employment would be restored by cutting real wage below where it was prior to a particular negative demand shock. The assumption is also made that workers can determine their real wages as opposed to simply their nominal wages.

In terms of the narrative of this chapter, what's critical for causal analysis and policy, is whether or not decisions-makers are rational and the implications of this for analysis and policy. The pre-Keynesian and new classical economics perspectives assume that rational agents would endeavour to clear all markets (prices are flexible) and behave as if prices are flexible. Hence, if unemployment exists or if it increases, this is related to the rational decision to keep real wages too high, for example. Here, unemployment or increases in unemployment are voluntary. There can no substantive demand side problem, especially in the longer run. The assumption here is that increases in the unemployment rate is a product of changing preferences of workers in favour of more leisure or non-labour market activities or government interventions that make labour markets less flexible and/or increase the real wage above what would be generated in a 'pure' market economy. The increased real wage is predicted to increase the rate of unemployment. Such institutional interventions (minimum wages and unions) increase the structural rate of unemployment. Here too the demand side is not of importance.

A popular rendition of this perspective was put forth in Friedman's classic (1968) article, making a case for supply side determinants of macro outcomes. He focuses on what he refers to as the natural rate of unemployment, which is determined by structure of real wages. Not much attention is paid to severe negative demand shocks. Ultimately, if workers wanted more employment they should and would cut their real wages. It is assumed that this would not have a knock-on affect of reducing aggregate demand and therefore further increasing the rate of unemployment. Moreover, as unemployment increases, even dramatically so, it can be attributed to changing preferences of workers in favour of more leisure time or changing government policy that permanently increases real wages to higher levels—facilitating workers' preferences for more leisure time.

Notice that amongst the old and new classical economists and, amongst many Keynesian economists, there is a prior assumption that decision-makers are rational, but the understanding of rationality differs across schools of thought, with significant implications for policy. Across the board, Keynesians regard spikes in unemployment yielding substantive increases in the unemployment rate to be involuntary. These increases in unemployment would be impossible for the market to deal with quickly and efficiently; that is in the real world of complex and asymmetric information, limited foresight, inflexible prices and the consequential reliance (to a lesser or greater extent) on decision decision-making heuristics, such as herding. There is no evidence that markets naturally clear swiftly after a severe demand-side shock. But the classicals assume that this reflects the preferences of decision-makers (there is very little modelling attention paid to different preferences and different power relationships across agents). This adds weight to the argument that one's definition of rationality, what it means to be a smart decision-maker, and the realism of one's modelling of the decision making process, is vitally important for causal analysis and, in the macro domain, for public policy.

A core Keynesian argument is that increasing demand either through monetary or fiscal policy will restore the economy to full employment in a relatively quick and efficient manner. Hence, the excessive demand-side related unemployment would be eliminated, and the economy restored to the prior and lower natural rate of unemployment. The higher unemployment rate that is realized during a depression or deep recession is not the natural rate of unemployment—which is the claim of the classical economists, old and new.

A critical assumption made by Keynesian economists is that for involuntary unemployment to be eliminated, workers must accept lower real wages, as increasing employment requires the formerly employed less productive workers (lower marginal product) to accept lower real wages. It is assumed here that a downward sloping marginal product of labour curve, over its relevant portion, characterizes the representative firm, which is a very big short run assumption indeed. The decreased real wage must coincide with adequate increases in aggregate demand. Classical economists argue that accepting lower real wages would not be the rational response of the typical worker. Hence, increasing aggregate demand can have no real effect on the economy, measured by increased employment. But the side-effect of such activist demand-side policy would be increased prices or increasing the rate of inflation.

Akerlof has attempted to provide a scientific quasi-rational basis for government policy to restore employment towards its pre-recession levels (Akerlof, 2002). He maintains that workers' in some sense suffer from money illusion (quasi-rationality) and will therefore not pay attention to reductions in real wages that is a function of low rates of inflation. Basically, the transaction costs of computing the impact of low rates of inflation on real wages are not worth the benefits. Hence, increasing aggregate demand to increase employment should be effective so long as one buys into the realism of this transaction cost-based money illusion argument.

Decades earlier, Keynes rejected any presumption of money illusion on the part of workers, although he accepted the assumption that real wages need to be decreased for pre-recession or depression rates of unemployed to be restored. Workers would accept cuts to real wages that were generalized across sectors and occupations as these would be seen as fair especially when accompanied by increased employment. This could be achieved through aggregate demand-side induced inflation. Workers, themselves, could not orchestrate such a cut in real wages. This would have to be affected through macroeconomic government policy. There is no money illusion here at all. Moreover, Keynes theorizes that self-imposed cuts to money wages would simply reduce aggregate demand, further dampening animal spirits and thereby, further increasing unemployment. Keynes (1936, pp. 14–15) argues:

> ...they [workers] do not resist reductions of real wages, which are associated with increases in aggregate employment and leave relative money-wages unchanged, unless the reduction proceeds so far as to threaten a reduction of the real wage below the marginal disutility of the existing volume of employment. Every trade union will put up some resistance to a cut in money-wages, however, small. But since no trade union would dream of striking on every occasion of a rise in the cost of living, they do not raise the obstacle to any increase in aggregate employment which is attributed to them by the classical school.

Simply because nominal wages are sticky in no way implies that real wages are not flexible enough in a world of rational (smart) agents, for employment to restored to pre-recession levels through monetary and fiscal policy. Increased longer term unemployment need not be a product of workers suddenly shifting their preferences towards more leisure, but rather of misconstrued macro policy that misreads sticky nominal prices (especially wages) with sticky real wages.

On a related note, given the empirics and theory underlying x-efficiency theory, even if real wages increase as aggregate demand increases, if this is accompanied by compensating increasing in labour productivity (a rational response by economic agents), increasing real wages would not impede the employment of more workers as aggregate demand increases. In this case, increasing real wages will not affect economic capacity of the firm to hire more workers on the margin. The marginal product of labour curve shifts to the right as real wages increase (Altman, 2006a, 2006b). Here too, by assuming rational individuals, one cannot logically deduce that increasing unemployment is a function workers' preference for more leisure. Rather, a large reduction of aggregate demand requires a compensating increase in aggregate demand, given that rational or smart workers pose no fundamental obstacle to restoring employment to its pre-recession levels. This x-efficiency perspective strengthens the rational worker approach presented by Keynes in his narrative on workers accepting generalized, fair cuts to real wages, given the expectation that employment will increase as a consequence.

In this instance, rational inefficiency becomes a product of government *not* pursuing policy that restores aggregate demand, in the face of rational decision-making at the firm level. The latter is a product of the belief by government decision-makers in the capacity of markets to self-correct and that the ultimate source of the persistence in the *increased* level of unemployment following a severe economic downturn is the unwillingness of workers to reduce their real wages. This belief in the classical model might be rational given the information set of decision-makers. But they yield economic inefficiencies at the macroeconomic level, keeping unemployment rates unnecessarily high and output well below what it might otherwise be. Thus, government unnecessarily causes great economic and social harm to large segments of its population in the pursuit of a misconstrued economic model.

Conclusion

A key argument presented in this chapter is that smart individuals (economic agents) can make decisions that are economically inefficient in the realm of production and consumption and at both the micro and macro level. Being smart and being rational, from this boundedly rational perspective, does preclude outcomes being inefficient and sub-optimal. In the conventional wisdom rational efficiencies are assumed away at the micro level. Rational agents behaving in accordance to the dictates of neoclassical theory should produce results that are both economically efficient in production and utility maximizing, reflecting the true preferences of consumers, in the realm of consumption. But if individuals were to deviate from neoclassical behavioural norms one would expect inefficiencies in both production and consumption, as they would be behaving irrationally at least from the perspective of the conventional wisdom. But the more empirically based smart agent approach, redefines rationality more broadly in terms of smart decision-making. This builds upon the contributions of Simon and bounded rationality/procedural rationality modelling platform that he developed. Here, a rational baseline for decision-making is predicated on the capabilities of the individual and the decision-making environment. This introduces a different set of norms for what is rational and even what is efficient.

Moreover, in the narrative presented in this chapter, economic inefficiencies can flow from rational or smart behaviour in both the realm of production and consumption. Such inefficiencies can be a function of the preferences of decision-makers and from the decision-making capabilities of smart individuals and their decision-making environment. In fact, even given optimal decision-making capabilities and optimal decision-making environments, inefficiencies can arise given the preferences of smart decision-makers. But economic efficiency cannot be achieved simply by constructing appropriate decision-making capabilities and environments. The latter two serve as the necessary but not sufficient conditions for economic efficiency.

Overall, the different approaches to behavioural economics empirically unmask the fact that individuals typically don't behave as predicted and as is normatively preferred by conventional economics. But the errors and heuristics approach to behavioural economics, which feeds into and overlaps with the nudging approach, regards such deviations from conventional norms as indicators of suboptimal behaviour, typically hardwired into the human brain. From this perspective, modelling choice behaviour requires investigating and documenting deviations from the conventional norms and determining means of inducing decision-makers to behave in accordance with these norms for optimal behaviour. Hence, the errors and heuristics approach, although critical of the conventional assumption that individual behave 'rationally', typically retains the conventional economic benchmarks for rationality.

Building upon the evidence, the argument presented in this chapter is that although smart people don't behave in accordance with conventional economic norms, this should not imply that such behaviour and the choices flowing from this, are irrational, sub-optimal, or inefficient, given individuals' capabilities and their decision-making environment. Smart people make boundedly rational decisions. Benchmarks for what is rational, smart, and intelligent, need to be based upon what makes sense given the decision-makers capabilities and their decision-making environment. There are no specific optimal decision-making norms that apply across time, space, and individuals, although there might be general behavioural normative rules of thumb.

The approach taken in this chapter and implicit in Simon's notion of bounded and procedural rationality, is that individuals can make mistakes and can even be biased, but this is not part and parcel of the human condition—hardwired in the human brain. Environmental factors and decision-making capabilities, which can be altered, play a determining role. And, one can determine the conditions under which optimal decisions can be achieved by individuals, households, and firms. Herein lies a critical role for societal (from community to state to international) interventions in economy and society; to facilitate the provision of improved decision-making environments and capabilities. Also, important is to correct for externalities, positive and negative, many of which are related to information imperfections and coordination failures as well as preferences that, if realized, cause harm to others.

Some of the differences and similarities of the different approaches to rationality and their implications for understanding the source and determinants of the relative inefficiencies in production and consumption are illustrated in Fig. 5.2. Conventional economics presumes that narrowly defined rationality best explains human behaviour, yields substantive predictions of production and consumption efficiencies, across time and space. Public policy is of limited importance apart from assuring competitive markets and secure property rights. The heuristics and biases approach, whilst retaining conventional normative benchmarks for optimal behaviour and efficient choice outcomes, documents the persistent deviations from conventional norms. Hence, one has persistent inefficiencies (errors and biases in decision-making), typically a function of behaviours hardwired into the human brain. This yields policy prescriptions designed to nudge individuals towards what experts (choice architects) deem to be in the best interest of the decision-maker.

The smart agent approach, building upon the bounded rationality contributions to the decision-making literature, rejects many of the conventional norms for optimal behaviour, whilst agreeing with the heuristic and biases proponents that humans typically don't behave in accordance with these norms. But here rationality is defined relative to the capabilities of the decision-makers, the decision-making environment, preferences, and power relationships, as well as recognizing differences in these variables across agents and across time and space.

In this smart agent modelling, rational agents can make errors and be biased in their decisions and generate inefficiencies in the domain of production and consumption. But these sub-optimal outcomes can be affected by changes to individual capabilities and the overall decision-making environment, for example. This

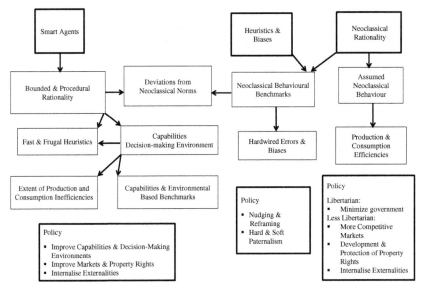

FIG. 5.2   Rationality and inefficiency.

underlines the significance of public policy in facilitating choices that yield more efficient outcomes whilst increasing the ability of agents to form and realize their true preferences thereby increasing their level of welfare or and even happiness.

References

Akerlof, G. A. (1970). The market for 'lemons': Quality uncertainty and the market mechanism. *Quarterly Journal of Economics, 84*, 488–500.

Akerlof, G. A. (2002). Behavioral macroeconomics and macroeconomic behavior. *American Economic Review, 92*, 411–433.

Akerlof, G. A., & Kranton, R. E. (2010). *Identity economics: How our identities shape our work, wages, and well-being.* Princeton, NJ: Princeton University Press.

Akerlof, G. A., & Shiller, R. J. (2009). *Animal spirits: How human psychology drives the economy, and why it matters for global capitalism.* Princeton NJ: Princeton University Press.

Alchian, A. A. (1950). Uncertainty, evolution, and economic theory. *Journal of Political Economy, 63*, 211–221.

Altman, M. (1999). The methodology of economics and the survivor principle revisited and revised: Some welfare and public policy implications of modeling the economic agent. *Review of Social Economics, 57*, 427–449.

Altman, M. (2002). Economic theory, public policy and the challenge of innovative work practices. *Economic and Industrial Democracy: An International Journal, 23*, 271–290.

Altman, M. (2005). Behavioral economics, power, rational inefficiencies, fuzzy sets, and public policy. *Journal of Economic Issues, 39*, 683–706.

Altman, M. (2006a). What a difference an assumption makes: Effort discretion, economic theory, and public policy. In M. Altman (Ed.), *Handbook of contemporary Behavioral economics: Foundations and developments* (pp. 125–164). New York: Armonk.

Altman, M. (2006b). Involuntary unemployment, macroeconomic policy, and a behavioral model of the firm: Why high real wages need not cause high unemployment. *Research in Economics, 60,* 97–111.

Altman, M. (2009). A behavioral-institutional model of endogenous growth and induced technical change. *Journal of Economic Issues, 63,* 685–713.

Altman, M. (2010). A behavioral and institutional foundation of preference and choice behavior: Freedom to choose and choice X-inefficiencies. *Review of Social Economy, 69,* 395–411.

Altman, M. (2011). Behavioural economics, ethics, and public policy: Paving the road to freedom or serfdom? In J. Boston (Ed.), *Ethics and public policy: Contemporary issues* (pp. 23–48). Wellington: Victoria University Press.

Altman, M. (2012). *Behavioral economics for dummies.* Mississauga, Ontario: Wiley.

Altman, M. (2015). Introduction. In M. Altman (Ed.), *Real-world decision making: An encyclopedia of behavioral economics.* Santa Barbara, USA: Greenwood, ABC-CLIO.

Altman, M. (2016). *Multiple equilibria, bounded rationality, and the indeterminacy of economic outcomes: Closing the system with institutional parameters.* In R. Frantz & L. Roger (Eds.), *Minds, models and Milieux commemorating the centennial of the birth of Herbert Simon* (pp. 167–185).

Altman, M. (2017). A bounded rationality assessment of the new behavioral economics. In R. Frantz, S.-H. Chen, K. Dopfer, F. Heukelom, & S. Mousavi (Eds.), *Routledge handbook of behavioral economics* (pp. 179–194). New York: Routledge.

Altman, H. J. R. (2019). *The behavioural economics of organizational inefficiency: The example of the New Zealand fitness industry.* Australia: Masters of Philosophy (Research), School of Economics and Finance Faculty of Business, Queensland University of Technology.

Becker, G. S. (1996). *Accounting for tastes.* Cambridge, MA: Harvard University Press.

Berg, N. (2014). The consistency and ecological rationality approaches to normative bounded rationality. *Journal of Economic Methodology, 21,* 375–395.

Berg, N., & Gigerenzer, G. (2010). As-if behavioral economics: Neoclassical economics in disguise? *History of Economic Ideas, 18*(133–166), 2010.

Bewley, T. F. (1999). *Why wages don't fall during a recession.* Cambridge, MA/London: Harvard University Press.

Cyert, R. M., & March, J. C. (1963). *A behavioral theory of the firm.* Englewood Cliffs, NJ: Prentice-Hall.

Frantz, R. S. (1997). *X-efficiency theory, evidence and applications. Topics in regulatory economics and policy. Vol. 23.* Boston, Dordrecht, and London: Kluwer Academic.

Friedman, M. (1953). *The methodology of positive economics.* In *Essays in positive economics* (pp. 3–43). Chicago: University of Chicago Press.

Friedman, M. (1968). The role of monetary policy. *American Economic Review, 58,* 1–17.

Gigerenzer, G. (2007). *Gut feelings: The intelligence of the unconscious.* New York: Viking.

Harsanyi, J. (1982). Morality and the theory of rational behavior. In A. Sen & B. Williams (Eds.), *Utilitarianism and beyond* (pp. 39–62). Cambridge, England: Cambridge University Press.

Hayek, F. A. (1944). *The road to serfdom.* Chicago: University of Chicago Press.

Hayek, F. A. (1945). The use of knowledge in society. *American Economic Review, 35,* 519–530.

Hayek, F. A. (1948). *Individualism and the economic order.* Chicago: University of Chicago Press.

Hume, D. (2014 [1738]). *A treatise on human nature.* Some Good Press. Kindle file.

Kahneman, D. (2003). Maps of bounded rationality: Psychology for behavioral economics. *American Economic Review, 93,* 1449–1475.

Kahneman, D. (2011). *Thinking, fast and slow.* New York: Farrar, Straus and Giroux.

Kahneman, D., & Tversky, A. (1979). Prospect theory: An analysis of decision under risk. *Econometrica, 47*, 263–291.

Keynes, J. M. (1936). *The general theory of employment, interest, and money.* New York: Harcourt, Brace and Company.

Leibenstein, H. (1957). *Economic backwardness and economic growth.* New York: J. Wiley and Sons.

Leibenstein, H. (1966). Allocative efficiency vs. 'X-efficiency'. *American Economic Review, 56*, 392–415.

Leibenstein, H. (1979). A branch of economics is missing: Micro-micro theory. *Journal of Economic Literature, 17*, 477–502.

March, J. G. (1978). Bounded rationality, ambiguity, and the engineering of choice. *Bell Journal of Economics, 9*, 587–608.

North, D. C. (1971). Institutional change and economic growth. *Journal of Economic History, 31*, 118–125.

North, D. (1991). Institutions. *Journal of Economic Perspectives, 5*, 97–112.

North, D. (1994). Economic performance through time. *American Economic Review, 84*, 359–368.

Nussbaum, M. (2011). *Creating capabilities: The human development approach.* Cambridge, MA: Harvard University Press.

Olson, M. (1996). Distinguished lecture on economics in government: Big bills left on the sidewalk: Why some nations are rich, and others poor. *Journal of Economic Perspectives, 10*, 3–24.

Posner, R. A. (2009). *A failure of capitalism: The crisis of '08 and the descent into depression.* Cambridge/London: Harvard University Press.

Reder, M. W. (1982). Chicago economics: Permanence and change. *Journal of Economic Literature, 20*, 1–38.

Sen, A. (1985). *Commodities and capabilities.* Amsterdam: North-Holland.

Shiller, R. J. (2008). *The subprime solution: How today's global financial crisis happened, and what to do about it.* Princeton: Princeton University Press.

Shiller, R. J. (2012). *Finance and the good society.* Princeton: Princeton University Press.

Simon, H. A. (1959). Theories of decision making in economics and behavioral science. *American Economic Review, 49*, 252–283.

Simon, H. A. (1978). Rationality as a process and as a product of thought. *American Economic Review, 70*, 1–16.

Simon, H. A. (1986). Rationality in psychology and economics. *Journal of Business, 59*, S209–S224.

Simon, H. A. (1987). Behavioral economics. In J. Eatwell, M. Millgate, & P. Newman (Eds.), *The new Palgrave: A dictionary of economics* (pp. 221–225). London: Macmillan.

Smith, V. L. (2003). Constructivist and ecological rationality in economics. *American Economic Review, 93*, 465–508.

Smith, V. L. (2005). Behavioral economics research and the foundations of economics. *Journal of Socio-Economics, 34*, 135–150.

Thaler, R. H., & Sunstein, C. (2008). *Nudge: Improving decisions about health, wealth, and happiness.* New Haven and London: Yale University Press.

Todd, P. M., & Gigerenzer, G. (2003). Bounding rationality to the world. *Journal of Economic Psychology, 24*, 143–165.

Tversky, A., & Kahneman, D. (1981). The framing of decisions and the psychology of choice. *Science, 211*, 453–458.

Chapter 6

How consumers can achieve freedom of choice: When consumers are truly sovereign

Chapter outline

Introduction   131
An alternative model of
     preference formation   132
Conventional perspectives and
     critiques   134
Constructing an alternative theory
     of welfare maximization   136

Choice x-inefficiency and
     x-inefficiency in production   142
Conclusion   142
References   144

Introduction

It is important to model choice behaviour in a manner that captures the reality that choices made by individuals are often not utility maximizing or satisficing from the perspective of the person doing the choosing. If an individual's choice behaviour is not welfare maximizing, as it is always assumed to be in the traditional economics narrative, then the revealed preferences of individuals need not be a metric for the good life. Rather, choice behaviour might instead reflect the preferences of others, misleading or incomplete information, or poor education. A key point made in this chapter is that only in an environment where individuals are free to choose and have effective voice, irrespective of income, gender, ethnicity, or religion, can choice behaviour be a metric for the good life. It is possible for rational agents who are characterized by optimal or true preferences to be unable to realize or manifest these preferences for social or institutional reasons. This has important implications for economic theory as well as for public policy, especially for institutional design. The perspective adopted in this chapter also explicitly takes the ethical and normative stance that one should respect the free choices of individuals and that free choice is an important component of the good life or socio-economic wellbeing (Sen, 2009). The narrative model builds on insights from Berlin (1968), Harsanyi (1982), Nussbaum (1999, 2000), and Sen (1990, 1999, 2000, 2009), amongst others,

Smart Economic Decision-Making in a Complex World. https://doi.org/10.1016/B978-0-12-811461-2.00006-7
131

who argue that the manner in which preferences are formed and expressed is important for understanding the welfare implications of expressed preferences and the choices made by individuals. Insights of contemporary behavioural economics, which find that the manner in which choices are framed impact on the choices individuals make, need to be considered as well (Thaler & Sunstein, 2003, 2008; Tversky & Kahneman, 1981).

In the alternative modelling, the preferences of agents are not necessarily the true or objective preferences that reflect the objective wants and desires of the individual. True preferences are those preferences individuals would construct under ideal but reasonably practical circumstances (Harsanyi, 1982; Tomer, 1995). Even if the individual is characterized by true preferences, individuals may lack the capacity to realize these preferences. Not unlike the conventional wisdom, however, it is argued that individuals have the capacity to engage in reasoned choice, which can be realized under particular circumstances. The alternative model of preference formation and choice asks: 'What are necessary conditions under which true or objective preferences can be constructed?'

An alternative model of preference formation

A fundamental conclusion flowing from this alternative formulation of preference formation and choice is that a necessary condition for an individual's capacity to construct and realize her or his objective preferences is an environment of political freedom, human rights, full and truthful information, and transparency. This brings to the fore the question of the importance of core capabilities (Nussbaum, 2000 and Sen, 2000 on the capabilities approach) as a necessary condition for the construction and realization of individuals' true or objective preferences, and the extent to which such capacities are universal in nature—crossing boundaries of cultural, national and social values (Ignatieff, 2001; Nussbaum, 1999, 2000; Sen, 1990, 1999, 2000).

A critical difference between this alternative theoretical framework and the conventional one is not that individuals cannot and do not make rational choices, but rather that such choices can be so constrained and preferences so distorted from their true or objective counterparts, that the actual choices made need not reflect welfare maximizing choices. If the assumptions of the neoclassical worldview do not hold, especially the assumptions that individuals' existing preferences are their true preferences and that their revealed preferences reflect their true preferences, the choices made by individuals can be critiqued internally: individual choices and preferences may deviate from what they would be in an ideal environment.

The perspective that individuals can behave rationally and can exercise some choice in their preferences, differs from a view that assumes that individuals are completely constrained by their external environment in terms of what their preferences are and are thus devoid of true choice. Such individuals' choices are more akin to 'choices' made by a robot whose choices are pre-determined by its programmer. Pre-programmed choices may be 'bad' choices that may need to be corrected for by government or other forms of intervention, which serve to re-construct the 'bad' preferences into 'good' preferences and thereby into 'good' choices. The question is which set of select individuals determines what are the 'good' preferences and choices (Altman, 2006; Twitchell, 1999).

Related to the no-choice school, in terms of its emphasis on the importance of culture and larger social variables as determinants of preferences and choice, are those who argue that choices made by individuals are influenced by one's cultural and social milieu (Davis, 2003; Dolfsma, 2002; George, 2001a, 2001b). Criticizing such choices may then be more circumspect. If social preferences are imposed on individuals, one cannot conclude that these preferences are optimal from either an individual or social perspective (see also Sen, 1999, 2009 on this point). In contrast, if individuals are actually not free to choose their preferred preferences, then the choices made by individuals may not be optimal from the individual's or society's point of view, and the choices made by individuals can then be critiqued on the basis of what the preferences and choices of individuals would be in an ideal choice environment.

Extending the theoretical frameworks of both capabilities and capacities, and ideas of x-efficiency and efficiency wage, this chapter argues that suboptimal preferences and choices can negatively impact the level of socioeconomic wellbeing of individuals, the potential level of economic efficiency and productivity. Moreover, in a world of heterogeneous preferences (Berlin, 1968), as opposed to the world of homogeneous preferences of the conventional economic wisdom, the capacity of one group to realize their preferences over and above another group or groups results in only one group's preferences dominating. I argue that a framework for critiquing this group approach to preference dominance is also required.

This chapter links preferences and choices with the socio-economic effects that these preferences and choices might generate. Borrowing from Leibenstein's (1966, 1979; see also Altman, 1999a, 2001a, 2001b, 2005) production-side theory, the difference between the preferences and related choices made under ideal circumstances and those made under less ideal conditions as consumption or choice x-inefficiency is a measure of the welfare costs incurred when an individual's preferences and choices deviate from their true preferences and related choices. In the conventional worldview there can exist no consumption or choice x-inefficiencies.

A fundamental question addressed is under what conditions can individuals construct true or objective preferences and effectively realize these preferences. Only under specific but realistic circumstances can true preferences be constructed and realized. I argue that only when individuals are free to construct and realize their true preferences can welfare be maximized. This, of course, has policy implications relating to institutional design.

If individual choice based on true preferences is assumed a primary human value to be respected and protected (an assumption of neoclassical theory), then any critique of choices cannot be based on criteria external to the individual's true preferences, except for situations where clear negative externalities exist (Mill, 2002, pp. 11–12). Needless to say, this argument does not imply that the expert's opinion is of no value. Individuals may not have specialized knowledge and must sometimes rely on expert advice. This is distinct from experts dictating the day-to-day choices of individuals. The expert as advisor is different from the expert as dictator.

Conventional perspectives and critiques

Conventional economic theory assumes that the preferences of the individual are the true or objective preferences of the individual. The choices of the individual are utility or welfare maximizing, despite various constraints faced (cf. March, 1978). Although individual choice is constrained, the constraints do not completely determine choice—individuals have a substantive degree of freedom in making choices.

This theory is normative in the sense that it prescribes that such behaviour is the most effective method of maximizing an individual's utility, welfare, or wellbeing. However, this theory is also taken to be descriptive by many of its adherents. Moreover, it is argued that one cannot make interpersonal comparisons of choice behaviour. The result is a rational choice outcome that can, by definition, not be evaluated in terms of an external metric. Choice outcomes are always utility and welfare maximizing. Any change in preferences and choices predicated upon exogenous interventions will be welfare and utility reducing.[a]

It is assumed here, however, that the actualisation of preferences yields optimal or welfare maximizing choices only under a specific set of social and institutional circumstances. The conventional wisdom typically pays little heed to how preferences are formed and how choices are made, assuming implicitly that the conditions underlying preference formation and the actualisation of choice are either of no substantive consequence, or that whatever the underlying conditions might be they are consistent with utility and welfare maximizing preferences and choices. If the necessary conditions for the development of true preferences are not present, one could critique the preferences and choices of the individual on the basis of the preferences and choices that can be expected to be obtained under a relatively ideal social and institutional environment, as Harsanyi (1982) has recognized.

Harsanyi (1982, p. 56) posits, however, that not all true preferences should be included in the social welfare function, as not all true or rational preferences

---

a. Individuals engage in constrained utility maximization, given their income and relative prices. Although not paid much attention to by the conventional wisdom, increasing the real income of individual, increasing real income by increasing minimum wages or improving the bargaining power of labour, can be predicted to increase the welfare of the affected individuals. This is not the same thing as interventions that push or nudge individuals to make should which they would not otherwise make.

are consistent with social utility or welfare maximization, even though the actualisation of such true preferences is consistent with individual utility or welfare maximization. Preferences that are antisocial, such as 'sadism, envy, resentment, and malice', should, according to Harsanyi, be excluded from the construction of a social welfare function. This is very much akin to Mill's utilitarian view.

An individual's actual preferences need not represent the true welfare maximizing preferences of the individual unless certain conditions are met. Harsanyi's focus is on the availability of all relevant information necessary to the formation of preferences and to the making of particular decisions, whether this information is always reasoned with the greatest possible care, and if the individual's state of mind is most conducive to rational choice. A list of what, in effect, are necessary conditions for the formation of true preferences and their actualisation can be expanded and elaborated upon without in anyway undermining the core message of rational choice theory (see Becker, 1996; Gigerenzer, 2007; Nussbaum, 1999, 2000; Sen, 1999, 2000; Simon, 1987). Given that we are boundedly rational, our decisions can be affected by how our information is structured and presented or framed (Tversky & Kahneman, 1981). Our decision-making is also affected by the costliness and asymmetries of information (Stigler, 1961; Stiglitz, 1985). Such broadening of the traditional model of the rational economic agent does not detract from the core assumption of rational choice theory, that individuals engage in intelligent decision-making given the constraints they face.

Sen (1999) speaks directly to one critique of rational choice theory, which maintains that the fact that individuals are faced by constraints precludes individual choice. There can be no individual choice, inclusive of rational choice, in a world of constraints. What follows from this worldview is that choice must be made for the individual by circumstances. Sen has been a consistent critic of narrow rational choice theory which, unlike Becker's perspective, provides no scope for non-economic variables conditioning and informing the preferences formed and choices made by individuals. However, that preferences are not formed and choices are not made in a vacuum, does not imply that rational choice is an impossibility in a world of constraints (Sen, 1999). Sen (1999, pp. 26–27) elaborates that

> ...important as the perceptual role of community and identity may be, it cannot be presumed that the possibility of reasoned choice is ruled out by these influences ... Choices do exist; the possibility of reasoning does too; and nothing imprisons the mind as much as a false belief in an unalterable lack of choice and the impossibility of reasoning.

Conventional economic theory assumes that circumstances are typically conducive to the formation of true preferences and choices by rational or intelligent individuals. It is, moreover, assumed that the typical individual is subsumed in an environment conducive to rational or intelligent behaviour.

This view is distinct from the metapreference view articulated, for example, by George (2001a, 2001b). In this perspective, metapreferences—which represent the preferences that an individual would like to have (second-order preferences)—and the actual preferences of the individual (first-order preferences), may or may not match.

Constructing an alternative theory of welfare maximization

Nussbaum and Sen do not critique the conventional rational choice theory because of its assumption that individuals are rational agents who have the capacity to make and actually do make intelligent choices. They accept this core assumption. This core assumption is also accepted here as one of the building blocks of an alternative theory of welfare maximization presented. Instead, I argue against the assumption of conventional choice theory that rational or intelligent behaviour should necessarily result in the formation of true preferences and, thereby, in the maximization of either individual or social welfare. Manifest or revealed preferences of intelligent individuals might yield sub-optimal welfare at both an individual and social level. In the alternative theory of welfare maximization, true preferences can be constructed only under specific circumstances. If these conditions are not met, the narrative of traditional economic theory identifying revealed or manifest preferences with true preferences, and thus with welfare maximization, is false and misleading.

Conceptually, I refer to a scenario characterized by choices emanating from true preferences as choice x-efficiency. This borrows from Leibenstein's (1966, 1979); Altman, 1999a, 2005; Frantz, 1997) notion of production x-efficiency, which is actualised only under particular conditions of industrial relations and market forces. Just as production x-inefficiencies prevail when conditions are not appropriate, so too can there be choice x-inefficiencies when choices are derived from false preferences or when an individual does not have the capacity to actualise her or his true preferences. Thus, there are clearly two potential sources of choice inefficiencies. One is based on the formation of false preferences which, when realized, yield sub-optimal welfare results or choice x-inefficiency. Being able to construct true preferences is no guarantee of choice x-efficiency, however. If individuals do not have the capacity to translate their true preferences into choice behaviour, choice x-inefficiencies will prevail. Choice x-inefficiencies yield individual welfare losses, possibly translating into social welfare losses unless choices derived from true preferences yield significant negative externalities.

The difference between choice x-efficiency and choice x-inefficiency is a measure of individual welfare losses and of sub-optimal choice behaviour. This type of modelling of choice behaviour focuses attention on conditions required for the elimination of any choice x-inefficiencies and for the realization of maximum social welfare as well. Only when choice x-inefficiencies are eliminated are the revealed or manifested preferences of the individual consistent with the conventional theory's assumption that rational individual choice yields individual welfare maximization.

Conditions for the formation of true preferences are an open-ended set that can be extended and revised as required. Of critical importance in a world of imperfect information, is for decision makers to have easy access to accurate and understandable information relevant to choice decisions individuals engage in. Related to the information set is education. Depending upon the information set, different levels of education might be required to access or to process the relevant information. The true set of preferences would be that set chosen when all relevant information and related educational sets are available. Otherwise, the individual would form false, sub-optimal, preferences. Consistent with the satisficing and bounded rationality narrative, uneducated folk can, of course, form rational preferences and engage in rational choice, albeit these choices might be sub-optimal given the constraints faced (Altman, 2001a; Simon, 1987).

On the importance of education, more education of women, ceteris paribus, tends to reduce child mortality through its effect on the preferences cum choices that the more informed women make (Altman, 1999b; Altman & Lamontagne, 2004; Sen, 1999). Another example would be: if a woman believes that she should be deprived of resources then she tends to develop a preference for relative deprivation. New information and education sets may result in women changing their preferences (Mill, 2002; Nussbaum, 1999, 2000; Sen, 1999). Thus, the initial set of preferences could be false. At an abstract level, if one believed that a particular product is good for you, you would form a preference for such products. However, these would be false preferences, if they are based upon false information of the effects of these products on your wellbeing. If information and education are critical to the formation of true preferences, institutions must be in place such that individuals have access to the necessary information and related education sets required to construct true preferences.

Related to the importance of information and education to the formation of true preferences, is the impact of social interaction to preference formation—conventional economic theory tends to assume that preferences are formed by individuals independently. It is, therefore, assumed that there exists no 'jointness' or interaction across individuals when preferences are formed. To the extent that there is jointness, if one individual is provided with better information and educational sets by being exposed to and engaged in conversation with individuals with lesser information and education sets, these latter individuals might develop preferences that are different from and preferred—and thus superior—to the old preferences constructed in isolation. Even if all individuals have access to the same information sets, an individual's true preferences are affected by her or his desire to match the preferences of others. Improvements in preferences for one individual might, additionally, yield positive externalities or spillovers that influence the preferences constructed by the other individual.

For example, if the wife's true preference is to smoke, while the husband's true preference is for there to be no smoking in the family, and with the credible default being divorce, the wife might choose not to smoke since maintaining the marriage is the higher order preference, subsuming the individual's initial true preference of smoking. In the context of a world where preference formation and choice is part of a social context, the utility maximizing choice of the individual is affected by the preferences of others whose utility is in fact part of the individual's objective function. The true preference of the individual in a social context might, therefore, be different from her or his true preference formed in isolation. But for a partnership to generate different but higher order preferences requires an environment where the parties to a relationship have effective voice in, and access to effective exit from, the relationship—this must an egalitarian and democratic relationship.

Also important to the formation of true preferences is an environment where the individual is free from coercion (Harsanyi's point) (see also Sen, 2009). In a coercive environment, the individual has less capacity for contemplating options and opportunities when constructing preferences and has less access to accurate information. Coercion may preclude the realization of true preferences, as the individual is subject to the preferences and choices of others that are imposed.

Some might argue that certain levels of economic wellbeing are required for true preferences to be formed, implying poor people cannot be rational and should be treated as minors by government and the experts until they achieve a 'high enough' level of material wellbeing. Although poverty levels and the like are critically important issues, low real-income levels do not preclude rational thought. Rational choices are always, and must always be, constrained choices. Income is one such constraint, affecting both preferences and choices. If the analyst or expert assumes that choice is not possible on the basis of pervasive constraints such as income or education, even though in reality this not does preclude choice, the analyst or expert illegitimates the preferences and choices of particular individuals (Sen, 1999, 2009).

Even when optimal conditions for the construction of true preferences are met, these are not sufficient for the actualisation of these preferences. Once true preferences are constructed, individuals might be precluded from actualising their preferences for legal, cultural, or bargaining power reasons, for example (for a similar point see Kuran, 1995). These factors might also serve to prevent adequate access to the information and education sets needed for the formation of true preferences. This raises the question of what are the core capacities required for individuals to actualise their true preferences, and when might these core capacities have a dynamic effect on the ability of individuals to construct true preferences. Nussbaum (1999, chs 1 and 2; 2000, ch. 2), for example, believes it is critical that an institutional setting be constructed that protects and promotes free choice amongst individuals as long as such free choices do not generate negative externalities. This includes political freedoms as well as material conditions necessary for individuals to engage in free choice given their preferences, as well as to enhance their capacity to construct true preferences.

Free choice does not arise spontaneously in a vacuum. Nussbaum (1999, p. 49) points to the importance of developing the appropriate institutional setting, encompassing the necessary capabilities, wherein free choice can both exist and be sustained. Government has an important role to play 'by making opportunities available, government enhances, and does not remove, choice'. Ignatieff (2001) presents an elaborate argument that speaks to the importance of human rights as necessary for the existence of free choice, an argument that overlaps with Nussbaum's. He finds that human rights must be constructed and do not necessarily or naturally arise, for example, either from the existence of more or freer trade or from a democracy wherein a majoritarian tyranny might arise and prevail. Free markets and democracy are not sufficient in and of themselves for human rights to be sustained. And without human rights, the extent to which individuals are free to choose is severely circumscribed. Human rights, argues Ignatieff (2001, p. 57) are necessary to protect the exercise of human agency— 'the capacity of each individual to achieve rational intentions [those that do not impose obvious harm to others] without let or hindrance … To protect human agency necessarily requires us to protect all individuals' right to choose the life they see fit to lead'.

Apart from protecting individuals from the negative externalities that might be generated by the free choices of other individuals, human rights do not dictate nor constrain the choices of individuals. Rather, human rights are a priori to agency and free choice and, thus to the actualisation and formation of what has been referred to in this chapter as true preferences (Ignatieff, 2001, pp. 89–90). Additionally, human rights and the free choice allowed for by core human rights are necessary to democratic economic development and to the process of economic development itself. Thus, Ignatieff directly links the capacity of individuals to actualise their preferences as not only a good in and off itself, in terms of individuals maximizing their own wellbeing, but also as the sin qua non of economic development which, obviously, impacts upon the level of wellbeing achievable by individuals. It can be argued that a critical necessary condition, although not a sufficient condition, for the formation of true preferences and their actualisation is the protection and fostering of agency or free choice.

If the conditions for the formation of real preferences and their actualisation are not met, then the revealed preferences of individuals are not welfare maximizing. The revealed preferences of individuals would then be choice x-inefficient and yield suboptimal welfare results.

Relatively free and competitive markets are no guarantee that the necessary conditions for the formation and realization of true preferences will be constructed. The necessary information flows, investment in human capital, and guarantees of core human rights needed, are more often than not a product of political interventions in the economy, interventions that ultimately set a frame for individuals' preference formation and choices. To the extent that the market cannot and does not generate the institutional environment necessary for the formation and realization of true preferences, one ends up with a market failure. Thus, for choice x-inefficiency to be eliminated and for social welfare to be maximized requires government intervention, just as government intervention is needed to establish the rules of the game for a market economy to become operational and approach its potential production efficiencies. The importance of private property rights as a requirement for economic wellbeing has appropriately drawn a lot of attention in economic literature. However, while one might have adequate property rights, one could still fall well below a reasonable benchmark of choice x-efficiency.

Some of the points discussed here can be illustrated in Fig. 6.1, where a standard indifference curve and a budget line are plotted. Assume that TR_A represents the true preferences of an individual and that no preference externalities exist. In standard conventional economic theory, this would be the prevailing indifference curve irrespective of the conditions underlying preference formation and execution of preferences. Thus TR_A is the welfare maximizing indifference curve and the welfare maximizing rational individual will choose a point along this indifference curve that is tangential to the budget line CD. At the point of tangency, XE, there is choice x-efficiency. However, if FR represents the revealed preferences of an individual and these are false preferences, making choices based on FR cannot yield maximum welfare. And FR yields a lower

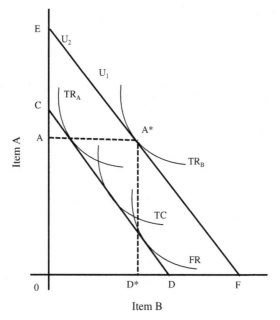

FIG. 6.1 Preferences and choices.

level of utility for a given level of income than TR_A, at equilibrium point XI_0. The institutional environment might change such that an individual might be able to form true preferences, TR_A, but the individual's agency might be constrained such that her or his preferences are at TC. Utility is maximized, given constraints, at XI_1. Given income, utility is above what it was when only false preferences were formed. But still, choice x-inefficiency prevails and individual welfare is not maximized since the choices of the individual are constrained such that the individual cannot actualise her or his true preferences.

Only when the institutional setting is such that true preferences can be formed and actualised can individual welfare be maximized and only then can the choices actually made by the individual be said to represent and reveal welfare maximizing preferences and choices. The gap between TR_A and TC and FR is a measure of choice x-inefficiency. When choice x-inefficiency exists, a greater level of real income is required, for example, if the x-inefficient choice is to yield the same level of utility as the x-efficient choice. The greater the extent of choice x-inefficiency, ceteris paribus, the greater the amount of real income required to yield the same level of utility as is generated by the x-efficient choice. The utility gap generated by x-efficient and x-inefficient choices closes as conditions change to allow for the formation of true preferences and their realization.

From a meta-preferences perspective (George, 2001a, 2001b) free individuals may not be capable of making welfare maximizing choices. In a regime where individuals know their true preferences and are free to actualise them, how can their choices not represent welfare maximizing choices? George argues that the 'costs' of shifting from first-order to second-order preferences, might explain this. But this approach suggests that the weakness of will must be overwhelming in this scenario as must be the psychological costs of realizing one's true preferences in a world without coercion. I would argue that this outcome is unlikely given that individuals are free to choose, especially in the longer run. It is more likely that first order preferences are not chosen when individuals are embedded in environment wherein free choice is highly constrained.

It is important to note that the above discussion relates especially to hypothetical situations where one is comparing the utility of 'identical' individuals in different choice scenarios. We are not comparing the utility of an individual who is moving in real time from an x-inefficient to an x-efficient choice scenario. As Becker (1996, pp. 20–22), points out, if individuals are unhappy with their actual preferences, they may not shift to their desired or true preferences if it is too costly to do so. Actual inherited personal and social capital, predicated upon their actual preferences ' … constrains their utility maximising choices, no matter how much they may regret the amount and kind of capital they inherited from the past. Their utility would be lower, perhaps much lower, if their "desired" preferences alone guided choices'.

This does not imply that such individuals will not act to realize their true preferences once they are known and the institutional preconditions for actualising their true preferences are in place. However, initial utility start-up costs would be incurred—this point is in many ways similar to George's.

Choice x-inefficiency and x-inefficiency in production

Choice x-inefficiency results not only in suboptimal levels of individual welfare or utility but can also result in significant economic inefficiencies reducing the level of material wellbeing from what it would be in a world of choice x-efficiencies. This particular line of reasoning extends the work of Leibenstein (1957) on efficiency wages and of Altman (1998, 2001a, 2005) and Leibenstein (1966, 1979) on the behavioural model of the firm and x-inefficiency theory. A case in point would be that the false preferences of women favouring biases against women with regards to nutritional, health, and educational standards and resources. Such biases negatively impact upon the potential capabilities of women in terms of how hard and how well they can work, as well as on their level of human capital formation. This, in turn, negatively impacts upon their level of material and social wellbeing. Moreover, at a macro-level, such reduced capacities serve to reduce the level of per capita output in the economy.

There can be market failure in preference formation similar to the realm of production wherein the revealed and actualised preferences of agents are such that the level of per capita output and the level of agents' material and social wellbeing is less than it would be if optimal preferences were constructed. This raises the public policy question of how to correct for such market failures. Such market failures contribute directly to development failures and, more specifically, to poverty with particular biases against individuals who do not have the power to actualise their already constructed optimal preferences, or who do not have the capacity to construct such preferences. A further critical point made with regards to the linkage between preference formation and economic efficiency is that there need not be a trade-off between increasing the extent of choice x-efficiency and increasing production x-efficiency. There need not be a zero-sum game.

Needless to say, however, conflict might arise amongst individuals where optimal preferences differ amongst individuals; women, for example, might wish to expend income on food and education, as opposed to a male preference for allocating marginal family income on drink and entertainment. In this sense, the optimal preferences of one group that serves to enhance economic efficiency might be in direct conflict with the optimal preferences of another group whose actualised preferences would serve to reduce the level of efficiency. The resolution to this type of conflict can be critical in furthering the process of development, reducing poverty in general, and gender-biased poverty in particular.

Conclusion

Conventional economic theory assumes that the choices made by individuals are necessarily welfare maximizing choices. But this need not be the case if such choices critically depend on the capacity of individuals to both construct and actualise their true preferences. Absent these conditions, individual welfare cannot be maximized, yielding choice inefficiencies. A critical public policy implication flowing from this is the importance of governance to developing a milieu wherein welfare can be maximized. To the extent that choice inefficiencies exist, this might also yield inefficiencies in production, lowering the level of material wellbeing from what it would be in a world of choice x-efficiencies. Moreover, choice x-inefficiencies can also contribute to lower overall welfare levels, examples of which might include higher rates of mortality, lower levels of life expectancy, or gender biases that yield missing females. Correcting for choice x-inefficiencies can, therefore, be welfare improving from a variety of perspectives. The conventional worldview, by denying the possibility of choice x-inefficiencies, overlooks the potential and substantive welfare losses that might arise from an institutional setting that is not conducive to the formation of true preferences and the capacity of individuals to actualise these preferences.

An alternative theory also provides an underlying theoretical framework with which to construct empirical measures of the extent of choice x-inefficiencies across societies and groups of individuals and thereby measure the gaps in the socio-economic and legal environment that serve to generate choice x-inefficiencies. It would be possible to construct an ideal preference index (IPI)—analogous to the United Nations' *Human Development Index*. An IPI would, in part, be based on various measures of human and consumer rights and educational attainment. This endeavour is part of my ongoing research agenda. Deviations from some ideal would be one measure of choice x-inefficiency. One can argue that societies weak in the realm of human, consumer and gender rights will be characterized by relatively high levels of choice x-inefficiency and, therefore, by lower levels of socio-economic wellbeing. Such societies and the individuals living in such societies would be operating below their ideal (x-efficient) choice possibility frontier (theoretically analogous to the production possibility frontier).

In reality, given that individuals are characterized by heterogeneous preferences, not everyone can be expected to achieve their preferred or true preferences, when the realization of one person's preference precludes the realization of another person's. This point, it is worth reiterating, is largely assumed away in the conventional wisdom. Such zero-sum games do not occur, however, with regards to different preferences for most goods and services. My consumption of 'health foods' does not preclude your consumption of 'fast foods'. But a person's desire for fewer children might conflict with their partner's desire for more children. The most that can be hoped for in the real world of scarcity is that individuals are provided with the capacity to construct their true preferences and are provided with the opportunities to realize them. When conflicts arise, the best that can be expected is that individuals will be provided with the ability to freely debate and discuss their differences and arrive at compromises, all of which can be expected, in turn, to impact on their final preferences as they evolve over historical time. This can, but need not, result in some convergence, in preferences. The alternative is the authoritarian one, where preferences and choices are imposed. What becomes critical for human wellbeing is the capacity and freedom to construct true preferences and the capacity and freedom to realize these preferences.

Perhaps Berlin (1968, p. 168) said it best:

> *The world that we encounter in ordinary experience is one in which we are faced with choices between ends equally ultimate and choices equally absolute, and the realization of some which must inevitably involve the sacrifice of others. Indeed, it is because this is their situation that man must place such immense value upon the freedom to choose.*

References

Altman, M. (1998). A high wage path to economic growth and development. *Challenge: The Magazine of Economic Affairs, 41*, 91–104.

Altman, M. (1999a). X-efficiency. In P. O'Hara (Ed.), *Encyclopedia of political economy* (pp. 1271–1273). London: Routledge.

Altman, M. (1999b). A theory of population growth when women really count. *Kyklos, 52*, 27–43.

Altman, M. (2001a). *Worker satisfaction and economic performance.* Armonk, NY: M.E. Sharpe Publishers.

Altman, M. (2001b). Behavioural economics. In J. Michie (Ed.), *Reader's guide to the social sciences.* London: Fitzroy Dearborn Publishers.

Altman, M. (2005). Behavioral economics, rational inefficiencies, fuzzy sets, and public policy. *Journal of Economic Issues, 34*, 683–706.

Altman, M. (2006). Human agency and free will: Choice and determinism in economics. *International Journal of Social Economics, 33*, 677–697.

Altman, M., & Lamontagne, L. (2004). Gender, human capabilities and culture within the household economy: Different path to socio-economic well-being? *International Journal of Socio-Economics, 31*, 325–364.

Becker, G. S. (1996). *Accounting for tastes.* Cambridge, MA: Harvard University Press.

Berlin, I. (1968). *Four essays on liberty.* Oxford, New York, London: Oxford University Press.

Davis, J. B. (2003). *The theory of the individual in economics: Identity and value.* London, New York: Routledge.

Dolfsma, W. (2002). Mediated preferences—How institutions affect consumption. *Journal of Economic Issues, 36*, 449–457.

Frantz, R. (1997). *X-efficiency: Theory, evidence and applications* (2nd ed.). Boston/Dordrecht/London: Kluwer Academic Publishers.

George, D. (2001a). *Preference pollution: How markets create desires we dislike.* Ann Arbor: University of Michigan Press.

George, D. (2001b). Unpreferred preferences: Unavoidable or a failure of the market? *Eastern Economic Journal, 27*, 463–479.

Gigerenzer, G. (2007). *Gut feelings: The intelligence of the unconscious.* New York: Viking.

Harsanyi, J. (1982). Morality and the theory of rational behavior. In A. Sen & B. Williams (Eds.), *Utilitarianism and beyond* (pp. 39–62). Cambridge, UK: Cambridge University Press.

Ignatieff, M. (2001). *Human rights as politics and idolatry.* Princeton, NJ: Princeton University Press.

Kuran, T. (1995). *Private truths, public lies: The social consequences of preference falsification.* Cambridge, MA: Harvard University Press.

Leibenstein, H. (1957). The theory of underemployment in densely populated backward areas. In H. Leibenstein (Ed.), *Economic backwardness and economic growth: Studies in the theory of economic development* (pp. 58–76). New York: Wiley.

Leibenstein, H. (1966). Allocative efficiency vs. X-efficiency. *American Economic Review, 56,* 392–415.

Leibenstein, H. (1979). A branch of economics is missing: Micro-micro theory. *Journal of Economic Literature, 17,* 477–502.

March, J. J. (1978). Bounded rationality, ambiguity, and the engineering of choice. *Bell Journal of Economics, 9,* 587–608.

Mill, J. S. (2002). *The basic writings of John Stuart Mill: On liberty, the subjection of women, and Utilitatrianism.* New York: Modern Library.

Nussbaum, M. (1999). *Sex and social justice.* Oxford: Oxford University Press.

Nussbaum, M. (2000). *Women and human development: The capabilities approach.* New York: Cambridge University Press.

Sen, A. (1990). Gender and cooperative conflicts. In I. Tinker (Ed.), *Persistent inequalities: Women and world development* (pp. 123–149). New York and Oxford: Oxford University Press.

Sen, A. (1999). *Reason before identity.* Oxford: Oxford University Press.

Sen, A. (2000). *Development as freedom.* New York: Anchor Books.

Sen, A. (2009). *The idea of justice.* London, New York: Allen Lane.

Simon, H. A. (1987). Behavioral economics. In J. Eatwell, M. Millgate, & P. Newman (Eds.), *The new Palgrave: A dictionary of economics.* Macmillan: London and Basingstoke.

Stigler, G. J. (1961). The economics of information. *Journal of Political Economy, 69,* 213–225.

Stiglitz, J. (1985). Information and economic analysis: A perspective. *Economic Journal, Supplement: Conference Papers, 95,* 21–41.

Thaler, R. H., & Sunstein, C. R. (2003). Libertarian paternalism. *American Economic Review, 93*(2), 175–179.

Thaler, R. H., & Sunstein, C. R. (2008). *Nudge: Improving decisions about health, wealth, and happiness.* Yale University Press.

Tomer, J. (1995). Good habits and bad habits: A new age model of preference formation. *Journal of Socio-Economics, 25,* 619–638.

Tversky, A., & Kahneman, D. (1981). The framing of decisions and the psychology of choice. *Science, 211,* 453–458.

Twitchell, J. B. (1999). *Lead us not into temptation: The triumph of American materialism.* New York: Columbia University Press.

Chapter 7

Inside the black box of the firm: Why choice, power and preferences matter for productivity and efficiency

Chapter outline

Introduction	147	Foundations of x-efficiency theory	163
Origins of efficiency wage theory	150	Linking x-efficiency and	
Real wages, effort variability, and		efficiency theories	178
efficiency wages	151	Conclusion	183
Efficiency wage theory revised	156	References	185

Introduction

In this chapter, expanding and elaborating on points discussed in Chapter 5, I present a more detailed and nuanced discussion of the role played by making the realistic assumption about effort discretion (how smart and hard one works) for an understanding of economic efficiency and economic or material wellbeing. This also has implications for public policy that could facilitate increased economic efficiency. This discussion is important if one is to integrate the decisions that individuals make inside the firm with regards to effort input to an understanding of the determinants of economic efficiency. In this narrative, individuals have a choice over how smart and hard they work, unlike in the conventional economic narrative. And, this allows for a discussion of the complexity of decision-making inside real world firms.

Harvey Leibenstein made critical contributions to the theory of the firm and our appreciation of the importance of human agency to economic performance through his development of efficiency wage and x-efficiency theories. The former set the basis for contemporary efficiency wage theory such as developed by Akerlof (1980, 1982, 1984), Shapiro and Stiglitz (1984), and Stiglitz (1976, 1987). Although x-efficiency theory has not received the same press as efficiency wage theory, the latter is a sub-set of the former and has become central to a multitude of empirical works attempting to measure the extent to which efficiency deviates from the neoclassical ideal where it is assumed that effort input is maximized by economic agents (Frantz, 1997).

X-efficiency theory raises critical questions with regards to the modus operandi of the firm in the real economy. Moreover, it presents an approach to the theory of the firm which differs in important domains from the behavioural economics of Simon (1987a, 1987b) where bounded rationality and satisficing behaviours reign supreme (Altman, 2001b). Leibenstein pays more focused and nuanced attention to incentives, individual or micro–micro motivations, and competitive pressures in determining individual choice within the firm and thereby economic outcomes. Leibenstein's approach to the firm and to agency also differs substantively from the transaction cost analysis pioneered by Williamson (1975, 1985). For Leibenstein, the economic problems which he identifies cannot be explained by bounded rationality or transaction costs per se and would remain in place even in their absence.

Both his x-efficiency and efficiency wage theories yield analytical predictions which differ substantively from those yielded by the conventional wisdom which, in turn, suggest alternative firm-level and public policy. Moreover, unlike contemporary efficiency wage theories, Lebeinstein's narrative raises the possibility for there being a full employment efficiency wage equilibrium. Contemporary efficiency wage theory, on the other hand, purports to explain persistent levels of involuntary unemployment as a product of rational firms choosing a unique efficiency (real) wage which is above what is required to clear the labour market.

Leibenstein's work on x-efficiency and efficiency wage theory also presents a face of behavioural economics which is largely absent from the current discourse on the subject (Altman, 2003) wherein the focus is upon biases and errors in behaviour as demonstrated in experimental or hypothetical settings, exemplified in the work of Kahneman and Tversky (1979; Tversky & Kahneman, 1981). Leibenstein's focus is on how firms and agents within the firm actually function and how theory should be revised so that the underlying assumptions of theory best reflect the realistic behavioural assumptions of human agents. This approach is adopted in response to what Leibenstein regards as serious flaws in the contemporary theory of the firm, and his efforts to design theory that yields greater explanatory power and more reasonable public policy. In this case, the good predictors are mapped on reasonable behavioural assumptions of the economic agents relevant to the modelling question. Theories, wherein good analytical predictions are disconnected from the underlying behavioural modelling assumptions need be questioned, revisited and revised. In conventional economics, assumptions do not matter. Only the precision of the predictions is of analytical importance (Altman, 1999; Friedman, 1953; Reder, 1982).

Although Leibenstein's adopts the neoclassical benchmark of rationality in his theoretical discourse with regards to optimal behavioural, referring to deviations form this norm as being irrational or quasi-rational, this is not core to his theoretical narrative as compared to its centrality for the Kahneman–Tversky approach to behavioural economics. Deviation from the neoclassical theoretical 'ideal' is not considered to represent a bias or error in decision making nor is the economic agent who deviates from neoclassical rationality in the realm of production considered to be lacking in substantive intelligence—which is what can be inferred from the Kahneman–Tversky approach. The language of quasi-rationality and irrationality, which has caused Leibenstein's work so much grief amongst mainstream economists, can easily be replaced with the assumption of rational and even maximizing agents (in terms of utility or profit) engaging in either x-efficient or x-inefficient behaviour. Neither behaviours need be irrational no matter how or the extent to which they differ from neoclassical norms. The point of Leibenstein's modelling is to provide space for the reality that economic agents can quite readily and for good reason deviate from what many neoclassical economists tend to refer to as rational behaviour. What many neoclassical economists refer to as rational behaviour often is not all related to substantive rationality and is simply and arbitrarily definitional. Related to the discourse on efficiency wage and x-efficiency theory there is nothing rational about maximizing effort if the necessary incentives and constraints necessary to do so are not.

In this chapter, I examine the basic premises of Leibenstein's x-efficiency and efficiency wage theories and how these contrast with the conventional wisdom. Leibenstein's basic modelling is critically assessed in the context of some of the contemporary elaborations of his work. I also extend x-efficiency and efficiency wage theory, based upon my own research. I discuss more nuanced definitions and applications of x-efficiency and efficiency wages. This brings us to a discussion of the implications and conditions for the existence of multiple equilibria in levels of x-efficiency and in efficiency wages achieved by rational optimizing economic agents operating in a variety of market structure ranging from competitive to monopoly. I argue that rational economic agents can be x-inefficient irrespective of product conditions or transaction costs and efficiency wages need not be causally related to sub-optimal levels of unemployment. Given that neither markets nor the underlying character of the economic agent guarantees economic efficiency the door is left wide open for the inclusion of macro and micro level institutional parameters as well as cultural and power relationships as critical determinants of a society's level of material wellbeing.

Key to Leibenstein's contribution to economic theory is his insistence on the dynamic or dialectical linkage between theory and reality or the deductive and inductive sides of economics. Just in terms of effort discretion this approach to economic reasoning forces significant revisions to economic theory, analysis and public policy. The analytical world becomes more complex and economic theory is reconfigured so that it is better able to analyse a world of human agents engaged in choice behaviour, where choice cannot be modelled usefully as given by some 'ideal' which is unrelated to the real world of choice behaviour and the complex decision-making environment within which it is embedded. Leibenstein does not deny the importance of simplifying assumptions in the construction of economic theory, which by definition will not be 'realistic'. Rather what is of concern to Leibenstein is that such simplifying assumptions be reasonable given the analytical questions one's theory is designed to address. Otherwise, such building-block assumptions yield theories which generate poor analytical predictions or theories which cannot explain cause and effect.

Leibenstein breaks with the conventional literature by assuming that effort is a discretionary variable in the process of production in both its quality and quantity dimensions. Although emphasis has often been placed in the derived literature on the quantity of effort inputs, for Leibenstein both dimensions are of critical importance. Indeed, one might maximize the quantity of effort without even coming close to x-efficiency in production given critical gaps on the quality side of effort inputs; this quality dimension has always been important throughout economic history. Leibenstein argues that effort need not be maximized at some ideal level. Contrary to the assumptions of the conventional wisdom, neither market forces nor the inherent disposition of economic agents (part of her/his utility maximizing function) guarantee that effort is fixed at some ideal maximum.[a] If effort is not maximized neither is material welfare—an analytical prediction which contravenes the conventional economic wisdom. In this case human agency, the freedom and ability to choose different effort levels becomes fundamental to any understanding of an economy's level of overall economic efficiency. Leibenstein's modelling suggests and provides a framework for analysing a genre of sub-optimal economic performance which has no place in the conventional worldview where 'price distortions' predicated upon deviations from a perfectly competitive ideal is the key culprit yielding 'deadweight' losses, which only type of economic inefficiency.

Origins of efficiency wage theory

The prospective positive causal relationship between wages and labour efficiency was made by economic luminaries such as Adam Smith and Arthur Cecil Pigou. Smith (1937, p. 81) argues in the *Wealth of Nations*:

> *The liberal reward for labour, as it encourages the propagation, so it increases the industry of the common people. The wages of labour are the encouragement of industry, which, like every other human quality, improves in proportion to the encouragement it receives. A plentiful subsistence increases the bodily strength of*

---

a. Leibenstein, himself, places considerable to weight on the extent to which product markets are competitive to the determination of the level of x-efficiency, given the preferences of decision-makers. In my extension of x-efficiency theory, I argue that even with highly competitive product markets, high levels of x-inefficiency are sustainable if the firm can compensate for high levels of x-inefficiency by reducing various production costs. Given the preference or utility function of many firm decision-makers, this alternative to x-efficient but higher wage firm performance, is preferred as it can be deemed easier to achieve in the short term and is consistent with the mental models used more often than not wherein cutting labour-related costs is regarded as the key to corporate success.

the labourer, and comfortable hope of bettering his condition, and of ending his days perhaps in ease and plenty, animates him to exert that strength to the utmost. Where wages are high, accordingly, we shall always find the workmen more active, diligent, and expeditious, than where they are low...

Thus, for Smith effort was not fixed at some pre-determined maximum. Rather effort is a dependant variable affected by conditions of work.

Pigou (1952, Chapter 10), in *The Economics of Welfare*, argues that increasing the income of the less well to do, serves to improve their productivity by improving their nutritional levels and health. As well, labour productivity is increased as one invests in the education and skill upgrading of labour through the transfer of income from the well to do to the less-well-to-do. Pigou was arguing against the dominant worldview that an individual's capabilities were predetermined biologically. For Pigou, increasing wages is not the ideal means of improving the capabilities of the poor, although he notes that improvements in wages might encourage employers to increase productivity through organizational and technological change (Pigou, 1952, Chapter 17).

Leibenstein's resurrects the notion that wages and labour productivity are positively and causally correlated to address the apparent empirical paradox of the simultaneous existence of persistent unemployment and positive real wages in less developed countries. He argues that 'surplus' labour should drive real wages downwards to clear the labour market. Surplus labour cannot exist in long run equilibrium as long as real wages are flexible downwards. Thus, Leibenstein assumes that persistent unemployment in less developed economies is largely a supply side problem, one which is largely a product of the downward inflexibility of real wage rates. Leibenstein writes (1957, p. 91): 'It is observed that agricultural workers in underdeveloped areas do receive a positive wage, yet the notion of surplus labour receiving a positive wage or income is a contradiction in the light of the received theory. There is clearly some need to reconcile what are presumed to be the broad facts and our theory on the matter.' Moreover, if clearing the labour market requires that real wages be depressed to zero, this possibility, argues Leibenstein (1958, p. 92), 'cannot be seriously entertained'. Empirically, in the long run we have neither full employment nor zero wages. Rather we have both unemployment and positive real wages which do not vary to clear the labour market. Leibenstein's way out of this dilemma is re-focus our attention to the (Leibenstein 1958, p. 94), 'often-neglected relationship between the wage level and productivity'. But in this narrative, workers do not have discretion over their effort inputs. Rather, it is determined more or less mechanically by the level of nutritional inputs consumed by workers.

Real wages, effort variability, and efficiency wages

Leibenstein, basing himself upon the contemporary empirical evidence, makes the case that there is clear relationship between labour income and caloric intake and thereby between labour income and productivity. He also points out that there is evidence for a strong statistical relationship between caloric intake and productivity, albeit Leibenstein does not explain why healthier workers (employees as opposed to self-employed) should work harder. Leibenstein appears to use higher real wages as a proxy for increasing the nutritional wellbeing of workers, assuming that higher wages will be translated into a higher nutritional intake by workers and that the latter will yield higher effort levels. But in terms of causation, it would be important to determine what motivates workers who can work harder—because of their higher caloric intake—to actually work harder. Here workers have agency or dioscretion over how hard or well they work. Do higher real wages serve as a dual mechanism which serves to both allow for a higher caloric intake by workers and to motivate them to actually work harder? Lebeinstein only confronts the issue of incentives in his narratives on x-efficiency theory.

With regards to the empirical relationship between effort input and nutritional levels Leibenstein (1958, p. 96) concludes: 'There is an obvious relationship between income and output, and, furthermore, it is clear that up to some point the amount of effective work is increased as wages are increased'. For this reason, it is critical to abandon the conventional assumption that labour supply is one dimensional and given by labour supply in terms of hours of work. It is necessary to recognize that labour supply is comprised of both a time and an effort dimension where the latter cannot be assumed to be fixed or invariant to changes in labour income. Therefore, the amount of effective labour supply is variable even if the amount of labour supply measured in terms of hours of work or number of workers weighted by hours worked per worker is fixed. Once effort is recognized as a variable input one can resolve the paradox of there being persistent unemployment with positive (or at least non-diminishing) real wages. Leibenstein (1958, p. 97) emphasizes, however, that his assumed positive relationship between real wages and productivity has its limit so that after workers realize a certain standard of living and therefore a particular level of caloric intake, effort input becomes perfectly inelastic to changes in real wages.

Leibenstein argues that since changes in the wage rate positively affect productivity, changes in the wage rates also affects the net revenue to the firm (or landlord in an agricultural society) in a much more complex fashion than what is modelled in the conventional model where effort inputs are invariant to changes in wages. Changing the wage rate up or down affects total cost given total revenue which it cannot do in a world where effort input is invariant to wages. Leibenstein (1958, p. 101) maintains that given this relationship:

> ...up to some [real] wage rate, net revenue is likely to increase. However, beyond some wage rate there must certainly be a reversal of this tendency. At some point an increase in wages will bring with it no increase in the amount of work supplied [in terms of effort input] per man. Even before this point is reached, as wages rise, the amount of work done per man will increase less than proportionately. Hence, beyond some point, the higher the wage rate, the lower the net revenue.

Leibenstein in fact postulates diminishing returns of effort input to increasing wages such that there exists one unique wage rate which maximizes the net revenue to the firm. Any other wage rate yields lower net revenue. If the firm chooses such a wage and this wage exceeds the market clearing wage than unemployment will exist. A drop in real wages would be resisted by profit maximizing firms since a fall in wages results in a drop in net revenue given the positive relationship between effort input and wages. Unemployment can be reduced only if lower real wages are paid; but this would be inconsistent with profit maximizing firm behaviour. Therefore, involuntary unemployment persists. Such an argument is quite similar to the contemporary efficiency wage theories of persistent involuntary unemployment in developed market economies, pioneered by Akerlof (1984), Akerlof and Yellen (1986, 1988, 1990), Bewley (1999), Shapiro and Stiglitz (1984), and Solow (1979). The latter pay little heed to Leibenstein's pioneering contribution.

Leibenstein's specific argument is built around a set of very special assumptions wherein not only is effort a variable input which is positively affected by the level of real wages, but also each real wage rate is attached to a particular marginal product of labour curve and that each such curve is related in a particular fashion to one another. Not all of Leibenstein's special assumptions are required to make an 'efficiency wage' case for persistent unemployment. Moreover, Leibenstein's modelling of the labour market just like the contemporary efficiency wage literature is constructed to 'explain' involuntary unemployment as a product of real wages which persist above the market clearing real wage. Ergo, for there to be lower levels of involuntary unemployment, there must be lower real wages, given that the level of effective demand suffices to render employment to the number of workers which firms would employ at the market clearing real wage.

In Fig. 7.1 which is based on Leibenstein (1958, p. 101, Fig. 6), there are four marginal product of labour curves each associated with different wage rates. The higher the wage rate the higher the marginal product curve. But Leibenstein (1958, p. 98) constructs these curves, arbitrarily assuming (without evidence) that the rate of decline in marginal product should be greater for the higher marginal product curve. Thus, the marginal product curves cross and moreover the curves are constructed in such a manner that higher wages are positively related to lower equilibrium (marginal product equals the wage) levels of employment. Moreover, the marginal product curves are constructed so that the net revenue generated by each curve is different, where net revenue is given by the area above the equilibrium wage rate. Each such net revenue is referred to by Leibenstein as optimal revenue. Thus, each real wage yields a different optimal revenue. Leibenstein assumes that there are diminishing returns to effort, conforming to classic textbook formulations of diminishing returns. This yields a U-shaped optimal revenue curve with one unique maximum optimal (net) revenue corresponding with one unique real wage rate. This is illustrated in Fig. 7.2 by optimal revenue curve $e_0 e_1 e_2 e_3$. The maximum net revenue is given

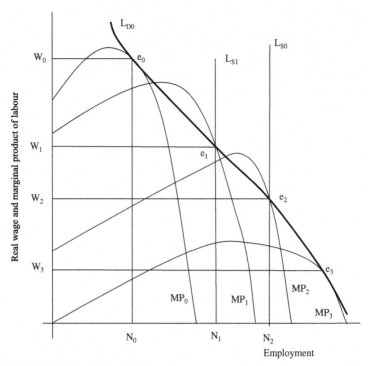

FIG. 7.1 Labour demand and marginal product.

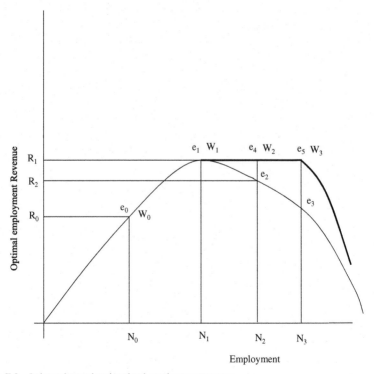

FIG. 7.2 Labour demand and optimal employment revenue.

by N_0 employment and W_1 wages. Thus, there is one unique wage rate which maximizes net revenue, but the unique wage rate need not be consistent with full employment. Deviations, up or down, from this net revenue maximizing wage and level of employment yields lower levels of employment.

In Leibenstein's modelling, employment is negatively related to the real wage rate as it is in the conventional wisdom wherein no effort variability is assumed. In Fig. 7.1, L_{D0} is the negatively sloped demand curve for labour generated by Leibenstein's construction of marginal product curves and the equilibrium wage rates which generate them. This demand curve is a type of envelope curve, one which is constructed by connecting each unique equilibrium point, where the wage rate equals the marginal product of labour, for every given marginal product curve. In the conventional modelling, the demand curve for labour is given by a unique and negatively sloped marginal product of labour curve which is invariant to changes in the wage rate. By construction Leibenstein identifies W_2 as the market clearing wage and its associated marginal product curve as the de facto market clearing marginal product of labour curve. At W_2, N_2 of labour or full employment is achieved. But the MP_2, W_2's marginal product curve, does not yield maximum net revenue. Thus, there is a disjuncture between the full employment and the real wage rate. For full employment to be achieved employers would have to accept less than maximum net revenue by paying out lower real wages which, in turn, generates lower levels of effort input.

Leibenstein argues that given the existence of excess labour supply at maximum net revenue—labour demand, N_1, is less than full employment labour supply N_2—market forces generate downward pressure on the real wage. If market forces are allowed to come into play, net revenue will diminish. Leibenstein argues that in order to prevent market forces from bidding real wages down and thereby diminishing net revenue to employers, employers, as a group, must devise institutional arrangements which will absorb the surplus labour even if this surplus is not actually effectively employed and represent no more than disguised unemployment or featherbedding. Thus, employers can be expected to employ some workers at a higher than 'market clearing' real wage.

Employers choose a real wage-marginal product of labour combination which is greater than what would be chosen had the market clearing real wage prevailed. But employers employ more workers than can be justified in terms of the equality between the real wage and the marginal product of labour. There will be some workers who are employed whose marginal product is less than their real wage. Still, Leibenstein argues, employers are better off in terms of net revenue than if the lower market clearing real wage prevailed. Employing workers whose real wage is greater than their marginal product wherein this wage is greater than the market clearing wage yields net revenue above what would be generated by the lower market clearing real wage. Net revenue is below the maximum, however, since a percentage of the net revenue accruing to employers must be dispersed to the relative low productivity 'surplus' employees. Leibenstein (1958, p. 102) writes:

The essential aspect of the argument is that, where the amount of work put forth is related to the wage, landlords can improve their position by employing excess labor rather than by employing the 'optimum' amount of labor and permitting the unemployed to drive wages down. If wages are driven down, they may reach a level at which the amount of work done is so reduced [this would be a product of a diminution in the level of effort inputs] that landlords' net revenue decreases.

Leibenstein effectively assumes that an 'efficiency wage' is paid only because employees (landlords in Leibenstein's narrative), can effectively collude over the long term to absorb the surplus labour. He even argues that serfdom represent a type of institutional arrangement designed to keep real wages relatively high (Leibenstein 1958, p. 99). If such collusion does not take place or is unstable there can be no efficiency wage. Leibenstein does not discuss why such collusive arrangements should be stable or even if they existed historically. Nor does he discuss whether an empirical case can be made for serfdom as a form of high wage institutional arrangement or even for employers inclusive of landlords working towards keeping real wages relatively high. Leibenstein's modelling predicts that employers will act in manner (in his narrative, collectively) to keep wages high relative to the market clearing wage and should therefore be advocates of 'high wage' economies (in the context or relatively poor economies).

In Leibenstein's modelling, surplus labour is not a product of low wages per se, it is rather a problem of labour displaced as a product of increased labour productivity engendered by higher real wage induced effort inputs and society's inability to absorb this surplus at the high wage rates. This points one back in the direction of lower wage rates as the solution to the surplus labour problem where this solution need not be obtained if profit maximizing employers pay workers the above market clearing real wage which is what maximizes employers' net revenue. In this model, where effort is a function of nutritional inputs, too high wages generates problems in the employment market given profit maximizing firms.

But it is important to note that the assumption of surplus labour, which was quite prevalent in the 1950s and early 1960s, especially following Lewis' (1954) classic work on the subject, has been seriously questioned in the empirical literature (Little, 1982, Chapter 6). Moreover, there is strong contemporary evidence suggesting a negative empirical relationship between real wages and unemployment—as real wages rise or are relatively high, unemployment rates fall or are relatively low (Blanchflower & Oswald, 1995).

Efficiency wage theory revised

The contemporary efficiency (Akerlof, 1980, 1982, 1984; Akerlof & Yellen, 1986, 1988, 1990) wage literature attempts to address the stability of efficiency wages in the face of persistent unemployment or access supply on the labour market. The essence of the argument is that efficiency wages are stable given that they are consistent with the profit maximizing objective function of firms or employers. If employers as a group can be assumed to be profit maximizers than any deviations from efficiency wages will generate lower profits. The latter scenario is completely consistent with Leibenstein's modelling. In this case, each firm acting independently—no collusion is required—will pay efficiency wages. Thus, even if surplus labour attempts to bid wages down, employers will not accept these bids since lower wage offers would negatively affect profits (net revenues in Leibenstein 1958) through their negative impact upon the level of effort inputs.

I reconstruct the case for the stability of efficiency wages, absent collusion, adapting with some liberty Leibenstein's graphic representation of 'efficiency wages'. In standard neoclassical theory surplus labour results in lower real wages and more labour is employed, given the existence of effective demand for labour's output, along the economy's labour demand curve which is derived from the individual firms' marginal product of labour curve. Profit maximizing firms accept lower real wage bids by the unemployed for employment. But in the traditional neoclassical narrative, the marginal product of labour curve is invariant to changes in the wage rate. In Fig. 7.3, for markets to clear at labour supply N_2, the wage diminishes to W_2 along marginal product of labour curve MP_1. But according to the 'efficiency wage' story, the marginal product of labour curve shifts inward with decreases to real wages. In this scenario, where

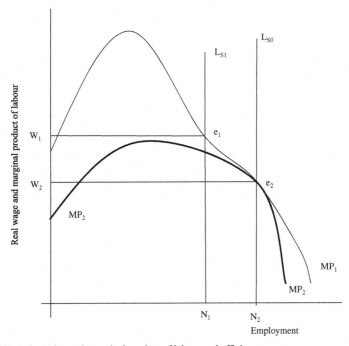

FIG. 7.3 Labour demand, marginal product of labour and efficiency wages.

the marginal product of labour curve shifts to MP_2, the market clearing wage remains at W_2. But this is no longer the revenue maximizing real wage, which in Leibenstein's narrative determines the preferred real which wage of rational maximizing employers. Rational employers would choose wage rate W_1 which is associated with marginal revenue curve MP_1, since this wage-marginal revenue combination maximizes net revenue—the area above W_2 in MP_1 is less than the area above W_1 in MP_2. However, with the higher real wage there are fewer workers employed (N_1 as opposed to N_2), even though they are willing to work for a lower real wage. Employers, acting independently, have no economic incentive accept lower real wage bids since this would yield lower net revenue. Thus, the non-market clearing higher real wage is sustainable without any collusion on the part employers. In stark contrast, in the conventional neoclassical model lower real wages are always better than higher real wages, from the perspective of the net revenue or profit maximizing employers, since this always yields higher net revenue.

The contemporary efficiency wage literature, especially that related to the work of Akerlof, ties the notion of efficiency wages to the world of developed economies wherein wages affect the level of effort input through their motivational effects on workers. In Leibenstein's narrative the latter step is missing, at least explicitly, as he draws a direct and tight link between wages to caloric and related nutritional intake to effort input. In the contemporary narrative effort input is increased with higher wages as higher wages are a proxy for fairness and the like. But no detailed discussion is provided with regards to how wages per se fit into the overall industrial relations bundle. At best, the wage rate is viewed as a proxy for all that which motivates workers (Altman, 2002). But the bottom line in this literature, as in the Leibenstein narrative, is that there is a unique net revenue or profit maximizing 'efficiency wage', whatever its psychological or sociological determinants.

It is also important to note an important distinction between Leibenstein's solution to the involuntary unemployment, which amounts to featherbedding, and one proposed in the contemporary efficiency wage literature such as is articulated in Akerlof, Dickens, and Perry (2000). Leibenstein argues that firms must hire more workers than would be consistent with profit maximizing so as to prevent real wages from being bid downwards through the excess supply of labour. Therefore, workers would be employed whose marginal product is less than their real wage. If employers fail to do so—and failure is assured absent a resolution to fundamental coordination problems—real wages and net revenue would fall. In the contemporary efficiency wage literature, no coordination problem presents itself so that the efficiency wage is stable as would be a certain amount of involuntary unemployment. But Akerlof et al. (2000) argue that workers are only quasi-rational and that if government institutes a policy of mild inflation workers would accept the lower real wage without reducing their effort inputs into the production process, believing that real wages have not fallen at all—workers are subject to money illusion—yielding higher levels of employment. Thus, government policy can affect the supply side obstacles to full employment by designing policy which causes real wages to fall without workers reacting negatively to this, exactly as would be the case in a world without effort discretion.

Critical to Leibenstein's narrative and that of contemporary efficiency wage theory is the assumption that one needs to explain involuntary unemployment as a product of the downward inflexibility of real wages. Efficiency wage theory is a model designed to explain such downward inflexibility by rational profit maximizing landlords or firm managers/owners. Contemporary efficiency wage theory helps to explain why such downward inflexibility might persist even in the absence of collusion amongst employers and why effort variability might be an important analytical assumption even in higher wage developed economies.

A fundamental attribute of the value added contributed by the efficiency wage literature as it has been articulated by Leibenstein for less developed economies and by Akerlof and others for contemporary economies, is that the downward stickiness is a key obstacle to reducing unemployment. Of course, for Leibenstein the reality of effort variability is of critical importance in other analytical domains, giving rise to his x-efficiency narrative. Be this as it may, the evidence does not provide strong support to the wage stickiness hypothesis nor to the notion of a unique efficiency wage to which all rational employers must converge. The question therefore arises as to how might the reality of effort variability fit into the model of the firm and rational cum maximizing behaviour wherein higher real wages are not a necessary condition for involuntary unemployment and firms need not converge to some unique profit maximizing wage.

What binds the different strands of efficiency wage theory together is that although effort is a variable, this variable adjusts up or down rather mechanistically, ultimately yielding a unique profit maximizing efficiency wage. But human agency, individuals actually choosing their effort levels, is not clearly evident in this modelling of the labour market. But this model differs from the conventional model because effort levels are not fixed; are not independent of movements in other variables in the model.

It is important to recall that the efficiency wage model's predictions flow from the underlying assumptions of the model, where a key assumption is smooth concavity in the marginal effort input-marginal effort product to wage function. In other words, diminishing returns (marginal effort product) to wages is assumed such that net revenue is maximized at some unique wage rate. The mirror image of this postulate is that the marginal product and average product of labour relative to effort input are each maximized at some unique wage. An alternative set of assumptions—the underlying reasoning of which is developed in great detail elsewhere (Altman, 1996, 2001a, 2001b, 2001c, 2001d)—model a world where an array of real wage rates yield the same net profits or unit costs and where higher wages might even be necessary to higher levels of employment. Such scenarios are possible if effort levels are a discretionary variable, but less mechanistically so, as in the efficiency wage literature.

In Fig. 7.4, the marginal product of labour curves are drawn such that they shift upwards with the higher wage—the higher the wage the higher the level of effort inputs. And there is a unique wage associated with each marginal product curve yielding an equilibrium level of employment. The marginal product curves are also constructed such that for each equilibrium level of employment net revenue is equal up to e_1—the area above the wage line is identical. By construction we generate a demand curve for labour which is upward sloping up to equilibrium point e_1. Thereafter, diminishing returns to effort relative to wage increases set in yielding both a lower equilibrium level of employment and lower net revenue at e_0—here we have a backward-bending demand curve for labour. Alternatively, one can model a further employment increase as consistent with the higher wage, but at a lower net revenue. Either way, employment can be maximized for the net revenue maximizing employer at e_1 and N_2. Thus, from the supply side, to increase employment requires higher wages and such higher wages could be paid by net revenue maximizing employers. In this case, employees, are not forced, by their profit maximizing preferences, into paying an efficiency wage that yields sub-optimal levels of employment. Which model should be chosen should be a function of which one best reflects the reality of labour market behaviour.

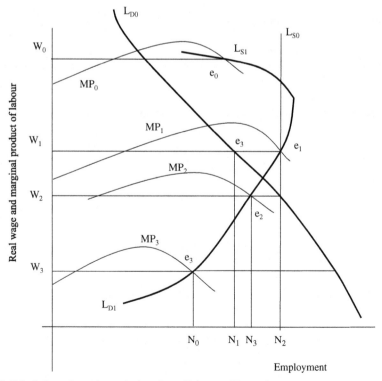

FIG. 7.4   Labour demand, marginal product of labour and increasing wages.

Superimposed, in Fig. 7.4, is the downward sloping labour demand curve generated by Leibenstein's assumptions as illustrated in Fig. 7.1, which is consistent with the contemporary efficiency wage narrative. In the latter scenario equilibrium employment is given by the efficiency wage W_1 at N_1 and a lower wage is required is clear the labour market. From the supply side, for the labour market to clear requires finding a procedure for reducing real wages without such a reduction negatively impacting upon the level of effort inputs such as is suggested by Akerlof et al. (2000), which assumes money illusion on the part of workers.

In the alternative effort variability scenario, employers should be indifferent from the perspective of net profits as to which wage rate from the $W_1W_2W_3$ set to choose. Here, employment is constrained by market or institutional forces which keep real wages relatively low or by demand side constraints. Moreover, given the market and institutional parameters faced by employers, to the extent that they have a preference for lower real wages for psychological reasons or power considerations or because of the short term costs involved in securing productivity increases to compensate for increases in real wages, such preferences can serve to keep real wages relatively low and thereby employment relatively low. Agency becomes fundamentally important. This type of modelling is consistent with the empirics suggesting a positive relationship between real wages and employment (Blanchflower & Oswald, 1995). Higher real wages pose a supply side obstacle to more employment only when productivity does not rise sufficiently to compensate for relatively higher wages. Moreover, in this modelling of effort variability there is no one efficiency wage which employers can be expected to converge towards, since there is an array of wage rates consistent with some unique maximum level of net revenue.

This point is illustrated in Fig. 7.2, where the conventional efficiency wage narrative is contrasted to the alternative mapping. In the alterative scenario, there is an array of employment levels correlated with one maximum net revenue whereas in the conventional model there can be only one level of employment, specified as less than 'full' employment, which is consistent with maximum net revenue. In both scenarios, the higher levels of employment are linked with higher real wages, but not in a causative manner. In the conventional Leibenstein type effort discretion modelling these are not all equilibrium levels of employment. Rather only one level of employment is consistent with equilibrium in terms of maximizing net revenue, but this is not full employment. In the alternative modelling, 'full' employment is realizable at the higher real wage as 'full' employment is consistent with maximum net revenue. Moreover, the alternative modelling is consistent with there being an array of real wages correlated with an array of realizable levels of employment as determined by supply side considerations since an array of real wages yields, up to a point, an identical level of net revenue. And a relatively high wage would here be linked to the full employment rate of unemployment given that aggregate demand side factors suffice to support this unemployment rate allowed for by supply side considerations.

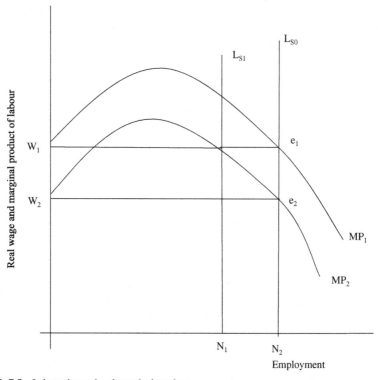

FIG. 7.5   Labour demand and marginal product.

Another take on the alternative model is illustrated in Fig. 7.5, where increasing wages has no negative impact on employment or the marginal revenue of the firm (given by area contained between the marginal product curve and the wage line). Moreover, lowering wages has no positive effect. This is a product of the assumed positive relationship between wages, effort input, and productivity. N2 employment is consistent with W1 and W2. Increasing the wage from W2 to W1 will not reduce employment. If no such relationship exists between wages, effort input, and productivity, this wage increase reduces employment, along MP2 to N1. The labour market clears only if labour supply shifts to LS1 from LS0. Given the above positive relationship between wages, effort input, and productivity, maintaining a particular rate of employment need not be contingent upon keeping wages fixed. Moreover, increasing employment would not be contoingent upon reducing real wages.

In the alternative effort variability modelling of the firm, the persistence of surplus labour (or of involuntary unemployment) is not explained from the supply side as a function of the downward stickiness of real wages. Rather, it points to relatively low real wages as a possible supply side constraint to full employment. In terms of public policy, the alternative modelling suggests that the supply side key to full employment need not be located in mechanisms that serve to lower real wages without generating a negative effort input response. Rather, surplus labour might very well be a product of workers being too unproductive to be employed profitability given their low effort inputs which, in turn, flow from their low real wages.

Foundations of x-efficiency theory

In his discussion of what we now refer to as efficiency wages, Leibenstein focuses upon the relationship between wages and productivity with effort input as the key intermediary variable. In contrast, Leibenstein's focus in his x-efficiency theory is effort variability, holding wages and related variables constant. Leibenstein's x-efficiency theory therefore zeros in upon how effort variability, ceteris paribus, impacts upon costs when effort inputs deviate from some 'ideal' realizable level; a possibility denied in the conventional neoclassical modelling of the firm. Driving effort variability in much of Leibenstein's discourse is the variability of management efficiency and the deviation of much management performance from some optimal level.

Significant to Leibenstein's narrative on x-efficiency theory is his view that the conventional assumption that the firm constitutes the basic or atomic decision making unit in production theory is inappropriate in addressing many key microeconomic issues. Rather he argues the basic decision making unit is the individual wherein an array of individuals comprise the firm. He pays keen attention to the importance which heterogeneous and conflicting preferences amongst firm members can result in deviations from some optimal level of average effort input and thus to the issue of how effort input can be increased where such conflicts exist and how conflict resolution can contribute towards increasing effort input and thereby the degree of x-efficiency. Here agency is of paramount importance. Only when all firm members behave as if they are of one mind—homogeneous preferences dominate across agents—would the conventional and x-efficiency perspective on the firm's decision making process converge.

Leibenstein's focus also tends towards the notion that the absence of adequate competitive pressures is what allows for effort inputs to deviate from some ideal maximum. Thus x-inefficiency can be expected when competitive pressures are slack especially over the long run. Conventional theory tends to assume that competitive pressures are sufficiently tight over the long haul (inclusive of Baumol's (1982) notion of contestable markets) to force agents to behave x-efficiency. Thus, Leibenstein's x-efficiency model presumes that sufficient competitive pressure is critical to the existence of x-efficiency. In the conventional view even in the absence of strong competitive pressures x-inefficiency cannot exist—only allocative inefficiency might result. For Leibenstein absent adequate competitive pressures *both* allocative and x-inefficiencies are generated. This type of modelling can be extended, as it is in Altman (1992, 1996, 1998, 2001a), such that competitive pressures become a contributing variable in generating higher levels of x-efficiency, but need not represent the necessary or sufficient conditions to achieve x-efficiency. In this scenario x-inefficiency can be realized even if markets are contestable and x-efficiency can also be achieved even when competitive pressures are relatively slack. However, ceteris paribus, competitive pressures reduce the degree of freedom afforded to agents with preferences for x-inefficient behaviour.

Once effort variability is recognized of being of some potential analytical importance, given the sustainable existence of slack in competitive pressures, x-efficiency theory suggests the implications of sub-optimal effort inputs upon costs and competitiveness and opens the door to an alternative measure of economic inefficiency, which Leibenstein dubs x-inefficiency, in contrast to allocative inefficiency. Moreover, Leibenstein argues that x-efficiency theory forces us to delve into the micro–micro economics of the firm and thereby into an understanding of how the details of the behaviour of individual agency, of heterogeneous agents, contributes to an understanding of economic outcomes, outcomes which by no means need by optimal even from the conventional perspective. However, by delinking the x-efficiency narrative from a discourse of wages, Leibenstein fails to examine important aspects of x-inefficiency and x-efficiency. But such a delinking is not necessary to x-efficiency theory. One can model x-efficiency and x-inefficiency from the perspective of fixed and changing real wages—which links efficiency wage and x-efficiency theories—allowing for analyses of different aspects of firm behaviour and competitive strategy.

Leibenstein sets up the basic model of x-inefficiency/x-efficiency in his classic 1966 *American Economic Review* publication, where his alternative modelling of economic efficiency is derived from his evaluation of the evidence on economic efficiency. Although Leibenstein builds upon his initial modelling over the course of the next two decades, often in response to critics, the essence of his x-efficiency theory remains true to the 1966 vintage model. X-efficiency is all about making the best use of resources with regards to effort inputs, where the latter is not a guaranteed outcome of the optimal (allocatively efficient) combination of inputs, property rights, or information flows.

As with efficiency wage theory, Leibenstein developed x-efficiency theory in an attempt to better come to terms with economic reality. He points out that in his view, efficiency is at the core of economics, however conventional theory is beset with concern for allocative efficiency which Leibenstein concludes, from the evidence, is of trivial importance with regards to its size effect, being much less than 1% in market economies (Leibenstein, 1966, p. 392). However, Leibenstein (1966, p. 392) argues that economic inefficiency is of no doubt of considerable importance but conventional microeconomics focuses on the relatively insignificant allocative inefficiencies to the exclusion of non-allocative inefficiencies. Leibenstein refers to the latter as x-inefficiencies, which encompasses effort variability and its determinants. He (Leibenstein, 1966, p. 408) argues that:

> *The data suggest that cost reduction that is essentially a result of improvement*
> *in X-efficiency is likely to be an important component of the observed [Solow]*

residual in economic growth...a significant part of the residual does not depend on the type of considerations that have been prominent in the literature in recent years, such as those that are embodied in capital accumulation of invention.

Any reduction in x-inefficiency serves to increase growth by increasing output per unit of input. Leibenstein hypothesizes that a large portion of Solow's residual can be accounted for by firms becoming more x-efficient. But such a contribution to growth cannot be contemplated in the context of the conventional wisdom, with implications for analyses and public policy.

A key point made by Leibenstein is that conventional theory is structured in a manner which precludes a determination of whether or not non-allocative inefficiencies exist since it is assumed that firms are at all times x-efficient in production. Leibenstein (1966, p. 407) argues:

The conventional theoretical assumption, although it is rarely stated, is that inputs have a fixed specification and yield a fixed performance. This ignores other likely possibilities. Inputs may have a fixed specification that yields a variable performance, or they may be of a variable specification and yield a variable performance...The most common case is that of labor services of various kinds that have variable specifications and variable performance—although labor markets sometimes operate as if much of the labor of a given class has a fixed specification. Moreover, it is exceedingly rare for all elements of performance in a labor contract to be spelled out. A good deal is left to custom, authority, and whatever institutional techniques are available to management as well as to individual discretion and judgment...For these and other reasons it seems clear that it is one thing to purchase or hire inputs in a given combination; it is something else to get a predetermined output out of them.

Thus, the conventional assumption of there being a fixed and optimal relationship between inputs and output appears to fly in the face of an abundance of evidence. Microeconomic theory should be constructed to incorporate the possibility of both allocative and non-allocative inefficiencies. The conventional worldview then becomes a sub-set of the broader encompassing theoretical framework suggested by Leibenstein.

From his perusal of a wide array of empirical results Leibenstein (1966, p. 404) concludes that: '...there is a great deal of possible variation in output of similar amounts of capital and labor and for similar techniques, in the broad sense, to the extent that technique is determined by similar types of equipment'. Such variation in output cannot be explained for the most part by variations in human capital, transaction costs, or property rights, for example (Leibenstein, 1966, 1978, 1979, 1983). In other words, output can vary considerably across firms and economies even when one controls for technology, human capital, transaction costs, and property rights. Leibenstein (1966, p. 407) concludes from the available data that: 'The simple fact is that neither individuals nor firms work as hard, nor do they search for information as effectively, as they could. The importance of motivation and its association with degree of effort and search arises because the relation between inputs and outputs is *not* a determinate one'. Therefore, firms and economies typically do not operate on the outer bound of their production possibility frontier; rather they operate well within the outer bound (Leibenstein, 1966, p. 413).

Related to this point, Leibenstein (1973, p. 766) reiterates that many economists are want to think of x-efficiency as equivalent to technical efficiency or engineering efficiency. He reject the term of technical efficiency since it has come to imply, in conventional microtheory, '...that there is some sort of 'central controller' of inputs who, at least in principle, is able to determine how the inputs are to be combined in order to pursue the objectives of the firm (i.e. minimize costs)'. The term x-efficiency does not imply, as does technical efficiency, that firms will typically achieve technical efficiency and that there is some central controller or planner who acts as a representative agent who realizes x-efficiency in production as a byproduct of her or his objective function irrespective of market structure and firm culture. Given the presumption of technical efficiency, conventional theory focuses upon movements along the production possibility frontier to the optimal point yielding allocative efficiency. But of much greater importance are movements from the inner to the outer bound of the frontier; which amounts to reductions in the level and extent of x-inefficiency. The central planner, however this agent is constituted, does not have the capacity or even the desire to achieve x-efficiency.

Critical to the existence of x-inefficiency, given imperfect product markets, is the assumption that in the real world economic agents have discretion over effort inputs in both their quantity and quality dimensions. One has agency. Effort discretion is a result of real world constraints on the construction of contracts with regards to work inclusive of effort inputs (imperfect contracts) and the related imperfections in monitoring and enforcement of effort behaviour, and the heterogeneity amongst agents of effort objectives. Ultimately effort discretion is combined with non-cost minimizing objective functions of all firm members inclusive of decision makers. This yields x-inefficiency (Leibenstein, 1979, pp. 486–487).

Leibenstein (1973, p. 767) summarizes some of his key foundational points thusly:

> *The assumptions about firms on which the theory rests are: (1) that labor contracts are vague and incomplete: (2) that detailed supervision of labor is impractical and or inefficient; hence, (3) there are normally many areas of choice open to managerial as well as other employees in determining how to fulfill their work roles. Legally, the firm makes contractual arrangements in its name, but the formal and informal contracts through which firms hire human inputs have significant gaps. The activities an individual is expected to carry out are rarely completely specified, and sometimes they are almost completely unspecified. Hence, it is necessary for individuals to interpret their jobs.*

Unless jobs are interpreted by decision makers in terms of x-efficiency and workers concur, x-efficiency in production will not obtain. Once again, for

Leibenstein, competitive pressures force economic agents to change their preferences towards x-efficient ones in so far as current preferences are inconsistent with the survival of the firm.

Given the existence of effort discretion, Leibenstein argues that (1973, p. 767):

> *Each individual decides (1) the activities he will carry out, (2) the pace at which he will carry out these activities, (3) the quality of the activities, and (4) the time spent on the activities. Thus each individual chooses an activity-pace-quality-time (APQT) bundle. Since most individuals interact with others in their work, the nature of the interactions and job interpretations set constraints on the APQT bundles each can choose. The formal system of financial payoffs, promotions, and potential dismissals determined by the contract is only part of the incentive system operative within the firm. Each person hired brings, in addition to his work potential, a set of desires, attitudes, and sense of responsibility about the activities of others around him, and contributes to the creation of an atmosphere of approval or disapproval which determines in part the nature of the APQT bundles that are chosen...*

Thus, the level and quality of effort inputs is contingent upon a complex set of incentives which, for Leibenstein, is critically primed by the extent of competitive pressures.

Underlying Leibenstein's early concern with the role management plays in the determination of the extent of X-efficiency, Leibenstein writes (1966, p. 397):

> *There is one important type of distortion that cannot easily be handled by existing microeconomic theory. This has to do with the allocation of managers. It is conceivable that in practice a situation would arise in which managers are exceedingly poor, that is, others are available who do not obtain management posts, and would be very much superior. Managers determine not only their own productivity but the productivity of all cooperating units in the organization. It is therefore possible that the actual loss due to such a misallocation might be large. But the theory does not allow us to examine this matter because firms are presumed to exist as entities that make optimal input decisions, apart from the decisions of its managers. This is obviously a contradiction and therefore cannot be handled [by conventional microeconomic theory].*

To this, Leibenstein adds (1966, p. 401): 'Clearly there is more to the determination of output than the obviously observable inputs. The nature of the management, the environment in which it operates, and the incentives employed are significant'.

Leibenstein's understanding of x-efficiency can be illustrated in Fig. 7.6 where x-efficiency and x-inefficiency are illustrated in terms of the production isoquant and production possibility frontier narratives. In Panel A, point C along production possibility frontier 1 is consistent with x-efficiency or technical efficiency. It represents the maximum output that can be produced given inputs and technology. But firms typically produce at point such as B or A in the interior of the x-efficiency production possibility frontier thereby producing less

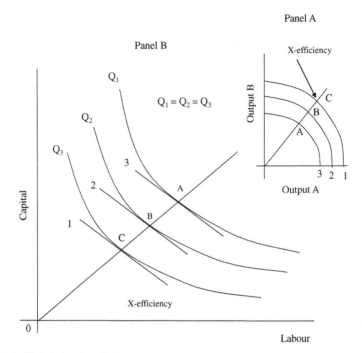

FIG. 7.6 Technical and x-efficiency.

output than technically feasible. The measured output gap between, A and C, for example, would be a measure of x-inefficiency. One should note that there need be no reference here to production costs, albeit this is what Leibenstein emphasizes. X-inefficiency can be specified simply in terms of output foregone as a consequence of sub-optimal effort inputs. Whether or not costs change as a consequence of changes in effort inputs critically hinges upon what one assumes is happening to input costs (such as wages) as effort inputs change.

This point is illustrated in Eq. (7.1) which flows from the basic production function of conventional micro theory. In this instance, it is assumed for simplicity that there is only one factor input (labour).

$$AC = \frac{wL}{Q} = \frac{w}{\dfrac{Q}{L}}, \tag{7.1}$$

AC is average cost, w is the wage rate, L is labour inputs, and Q is output. If the wage rate is fixed (which is implicitly assumed in Leibenstein, 1966 vintage model), any decrease in output, such as would follow from an increased level of x-inefficiency, would result in a higher level of average costs.

In terms of the production isoquant (Fig. 7.6, Panel B), x-efficiency is illustrated at point C where a given level of output is produced using the least amount of inputs. Given some fixed capital to labour ratio in the long run, if the x-inefficiency exists, a higher level of output can only be produced using more factor inputs as more labour and capital need be employed. Ceteris paribus, this yields a higher cost of production. One measure of x-inefficiency is the extent to which extra factor inputs are required to produce a given level of output relative to what is technically required if x-efficiency prevails. For practical purposes one can measure the extent of x-efficiency in terms of best practice performance where the latter might be inferior to some ideal measure of x-efficiency such as what neoclassical theory might predict. Leibenstein (1983, p. 840) writes: '…we need not compare an actual situation with a pie in the sky ideal, but rather with some particular performance such as best practice performance. The ideal may be superior to best practice'.

Given the assumption that x-inefficiency results in higher costs, Leibenstein (1966, p. 410) argues that, 'Both competition and adversity create some pressure for change…Thus we have instances where competitive pressures from other firms or adversity lead to efforts toward cost reduction, and the absence of such pressure tends to cause costs to rise'. Given that high cost x-efficient firms persist in equilibrium, according to Leibenstein (1979, pp. 489–491), this can be explained and help explain what Leibenstein refers to as sheltering activities which is a substitute for reducing costs in terms of becoming more x-efficient. Some examples of sheltering activity would be (Leibenstein, 1979, p. 490):

> …entering into price agreements, activities that help maintain price agreements, product differentiation, activities such as advertising, developing trademarks, engaging in market share agreements, entering into mergers, political activities to obtain price supports, tariffs or other restrictions on trade, and so on. The function of such sheltering activities is to reduce the impact of competition in the industry, or by possible entrants, in order to maintain or raise the existing price or prices charged by the firm in question. Thus, in general, the aim of sheltering activities is to increase the capacity to raise prices without excessive loss of sales. Of course, the firm in question need not initiate such activities. In part it may engage in such activities by acquiescing to or supporting the sheltering activities of others. Thus, in the price leadership situation following the price leader is a type of sheltering activity. Similarly, supporting political activities to increase a particular tariff is a sheltering activity that is likely to be approved by both management and trade unions that represent some or all of the workers within the firm. Thus sheltering activities are facilitated by various organizational networks, which permits the flow of support from inside the firm to industry-wide organizations, to political parties, and to governments.

What Leibenstein fails to consider as a form of sheltering activity are efforts to reduce labour benefits. As we shall see, one can specify a dynamic relationship between labour compensation and x-efficiency such that x-inefficiency in production is sheltered by weak labour markets and low levels of labour compensation analogous to the effects of subsidies and tariffs in Leibenstein's narrative.

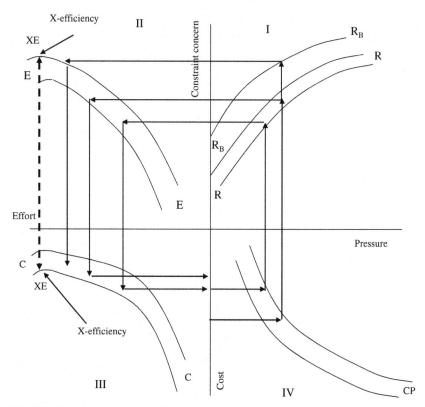

FIG. 7.7 Pressure, effort inputs and costs.

Leibenstein illustrates some of the key behavioural elements of his x-efficiency theory in one his summary articles from which our Fig. 7.7 is derived (Leibenstein, 1979, pp. 485–487). First note that in this figure all curves are 'fat' to reflect what Liebenstein refers to the inertia inherent in human behaviour. Leibenstein argues (1979, p. 486):

> *The idea of inert areas indicates the existence of effort points or of 'positions' (whether effort positions or other types of option choices), so that if one is at one position associated with a certain utility one does not move to another position associated with a higher utility. The reason is that there is an 'inertial cost' in moving from one position to another, and for the positions in the inert area, the inertial cost of moving is greater than or equal to the utility gain.*

So, for example, if there is more pressure on the individual, this need not imply that the individual will work harder unless the increase in pressure is large enough to induce the individual to change her or his behaviour in terms of net utility gain. Thus, individuals are stuck in their choice behaviour unless the gain in utility in changing one's behaviour exceeds the utility costs incurred.

However, the causal direction of Leibenstein's narrative is not much affected if one assumes for simplicity zero inertial costs.

In Fig. 7.7, Leibenstein, postulates a positive relationship between pressure and constraint concern where the latter is the dependant variable (Quadrant I). Constraint concern determines the effort level chosen by the economic agent and each agent can be expected to have different constraint concern functions. Pressure can be internal to the firm in terms of peer pressure or external such as would stem from competitive pressure. The level of the constraint concern function (RR) can be affected by the culture of the firm or the demeanour of the economic agent. A more cooperative less confrontation and trusting firm culture tends to be characterized by a higher constraint concern function (R_BR_B), yielding more constraint concern per level of pressure. Given more pressure, there is more effort input (Quandrant II), through the intermediate variable of constraint concern, subject to diminishing returns. Effort input is the dependent variable. Note that effort increases as the constraint concern function shifts up and diminishes if it shifts down. Effort can be maximized by either increasing pressure or by shifting the constraint concern function, albeit Leibenstein does not consistently pay adequate to the latter which draws attention to the culture of the firm and its related incentive environment. In Quadrant III, the relationship between effort and unit costs is specified. Leibenstein focuses on the manner in which increased pressure yields lower unit costs. A level of pressure which generates maximum effort yields x-efficiency in production. However, Leibeinstein's modelling opens the door to the possibility of x-efficiency being obtained at any given level of pressure; this being contingent on the position of the constraint concern function which in turn is a function of the culture of the firm. In Quadrant IV, the relationship between unit cost and pressure is illustrated, with pressure being the independent variable.

With regards to unit cost, Leibenstein pays little attention to the implicit relationship between average or unit cost and labour productivity which is illustrated in Fig. 7.8. Effort affects unit cost through its impact upon labour productivity (holding the quality dimension of effort input constant). Assuming there is diminishing returns to effort inputs, there is some maximum to average product such as point A in the top panel of the figure. This can be referred to as the x-efficient level of labour productivity which corresponds to an x-efficient level of effort input, B. Ceteris paribus, it is the increasing labour productivity which yields diminishing unit production costs down to some minimum point D, in the bottom panel of the figure, where D corresponds with the x-efficient level of labour productivity. From Fig. 7.8, what is critical to x-efficiency in production is labour productivity. Maximizing labour productivity through maximizing effort input is what x-efficiency is all about. Leibenstein assumes that x-efficiency in production automatically translates into cost minimisation since he assumes that input costs are invariant to changes in effort and that input costs are not causal determinants (independent variables) with respect to effort variability. In terms of Fig. 7.7, the vertical XE line joins the x-efficient point along the effort

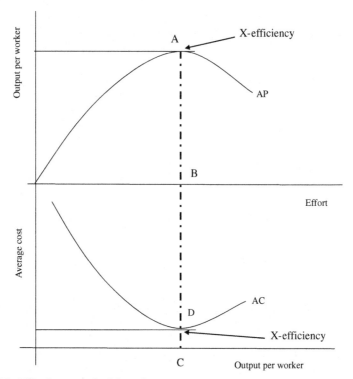

FIG. 7.8 Effort inputs, productivity, units costs.

function EE and cost function CC where an x-efficient level of effort yields an x-efficient level of unit cost.

As average cost increases relative to other competing firms there is more pressure. Lower relative average cost yield less pressure. If average cost increases and this yields more pressure, more constraint concern, more effort and, thereby, lower costs, pressure will be reduced, allowing some relaxation in pressure, constraint concern, and effort input. And the cycle begins again. But if there exists some equilibrium average cost which meets the competitive test of a particular market structure, effort input must be such as to allow for the realization of such a competitive average cost. Competitive pressure push agents, no matter their original preferences with regards to effort input, to behave relatively x-efficiently. This is perhaps the key underlying determinant of equilibrium effort input in Leibenstein's narrative. Lower effort levels would be unsustainable and therefore not consistent with equilibrium. Moreover, equilibrium will be upset if firms behave in an entrepreneurial fashion, increasing effort levels and driving unit cost down. Competing firms must either increase effort levels to survive or increase sheltering activity. If the firm's relative unit cost is increasing, one alternative to becoming more x-efficient is to increase the extent of the firm's shelter from competitive pressure, keeping mounting external pressures at bay.

This aspect of Leibenstein's modelling can be illustrated in the series of equations below which reflect the variables mapped out in Fig. 7.7.

$$CC = f(\text{Pr}) \qquad (7.2)$$

$$E = f(CC) \qquad (7.3)$$

$$AC = f(E) \qquad (7.4)$$

$$\text{Pr} = f(AC) \qquad (7.5)$$

where CC is constraint concern, Pr is pressure, E is effort input, and AC is average or unit cost. Given some competitive AC, the values of the other variables are determined given the functional form for the above specified relationships assumed by Leibenstein in Fig. 7.7. As the competitive average cost changes so does the sustainable level of effort input and thus the sustainable level of x-inefficiency.

Given the specified sustainable unit cost, Leibenstein argues that x-efficiency theory is consistent with the conventional modelling of firms as profit maximizers. For example, Leibenstein writes (1973, pp. 773–774):

For present purposes, it is not really necessary to depart from the profit maximization assumption. The pursuit of profit maximization does not imply cost minimization if the top management cannot control costs but can control the quantity of output and price. For each alternative cost level, profits would be maximized on the marginal revenue curve...

Thus, profit maximization is consistent with x-inefficiency in production and moreover profit maximization per se is no guarantee for the realization of x-efficiency. Analytically one can separate the notion of profit maximization from that of effort variation and x-efficiency. In other words, x-efficiency can be modelled in the context of the conventional economic wisdom wherein x-efficiency theory broadens, with good effect, the analytical parameters of the conventional narrative.

In many of the variations on the x-efficiency narrative presented by Leibenstein, the sustainable competitive level of x-inefficiency appears to be consistent with utility maximization on the part of economic agents given the constraints which they face which include external competitive pressures as well as the culture of the firm and the individual's personal demeanour. Moreover, at times Leibenstein assumes that economic agents prefer to work less hard and absent sufficient external pressures will drift towards x-inefficient behaviour. On other occasions, Leibenstein makes the case that increasing effort input along either the quantity or quality dimension can be net utility enhancing. However, a fundamental thread running throughout his discourse is that both management and workers have a preference to work less hard, ceteris paribus. This is why, to his mind, competitive pressure is so critical to the realization of x-efficiency in production. Although agents might be maximizing utility by working harder and smarter when the external environment is tight—they are doing the best they can given their constraints—this would be an unstable utility maximizing equilibrium, with individuals reverting to x-inefficient behaviour when the external environment slackens.

Given that choice behaviour is critical to Leibenstein's argument, it would be useful clarify and expand upon his notion of utility maximization and the preferences of economics agents. First, if Leibenstein's oft-made assumption of a preference by both workers and management for x-inefficient behaviour holds than economic efficiency must be an unstable economic condition that can be maintained only when product market competitive conditions are severe. In this case, utility is maximized by agents only in the sense that they are doing the best they can within the bounds of *unpreferred* constraints. Workers and managers would then have the incentive to relax such constraints so that they could work less hard which would yield a higher level of utility at the maximum of the individual's preferred utility function. In Fig. 7.9, a series of utility functions are drawn all subject to diminishing returns. With reference to U_1 and U_2, utility is highest along U_1. Utility curves above U_1, wherein individuals obtain higher utility at the maximum of the utility curves with more effort input, are not within the parameters of the dominant Leibenstein x-efficiency narrative. Given a slack external environment, the typical economic agent might work up to A in terms of effort input, realizing utility E along utility function U_1. In this case, we have x-inefficiency in production. In a tight external environment,

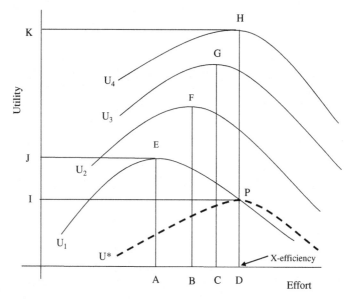

FIG. 7.9 Effort inputs and utility.

the typical economic agent is forced to work x-efficiently with D effort input along a different utility function U*, maximizing utility at P, which is less than the maximum obtained at E of utility function U_1. U* is a sub-utility function, inferior to U_1. This is an unstable equilibrium since individuals have a utility incentive to revert to A effort input once competitive pressures relax.

In this scenario, the economy tends towards x-inefficiency and related to this, sheltering activity. Differences in degrees of x-inefficiency can then be explained largely in terms of differences in competitive pressures faced by firms. A serious hole in Leibenstein's foundational x-efficiency narrative relates to the determinants of competitive pressures, and more precisely the slackness in such pressures, which allow for the persistence of x-inefficiency. Of course, Leibenstein argues that firms engage in sheltering activity to reduce competitive pressure. But other firms engage in entrepreneurial activities which could offset and even dominate the latter.

Leibenstein (1979, 1982, 1983), opens the door to determinants of x-inefficiency other than competitive pressures in his discussion of prisoner dilemma scenarios in the context of his multiple agent firm. In this narrative, Leibenstein's focus is no longer on competitive pressures as the key determinant of the degree of x-efficiency; albeit the tightness of the external environment stills lurks in the background as a causal and independent variable since it is the absence of sufficient competitive pressure which remains for Leibenstein a necessary condition for the existence and persistence of x-inefficiency. Rather, Leibenstein argues that the typical firm should be modelled as consisting of heterogeneous individuals often characterized by conflicting objective functions in the domain of effort input. Given the space for effort discretion as determined by the degree of competitive pressure on the firm, the culture of the firm and the psychology of the individual have a significant effect on the degree of x-efficiency.

One important insight ensues from this discourse. The realization of x-efficiency is closely tied to the culture of production within the firm. Leibenstein argues that typically firms tend towards prisoner dilemma type solutions to the productivity problem. But he also argues that prisoner dilemma type solutions are not the only available solution. There are higher productivity solutions as well, irrespective of competitive conditions. Low productivity prisoner's dilemma outcomes ensue when potential conflict amongst economic agents cannot be contained or resolved. In this case (Leibenstein, 1982, p. 96), '...joint choices which are adversarial lead to smaller joint payoffs than would otherwise be the case'. Leibenstein argues (1978, p. 329): '...because of differential principal-agent interests we would normally expect most individuals to choose noncost-minimising positions. Furthermore, the existence of inert areas will imply some degree of persistence of such positions.' Moreover (Leibenstein, 1982, p. 94):

> A basic criterion is that a prisoners' dilemma occurs wherever there are possibilities for adversarial behavior between the parties, and by all parties, which reduces the joint cooperative outcome. Now, it seems reasonable to presume

that adversarial behavior between employees and the firm will usually decrease productivity, while cooperative behavior will increase it. This is certainly not the case in all types of games. But this is the case for the particular 'game' set where productivity is the outcome.

Leibenstein argues that given adversarial environments, the incentive exists for agents to make prisoner dilemma type effort choices. Such choices can be and often are abated by conventions which allow agents to rally around effort inputs which yield more x-efficient firm performance.

Most conducive to effort maximization is cooperative and trusting behaviour amongst firm members, inclusive of owners, managers and workers. In this instance the potential conflict inherent amongst such groups of economic agents is honed. Leibenstein (1978, p. 206) argues that x-efficiency can best be realized (1978, p. 206) when firm members '…interpret their jobs in such a way that they made effort choices which involved cooperation with peers, superiors, and subordinates, in such a way as to maximise their contribution to output.' Moreover, (Leibenstein, 1983, p. 838):

The main general point is that merely obtaining an acquiescent nonshirking effort is of limited value. Freely offered effort, inclusive of attentiveness and caring about the quality of effort, in return for what is viewed as a good deal (in the long run) is likely to result in higher productivity.

This involves, argues Leibenstein (1983, p. 838), a limited use of monitoring, '…and instead resorts to other motivating forces, which in essence involve higher levels of trust and lower implicit adversarial relations. But such relations are likely to involve quite a bit of discretion on all sides'. When contracts are incomplete and effort discretion exist, effort input can only move beyond prisoner dilemma type outcomes if agents develop conventions which are based on trust and which are therefore self-enforcing via peer pressures or constraint concern emanating from the individual her or himself.

As part of this narrative, Leibenstein argues that relatively more x-efficient behaviour can be consistent with utility maximizing behaviour. In other words, working harder and smarter can yield higher levels of utility. Leibenstein argues that (1983, p. 834):

The basic question is whether an individual receives less satisfaction from his work qua work when he puts forth more effort. In my view, this depends on the nature of the work, whether others are working equally hard, and whether approval is associated with the marginal effort…Thus there may be circumstances… where an increase in effort is not associated with any loss in satisfaction. In other cases there is such a loss, and other things equal, the incentives for individuals are towards putting forth less effort. In general we should keep in mind that effort satisfaction is likely to depend on whether relevant others are putting forth more or less effort, as well as the simultaneous approval or disapproval of others associated with marginal effort.

Leibenstein perspective on utility and effort is not consistent since critical to much of his argumentation is the assumption that agents maximize utility at low x-inefficient levels of effort input. But agents choose, irrespective of the extent of external environmental tightness, higher levels of effort input in cooperative work settings in Leibenstein's game theoretic discourse on x-efficiency theory.

I model the notion that utility can be increased with more effort input—otherwise why would agents voluntarily increase effort input—in terms of Fig. 7.9, whereby U_4 is consistent with a more cooperative work environment and D effort input is consistent with utility maximization. D effort input is also a stable equilibrium given the relatively cooperative work environment. This is in contrast to D at utility curve U^*, wherein D effort is supplied only because of exceptionally severe competitive pressures. More adversarial work environments yield less utility at the maximum of the relevant utility functions, such as U_3, U_2, and U_1. Effort discretion, which is the reality of typical real world firms, is quite consistent with x-efficient utility maximizing behaviour under the appropriate human relations environment even under slack competitive conditions.[b]

But this raises a paradox within Leibenstein's narrative of x-efficiency theory wherein x-efficiency can be potentially realized even without severe competitive conditions being in place. If firms are x-efficient, ceteris paribus they should produce at lower unit cost thereby pressuring x-inefficient firms, where the work culture is relatively antagonist, into being more x-efficient. How does one then explain the persistence of x-inefficient firms, where such persistence is a stylized fact of economic life? Leibenstein suggests one possible explanation for this paradox in his discourse on the supply of entrepreneurship (Leibenstein, 1968, 1979, pp. 490–492). A shortage in the supply of x-efficiency goal oriented entrepreneurs relative to demand would result in the persistence of x-inefficient firms. However, in Leibenstein's narrative, because different levels of x-inefficiency result in different levels of unit costs, one would expect that the x-efficient firms should eventually dominate the market place. Altman (1992, 1996, 2001a, 2001b, 2001c, 2001d) shows how x-inefficient firms can survive in long run competitive equilibrium; but this requires linking movements in rates of labour compensation, firm culture to different degrees of x-efficiency and thereby linking efficiency wage and x-efficiency theories. This critical linkage, discussed briefly below, is absent from Leibenstein's narrative.

---

b. Most discussions of the firm are focused on investor-owned firms, where conflictual preferences all too often dominate the firm and are even entrenched in the culture of the firm (Gordon, 1996). Although even here more co-operative forms of firm government can evolve (Altman, 2002; Gordon, 1996) However, it is critically important to note that there are other firm types such as a member-owned firms or co-operatives, wherein co-operation and trust across economic agents should be the natural outcome of this type of firm structure, if co-operative principles are abided by (Altman, 2014, 2015).

Linking x-efficiency and efficiency theories

As discussed, Leibenstein assumes that labour compensation is constant as effort input varies, generating different unit costs for different levels of effort inputs. However, Leibenstein's game theoretic narratives speak to but in no way elaborates upon a connection between higher rates of labour compensation and higher rates of effort input. Once one introduces variations in labour compensation which are causally and positively correlated with variations in the level of effort input, the analytical prediction that unit cost positively varies with different levels of x-efficiency no longer holds with any degree of precision. Indeed, it becomes possible for unit cost to be invariant to changes in the level of x-efficiency and for levels x-efficiency to be much less constrained by competitive pressures than is argued by Leibenstein.

As elaborated upon in Altman (1992, 1996, 2001a, 2001b, 2001c, 2001d, 2002), there is a large literature suggesting that different levels of x-efficiency are causally related different work environments of which working conditions and related rates of labour compensation is one important component. It is quite possible for different levels of x-efficiency to be consistent with the same level of unit cost. Therefore, there might be an array of levels of x-efficiency associated with some unique average cost if the level of x-efficiency changes just enough to offset any change in labour compensation where labour compensation is a proxy for working conditions. Being more x-efficient need not result in firms being more competitive. Thus, cooperative firms need not be lower cost than prisoner dilemma type firms if the cooperative firms provide higher pecuniary benefits to firm members. In this case, the economic losses to society attributable to x-inefficient production would not be measured in terms of higher unit costs but rather in terms of loses in productivity.

In Fig. 7.10, possible relationships between wages and related costs and unit costs are mapped out. In the conventional model of the firm, where effort discretion does not exist, increasing wages yields higher unit cost, ceteris paribus, as per CO_0S. However, if labour compensation and effort input are causally and positively related, increasing labour compensation need not yield any increase in unit cost to the extent effort related increases in productivity suffice to offset increased labour cost. On the other hand, reducing labour compensation need not result in lower unit cost to the extent that effort related productivity decreases suffice to neutralize the impact of lower labour cost. Thus, along CO_0A unit cost is constant as labour cost increases. In the background, effort changes in response to changes in labour compensation. Past point A, effort-related increases in productivity no longer suffice to compensate for increasing rates of labour compensation and unit cost increase. Point A might represent the x-efficient level of effort input. Further increases in labour compensation simply increase unit cost as it would in the conventional model. The mechanics of this point is further illustrated in equation one above where it is assumed for simplicity that labour is the only factor input. In this scenario, productivity must

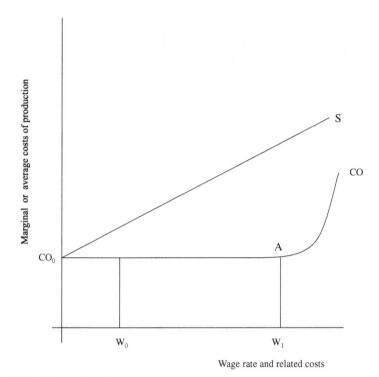

FIG. 7.10 Labour and production costs.

increase proportionally to wage increases for unit cost to remain constant. If labour is not the only factor input, which is typical, productivity increases need be less than the increase in wages, determined by the ratio of labour to total costs. Thus, if labour represents 40% of total cost, productivity need increase by only 40% of the wage increase if unit cost is to remain constant.

In this scenario, being relatively more or less x-efficient need not affect the competitive position of the firm. To remain competitive the firm need only maintain unit cost at a competitive level, controlling for quality. Since x-efficient firms need not be any less competitive than x-efficient firms there need not be any market pressure on the x-inefficient firms to become more x-efficient. In the Leibenstein narrative, x-inefficient firms must be sheltered from competitive pressures to survive x-inefficiently. Otherwise, the firm must become more x-efficient even if this results in economic agents expending more effort than desired. The level of x-inefficiency is in Leibenstein's modelling, to an important extent, a function of the extent of competitive pressures. In the alternative x-efficiency modelling scenario low wages and poor working conditions become a form of sheltering x-inefficient firms whereas higher wages and better working conditions serve to pressure firms into becoming more x-efficient irrespective of the competitive environment. Moreover, in the alternative scenario x-inefficient behaviour is not a corollary derivative of agents' utility being maximised at low levels of effort input. Utility can be maximised at x-efficient levels of effort input, where such a choice of effort input is stable, given an appropriate firm culture. Indeed, utility can be maximised at alternative levels of effort input, depending on the culture of the firm. Therefore, the utility function of agents cannot explain the level of x-efficiency in any way independent of the work environment of the firm.

When labour compensation and effort input move hand in hand and effort changes simply to compensate for changes in labour compensation there is no incentive for firm decision makers to become more x-efficient unless pressured to do—increasing x-efficiency does not reduce unit cost or increase profits. To the extent that shifting towards more x-efficiency causes any increase in short term pecuniary or non-pecuniary costs (inclusive of disutility) to firm managers or owners, building x-efficiency might be resisted by firm decision makers unless their utility functions incorporate aspects of workers' utility function. Moreover, firm decision makers would favour lower rates of labour compensation and less cooperative work environments even if this comes at the cost of more x-inefficiency (holding unit cost and profits constant), when a more x-efficient work culture reduces the utility of firm decision makers. In this case, x-efficiency might be unstable if firm decision makers are not maximizing their utility in an x-efficient firm environment. What makes for x-efficiency in this scenario is the capacity of workers to pressure for improved working conditions, for this pressure forces firms into becoming more x-efficient if they are to remain competitive. Relaxation of such pressure revert firms into x-inefficiency analogous to the effect which the loosening of markets pressures is predicted to have on x-efficiency in Leibenstein's foundational model. To the extent that improvements in x-efficiency benefit all economic agents including both workers and managers there is an incentive for agents to work towards this end. But if improvements in productivity simply serve to cover the increased costs of obtaining higher levels of x-efficiency, such as improvements in labour and managerial benefits, unit cost would not change as a consequence of improvements in x-efficiency. In this case competitive pressures cannot force firms into becoming more x-efficient. Rather, it is the ability of economic agents to develop a joint productivity enhancing firm culture which contributes to this end. In addition, there must be an adequate supply of x-efficiency oriented entrepreneurs for x-efficiency to obtain. However, deficiency in supply of this factor input is sustainable given that x-inefficient firms cannot drive out their x-inefficient counterparts if both types of firms are producing at the same unit cost.

In Leibenstein's original formulation of x-efficiency theory, x-inefficiency is explained by preferences of economic agents to minimize their effort inputs for any given rate of labour or managerial compensation. This allows Leibenstein to predict that any relaxation in competitive pressures will result in a reduction in effort inputs the increased cost of which is passed onto the consumer. This is the case Leibenstein makes with regards to the cost of monopoly and corporate bigness in general whereby allocative efficiency is small as compared to resulting x-inefficiency. Increasing competitive pressure has the opposite effect. But under Leibenstein's assumptions x-efficiency remains unstable, always in danger of collapsing into x-inefficiency given the absence of adequate competitive pressures. By integrating labour compensation and related working conditions into modelling x-efficiency—which is already implicit in Leibenstein's game theoretic discourse—the existence and persistence of x-inefficiency as well as that of x-efficiency can be explained as a consequence of more complex scenarios in the context of utility and profit maximizing economic agents. Such an x-efficiency/efficiency wage modelling of the firm incorporates and extends Leibenstein foundational analytical predictions.

The extended model developed in Altman (1992, 1996, 1998, 2001a, 2001b, 2001c, 2001d, 2002, 2012), easily collapses into Leibenstein's basic model (factor prices are held constant and managers and owners have preferences for less own effort input) to help explain instances of increasing cost in a more relaxed competitive environment (Altman, 1990). Given particular objective functions amongst economic agents, less competition which can result from corporate bigness, will yield more x-inefficiency. Moreover, firms can pass on to consumers higher benefits to firm members, as opposed to increasing x-efficiency, when the competitive environment is lax. But in the extended model, more competitive pressure need not result in more x-efficiency if costs can be reduced by cutting pay and benefits to economic agents without resulting in a corresponding reduction in effort input. Low wages become a form of sheltering.

More generally, in the extended model, one cannot predict the impact of changing levels of x-efficiency upon unit costs or the impact of differential levels of competitiveness upon levels of x-efficiency or unit cost. Nevertheless, a tighter external environment is more conducive to higher levels of x-efficiency than a more lax external environment, ceteris paribus. Moreover, in the extended model x-inefficiency need not result from objective functions which are prejudiced against higher levels of effort in terms of quantity and quality. The level of x-efficiency can be affected by the latter, but of even greater significance would be differential objective functions between economic agents and groups of economics agents, such as workers, managers and owners, and the differential capacity of firm members to realize their preferences. For example, if workers have the capacity to realize their demand for improved working conditions and these costs cannot be passed on to consumer via higher prices, the organization of the firm might be transformed into a more cooperative setting, even if this is not the preferred organizational form of owners and managers. However, if workers do not have such capacity and the preferences of owners prevail (and these are for a low wage environment), x-inefficiency would prevail (Altman, 2012). This modelling is informed by Leibenstein's game theoretic narrative.

In the extended model, unlike in Leibenstein's basic model, firms can be x-efficient or x-inefficient irrespective of competitive conditions since, consistent with the facts, wages and working conditions are closely tied to movements in effort input and thereby to different levels of x-efficiency. Unit cost need not change with variations in the level of x-efficiency and x-inefficient firms can be competitive with x-efficient firms. In this case, differential unit costs need not be a marker for x-inefficiency for firms producing like products and using like technologies. Moreover, in the extended model, competitive conditions is not the only or most important independent variable driving the extent of a firm's and an economy's level of x-efficiency. At least as important, is the capacity of workers to realize their preferences for higher levels of material wellbeing and improved working conditions which force firms into becoming for x-efficient in a reasonably competitive environment. This speaks to issues related firm to governance, bargaining power, and institutional determinants of both of these variables. If workers preferences are not met, society is worse off materially, but firms need not be any less competitive. Indeed, low wage highly x-inefficient firms can be competitive with high wage x-efficient firms. Moreover, efforts by firms to become more competitive on the basis of low wages might very well be frustrated by reactive reductions in effort input and thereby productivity. Whereas fears that higher wages and improved working conditions will cause firms to become uncompetitive might be misleading and misplaced when such improvements can be accompanied by sufficient increases in x-efficiency. Linking Leibenstein's foundational model with the extended x-efficiency/efficiency wage model, heightened competitive pressures will force x-inefficient firms into being more x-efficient if they are higher cost producers in the first instance and driving wage downward is not an option if this is accompanied by a neutralizing diminution in productivity.

Leibenstein's x-efficiency theory opens the door to fundamental socioeconomic questions relating to the determinants of material wellbeing and the multiplicity of options available to improve economic welfare without damaging the competitiveness of firms and economies (see for example Altman, 1998, 2000, 2001a, 2001c, 2002, 2004, 2012). Leibenstein's key break with conventional theory is the assumption of effort variability as a common feature of economic reality.

His x-efficiency theory focuses on effort variability in the context of fixed labour and other factor costs. In Leibenstein's modelling one can write his dependent and dependant variables as follows:

$$XE = F\left(ET\right) \tag{7.6}$$

where XE is the level of x-efficiency and ET is the extent of environmental tightness. The extent of x-inefficiency is determined by the extent to which competitive pressures are slack. Given slack in the external environment, x-inefficiency arises as a result of economic agents having a preference for non-maximizing levels of effort input. So, given that the actual ET or ET_A is less than maximally tight or ET_{MAX}, the extent of x-inefficiency is determined by preferences of economic agents with regards to effort input. Given slack in environmental tightness human agency becomes important. Therefore, given that $ET_A < ET_{MAX}$:

$$XE = F\left(EP\right) \tag{7.7}$$

where EP is effort preferences. Effort input cannot drop below what is required to keep firms competitive, given EP_A. But Leibenstein assumes that EP is always below the level consistent with x-efficiency in production.

In the extended model, XE is still the dependant variable but the independent variable structure is more complex:

$$XE = F\left(ET, LB\right) \tag{7.8}$$

The level of x-efficiency can be affected by the degree of environmental tightness, but even if the coefficient for ET is at a maximum and there can still be considerable x-inefficiency, where the latter is determined by the level of labour benefits. This brings into the modelling of x-efficiency the efficiency wage causal narrative. Hence, in the extended model, there more room for human agency in decision-making—an additional degree of freedom. The role of effort preferences is also more complex in extended model since economic agents are not assumed to prefer lower levels of effort input irrespective of the culture of the firm and the expected pecuniary and non-pecuniary benefits derived from work. Therefore, in this model, even with slack in environmental tightness (ET), one can achieve x-efficiency, contingent upon the preferences of economic agents. Moreover, the realized effort preference depends on whether there is a stable consensus amongst economic agents or groups of economic agents on what the ideal level of effort input should be (at least in the rough) or, if such a stable consensus cannot be achieved, the realized effort preference depends on which group of economic agents can impose their preferences on the firm. However, effort input cannot fall below the level required to keep the firm competitive given ET and LB.

One should note that in the extended model, economic agents can be assumed to be behaving rationally given their objective functions and the constraints which they face even though individuals are not maximizing effort input as is oft-assumed in the conventional wisdom. Effort maximization and related to this the maximization of productivity per unit of effort is as rational as x-inefficient related effort inputs. Much depends on the incentives in place to maximize effort and this is also related to the culture of the firm (March, 1978).

Conclusion

Harvey Leibenstein contributed to and set the foundations for some of the most innovative theoretical advancements in twentieth century economics.

Both efficiency wage theory and x-efficiency and related theories have their contemporary origins in Leibenstein's pioneering contributions. In both paradigms the underlying theme is the assumption that economic models should be designed to address real world economic issues and quandaries and that the models' underlying assumptions should be realistic. Leibenstein fundamental break with the conventional wisdom is his introduction of effort discretion as a core behavioural assumption. Hence, importantly Leibenstein introduced human agency as an indepdent variable especially in his x-efficiency narrative. Once effort is a discretionary variable, this significantly affects our understanding of the determinants of employment as well as of economic efficiency.

Leibenstein's narrative on what we now refer to as efficiency wages has been little affected in substance (although enriched) by contemporary contributions by Akerlof, for example. The essence of the argument remains that effort discretion causes real wages to be sticky downwards preventing 'full' employment from being realized. Building on Leibenstein's and Akerlof's modelling of efficiency wage, I make the case that the prediction that effort variability, where effort input and wages are positively correlated, need not imply that too high real wages is the ultimate supply side cause of employment being lower than it need be. Rather the argument is presented that under reasonable modelling assumptions, higher real wages can contribute to higher levels of employment though its positive productivity (or x-efficiency) effect. Instead of being an obstacle to higher levels of employment in a world of effort variability, high real wages can be an enabling supply side variable generating high enough productivity levels for more workers to be employed than would be possible in low wage environments.

As Roger Frantz (1997, see also Tong, 2019) thoroughly documents, Leibenstein's x-efficiency theory has significantly affected the empirical and theoretical discourse on economic inefficiency as a consequence of less than realizable effort input and the importance of market structure as an important determinant of such inefficiency (see also, Tong, 2019). The conventional wisdom largely assumes x-inefficiency away through its assumption of fixed and optimal effort input irrespective of circumstance. But Leibenstein's x-efficiency analysis can be extended well beyond the notion that market imperfections determine the extent to which economic losses are systematically incurred by society from the supply side. Introducing efficiency wage considerations, firm culture, bargaining power, and institutional parameters, for example, into the modelling framework allows one to appreciate the complexity of the determinants of x-efficiency and the multiplicity of important paradoxes which an extended version of x-efficiency theory can help resolve within the framework of rational (smart or intelligent) decision making in the real world of bounded rationality. This is vitally important as productivity is largely determined inside of the firm, given the constraints and opportunities it faces. And, productivity and, relatedly the extent of x-efficiency plays a critical in role in determining the level of material wellbeing of society at large as well as the distribution of income.

References

Akerlof, G. A. (1980). A theory of social custom, of which unemployment may be one consequence. *Quarterly Journal of Economics, 94,* 749–775.

Akerlof, G. A. (1982). Labor contracts as partial gift exchange. *Quarterly Journal of Economics, 97,* 543–569.

Akerlof, G. A. (1984). Gift exchange and efficiency wage theory: Four views. *American Economic Review: Papers and Proceedings, 74,* 79–83.

Akerlof, G. A., Dickens, W., & Perry, P. (2000). Near-rational wage and price setting and the long-run Phillips curve. *Brookings Papers on Economic Activity, 1,* 1–59.

Akerlof, G. A. & Yellen, J. L. (Eds.), (1986). *Efficiency wage models of the labor market.* Cambridge, England: Cambridge University Press.

Akerlof, G. A., & Yellen, J. L. (1988). Fairness and unemployment. *American Economic Review: Papers and Proceedings, 78,* 44–49.

Akerlof, G. A., & Yellen, J. L. (1990). The fair wage hypothesis and unemployment. *Quarterly Journal of Economics, 105,* 255–283.

Altman, M. (1990). A critical appraisal of corporate bigness and the transactions cost economizing paradigm. In R. Frantz (Ed.), *Handbook on behavioral economics* (pp. 217–232). 2A, London: JAI Press.

Altman, M. (1992). The economics of exogenous increases in wage rates in a behavioral/x-efficiency model of the firm. *Review of Social Economy, 50,* 163–192.

Altman, M. (1996). *Human agency and material welfare: Revisions in microeconomics and their implications for public policy.* 1996. Boston, Dordrecht, London: Kluwer Academic Publishers.

Altman, M. (1998). High path to economic growth and development. *Challenge: The Magazine of Economic Affairs, 41,* 91–104.

Altman, M. (1999). The methodology of economics and the survivor principle revisited and revised: Some welfare and public policy implications of modeling the economic agent. *Review of Social Economy, 57,* 427–449.

Altman, M. (2000). Labor rights and labor power and welfare maximization in a market economy: Revising the conventional wisdom. *International Journal of Social Economics, 27,* 1252–1269.

Altman, M. (2001a). When green isn't mean: Economic theory and the heuristics of the impact of environmental regulations on competitiveness and opportunity cost. *Ecological Economics, 36,* 31–44.

Altman, M. (2001b). *Worker satisfaction and economic performance.* Armonk, New York: M.E. Sharpe Publishers.

Altman, M. (2001c). A revisionist view of the economic implications of child labor regulations. *Forum for Social Economics, 30,* 1–23.

Altman, M. (2001d). Behavioural economics. In J. Michie (Ed.), *Reader's guide to the social sciences.* London: Fitzroy Dearborn Publishers.

Altman, M. (2002). Economic theory, public policy and the challenge of innovative work practices. *Economic and Industrial Democracy, 23,* 271–290.

Altman, M. (2003). The Nobel prize in behavioral and experimental economics: A contextual and critical appraisal of the contributions of Daniel Kahneman and Vernon Smith. *Review of Political Economy, 16,* 3–41.

Altman, M. (2004). Why unemployment insurance might not only good for the soul, it might also be good for the economy. *Review for Social Economy, 62,* 517–541.

Altman, M. (2012). *Economic growth and the high wage economy: Choices, constraints and opportunities in the market economy.* London, New York: Routledge.

Altman, M. (2014). Are cooperatives a viable business form? Lessons from behavioural economics. In S. Novkovic & T. Webb (Eds.), *Co-operatives in a post-growth era: Towards co-operative economics*. London: ZED Books.

Altman, M. (2015). Cooperative organizations as an engine of equitable rural economic development. *Journal of Co-operative Organization and Management, 3*, 14–23.

Baumol, W. (1982). Contestable markets: An uprising in the theory of industry structure. *American Economic Review, 72*, 1–15.

Bewley, T. F. (1999). *Why wages don't fall during a recession*. Cambridge, MA, London: Harvard University Press.

Blanchflower, D. G., & Oswald, A. J. (1995). An introduction to the wage curve. *Journal of Economic Perspectives, 9*, 153–167.

Frantz, R. (1997). *X-efficiency: Theory, evidence and applications* (2nd ed.). Boston/Dordrecht/London: Kluwer Academic Publishers.

Friedman, M. (1953). The methodology of positive economics. In M. Friedman (Ed.), *Essays in positive economics*. Chicago: University of Chicago Press.

Gordon, D. (1996). *Fat and mean: The corporate squeeze of working Americans and the myth of managerial 'downsizing'*. New York: Free Press.

Kahneman, D., & Tversky, A. (1979). Prospect theory: An analysis of decision under risk. *Econometrica, 47*, 263–291.

Leibenstein, H. (1957). *Economic backwardness and economic growth*. New York: J. Wiley and Sons.

Leibenstein, H. (1958). Underemployment in backward economies: Some additional notes. *Journal of Political Economy, 66*, 256.

Leibenstein, H. (1966). Allocative efficiency vs. 'X-efficiency. *American Economic Review, 56*, 392–415.

Leibenstein, H. (1968). Entrepreneurship and development. *American Economic Review: Papers and Proceedings, 58*, 72–78.

Leibenstein, H. (1973). Competition and X-efficiency: Reply. *Journal of Political Economy, 81*, 765–777.

Leibenstein, H. (1978). On the basic proposition of X-efficiency theory. *American Economic Review: Papers and Proceedings, 68*, 328–332.

Leibenstein, H. (1979). A branch of economics is missing: Micro-micro theory. *Journal of Economic Literature, 17*, 477–502.

Leibenstein, H. (1982). The prisoner's dilemma in the invisible hand: An analysis of intrafirm productivity. *American Economic Review, 72*, 92–97.

Leibenstein, H. (1983). Property rights and X-efficiency: Comment. *American Economic Review, 73*, 831–842.

Lewis, W. A. (1954). Economic development with unlimited supplies of labor. *Manchester School of Economic and Social Studies, 22*, 139–191.

Little, I. M. D. (1982). *Economic development: Theory, policy and international relations*. New York: Basic Books.

March, J. G. (1978). Bounded rationality, ambiguity, and the engineering of choice. *Bell Journal of Economics, 9*, 587–608.

Pigou, A. C. (1952). *The economics of welfare*. London: Macmillan.

Reder, M. (1982). Chicago economics: Permanence and change. *Journal of Economic Literature, 20*, 1–38.

Shapiro, C., & Stiglitz, J. E. (1984). Equilibrium unemployment as a worker discipline device. *American Economic Review, 74*, 433–444.

Simon, H. A. (1987a). Bounded rationality. In J. Eatwell, M. Millgate, & P. Newman (Eds.), *The new Palgrave: A dictionary of economics, London and Basingstoke*: Macmillan.

Simon, H. A. (1987b). Behavioral economics. In J. Eatwell, M. Millgate, & P. Newman (Eds.), *The new Palgrave: A dictionary of economics, London and Basingstoke*: Macmillan.

Smith, A. (1937). *An inquiry into the nature and causes of the wealth of nations*. New York: The Modern Library.

Solow, R. M. (1979). Another possible source of wage stickiness. *Journal of Macroeconomics, 1*, 79–82.

Stiglitz, J. E. (1976). The efficiency wage hypothesis, surplus labor and the distribution of income in L.D.C.'s. *Oxford Economic Papers, 28*, 185–207.

Stiglitz, J. E. (1987). The causes and consequences of the dependence of quantity on price. *Journal of Economic Literature, 25*, 1–48.

Tong, S. (2019). *Managerial quality, firm performance, technical efficiency and productivity in New Zealand*. Doctor of Philosophy in Economics, Australia: University of Newcastle.

Tversky, A., & Kahneman, D. (1981). The framing of decisions and the psychology of choice. *Science, 211*, 453–458.

Williamson, O. E. (1975). *Markets and hierarchies: Analysis and antitrust implications*. New York: Free Press.

Williamson, O. E. (1985). *The economic institutions of capitalism: Firms, markets, relational contracting*. New York: Free Press.

Chapter 8

How smart people can be involuntarily employment when misguided policy dominates decision-making

Chapter outline

Introduction 189
Keynes and the real
    wage rate 191
Keynes and the demand side 195
The behavioural model and
    employment 198
Conclusion 206
References 207

Introduction

This chapter provides a more detailed and elaborate narrative of the macroeconomic implications of introducing a greater degree of human agency when modelling the firm, some of which is discussed in Chapter 5. Human agency, the capacity of individuals to make choices given their capabilities and decision-making environment in a world of bounded rationality and therefore of complexity is as fundamentally important in the macro as it is in the micro level. And, moreover, the macro world, where aggregate employment and output is determined, has fundamentally important microeconomic foundations.

A common denominator running through the spectrum of modern macroeconomic theory, be it the new classical or old and new Keynesian, is that unemployment can be reduced only if real wages are cut and that relatively high rates of unemployment are a function of relatively high real wage rates. The key philosophical distinction between the new classical and Keynesian economics is that for the new classicals unemployment is voluntary whereas for the new Keynesians it is largely involuntary. The new Keynesian theorists, basing themselves on Keynes' own foundational contribution to the literature, argue that real wages must be cut in the short run (plant size and technology are held constant) for unemployment to fall. A reduction in real wages is a necessary condition for increasing the level of employment and, thereby, the rate of unemployment. This can be done most efficaciously through a mild inflationary

Smart Economic Decision-Making in a Complex World. https://doi.org/10.1016/B978-0-12-811461-2.00008-0

process and such cuts would be acceptable to workers at large in a world where prices are sticky downwards (Akerlof, 2002; Akerlof, Dickens, & Perry, 1996, 2000; Fortin, 2001). Thus, for the new Keynesians, a key explanatory variable to persistent high rates of unemployment and to increasing unemployment rates, is the downward stickiness of real wages. Critical here is that workers will choose to have their real wages (not nominal wages) cut through government policy given the expectation that this will increase employment and will increase the probability of the employed not losing their jobs.[a] The post Keynesians, on the other hand, focus on increasing aggregate demand, implicitly assuming that real wages will fall, as need be, in the process of demand-side expansion—the dynamics of necessary real wage adjustments are largely ignored in this discourse. The new classical economists reject the assumption that workers would accept any such real wage cuts, thereby maintaining, voluntarily, the prevailing macroeconomic rate of unemployment.

A behavioural model presented in this chapter suggests that changing real wages need not affect the marginal cost of output over a range of wage rates through its effect upon effort inputs and, in the longer term, upon technical change. The behavioural model, therefore, suggests that the production function is not determined independent of real wages or working conditions in the firm, as it is in its traditional rendering. In this scenario, reducing real wages is not a necessary condition for increasing employment. Nor need increasing real wages be a supply side obstacle to increasing employment (see also Chapter 5). In this scenario, unemployment, to the extent that it is demand-side driven, need not be related to movements in real wages. Therefore, restoring full employment after a negative demand shock becomes a matter for demand management, not demand management that must be coordinated with measures designed to reduce real wages. Moreover, in this scenario, maintaining an adequate level of aggregate demand becomes a necessary condition for maintaining low levels of unemployment. Demand management is also modelled as a corollary to increasing the efficiency of labour. In other words, a dynamic dialectical relationship is established between increasing and high real wages, increasing and high levels of economic efficiency, demand management and the rate of unemployment.

From this perspective, on the supply side, more attention need be placed on increasing the level of economic efficiency as opposed to reducing real wages. On the other hand, increasing efficiency, without corresponding increases in aggregate demand will generate increasing rates of unemployment. We are not concerned here with the important issue of wage flexibility as it pertains to shifts in the demand for labour across an economy's many labour markets due to structural change or changes in consumer tastes. In this case, wage flexibility relates to movements in wages about some average to accommodate relative shifts in supply and demand across product markets. This is not the same wage

---

a. The latter is implicitly assumed. The employed don't necessarily care about employment increasing. But they definitely do care about losing their jobs.

flexibility issue addressed in the macroeconomic discourse on the average flexibility of real wages to accommodate changes in aggregate demand across all labour and product markets.

Which economic theory is used to design macroeconomic policy is critically important. The gist of this chapter is to improve the standard modelling of the causes of involuntary unemployment by introducing alternative assumptions contained in a behaviour model presented here, that wages and working conditions impact upon the production function. The framework for this discussion is the macroeconomic demand model contained in the standard IS-LM framework and in the post-Keynesian rendition of Keynes' work and the macroeconomic supply model contained in the neoclassical production function parlayed into the labour market. Particular attention is paid to the importance of supply side factors in these models, specifically real wages, as a constraint to demand side efforts to reduce the rate of unemployment.

Keynes and the real wage rate

Since Keynes provided the foundational work for active and effective demand side management of the economy as it relates to determining the level of employment, for the many varieties of Keynesian economics that have developed over the last five decades, it is of some immediate importance to garner an appreciation of his theoretical perspective on the causal relationship between real wages and the level of employment. Keynes accepts the traditional world view that labour productivity is subject to diminishing returns and that diminishing returns occur incrementally as labour inputs increase in the short run. In this scenario, a reduction in demand results in an increase in the marginal product of labour and, in equilibrium, an increase in the real wage. On the other side of the coin, for increasing demand to generate an increase in employment requires a fall in real wage rates, restoring the real wages to its pre-demand reduction level. Hamilton (1942, 1952) makes the case that long term economic development requires inflation so as to cut real wages, thereby increasing the long run profitability of investment. Related to this point are the two definitions of involuntary unemployment put forth by Keynes, which he deems to be substitutes. It is important to first note that involuntary actually refers to unemployment that, in the first instance, is a direct consequence of deficient aggregate demand.

The first definition is (Keynes, 1936, p. 15): 'Men are involuntarily unemployed if, in the event of a small rise in the price of wage-goods relative to the money-wage, both the aggregate supply of labour willing to work for the current money-wage and the aggregate demand for it at that wage would be greater than the existing volume of employment'. In this scenario, for employment to increase as aggregate demand rises requires that real wages fall. The decline in real wages is caused by an increase in the price of wage-goods, which, in turn, is a product of an increase in aggregate demand. His second definition for involuntary unemployment is actually a definition for full employment.

Of course, at less than full employment, involuntary unemployment exists. Full employment exists when (Keynes, 1936, p. 26): '...aggregate employment is inelastic in response to an increase in the effective demand for its output'. The latter condition is met when workers resist cuts to real wages as aggregate or effective demand increases.

This point is clarified by one of the summary propositions of the general theory, as specified by Keynes (1936, p. 29): '(6) For every value of N [employment] there is a corresponding marginal productivity of labour in the wage-goods industries; and it is this which determines the real wage... N cannot exceed the value which reduces the real wage to equality with the marginal disutility of labor'. We have involuntary unemployment as long as workers are willing to accept cuts to real wages, determined by the production function, which coincide with increases in aggregate demand (Keynes, 1936, p. 289). Keynes (1936, p. 245) writes: 'Our independent variables are, in the first instance, the propensity to consume, the schedule of the marginal efficiency of capital and the rate of interest [which determine the level of effective demand]. Our dependent variables are the volume of employment and the national income (or national dividend) measured in wage-units'. For Keynes, the essence of the general theory (1936, pp. 29, 30) is contained in this proposition, whereby aggregate demand drives the system with regard to determining the level of employment while real wages accommodate and adjust to changes in demand. Involuntary unemployment is in the first instance a product of deficient aggregate demand, not of real wages being too high. Nevertheless, the real wage rate plays a determining role in achieving higher levels of employment, given Keynes' acceptance of the classical assumption of a diminishing marginal product of labour.

Keynes (1939) does not accept the empirical findings of Dunlop (1938) and Tarshis (1939) that suggest that real wages do not fluctuate over the course of the business cycle and that real wages need not drop off to restore full employment. Given the classical theoretical framework which assumes diminishing returns given capital stock and technology, Keynes (1939) suggests that, although Dunlop's and Tarshis' empirics would be convenient for his own argument related to demand side unemployment, he remains unconvinced and suggests estimation problems with the Dunlop and Tarshis results. Dunlop and Tarshis basically suggests an L-shaped marginal cost curve opposed to the negatively sloped one accepted by Keynes.[b]

Once workers are no longer willing to accept real wage cuts, full employment is achieved and further increases in aggregate demand, accommodated by increases in the supply of money, will result, in equilibrium, in proportional increases in wages and prices, leaving real values, such as real wages,

---

b. Marcuzzo (1996) discusses the theory underlying L-shaped marginal cost curves and McCombie (1985–1986) discusses the possible positive relationship between marginal cost curve shifts and changes in real wages. McCombie's argument would reinforce the argument derived from the behavioural model put forth in this chapter.

employment, and real output unaffected (Keynes, 1936, p. 289). Such a scenario is one that Friedman (1968), the founder of the new classical economics, maintains is typical. Increases in effective demand cannot change real values, inclusive of real wages, employment, and output, in any permanent sense. Friedman writes (1968, p. 8): 'At any moment of time, there is some level of unemployment which has the property that it is consistent with equilibrium in the structure of real wage rates'. This rate of employment will be realized without any active efforts on the part of government to affect aggregate demand. It is implicitly assumed that any existing level of unemployment is the equilibrium or 'natural' level. And this is so following from the assumption that efforts to reduce the level of unemployment through demand management serves to increase the real wage above the marginal product of labour at the new higher level of employment. In other words, nominal wage rates are assumed to increase at a faster pace than the price of wage-goods. Thus, it is assumed that workers will typically resist the cuts to real wages required to increase employment given the production function. To increase employment further, that is to reduce the natural level and rate of unemployment requires, according to Friedman (1968, p. 9), the reduction or elimination of minimum wages and the weakening or elimination of labour unions, which would allow market forces to drop real wages to a level consistent with a higher level of employment. The natural rate can also be reduced, given the real wage, by improving employment exchanges, information of job vacancies and labour supply, and the like. Keynes, of course, argues that we would not know what the equilibrium unemployment rate is until we experience it; until through demand management we experience employment inelasticity to increases in aggregate demand. Theory, per se, cannot determine the level of full employment or demand-determined employment.

Although, like the classical economists before him and the new classical economists today, Keynes believed that a fall in real wage rates is a necessary condition for an increase in employment, ceteris paribus. But Keynes did not believe that the employed or the unemployed could orchestrate the necessary fall in real wages independent of government intervention on the demand side. Keynes (1936, pp. 9–13; Chapter 19) argues that in a competitive economy a reduction in money wages would simply result in a proportional fall in prices, thus maintaining the real wage at its original excessive level. In other words, the real wage cannot be set in the firm through the wage bargain in isolation from the workings of the macroeconomy. Moreover, workers that resist nominal wage cuts does not imply that they are unwilling to accept a cut in real wages that is a function the increasing price of wage-goods (Keynes, 1936, pp. 8–9). In this case, the supply of labour would not be entirely a function of the real wage. Rather, labour supply would be a function of money wages over a certain range of real wage rates. As Keynes (1936, p. 8) writes: '…it may be the case that within a certain range the demand of labour is for a minimum money-wage and not for minimum real wage. Resisting reductions in the money wage, in this case, would not be the same thing as resisting a cut to the real wage'.

Keynes (1936, p. 14) argues that workers tend to behave in exactly this fashion for good rational reasons—workers do not suffer from money illusion or related forms of irrational or quasi-rational behaviour. Workers play an important role in determining the rate of unemployment but only in the context of accommodating government policy—which must be the case in the real world of complex and imperfect information.

Individual workers or groups of workers tend to resist cuts to money wages since such reductions by workers in an uncoordinated labour market will result in a reduction in the relative real wage of these workers. By resisting cuts to money wages, workers are simply resisting cuts to their relative real wage and are deemed to be unfair. However, workers tend to accept cuts to the real wage that is a product of aggregate demand induced price increases that are related to efforts to increase the level of employment. Keynes, 1936, pp. 14–15) argues: 'Every trade union will put up some resistance to a cut in money-wages, however, small. But since no trade union would dream of striking on every occasion of a rise in the cost of living, they do not raise the obstacle to any increase in aggregate employment which is attributed to them by the classical school'.

This Keynesian labour market narrative can be illustrated in Fig. 8.1, where all values are in real terms. Consistent with Keynes and with conventional economic theory, assume that a negatively sloped marginal product of labour (MPL) curve (L_D) is derived from a short run production function subject to

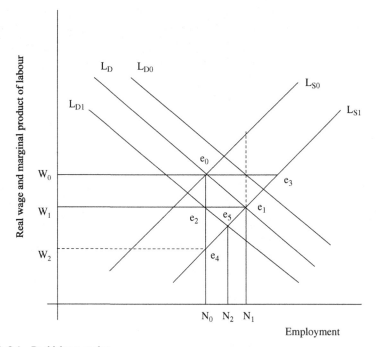

FIG. 8.1 Real labour market.

diminishing returns, where capital stock and technology are held constant. The MPL curve yields a supply side demand curve for labour, which indicates the maximum amount of labour a firm could employ at a given real wage if there exists the demand for the output produced by that labour. Also assume a conventional upward sloping labour supply curves given by L_{S0} and L_{S1}. Full employment is given by N_1, which is consistent with real wage W_1 at e_1. Assume that demand side problems, an inadequate demand for the output produced by labour, only allows for the employment of N_0 of labour. If product demand side problems result in deflation, the real wage climbs to W_0, along the MPL curve given by L_D. Keynes argues that this real wage rate at this low level of employment is greater than the marginal disutility of labour given by W_2, so that workers would accept real wages falling back to W_1, thereby making it possible for firms to hire N_1 of workers when aggregate demand reaches a level that would make this possible once again.

The drop in real wages is achieved by demand side induced price increases. If, on the other hand, real wages remain at W_1 as product demand diminishes, restoring full employment would not require any decrease in real wages.

In contrast, the old and new classical economists would argue that if we observe unemployment at N_0 at wage rate W_0, this would be the equilibrium wage with the labour supply curve at L_{S0}. Indeed, in this scenario, the lower level of employment is a product of the labour supply side driven higher real wage rate. Efforts to reduce the real wage through inflationary policy *will not shift* the labour supply curve outward to L_{S1}, thus maintaining the equilibrium employment level at the relatively lower level. But this narrative, which focuses largely on real wages as the causal variable determining the level of employment, represents only one side of the Keynesian coin. The other is the demand side.

Keynes and the demand side

It is the demand side that determines whether or not the maximum amount of labour is employed given the labour supply function and the production function. Keynes' treatment of the demand side of the economy is consistent with the graphic treatment of the demand side by the Post-Keynesians, well represented in the work of Davidson (Davidson, 1983a, 1983b, 1998; Davidson & Smolensky, 1964). Keynes introduces the aggregate supply function, which is built upon the aggregate supply price of output for a given level of employment. This supply price (Keynes, 1936, p. 24): '... is the expectation of proceeds which will just make it worth the while of entrepreneurs to give that employment'. These proceeds must cover the anticipated expenses from the employment of a given amount of labour, inclusive of labour income and payments for other factor inputs (Keynes, 1936, p. 23). It follows that different levels of employment yield a different supply price, where the supply price is a positive function of employment. The supply price of output is the minimum revenue required by the firm for it to realize a particular level of output.

On the other hand, the aggregate demand function stipulates that aggregate income to be expected by firms from sales generated from a particular level of employment. It is positively sloped given that more revenue tends to be generated as employment increases. If aggregate demand exceeds the supply price there is an incentive for firms to increase employment up to the point where the supply price equals aggregate demand income (Keynes, 1936, p. 25): '…for it is at this point that the entrepreneurs' expectation of profits will be maximized'. Where aggregate demand, that is the aggregate demand income, just equals the supply price, is referred to by Keynes as the point of effective demand. At the point of effective demand, firms just cover and expect to cover the expenses incurred from producing a given level of output associated with a given level of employment. The level of effective demand thus determines the level of employment assuming that the real wage rate, consistent with this level of employment, can be obtained. Keynes and Keynesians argue that the aggregate demand curve shifts for a variety of reasons, of particular importance would be shifts in investment spending. Thus, there may be an array of points of effective demand. The critical argument made by Keynes is that there no reason to expect that the level of effective demand should be the one which is consistent with the maximum employment point given by real wages and the production function, such as N_1 in Fig. 8.1. Nor can market forces be expected to adjust effective demand to its full employment position in either a world of flexible or inflexible prices.

In Fig. 8.2, where all values are in real terms, AD and AS are the aggregate demand and aggregate supply functions respectively. Davidson and Smolensky (1964) discuss the derivation of the macroeconomic aggregate demand and

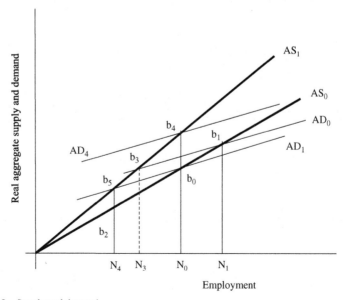

FIG. 8.2 Supply and demand.

supply curves further. AD is sloped upward as more aggregate expenditure is required to employ more workers, ceteris paribus. AS is positively sloped since on the aggregate it is more costly to employ more workers ceteris paribus. Introducing non-linear AD and AS curves would not affect the basic analytics. There is only one point of effective demand, b_1, where the aggregate supply curve AS_0 and the aggregate demand curve AD_0 intersect, which is consistent with full employment N_1, given by N_1 in Fig. 8.1. Any fall off in demand yields a drop in employment below the initial level. For example, a reduction in investment yields a shift in the aggregate demand curve to AD_1, yielding a lower level of effective demand (b_0) and a lower level of employment, N_0, consistent with N_0 in Fig. 8.1. What is driving the reduction in employment is a drop in effective demand, not a rise in real wages. For employment to increase, effective demand must rise. Of course, the real wage rate must be consistent with wage rate W_1 in Fig. 8.1 for full employment to be restored. In Fig. 8.2, it is also possible to show that, ceteris paribus, an increase in the real wage can result in a 'permanent' reduction in the level of employment. An increase in the real wage rate pivots the supply curve upwards to AS_1, yielding employment level N_3. In this scenario, simply increasing the level of effective demand could not increase the level of employment, since only by reducing the real wage rate could firms profitably hire more workers at a higher level of aggregate demand.

These arguments can also be illustrated in price-employment space, derived from a price-output space modelling, where the latter is the traditional venue of the conventional macroeconomic wisdom, built upon the IS-LM framework originated by Hicks (1957). Employment and output are directly linked through the production function. From the perspective of Keynes and Keynesian economics, the supply curve is positively sloped, wherein increasing prices result in lower real wages allowing for more workers to be employed as per Fig. 8.1. In Fig. 8.3, supply curve S_1 contains a vertical portion, reflecting the minimum real wage rate below which workers refuse to allow the wage rate to fall. The demand curve is negatively sloped, reflecting the impact that price changes have, for example, upon the real money supply. Where demand curve D_1 cuts supply curve S_1 at c_1 yields the full employment level of employment, N_1, consistent with N_1 in Fig. 8.1. Demand side unemployment is caused by a fall in demand given by an inward shift in the demand curve to D_0, yielding employment level N_0. The lower price level, P_0, yields a higher real wage, as per W_0 in Fig. 8.1, which will fall with a reversal in demand back to its full employment position at D_1. In a world in inflexible money wages, inflation serves to adjust real wages to its production function consistent values as aggregate demand fluctuates. Classical economists would argue that if employment is at N_0, this is full employment since the supply curve would be vertical reflecting the unwillingness of workers to allow real wages to fall to the extent necessary, given the production function, to generate a higher level of employment. Increasing demand from D_0 to D_1 would simply serve to increase the price level from P_0 to above the original P_1 such as to P_2.

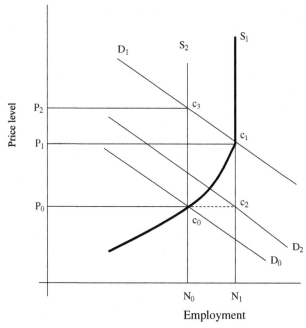

FIG. 8.3 Prices and employment.

The behavioural model and employment

The behavioural model of the firm, which I've developed in some detail else-where (for example, Altman, 1992, 1998, 1999, 2001, 2002; see also Chapter 5) introduces the assumption that wages and working conditions affect effort lev-els and technical change. The theoretical framework adopted is an extension and elaboration of Leibenstein (1966). Thus, effort is introduced into the short and long run production function as a variable, where the former is most relevant to the traditional Keynesian narrative. The standard assumption in macroeco-nomics is that effort is invariant to changes in wages and working conditions. Therefore, increases in wages induce lower levels of employment on the supply side. However, the assumption of effort variability and its positive relationship to wages and overall working conditions has substantial empirical support.

Economic theory should therefore incorporate the possibility of effort vari-ability and the implication of this for macroeconomics. Key empirical findings suggest that there is a positive relationship between wages and productivity given technology with effort input being the assumed intermediary variable and, moreover, that changes in wages induce changes in productivity. This positive relationship is strongest when the wage rate is embedded in a particular indus-trial relations setting (see, for example, Akerlof, 2002; Altman, 2002; Buchele & Christainsen, 1995, 1999; Fehr & Gachter, 2000; Ichniowski, Kochan, Levine,

Olson, & Strauss, 1996; Levine & Tyson, 1990, for some empirical backing for this type of modelling of the economic agent). Moreover, wages tend to be sticky downward over the business cycle because of this positive relationship between wages and effort (for example Akerlof, 2002; Bewley, 1999).

More recently, in the efficiency wage literature, effort variability is introduced to provide one explanation for downward nominal wage inflexibility (for example, Akerlof & Yellen, 1986, 1988, 1990; Bewley, 1999; Stiglitz, 1987; Yellen, 1984). The latter does not affect the standard analytical prediction that more employment requires lower real wages or that persistent high levels of unemployment are largely a product of high real wages or other supply side constraints to employment growth. Another strand of the efficiency wage literature suggests that a high level of unemployment is a product of firms having to pay above market clearing wages so as to minimize costs in world where workers shirk at low levels of unemployment when their bargaining power is greatest (Shapiro & Stiglitz, 1984; Weisskopf, Bowles, & Gordon, 1983; Yellen, 1984). The behavioural modelling of the firm presented here is distinct from what underlies efficiency wage theories, yielding distinct analytical predictions.

The assumption of effort variability is introduced here to examine its implications for employment in a world where real wages rise as employment increases and where workers resist real wage cuts even if they are a product of price increases. The standard efficiency wage literature as it relates to macroeconomic theory flows from Solow (1979), where he argues that a reduction in the real wage by the firm yields a reduction of effort inputs by labour. In this scenario, the firm chooses a real wage that minimizes labour costs per efficiency unit. There will be one such unique wage, which is deemed the efficiency wage.

If this wage is above the market-clearing wage on the labour market, there will be unemployment since the profit-maximizing firm has no incentive to cut the real wage in a monetary economy. Nevertheless, leading proponents of the efficiency wage hypothesis argue that inflationary policy can serve to reduce the real wage without any negative impact on the effort dimension, thus allowing for effective demand side policy to increase the level of employment (Akerlof et al., 2000). In this most recent articulation of the Keynesian perspective, it is assumed that workers are quasi-rational at low levels of inflation and thus suffer from money illusion. Quasi-rationality was, of course, a concept never adopted by Keynes to explain nominal wage rigidity.

Unlike what is assumed in the traditional efficiency wage literature, in the behavioural model presented here it is assumed that there exists some linearity with respect to the relationship between effort inputs and the wage rate which, for simplicity, is assumed to embody the entire system of industrial relations within the firm. In this scenario, there is an array of wage rates consistent with a unique marginal or average cost when productivity changes, brought about through effort changes, just sufficient to offset the cost impact that changes to the real wage might otherwise have. In the conventional efficiency wage view, by assumption, there exists only one unique wage that minimizes costs (Akerlof & Yellen, 1986; Altman, 2001, 2002; Solow, 1979). The behavioural perspective is illustrated in Eqs (8.1a), (8.1b) and Fig. 8.4.

$$MC = \frac{w}{(dQ/dL)} \ldots \tag{8.1a}$$

$$AC = \frac{w}{(Q/L)} \ldots \tag{8.1b}$$

where MC is marginal cost, w is the wage rate, (dQ/dL) is the marginal product of labour, AC is average cost, and (Q/L) is the average product of labour. Assuming, for simplicity, that labour is the only input, marginal cost and average cost do not increase in the face of an increasing wage rate nor do they fall when the wage rate falls, if there exist corresponding and proportional changes in the marginal and average product, respectively.

It is important to note that productivity need not increase proportionally to increases in labour costs when labour is only one amongst many inputs into the production process, which is typically the case. When labour is not the only compensated factor input, labour productivity increases less than proportionally

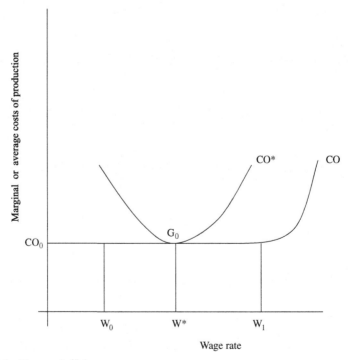

FIG. 8.4 Wages and efficiency.

to increases in labour costs so as to neutralize increases labour cost. This point is illustrated in Eq. (8.2)

$$\frac{dAC}{AC} = \left(\frac{dw}{w}\right)\left(\frac{w*L}{w*L+NLC}\right)\ldots \qquad (8.2)$$

where dAC is the change in average cost, dw is the change in the wage rate, and NLC is non-labour costs. If, for example, the wage rate is increased by 10% (dw/w) and wage costs (w×L) represent 100% of total costs, labour productivity must increase by 10% to compensate for what would otherwise be a 10% increase in average costs. However, if wage costs represent only 50% of total costs, labour productivity must increase by only 5% to compensate for what would otherwise be a 5% increase in average costs.

In Fig. 8.4, flowing from the behavioural model, an array of wage rates, including the relatively low real wage W_0 and the relatively high real wage W_1, result a unique marginal cost of CO_0. The conventional efficiency wage assumptions yield a unique efficiency wage W^*. Any other wage rate increases the marginal and average costs of production. In the behaviour model, firm owners have no immediate economic incentive to change the wage rate up or down from its original level. Productivity changes simply offset changes in labour costs. In other words, in this model, a firm hierarchy that does not voluntarily change real wage rates is behaving rationally. Moreover, in the short term, efforts to cut real wages can result in transitionally higher costs, which generate incentives to maintain the real wage at its original level. At any given wage rate, the wage rate cost curve, such as CO_0CO, shifts upward when wages are cut until adjustments are completed.

The behavioural model suggests that even if one assumes that workers resist cuts to their real wages, irrespective of whether these cuts are attempted directly by the firm hierarchy or indirectly through an inflationary process, this need not preclude effective demand side policy from increasing the level of employment. The conventional efficiency wage literature assumes that the efficiency wage yields a point along the marginal product curve of the firm that generates a relatively low level of employment and thus a relatively high rate of unemployment. Only cuts to the real wage will allow for more employment on the supply side. But this need not be the case. If a negative demand shock to the economy yields a higher real wage ($W_0–W_1$ in Fig. 8.1), as one moves along the negatively sloped marginal product of labour curve given by L_D, for example, (as one would in the standard Keynesian model) and this positively affects labour productivity (as would be the case in the behavioural model), the marginal product curve shifts outward to L_{D0}. The higher real wage would here be consistent with a higher level of employment, such as N_1 as opposed to N_0. This higher level of employment could be achieved only if aggregate demand increases sufficiently to absorb the increased output.

Price increases to reduce the real wage are not required to increase employment in this scenario. Thus, increasing employment from N_0 to N_1 occurs without any cut to real wage rates, with constant prices, as a product of the efficiency effect of increasing the real wage from W_1 to W_0. Moreover, in the context of an efficiency effect induced by increasing the real wage rate, a particular level of employment such as N_1, given by the production function, is associated with an array of wage rates. Higher real wages need not imply lower attainable levels of employment and lower real wages higher levels of attainable employment.

In Fig. 8.3, the increase in employment is illustrated using vertical supply curves wherein changes in employment are not affected by price changes. Holding the price level constant at P_0, employment increases from N_0 to N_1 as demand rises as a consequence of an outward shift of the marginal product of labour curve which compensates for any increases in real wages required to induce the requisite increases in labour supply underlying increasing employment. This is reflected in the movement of the employment supply curve from S_2 to S_1. The employment supply curve is thus perfectly inelastic with respect to price and employment becomes 'full employment' once employment is at a maximum given the labour supply and production functions.

In the short run, increasing demand from D_0 would simply increase price given employment curve S_2, such as to P_2 with demand curve D_1. In the longer run, as the supply curve shifts outward to S_1, employment increases to N_1. An employment supply curve can be given by $P_0c_0c_1$. In this scenario, a price increase can accompany the increase in employment if the demand increases sufficiently, for example to D_1. But it would not be the increase in the price level that actually causes the increase in employment to N_1. Rather, it is an increase in aggregate demand in the context of the real wage rate induced increase in labour productivity that is responsible for an increase in the level of employment. The supply curve shifts to the right for conventional reasons which should incorporate extraordinary increases in efficiency as well as technological change induced by increasing real wages—in the Keynesian short run it is the efficiency effect induced by increased wages which is most pertinent.

In the context of the behavioural model, the question of the potential impact of cutting real wages through inflation can also be addressed. Of course, the conventional wisdom suggests that this should result in more employment given a sufficient increase in aggregate demand. In Fig. 8.1, as wages fall from W_0 to W_1, along L_D, employment rises from N_0 to N_1, if there is an adequate increase in aggregate demand, where N_1 is the initial full employment level of employment and L_{S1} is the labour supply curve. But to the extent that lower real wages generates lower effort inputs and thus an inward shift in the marginal product of labour curve, lower wages do not make it possible for firms to profitably employ more workers given adequate aggregate demand. Ceteris paribus, lower real wages might result in the original or even a lesser number of workers being employed. Thus, if the marginal product of labour curve shifts inward to L_{D1}, W_1 of real wages will only allow for N_0 of employment. Cutting real wages is not a necessary condition for increasing employment when such cuts contribute towards reducing the level of labour productivity. Contrary to the conventional wisdom, cutting real wages, in this scenario, can instead serve to impede the process of employment growth. Thus, lower wages may yield higher rates of unemployment when effort is a variable in the production function. But recall that in the new-Keynesian approach, most recently articulated by Akerlof et al. (1996), Akerlof et al. (2000), Akerlof (2002), real wage cuts serve to increase employment only because workers are 'quasi-rational', suffering from money illusion.

At a more general level, the behavioural model suggests that increasing real wages and policies which contribute towards higher real wage rates, such as unionization, minimum wages, and unemployment insurance, need not contribute towards lower levels of sustainable employment and thus to higher levels of, what Friedman refers to, natural unemployment rates. To the extent that higher real wages can be causally related to higher levels of labour productivity, one cannot predict that real wage increases are an obstacle to full employment. In fact, such labour productivity increases can make for higher levels of sustainable employment. However, for the higher level of sustainable employment to be realized, aggregate demand must be increased sufficiently to absorb the increased output. A more productive workforce will, of course, be producing more than the less productive one. This is point is clarified in Eqs (8.3), (8.4):

$$Q = L \times \frac{Q}{L} \dots \tag{8.3}$$

where Q is total output and L is total employment and (Q/L) is labour productivity. Eqs (6.1a), (6.1b) can be transformed into:

$$L = \frac{Q}{(Q/L)} \dots \tag{8.4}$$

From Eqs (8.3), (8.4) it is clear that when workers become more productive, for the original number of workers to remain employed output must increased and unless output increases proportionally to labour productivity, employment falls. Referring back to Fig. 8.2, ceteris paribus, increasing aggregate supply through an increase in labour productivity, from AS_0 to AS_1, with the initial level of employment at N_0 given by aggregate demand curve AD_1 at b_0, will result in a lower level of employment at N_4 at b_5, unless accompanied by an increase in aggregate demand from AD_1 to AD_4 yielding a new level of effective demand at b_4. With this in mind, what should be of concern to policy makers is the extent to which real wage increases are matched or surpassed by increases in labour productivity and the extent to which related increases in output are matched by increases in aggregate demand. To the extent that increasing productivity is an option as employment increases, public policy need not focus on developing effective methods to reduce real wages or the growth of real wages, which is so much the focus of Keynesian, new Keynesian and of course the various iterations of Classical analysis.

Overall, the behavioural model suggests that increasing real wage rates or the failure of demand management policy to reduce real wages through the inflationary process need not pose an obstacle to increasing the level of employment. Rather, in the context of increasing real wage rates or the downward inflexibility of wage rates, employment growth might be held back most significantly by slow growth in labour productivity and by restrictive macroeconomic policies. Lombard (2000) suggests that restrictive macroeconomic policy in Western Europe played a determining role in driving unemployment rates here to historically high levels for the post world war two period. Freeman (1995) raises some doubt as the overall efficacy of real wage flexibility as a vehicle to reduce the rate of unemployment in Europe down to current, relatively low, American rates. That wage inflexibility per se need not pose an obstacle to the realization of relatively low rates of employment, see Galbraith, Conceicao, and Ferriera (1999) and Nickell (1997). Needless to say, the behavioural model suggests that higher real wages positively affect labour productivity through its impact upon effort inputs. In a more dynamic modelling of the labour market, higher real wages would also affect labour productivity through its impact on technical change—this would shift the aggregate supply curve in Fig. 8.3 outward (Altman, 1998, 2001). In this context, employment would be encouraged by efforts to promote increases in labour productivity and more aggressive demand management strategies designed to accommodate the resulting increase in aggregate output. Meltzer (1983, 1984) in his interpretation of the Keynes' general theory argues that labour productivity is also affected by investment in capital stock, which is slowed down during economic recessions. To the extent that capital stock represents an important embodiment of new technology, recessions serve to further constrain labour productivity growth and, thereby, the realization of the maximum level of employment as determined by the production function. Also, Darity and Goldsmith (1996) point out that extended exposure to unemployment might have a lasting and negative impact on the productivity of labour thereby reducing the maximum level of employment. In this scenario, active macroeconomic policy therefore generates the added benefit of increasing labour productivity which, ceteris paribus, allows for a higher level of employment to be realized than would be otherwise possible.

This model further suggests the possibility of lower levels of unemployment being associated with higher real wage rates whilst higher levels of unemployment are associated with lower real wages rates. This possibility is manifested in the research of Blanchflower and Oswald (1994, 1995, 2005), who find, using an international sample population, that regions with low unemployment rates are systematically correlated with high wage rates and vice versa. More specifically, they find that for all countries examined, reducing the unemployment rate by 1% is statistically correlated with a 0.1% increase in the wage rate. Blachflower and Oswald argue that bargaining and efficiency wage models—the model articulated in this article is of this genre—is most consistent with their empirics. In the model presented here, the level of unemployment associated with a particular level of real wages critically depends on the elasticity of labour productivity to the wage rate and the responsiveness of macroeconomic demand side variables to increasing output.

Of particular concern in this chapter is to address what appears to be an empirical paradox to the conventional wisdom: that higher real wages, both in the short and the long run, are consistent with higher levels of employment and lower rates of unemployment and that lowering real wages need not provide the microeconomic incentives for firms to employ more workers. When effort is a variable in the production function, this paradox can be addressed if not resolved (see also Altman, 2001).

The behavioural model presented here also suggests that a positive empirical relationship between the price level or the rate of inflation and employment need not be a causal one. Rather, it might simply reflect underlying dynamics in the economy wherein it is increasing labour productivity in conjunction with increasing aggregate demand that is driving the increase in employment. Inflation might simply be a reflection of an accommodating macroeconomic policy that allows for the absorption of the increasing output flowing from the increase in labour productivity. Inflation would here be a product of overshooting increases in aggregate demand in a world of uncertainty. In this sense, low rates of inflation are consistent with increasing the level of employment, although not the cause of such increases.

The traditional Keynesian perspective articulated early on in the game by Samuelson and Solow (1960) and manifested most recently by Akerlof et al. (1996, 2000) and Fortin (2001), is that price increases result in more employment and thus in lower levels of unemployment by reducing real wage rates or the rate of growth in real wage rates. This Phillips (1958) Curve type relationship is rejected by the new classical economists. But as we discuss in this chapter, lower real wages need not be a necessary condition to achieve lower unemployment rates.

Finally, the behavioural model is consistent with the assumption of 'rational' workers, that is workers who do not suffer from money illusion—'quasi-rational' workers is a critical assumption in much of the new Keynesian literature. This assumption of the 'rational' worker is consistent with the modelling articulated by Keynes in the general theory and in the works of the new classical macroeconomists following in the footsteps of Friedman's critical 1968 essay. Resisting cuts to real wages need not impede employment growth to the extent that efficiency changes are such that they prevent unit employment costs from rising as employment increases. Thus, workers do not have to be tricked or forced into accepting low overall rates of labour compensation for employment to be restored to its 'full employment' level. To the extent that effort is invariant to changes in labour costs and technological change is exogenous, the behavioural model collapses into the standard Keynesian model wherein real wages must fall to accommodate increases in employment.

To summarize, some of important testable analytical predictions that flow form the behavioural model are that, assuming rational agents:

1. If a downward demand shock to the economy yields higher real wages, restoring employment to its pre-shock equilibrium does not require an accommodating decrease in real wages if increasing real wages generates an offsetting efficiency effect.
2. Downward stickiness of nominal wages need not be an impediment to increasing employment, given the existence of sufficient aggregate demand, if increasing real wages yields an efficiency effect.
3. Positive demand shocks to the economy need not generate only nominal economics effects if subsequent increases in real wages generate offsetting efficiency effects.
4. In the long run, higher rates of employment would be positively correlated with higher levels of wages if the latter yields efficiency and induced technological change effects.

Conclusion

Keynes argued that in monetized market economies unemployment rates can reach high levels and get stuck at these high levels without active government macroeconomic intervention. However, he believed that although the key to achieving low rates of unemployment is demand management, he argued, basing himself on the conventional wisdom, that increasing demand must be and would be accompanied by a reduction in the real wage rate even if one assumes 'rational' economic agents. This perspective is echoed in the contemporary macroeconomic literature where persistent high rates of unemployment are typically attributed to the downward rigidity of real wages.

The behavioural model presented here suggests that higher real wage rates or the downward stickiness of real wages may have little to do with either generating or maintaining relatively high rates of unemployment if such wage rates positively affect labour productivity. Moreover, lower real wage rates might have the effect of reducing the maximum level of achievable employment by reducing labour productivity. Therefore, the existence of relatively high real wage rates and the downward inflexibility of real wage rates need not signify labour market obstacles to the realization of sustainable lower unemployment rates. In this scenario, the culprit responsible for high rates of unemployment might very well be restrictive and inadequately expansive macroeconomic policy. Efforts to make labour markets more flexible by weakening the bargaining power of labour so as to reduce the unemployment rate might be both unnecessary and counterproductive. It might be much more fruitful to pursue policy that would facilitate increases in productivity inclusive of policies that would facilitate firms adopting innovations, both managerial and technological, to increase productivity as real wages increase and working conditions improve. The behavioural model therefore suggests that more research effort be expended to better understand the relationship between wage rates and working conditions, and labour productivity, and how this relationship relates to demand-side policy. Simply assuming that labour productivity is determined independent of the wage rate and working conditions and that given diminishing returns real wages must be made flexible downward can very well generate economic policy that needlessly reduces the absolute or relative level of material wellbeing of workers while doing nothing to bring employment to the currently involuntarily unemployed.

References

Akerlof, G. A. (2002). Behavioral macroeconomics and macroeconomic behavior. *American Economic Review, 92*, 411–433.

Akerlof, G. A., Dickens, W., & Perry, G. (1996). Low inflation or no inflation: Should the Federal Reserve pursue complete price stability. *Challenge: the Magazine of Economic Affairs, 39*, 11–17.

Akerlof, G. A., Dickens, W., & Perry, G. (2000). Near-rational wage and price setting and the long-run Phillips curve. *Brookings Papers on Economic Activity, 1*, 1–60.

Akerlof, G. A. & Yellen, J. L. (Eds.), (1986). *Efficiency wage models of the labor market.* Cambridge, England and New York: Cambridge University Press.

Akerlof, G. A., & Yellen, J. L. (1988). Fairness and unemployment. *American Economic Review, Papers and Proceedings, 78*, 44–49.

Akerlof, G. A., & Yellen, J. L. (1990). The fair wage hypothesis and unemployment. *Quarterly Journal of Economics, 105*, 255–283.

Altman, M. (1992). The economics of exogenous increases in wage rates in a behavioral IX-efficiency model of the firm. *Review of Social Economy, 50*, 163–192.

Altman, M. (1998). A high wage path to economic growth and development. *Challenge: The Magazine of Economic Affairs, 41*, 91–104.

Altman, M. (1999). The methodology of economics and the survivor principle revisited and revised: Some welfare and public policy implications of modeling the economic agent. *Review of Social Economics, 57*, 427–429.

Altman, M. (2001). *Worker satisfaction and economic performance: The microfoundations of economic success and failure.* Armonk, New York: M.E. Sharpe.

Altman, M. (2002). Economic theory, public policy and the challenge of innovative work practices. *Economic and Industrial Democracy: An International Journal, 23*, 271–281.

Bewley, T. F. (1999). *Why wages don't fall during a recession.* Cambridge, MA/London: Harvard University Press.

Blanchflower, D. G., & Oswald, A. J. (1994). *The wage curve.* Cambridge, MA: MIT Press.

Blanchflower, D. G., & Oswald, A. J. (1995). An introduction to the wage curve. *Journal of Economic Perspectives, 9*, 153–167.

Blanchflower, D. G., & Oswald, A. J. (2005). The wage curve reloaded. In *National Bureau of Economic Research working paper #11338.* Cambridge: MA.

Buchele, R., & Christainsen, J. (1995). Worker rights promote productivity growth. *Challenge: The Magazine of Economic Affairs, 38*, 32–37.

Buchele, R., & Christainsen, J. (1999). Labor relations and productivity growth in advanced capitalist economies. *Review of Radical Political Economics, 31*, 87–110.

Darity, W., Jr., & Goldsmith, A. H. (1996). Unemployment, social psychology, and macroeconomics. *Journal of Economic Perspectives, 10*, 121–140.

Davidson, P. (1983a). The dubious labor market analysis in Meltzer's restatement of Keynes's theory. *Journal of Economic Literature, 21*, 52–56.

Davidson, P. (1983b). The marginal product curve is not the demand curve for labor and Lucas's labor supply function is not the supply curve for labor in the real world. *Journal of Post Keynesian Economics, 6*, 105–117.

Davidson, P. (1998). Post Keynesian employment analysis and the macroeconomics of OECD unemployment. *Economic Journal, 108*, 817–831.

Davidson, P., & Smolensky, E. (1964). *Aggregate supply and demand analysis.* New York: Harper and Row.

Dunlop, J. T. (1938). The movement of real and money wage rates. *Economic Journal, 48*, 413–434.

Fehr, E., & Gachter, S. (2000). Fairness and retaliation: The economics of reciprocity. *Journal of Economic Perspectives, 14*, 159–181.

Fortin, P. (2001). Inflation targeting: The three percent solution. *Policy Matters, 2*, 2–16.

Freeman, R. (1995). The limits of wage flexibility to curing unemployment. *Oxford Review of Economic Policy, 11*, 63–72.

Friedman, M. (1968). The role of monetary policy. *American Economic Review, 58*, 1–17.

Galbraith, J. K., Conceicao, P., & Ferriera, P. (1999). Inequality and unemployment in Europe: The American cure. *New Left Review, 253*, 28–51.

Hamilton, E. J. (1942). Profit inflation and the industrial revolution, 1751–1800. *Quarterly Journal of Economics, 56*, 256–273.

Hamilton, E. J. (1952). Prices as a factor in business growth: Prices and progress. *Journal of Economic History, 12*, 325–349.

Hicks, J. R. (1957). A rehabilitation of 'classical' economics. *Economic Journal, 67*, 278–289.

Ichniowski, C., Kochan, T. A., Levine, D., Olson, C., & Strauss, G. (1996). What works at work: Overview and assessment. *Industrial Relations, 35*, 299–333.

Keynes, J. M. (1936). *The general theory of employment, interest, and money.* Brace and Company, New York: Harcourt.

Keynes, J. M. (1939). Relative movements of real wages and output. *Economic Journal, 49*, 34–51.

Leibenstein, H. (1966). Allocative efficiency vs. 'x-efficiency'. *American Economic Review, 56*, 392–415.

Levine, D. I., & Tyson, L. D. (1990). Participation, productivity, and the firm's environment. In A. S. Blinder (Ed.), *Paying for productivity: A look at the evidence* (pp. 183–237). Washington, DC: Brookings Institute.

Lombard, M. (2000). Restrictive macroeconomic policies and unemployment in the European Union. *Review of Political Economy, 12*, 317–332.

Marcuzzo, M. C. (1996). Alternative microeconomic foundations for macroeconomics: The controversy over the L-shaped cost curve revisited. *Review of Political Economy, 8*, 7–22.

McCombie, J. S. L. (1985). Why cutting real wages will not necessarily reduce unemployment— Keynes and the 'postulates of the classical economists'. *Journal of Post Keynesian Economics, 8*, 233–248.

Meltzer, A. H. (1983). Interpreting Keynes. *Journal of Economic Literature, 21*, 66–78.

Meltzer, A. H. (1984). Keynes's labor market: A reply. *Journal of Post Keynesian Economics, 6*, 532–539.

Nickell, S. (1997). Unemployment and labor market rigidities: Europe versus North America. *Journal of Economic Perspectives, 11*, 55–74.

Phillips, W. A. (1958). The relation between unemployment and the rate of change of money wage rates in the United Kingdom, 1861–1957. *Economica, 25*, 283–299.

Samuelson, P. A., & Solow, R. M. (1960). Analytical aspects of anti-inflation policy. *American Economic Review, 50*, 177–194.

Shapiro, C., & Stiglitz, J. E. (1984). Equilibrium unemployment as a worker discipline device. *American Economic Review, 74*, 433–444.

Solow, R. M. (1979). Another possible source of wage stickiness. *Journal of Macroeconomics, 1*, 79–82.

Stiglitz, J. E. (1987). The causes and consequences of the dependence of quantity on price. *Journal of Economic Literature, 25*, 1–48.

Tarshis, L. (1939). Changes in real and money wages. *Economic Journal, 49*, 150–154.

Weisskopf, T. E., Bowles, S., & Gordon, D. M. (1983). Hearts and minds: A social model of US productivity growth. *Brookings Papers on Economic Activity, 2*, 381–441.

Yellen, J. L. (1984). Efficiency wage models of unemployment. *American Economic Review, Papers and Proceedings, 74*, 200–205.

Chapter 9

Why financial literacy matters for socio-economic wellbeing

Chapter outline

Introduction   211
The conventional wisdom   215
Fast and frugal decision-making and smart heuristics   216
Institutions matter   218
Errors and biases and 'irrational' heuristics   219
Financial education and literacy and the different faces of behavioural economics   222
Linkages between financial issues, financial education, and financial literacy   224
Pensions and saving   224
Investing in financial assets   227
Bubbles and busts: Animal spirits and decision-making   228
Informational problems and errors in decision making   232
The trust heuristic   233
Ponzi schemes and the trust heuristic   234
Conclusion: Economic theory, financial literacy and public policy   236
References   242

Introduction

This chapter discusses decision-making in the real world of complexity and bounded rationality in the context of financial literacy and its mirror image, financial illiteracy. This is a fundamentally important area of decision making. And, it relates to individuals across socio-economics groups and ages. A standard definition of financial literacy is 'having the knowledge, skills and confidence to make responsible financial decisions'. The institutional environment is also important to financial decision making and greatly affects choices, influencing the extent and quality of relevant information and incentives. Financial literacy is of increasing concern to government and other public policy makers. Surveys in OECD countries find that financial literacy is very low amongst individuals and households irrespective of income and education, but especially amongst groups with lower income and less education. Even stock ownership and trading in financial assets do not appear to improve the level of financial literacy. Most people have difficulty answering questions about compound interest, inflation, or risk diversification, and have difficulty understanding budgeting and saving programs and financial information in general. This appears

Smart Economic Decision-Making in a Complex World. https://doi.org/10.1016/B978-0-12-811461-2.00009-2

to be the case in Canada, the United States, the United Kingdom, Australia, New Zealand, Korea, and the Netherlands (Munshaw, 2008; OECD, 2005; Yoong, 2010). Serious gaps in financial literacy are of mounting concern, with the increasing number of financial products and services on the market, their increased complexity, and the escalating importance of financial decision-making to individuals and society at large, especially as life expectancy is increasing.

Estimates of the economic losses due to financial illiteracy are very rough and ready. But they amount to billions of American dollars per year, perhaps 1–2% of American GDP, perhaps the same for the rest of the world.[a] At best these estimates are lower-bound. They don't carefully take into consideration the losses in income due to not securing the best possible employment, for example. They don't take into consideration errors in voting behaviour due to financial illiteracy nor do they incorporate poor and misguided policy that's product of financial illiteracy. Moreover, these estimates don't take into account the extent which economic losses disproportionately hurt lower income groups.

The topic of financial literacy raises the issue of the potential role that might be played by education, quality information, and incentives in improving decisions. It can be argued that with a less than ideal education, information sets, and incentives, individuals cannot make the best decisions. By contributing to financial literacy, financial education should contribute to more informed and effective decisions on financial matters such as contributions to pensions, use of credit cards, household budgeting, mortgages, and investing in the stock market. Improvements to relevant information, with a focus on quality (and truthfulness), make possible the effective use of financial education. Financial education and quality information go hand and hand, forming key ingredients to effective financial literacy.

This perspective on financial literacy, I would argue, runs contrary to the standard or conventional economic wisdom. The conventional wisdom presumes that individuals have the physiological and psychological capabilities, and are in an informational, governance, and social environment, that will allow them to make optimal decisions. If the typical individual is so endowed, financial education can have little impact on improving choices. In effect, one might argue that in the conventional approach individuals either are assumed to be financially literate or that they make choices consistent with financial literacy. This approach does not allow for a robust discussion of the extent which financial illiteracy exists. Basically, this is the case, because individuals are assumed to be behaving optimally. This is analogous to our discussion of the firm where individuals are assumed to be behaving optimally, hence economic efficiency (x-efficiency) is assumed. In this conventional narrative of the firm, the possibility of x-inefficiency in the firm is assumed away. With regards to financial literacy, it is assumed that there is no x-inefficiency in the domain of financial

---

a. Author's estimates based on aggregate loss estimates from various sources. See especially, World Literacy Foundation (2015, 2018) and Lusardi and Mitchell (2014).

decision making. Therefore, there can be no room for improvement. We end up ignoring an important (well documented) cause of sub-optimal economic, indeed, socio-economic outcomes, which is a function of poor financial-related decision-making. Although, I argue that financial illiteracy is critically important in the real world of complexity and bounded rationality, this does not mean that decision-makers, themselves, are personally responsible for poor (sub-optimal) financial-related decision. I argue that much of financial illiteracy is related to the decision-making environment which the individual is not directly responsible for. Institutional change and investment in financial literature education can play an important role in reducing the extent of x-inefficiency in the domain of financial-related decisions.

Research in behavioural economics suggests quite different behavioural and institutional assumptions. There are two key perspectives in behavioural economics that yield distinct implications for financial literacy and financial education (Altman, 2008), both of which deny that individuals typically behave as rationally as assumed by conventional economics. Behavioural economics also questions the conventional assumption that the environment in which financial decisions are make is necessarily ideal (Altman, 2012).

This chapter discusses the implications of the two approaches of behavioural economics for possible improvements to financial literacy and, therefore, to financial decision making. What I refer to as the Kahneman–Tversky approach maintains that individuals often make systematic errors and biases in decision making that are largely rooted in the hard-wiring of the brain. Errors and biases occur when individuals deviate from conventional (neoclassical) decision-making rules. Education can have little effect on such behaviour. This approach is much more supportive of government policy that nudges consumers into making decisions that some might argue are in the best interest of consumers. Experts are assumed to know better than individual decision makers what is in their best interest (Thaler & Sunstein, 2003, 2008; see also Camerer, Issacharoff, Loewenstein, O'Donoghue, & Rabin, 2003; de Meza, Irlenbusch, & Reyniers, 2008; Shefrin, 2002; see Sugden, 2008, 2009, for a critique of Thaler and Sunstein).

What I refer to as the Simon-March approach (bounded rationality-smart decision maker), argues that individuals are physiologically incapable of behaving as prescribed and predicted by conventional economic wisdom. As a result, they develop heuristics, or experience-based decision-making shortcuts, to make choices that are rational and smart even though often inconsistent with the conventional behavioural norms. It is also recognized that the typical choice environment is characterized by asymmetric information, incomplete information, and even false information and poor education. Both physiological and environmental constraints can, but need not, result in errors in decision making, such as relatively poor investment decisions, poor household planning, and errors in labour market decisions. Because choice environments can be changed, this approach provides a much stronger rationale for enhancing the quality of financial decision making through improvements to financial education and the decision-making environment. This would include improved access to and improved availability of quality and pertinent information, appropriate decision-making rules and regulations, and appropriate financial education. On the whole, individual preferences, which are regarded as multi-faceted across decision makers, are respected and less attention is paid to nudging unless individual choices can be shown to cause social harm (negative externalities). This perspective is well reflected in the research of Shiller (2001, 2008, 2009, 2010), a leading behavioural finance scholar (see also Chapters 2 and 3).

These different approaches to financial decision-making are summarized in Table 9.1.

TABLE 9.1 Comparing different approaches to decision making.

1. Conventional economic theory	• Individuals make intelligent decisions, and they do not regret them. Their choices reveal informed and well-considered preferences. • An ideal decision-making environment is assumed. • Education and training (referred to as human capital formation) are regarded as important means of enhancing productivity. But no clear theoretical mechanism is specified linking improvements in the quantity and quality of education and improvements in decision making. • Human capital formation provides important theoretical space for explaining errors or less than ideal decisions, a space well-taken by behavioural economics. • Financial decision-making is assumed to be best-practice unless distorted by government interventions in the market and in decision making.
2. Behavioural economics: Kahneman–Tversky, errors and biases approach	• Individuals tend to make irrational, error-prone decisions, which they eventually regret. • Errors and biases in decision making are wired into the brain architecture. • It is possible for the decision-making environment to be less than ideal. • Individuals often do not know what is in their own best interest. • The benchmark for rationality in decision making is based on conventional economics and focuses upon calculating behaviour. • Decision-making shortcuts are regarded as typically error-prone. • Individuals are easily fooled and deceived by how questions are framed and often reverse their preferred decisions with inconsequential changes in how questions or options are framed. • Education can sometimes improve decision making. • Government intervention in decision making is often thought to be the best-practice route to take for ideal choices to be made. • Financial decision-making will be biased and error-prone without government intervention in choice behaviour. • Some success predicted for improvements in the decision-making environment, less for the improvements to financial education.

TABLE 9.1 Comparing different approaches to decision making—cont'd

3. Behavioural economics: Simon, bounded rationality, rational individuals approach	• Individuals are assumed to make rational decisions as a result of how the brain is wired and the decision-making environment. • Conventional benchmarks for rational or intelligent decisions are often rejected. • Decision-making shortcuts are rational more often than not, even when they contravene conventional economic benchmarks. • Individuals are not easily fooled, but they can be misled. • Individuals can make decision-making errors and these can lead to decisions that are subject to regret. • A major source of decision-making errors is a less than ideal institutional environment. • Education can have important effects on decision making. • Government plays an important role by establishing an ideal institutional environment and by providing the education required for ideal choices to be executed. • Government should not intervene in individual choices unless these choices can be shown to cause harm to others. • Financial decision-making can be improved by improving the decision-making environment and through improvement to financial education. • Government intervention in choice behaviour is not considered to be best-practice if individuals make decisions in an ideal decision-making environment and with appropriate levels of financial education.

The conventional wisdom

The standard set of assumptions of the conventional wisdom is well articulated by Simon (1987), who was awarded the Nobel Prize in Economics in 1978 for his contribution to the then nascent field of behavioural economics. He argues that the essence of the conventional economic decision-maker is embodied in the notion of *Homo Economicus*, which is characterized by: (1) a stable set of preferences or wants or desires; (2) perfect knowledge of alternatives relevant to a choice problem; (3) the ability to forecast the expected consequences of particular choices in the present and into the future even when the future is highly uncertain; (4) the ability to make use of this knowledge to maximize personal economic well-being or happiness; (5) rapid updating of behaviour based on new information (Baysian updating); (6) consistency in the choices made by the individual; and (7) the insubstantial role of emotions and intuition in decision making (p. 221).

An underlying assumption of these analytical assertions is that individuals have unbounded knowledge of relevant choice alternatives and unbounded computational capacities to determine outcomes of alternative choices. Individuals are assumed to make such choices independently of other individuals. They are unaffected by other people's choices. It is also assumed that individuals have the capability and power to make the choices that they prefer to make. Other individuals do not, therefore, interfere with these choices. Moreover, it is assumed that rational decision-making takes place independently of emotional and intuitive behavioural drivers. Finally, it is assumed that rational individuals are narrowly selfish, most interested in maximizing their own material well-being. Deviations from such narrowly self-interested behaviour will not be welfare-maximizing (or maximizing happiness) and hence would be irrational. It is further assumed that individuals' choices are sensitive to relative prices and income levels as well as to changes to these variables. The latter assumption refers to an underlying premise of the conventional wisdom, accepted by most behavioural economists, that economic incentives matter in decision making.

Fast and frugal decision-making and smart heuristics

With regards to the rationality or smartness of choice behaviour, March (1978), a close associate of Simon and one of the pioneers of behavioural economics, argues that individuals are typically rational or intelligent when it comes to engaging in decision making even if their behaviour is at odds with conventional benchmarks for optimal behaviour. What appears irrational from the perspective of the conventional wisdom might be very rational and intelligent if one digs a bit below the surface (p. 589).

Herbert Simon led the way in developing behavioural economics as an analytical perspective to better explain rational human choice behaviour or decision making that is consistent with real human beings, endowed with limited computational and processing capacity and limited memory, facing real world environmental constraints. He develops the concepts of bounded rationality and satisficing (as opposed to maximising) to better classify, describe, and analyse real-world choice behaviour. Keys points made by Simon (1987) include the notion that one's definition of rationality must be derived from an understanding of actual human behaviours and capabilities and environmental constraints and facilitators. Moreover, benchmarks for rational behaviours need be based upon an understanding of what human agents are capable of doing in the real world—a type of real-word modelling scenario to help identify best-practice decision-making rules to optimize human well-being or welfare.

Building on the research of Simon and March, Gigerenzer (2007) developed the notion of fast and frugal heuristics to highlight how non-conventional decision-making, often driven by emotional and intuitive variables, results in effective and efficient decisions. These can include decisions made on financial markets or dealing with financial matters in a complex world where uncertainty is prevalent, information is imperfect and asymmetric, and information processing costly. This approach to an understanding of choice behaviour or decision making is also referred to as ecological rationality. One should note that the fast and frugal approach to decision making stands the errors-and-biases approach on its head since what is irrational from the latter perspective, where emotion and intuition yield poor decisions, can be most rational in the fast and frugal narrative. Emotive and intuitive factors are part of the complex decision-making toolbox of the evolved human brain that helps generate relatively intelligent decisions in an efficient and effective fashion.

This type of analytical paradigm sits well with and is informed by ongoing pioneering brain research, which finds that optimal decision-making *cannot* be largely or typically based on rationality benchmarks that simply focus on calculating and logic-based behaviour, and where emotions and intuition are treated as obstacles to rational decision-making. Rather, emotion and intuition play a vital role in rational decision-making. Research has shown that individuals who suffer damage to the emotional part of the brain are no longer able to engage in rational decision-making. Previously successful individuals become socially inept even at making and delivering such basic decisions as deciding what to buy and what to do during the day.

Damasio (2006) pioneered the research identifying the positive importance of emotions to rational decision-making, referred to as the somatic marker hypothesis. In this modelling framework, emotions allow people to act smart without having to think smart, at least in many significant instances. But Damasio emphasizes that emotions work when based on one's past experience and those of others based on pertinent circumstances. In effect, one requires emotional human capital formation for emotion and intuition be an effective decision making tool.

Nobel Laureate Smith (2003, 2005), who pioneered the development of experimental economics, also makes the case, based on his empirical research and that of his colleagues, that individuals typically don't make decisions using prescribed conventional economic (neoclassical) decision-making rules. Smith argues that this is not a sign of irrationality in individual choice behaviour or of sub-optimal behaviour. Rather, non-conventional behaviour can even result in superior economic results.

Simon refers to the proposition that rationality (smart behaviour) is contingent upon environmental conditions and physiological constraints and not upon exogenous and arbitrary benchmarks, such as in the case with conventional economics, as process rationality. Smith, building on Gigerenzer's most recent research as well as earlier work by Friedrich Hayek, refers to this type of context-dependent rationality as ecological rationality. Behaviour is ecologically rational if it is adapted to the structure of the environment and is best suited to the physiological make-up of the individual (such as computational limitations). For Smith and Hayek, individuals typically do the best they can do (satisficing), and tend to naturally evolve towards optimal (best-practice) behaviour. However, even Smith argues, like Gigerenzer and Hayek before him, that whether or not best-practice behaviour evolves can be contingent upon institutional parameters and learning (see Chapter 3).

With regards to financial education, the concepts of procedural and ecological rationality open the doors to the possibility that education might affect and improve choice behaviour. However, at one extreme, the ecological (Smith-Hayek) perspective on behavioural economics suggests that decision makers and institutions naturally evolve towards best-practice decisions, albeit these decisions need not and typically will not be rational from a conventional economics (neoclassical) perspective. This extreme perspective, just like its conventional economics counterpart, would close the door to financial education as being of much value in generating better decisions from the individual decision-maker's point of view and for society at large.

In the behavioural economics paradigm pioneered by Simon, although individuals are typically rational, that is smart, when engaging in decision making, mistakes or errors can be made, which can be referred to as rational errors (Altman, 2008 and Chapters 1, 2, 4 and 5). These might include making poor investment decisions that could have been avoided, like not investing adequately in pensions, or choosing a poor credit card option. From this perspective, informational, information processing, and institutional parameters play a key role in generating such errors. Better information, greater clarity in how information is presented and framed, and improved incentives, could fix such rational errors.

But even when choice behaviour is at its smartest, outcomes from the decision-making process need not be optimal or rational from the perspective of society at large. Individual decision-makers in the financial sector, for example, might be satisficing and ecologically rational from their own perspective (maximizing their own wealth), but they might be bankrupting institutions (theirs and others') in the process if the institutional parameters are not appropriate. Such behaviour can result in exceptional financial bubbles and busts that might cause great social harm, severely damaging the financial well-being of the many while benefiting the few. Such bubbles and busts can be a product of the rational and even optimal decisions of a few key decision-makers. Another example of such privately rational but socially irrational decision-making is the problem a gambler creates her or his happiness while having a disastrous effect on the family's financing and well-being. In these instances, institutional change and the incentives embodied in institutional change might be of greater importance than education in affecting behaviour.

Institutions matter

The Simon-March tradition of behavioural economics makes an important contribution by assigning a key role to institutional parameters in producing optimal (or best) decisions, unlike scholars following in the Kahneman–Tversky (errors and biases) perspective, who focus almost exclusively on psychological variables. From the Simon-March perspective, satisficing and non-neoclassical rational behaviour (bounded rationality) takes place in the context of institutions within which individuals engage in decision-making and choice behaviour.

Once the importance of institutions and related incentives (which should include social norms and rules and regulations) are placed front and centre as part of the analytical discourse, one can make more sense of socially irrational but individually rational (satisficing) behaviour, such as behaviour that maximizes the wealth of individuals while leading to severe recessions and large-scale bankruptcies of financial institutions.

In fact, a pioneer of a highly libertarian approach to economics, Friedrich Hayek argues that appropriate institutions are a pre-requisite if rational individual choice in all its complexity and diversity is to yield optimal (welfare maximizing) or rational social outcomes. Hayek (1948) writes, in the tradition of Adam Smith, that individualism is 'a system under which bad men can do least harm' (p. 11). This requires institutions that induce people to voluntarily contribute to the social good. Without such institutions socially beneficial outcomes need not be obtained.

From this perspective, financial education can change behaviour. But the extent of this impact is mitigated by the institutional parameters in place at a given time. Improved decision-making requires appropriate financial education plus appropriate institutions. One cannot be expected to work without the other—they are two blades of the scissors required to produce ideal choices in financial matters from both an individual and social perspective. Therefore, financial education, without an appropriate decision-making environment will have a limited impact on reducing the extent of financial illiteracy.

Errors and biases and 'irrational' heuristics

Dominating behavioural economics at present is the perspective developed by Daniel Kahneman and Amos Tversky, that individual decision-making is too often characterized by persistent biases and errors in choice behaviour. Humans develop heuristics to engage in decision making. Because these differ from the neoclassically prescribed norms for choice behaviour, they are deemed to represent error-prone or biased ways of acting, and are considered by many scholars to be irrational (for a more recent rendition of this perspective see Kahneman, 2011).

Tversky and Kahneman (1974, p. 1130) stress the importance of neoclassical norms as the benchmarks for rational behaviour. What is critical to the popular and pervasive Kahneman and Tversky approach is the central role of emotion and intuition as the basis of choice irrationality in decision making, as opposed to the physiological and environmental variables stressed by the Simon-March approach to behavioural economics. Emotion and intuition can result in decision making that is short-sighted and subject to regret in the longer run; that is, in behaviour that is inconsistent with rationality, according to Tversky and Kahneman (1981). However, the emotional and intuitive side to the decision-making process might be subject to some control and re-education (Tversky & Kahneman, 1981, p. 458).

In a nutshell, Kahneman and Tversky's key proposition (see Kahneman, 2011, for an updated elaboration of this argument), much of it articulated in prospect theory, relates to how emotive factors, rather than objective decision-making benchmarks, drive the decision-making process. The critical empirics that underlie prospect theory are:

1. On average, individuals have a preference for outcomes that are certain, even if their monetary value is less than that of the uncertain outcome. For example, a person prefers a certain (100% probability) $100 option over an option where there is an 80% chance of obtaining $140 and a 20% chance of ending up with nothing. The latter yields an expected return of $112. Individuals are 'irrationally' willing to sacrifice $12 to gain a certain outcome.
2. On average, individuals weight losses more than gains. For example, based upon Kahneman's and Tversky's research, a $100 loss would be given a weight of 2.5 and a $100 gain would be given a weight of 1. If one gains $100 and loses $100, one ends up with no net change in income or wealth. Objectively speaking, from a materialist (neoclassical) perspective, this type of event does not and should not affect one's well-being. However, prospect theory suggests that an individual's well-being will fall by quite a lot in this scenario as a result of the subjective (emotionally based) weights that individuals differentially attach to losses and gains. This causes individuals to be loss-adverse—to feel particularly bad about losses.
3. Individuals' subjective well-being is affected by their relative standing and changes to their relative standing in terms of losses and gains. Absolute levels of wealth are less important than changes to wealth. For this reason, the reference point that the individual uses when making decisions is important, and these reference points are subjectively (thus not rationally) determined.
4. The framing of options or prospect affects decision making. When events are framed positively, individuals tend to choose them over the same events framed negatively. This should not happen when the different frames have no substantive effect on events—packaging should not affect decision making. Since such frames do affect decision making, individuals are subject to perceptual or cognitive illusions. Related to this, individuals can be easily manipulated by frames. This is referred to as the framing effect. Such behaviour is considered to be irrational or biased. However, one should note that it is not clear that differential framing will affect choice behaviour when prospects or rates of return are substantively different. People can be fooled when the cost of being tricked is not all that great. In the same vein, Gigerenzer (2007) makes the point that in a world of imperfect information and uncertainty or of bounded rationality (the real world), frames signal information about the event. When an event is positively or negatively framed, individuals read between the lines, attempting to extract surplus information from the frames. A positive frame suggests a better choice than a negative frame. This is a judgement call that might prove to be incorrect. But it is a rational choice in a world of bounded rationality and uncertainty. However,

this does not distract from the suggestion that frames can be manipulated such that smart people can end up making rational errors in their decisions, yielding choices that they might not have made had there been better cognitive frames in place (Gigerenzer, 2007, pp. 99–100).

As part of the Kahneman–Tversky perspective, the following are identified as key cognitive biases (there are said to be many others) in decision making:

1. Overconfidence: Individuals overestimate their decision-making capabilities. As a result, individuals engage in risky behaviour in activities beyond their objective capacity to succeed.
2. Herding: The tendency of individuals to mimic the behaviour of others can result in cascades of particular choices. Herd behaviour occurs even when other individuals' behaviours are error-prone in the long run.
3. Loss aversion (related to prospect theory).
4. Status quo bias and the endowment effect: Individuals show a preference for the status quo even when it does not yield higher levels of material welfare. One example would be an individual valuing an asset by more than its purchase price even though its market value is not increasing. Possession in itself increases the value of the item possessed in the eyes of the individual endowed with this asset.
5. Framing effect (related to prospect theory).
6. Anchoring: Individuals tend to anchor their choices to reference points that are not objectively relevant to the decision at hand. This relates to what is referred to as the recognition heuristic (see below).
7. Adopting the wrong heuristic: This represents a more recent contribution Kahneman (2011), in this thinking slow and thinking fast narrative. Thinking fast (analogous to fast and frugal heuristics), might be okay in some circumstances, but it can lead to disastrous or, at best, sub-optimal decisions in other circumstances when thinking slow, taking one's time to think things through can yield superior decisions and choices. Kahneman argues that which heuristic is best is context dependent. So, one has to re-focus on context to appreciate which system of thinking is most effective and efficient.

One important implication of the Kahneman and Tversky perspective to behavioural economics is that because individual decision-making is all too often irrational, error-prone or biased for emotive reasons—and, related to this, because of the role heuristics play in decision making (which can involve intuition)—external intervention can be justified in choice behaviour. Experts (or bureaucrats informed by experts), coming from a rational benchmark, can affect the decision outcomes or choices of individuals by regulating choice behaviour or by encouraging particular choices based upon what is taken by an expert to be optimal choices, which the expert believes to be in the best interest of the individual. Such intervention could take place even if an individual's choices are not encumbered by negative externalities and, therefore, cause no harm to others.

This line of thinking is expressed quite eloquently by Thaler and Sunstein (2008, p. 6): 'Individuals make pretty bad decisions in many cases because they do not pay full attention in their decision making (they make intuitive choices based on heuristics), they don't have self-control, they are lacking in full information, and they suffer from limited cognitive abilities'. As a consequence, individuals should be nudged towards rational choices. People who oppose choice architecture, they argue, do so because they make the false assumption that (Thaler & Sunstein, 2008, p. 11): 'almost all people, almost all of the time, make choices that are in their best interest or at the very least are better than the choices that would be made by someone else. We claim that this assumption is false. In fact, we do not think that anyone believes this on reflection'. This implies that education cannot be expected, with any degree of confidence, to do the trick in affecting choice behaviour. Choice architecture is a way of framing choice options so that people can be nudged or manipulated into making the 'correct' or rational choices.

Financial education and literacy and the different faces of behavioural economics

The different approaches to economics imply various attitudes towards the potential for education and learning to affect choice behaviour. Conventional economics suggests that financial education can do little substantively, since individuals are behaving neoclassically, making choices consistent with neoclassical behaviour, or are quickly forced into behaving neoclassically by market forces, Behavioural economics, on the other hand, has provided us with an abundance of evidence that individuals do not behave neoclassically (Altman, 2006; Akerlof & Shiller, 2009; de Meza et al., 2008; Gigerenzer, 2007; Kahneman, 2003; Roubini & Mihm, 2010; Shefrin, 2002; Shiller, 2001; Wärneryd, 2001). Whether that behaviour is rational, however, depends on what approach to behavioural economics one subscribes to. Therefore, these differing approaches proffer different prescriptions as to what can or should be done about current decision-making processes or outcomes that do not accord with the conventional economic or neoclassical benchmarks for what are considered rational behaviours and rational choices. Just as with conventional economics, what determines how the different strands of behavioural economics regard the potential impact of education on financial decision-making very much hinges upon which benchmark is used for determining rational behaviour and what are thought to be the critical determinants of individuals deviating from the acceptable rationality (smart decision-making or choice) benchmarks.

In other words, from the perspective of the conventional wisdom, education can do little to influence finance-related decision-making since it is assumed that individuals behave according to the dictums of optimal neoclassical rational behaviour or generate choice outcomes consistent with neoclassical rationality benchmarks. The mainstream of behavioural economics, dominated by the Kahneman–Tversky perspective on human choice behaviour, regards the average individual's decision making to be dominated by persistent errors and biases or irrational behaviour using conventional economic or neoclassical benchmarks for rational behaviour. Moreover, the average individual is thought to be, all too often, subject to persistent cognitive illusions and therefore easily manipulated by the framing of options or prospects. This opens the door to intervention in the realm of decision making and choice in many dimensions, including educating people to behave more rationally. Since emotion and intuition are regarded as key culprits in driving irrational decision-making and, therefore, irrational choice, educating people to better control their emotive side would be a critical function of financial education from the Kahneman–Tversky perspective in behavioural economics.

Simon's perspective on behavioural economics agrees with the Kahneman–Tversky worldview, that individuals do not behave neoclassically. But it disagrees in that it does not necessarily find decision making and resulting choices to be irrational. Rather, more often than not, choice behaviour is considered to be ecologically rational or rational from a process perspective. Neoclassical norms are typically not used as benchmarks for how rational people should behave. Moreover, emotion and intuition are viewed as often playing an important *positive* role in real world decision-making. But this does not imply that individuals cannot make errors in decision making (rational errors) or that rational individual choices cannot generate socially irrational results. Errors in decision making can be based, for example, on imperfect and misleading information, poor incentives, and the inability of individuals to make their preferred choices (see Chapters 2–6).

Financial education can improve decision making (result in fewer errors) by providing individuals with better information and understandings of decision problems and the means to be better able to process this information. Moreover, in the Simon-March (bounded rationality) worldview, such financial education would have most impact if it were structured to minimize processing time and designed to minimize the complexity of information. This recognizes the brain as a scarce resource and the human proclivity to use fast and frugal heuristics (Gigerenzer) in decision making (including information processing). Also, the bounded rationality approach is consistent with Kahneman's slow and fast thinking narrative, that individuals need to better understand when slow thinking is best to generate optimal choices form the individual's perspective. It is important choose the best possible heuristic given one's circumstances. Finally, in the Simon-March approach, institutions play a key role in determining the choices people make. This approach is one which would be much more libertarian in its interventions to improve financial decision-making compared to the Kahneman–Tversky approach to behavioural economics. It would be much less concerned with outcomes than with providing people with the means to make decisions and choices that they prefer to make, unless such privately maximizing decisions causes social harm.

Shiller (2008) provides an example of the Simon-March approach when making the case that one cause for bad investment decisions is bad information and bad arguments which are often a product of low quality and misleading information. He favours the provision of higher quality information and the better dissemination of such information as one very important mechanism to improve financial decision-making. And, he argues, government should subsidize this since it would be socially beneficial (Shiller, 2008, 2009). Shiller writes:

> *Financial advice is in some respects like medical advice: we need both on an ongoing basis, and failure to obtain either can impose costs on society when our health—physical or financial—suffers. There's a strong case to be made that the government should subsidize comprehensive financial advice ... to help prevent bubbly thinking and financial overextension.*

Getting into the specifics of quality information, Shiller (2010) argues for regulated labelling for financial products analogous to required nutritional labelling for food products as a means to improve financial decision-making. He argues that labels should be designed to provide consumers with basic information in a relatively easy to read and understand format, one that does not send false signals to potential buyers of financial products. Labels should include *understandable* information on risk and returns. Shiller (2010) maintains:

> *Including such information on financial products would give an enormous boost to the efficiency and efficacy of our financial products in serving customers' needs. The only reason that such labeling has not yet been required is the same reason that nutritional labels were not required long ago on foods. Public outcry at a time of scandal forced progressive change then; we should hope that it does so now.*

Linkages between financial issues, financial education, and financial literacy

The approaches to financial education and financial literacy that flow from the differing methodological perspectives within behavioural economics can be illustrated and highlighted by looking at how these different methodological narratives would engage financial education to tackle key areas of consumer decision-making on financial matters. Arguably, of particular importance to many is the underinvestment in pensions and business-cycle behaviour with regards to investments in the stock market. Also, of importance is the trust heuristic, a fast and frugal heuristic, often employed in financial decision-making.

Pensions and saving

It is well documented that, on average, individuals underinvest in savings for retirement (OECD, 2005; Thaler & Sunstein, 2008). Of critical importance in much of the behavioural literature, when people are relatively young they make consumption choices that result in pensions too low to meet their income needs after retirement. This is often explained as a product of a lack of self-control or lack of foresight. This perspective pays no attention to the possibility that inadequate levels of income drive relatively low investment in pensions. Later in life, many people would like to save more, but they find it much too late to compensate for inadequate savings earlier on in their life and they regret the savings-related decisions they made when they were young. This contravenes the conventional economic wisdom that predicts that rational decision-makers will adequately save for their retirement, such as is reflected in the life-cycle hypothesis, presently a dominant economics view of real-world saving behaviour.

Many behavioural economists have argued that savings behaviour is largely determined by how saving options are framed to the potential saver. It is also well documented that if the default option for a savings plan is that one is enrolled automatically, the vast majority of employees enrol, and will therefore not choose to fill out the forms allowing them to opt out. If the default option is not to participate in a savings plan, the vast majority will not, and will therefore not choose to fill out the form to opt in (Benartzi & Thaler, 2007; Thaler & Sunstein, 2003). This suggests that individuals are easily and willingly manipulated or nudged into savings behaviour that they will probably prefer to have later on in life. From the perspective of the Kahneman–Tversky approach to behavioural economics, changing the frame or default of a pension option is the ideal method of dealing with the irrational decision-making behaviour of the average individual. Financial education per se is not critically important in this instance in changing choice behaviour. What counts is the default option.

From the Simon-March bounded rationality perspective, the manner in which an option is framed provides rational individuals, in an uncertain world with imperfect information, with implicit data or signals about options. Changing the saving default option to saving signals that participating in a particular savings plan is the right and safe thing to do. It is therefore a moral imperative that if opting in is the default option, the state ensures that employees aren't unwittingly opting into high-risk savings plans. It is also important that employees are provided with reasonable opting-out mechanisms from possibly high-risk pension plans.

It also critical to note that changing the default option has the most success when employers or governments have provided funds, in some proportion, to match employee contributions. Changing the default, in itself, has often not been sufficient to flip employee decision-making in a dramatic manner. Therefore, it appears that incentives also play a critical role in changing savings behaviour. The relative role played by changing the default option, controlling for changes in economic incentives, remains a subject for future research.

Financial education can play a role in changing savings behaviour from the perspective of bounded rationality, but not by changing the behavioural traits of decision makers. Rather, by providing employees with improved information, it is possible that some employees will choose to invest more towards their retirement. Also, providing information on pension plan options can allow employees to better understand the risks involved in particular pension plans. But the evidence suggests that, on average, changing the default option, along with changing the economic incentives, is the most effective mechanism of changing savings behaviour.

An important study on financial literacy commissioned by the OECD (OECD, 2005, p. 57) found that financial education can, indeed, make a substantive difference to savings behaviour. This is most often the case when employers and financial advisors provide financial information that employees trust and present it in a manner that is easily understood. However, such advice is often provided by individuals who have a vested interest in encouraging employees to invest in particular pension plans. As a result, the advice is biased towards the advisors' preferred plans.

According to this same study (OECD, 2005, p. 46), 'Many consumers accept without question what their financial advisor recommends'. This suggests that in a world of bounded rationality and, more specifically, when given highly complex information, combined with limited knowledge, limited time to assess and analyse that information, and uncertainty, individuals often fall back on heuristics when making financial decisions when there are faced with changes in defaults for saving and, more specifically, for pension options. For this reason, a critical aspect of financial education is for there to be third parties who can attest to the accuracy and integrity of the financial information provided and who can be involved in determining which pension options are set as the default. This is especially important if the default option, in an unregulated market, is for high-return, high-risk pension fund options, where the trust heuristic can result in losses that employees do not expect. This same narrative also applies to other financial decisions where financial advisors' are the heuristic used to made critically important decisions.

As a contemporary footnote to this discussion of investments in pension-fund-related financial assets, in the recent past (pre-2010), leading financial rated agencies provided AAA credit ratings to very high-risk bundled assets, such as the Collateralized Debt Obligations (CDOs) that contained both safe and highly risky assets. This falsely signalled to consumers that these assets were judged to be safe by internationally renowned and trusted private sector rating agencies. In such a case, financial education and improved financial literacy could not have protected consumers or provided them with the means to make improved financial decisions when faced with misleading information that they trusted to be accurate. For rational decision-makers to make optimal decisions, the information at hand must also be as correct as possible (Lewis, 2010; Posner, 2009; Roubini & Mihm, 2010). Then proper financial education kicks in. Otherwise, financial education can be predicted to have limited effect.

Investing in financial assets

Investment in financial assets over the business cycle and across significant booms and busts provides another excellent platform from which to assess how the different behavioural economics narratives speak to the ability of financial education to affect decision-making. Investment in financial assets highlights behaviours that are inconsistent with conventional benchmarks for rational decision-making. These aberrant behaviours include greed, overconfidence, herding, and passive trading, or the absence of true Bayesian updating (constant updating of decision making based on new information). The Kahneman and Tversky approach to behavioural economics seeks to discover means to overcome such behaviours. However, research into investor behaviour suggests that individuals who do not behave neoclassically are financially better off on average than those who make their decisions based on conventional neoclassical prescriptions. This being said, it is important to determine the role financial education can play in improving financial decision-making by the average individual and, perhaps more poignantly, reducing the probability that the average individual, but also the unique individual in particular circumstances, will make disastrous investment decisions.

Wärneryd (2001, p. 6) finds that non-rational investors, from a neoclassical perspective, are typically more successful than relatively sophisticated (more neoclassically oriented) investors. These are passive investors who minimize buying selling of financial paper. They are interested in the long run and are not neoclassically calculating, but do relatively well in the long run.

Gigerenzer (2007, pp. 26–28) provides a concrete example of such behaviour in his analysis of the investment behaviour of Harry Markowitz, 1990 Nobel Prize Laureate in economics. Markowitz, was awarded the Nobel Prize for his research on optimal asset allocation. He argues that there is an algorithm to compute an asset portfolio that maximizes returns while minimizing risk. However, when putting together his own investment package, Markowitz uses what Gigerenzer refers to as the 1/N rule, which tells us to spread our money equally across each of the designated N funds. This is how many ordinary folk-type investors actually behave. These are the passive investors mentioned by Wärneryd. The 1/N heuristic actually outperforms the portfolios constructed using the optimal algorithms derived from economic theory. The complex algorithms outperform the 1/N asset allocation only over very long spans of time—50 assets distributed by the complex theory-based algorithm requires 500 years to outperform the 1/N rule asset distribution, so not in our or many lifetimes. As well, this and other heuristic-based investment portfolios typically outperform portfolios designed by major investment houses and fund managers.

The 1/N heuristic is a fast and frugal shortcut that jives with the computational capacities of the human brain working within the realm of imperfect, asymmetric, and uncertain information. It also overrides short-run emotional considerations that can drive an individual's investment decisions. This heuristic is not only a descriptor of individual behaviour; for some behavioural economists and economic psychologists it is also an optimal heuristic for investor behaviour if one isn't privy to insider information. One lesson from this type of analysis is that, for most people, passive investing strategies in a relatively diversified asset portfolio (such as is given by the 1/N rule) is optimal. Moreover, active investing (the neoclassical heuristic) is sub-optimal. Investing in a mutual fund and index investing, where trading is not aggressive, is a proxy to investing by the 1/N rule.

These findings sit quite nicely with the bounded rationality–satisficing approach to behavioural economics. In this instance financial education can play an important role in informing individuals about actual returns from different types of investment strategies. It can also provide information on the advantage of holding on to a diversified asset portfolio over the long term as asset prices, on average, tend to revert to the mean (the mean reversion hypothesis). One cannot expect the typical individual to have this information easily at hand in an easily comprehensible format.

An important question becomes who is best positioned to objectively provide such information. One should not expect private investment houses or banks to provide neutral information and education in this area if higher profits can be made attracting investment into funds with active fund managers. As previously discussed, Shiller (2008, 2009, 2010) makes the case for legislating and subsidizing the provision of such information.

Bubbles and busts: Animal spirits and decision-making

Many behavioural economists have tied both bubbles and busts to emotionally driven (and therefore irrational or biased) heuristics motivating decision-making. This is exemplified in the most recent (2008–09) crash in financial markets. Greed, animal spirits (decision-making driven by psychological factors), irrational exuberance (pro-active investment behaviour not based on economic fundamentals), and overconfidence are considered to be the key culprits (see, for example, Akerlof & Shiller, 2009; Shefrin, 2002). Behavioural economists coming from the Kahneman–Tversky perspective might argue that efforts to mitigate these behavioural traits, through education for example, could reduce the severity of severe booms and busts in average financial asset prices. Furthermore, individuals might be expected to learn from past experience so as not to repeat past behaviour that results in severe economic loses. Thaler, a key proponent of the Kahneman–Tversky approach, is not convinced of the efficacy of financial education in this domain, as many of these behaviours, he argues, are hard-wired. For this reason, he is a strong proponent of nudging as a means of changing the way individuals make choices (Palmer, 2008; Thaler & Sunstein, 2008).

From the Simon-March approach as well, to the extent that greed, animal spirits, and exuberance are part and parcel of the evolved human animal, education would do little to modify decision making that is predicated upon these human characteristics. But such behaviours would not necessarily be deemed irrational. For example, individuals who wish to improve their material well-being can be expected to invest in financial assets that are rising in value and divest financial assets whose value is falling. This can be referred to as greed, but it is not at all clear that this behaviour is irrational. Wanting more rather than less, such as wanting higher instead of lower returns from financial assets, would seem to be consistent with rational or intelligent behaviour.

How one decides to invest is often determined by animal spirits. Keynes (1936) refers to animal spirits as behaviour that is motivated by emotive factors, as opposed to calculating or hard-core economic rationality demanded by conventional economics. Keynes (1936, pp. 161–162) speculates:

> *Most, probably, for our decisions to do something positive, the full consequences of which will be drawn out over many days to come, can only be taken as the result of animal spirits – a spontaneous urge to action rather than inaction, and not as the outcome of a weighted average of quantitative benefits multiplied by quantitative probabilities.*

But animal spirits, although not calculating behaviour, is intuitive, based on a sense of what one expects to occur in the near future. It is a heuristic based on one's expectations in a world of uncertainty. Although not consistent with calculating behaviour, it is consistent with bounded rationality and satisficing. Nevertheless, animal spirits can serve to generate significant deviations from economic fundamentals.

Take the case when animal spirits are motivated by how other people behave or how one expects other people to behave on the market. In a world of uncertainty investors use proxies such as rumours or insights from experts to build their expectations. In this fashion, individuals follow the leader in their investment behaviour once these leaders are identified. This is an example of the recognition heuristic, Gigerenzer identified. Thus, individuals make choices based on what appears to be quality information or signals in the immediate absence of anything better. This particular type of recognition heuristic is referred to as herding. Herding can generate cascades in financial asset prices that deviate quite significantly from the economic fundamentals of the economic assets represented by financial paper (Shiller, 2001). Cascades can contribute to significant financial bubbles and busts in asset pricing. Is the application of this herding heuristic an example of irrational animal spirits or of irrational exuberance?

According to the Kahneman–Tversky perspective, this type of decision making is an example of irrationality because it runs contrary to behavioural norms of the conventional neoclassical wisdom. The solution here might be to convince people that herding behaviour is not the best strategy, and neither is the recognition heuristic or being influenced by rumours. But it is unlikely that people can be convinced of this when they operate in a world of bounded rationality. Such behaviour is, as mentioned above, individually rational, although it does, invariably in the long run, result in financial booms and busts. To put this another way, should people who want to make more money on their investments not invest in assets that are increasing in value, because they know that one day (which one can't identify with any precision) prices might fall? Would the counterfactual to this dilemma be that they should not invest in financial assets, including real estate or housing, when pricing are rising? Should this rule of thumb apply to financial advisors as well? Would this be rational? And is this what one would want financial education to propagate?

At this point, it is important to note that during financial asset price cascades individuals do not hold on to assets whose prices are falling relative to their fundamental values, nor do they dump assets whose prices are rising relative to their fundamental values. In other words, individuals do not behave as predicted by Kahneman–Tversky. Instead, many people are risk-adverse in losses (they dump bad assets) and risk-seeking in gains (they hold on to relatively high priced assets for too long) when there is a credible leader or rumour to justify such behaviour. In fact, one cause for booms and busts is animal spirits as driven by herding behaviour, such that bad assets are dumped quickly and assets with increasing prices are held for too long in the sense that they are kept at least until a crash seems imminent—a situation that no one can in fact predict with any calculable and precise probability.

Richard Posner (2009, p. 76), one the key proponents of the conventional economic wisdom but highly critical of economic theory's shortcomings with respect to the 2008–09 economic crisis, argues that institutional failures were largely to blame for the financial meltdown, *as opposed to the irrationality of decision makers*—even though decision makers were acting contrary to neoclassical first principles of decision making. Thus, for example, greed, irrational optimism, intellectual deficiencies, or mistakes and errors in decision making are not the main causal culprits in economic collapse. Posner also argues that emotive variables, so stringently critiqued by the Kahneman–Tversky perspective as well as by the conventional neoclassical outlook, should not be regarded as indicative of irrational drivers in the decision-making process. Posner (2009) maintains that emotions represent telescoping thinking that is often 'superior to conscious analytic procedures'. He also argues that buying at the peak and not selling at the trough of a cycle is not irrational since no one knows when the peak or tough occur in a world of uncertainty, and decision-making here is like firing a shot in the dark. With uncertainty there is no strict mathematical basis for decision making. We base actions on our intuition of what we think makes the most sense. This behaviour is neither irrational nor subject to change by education if it is based on what decision makers perceive to be solid information (Posner, 2009, pp. 82–85).

Posner (2009) argues that herding behaviour is also quite rational since in a world of imperfect information someone else might know something that you do not. Following a supposedly informed individual might be in your best interest, and not following might turn out not to be in your best interest. As Posner (2009, p. 84) argues:

> *It is risky but not irrational to follow the herd. (It is also risky to abandon the safety of the herd—ask any wildbeast). That is why buying a stock because others are buying it and thus forcing up the price is not irrational. And likewise while it can be very dangerous to be a prisoner of your preconceptions…it is irrational to think without preconceptions, because preconceptions impound vital knowledge as well as prejudice.*

Here again, from Posner's perspective, one cannot educate decision makers not to herd because herding is rational in a world of uncertainty, although herding invariably results in busts. Rational decision-makers can't predict when bubbles will burst or when there will be a recovery in the real world of bounded rationality. So, in Simon's methodological terminology, rational agents satisfice, they ride the tide and hope for the best while searching for easily identifiable and relatively trustworthy signals when engaging in financial decision-making.

Posner accepts that smart people can make errors in their decisions. But these are errors that smart people can make and not the product of Kahneman–Tversky-type irrationalities or systematic biases. For Posner, institutional failure was the key reason that non-conventional (but smart) behavioural heuristics did not work in 2008–09. Whether or not good or bad institutions are in place depends on public policy. This analysis fits into the Simon-March approach to behavioural economics that emphasizes rational behaviour in a world of bounded rationality and the importance of institutional parameters affecting decision making. Therefore, many significant but problematic financial choices from a social perspective are better addressed through institutional change than through financial education.

Posner's point of focus is the incentive environment created for different levels for decision makers within financial institutions as well as consumers prior to the 2008–09 financial crisis. This incentive environment minimized the risk or reduced the cost to rational individuals and large financial corporations of knowingly engaging in overly risky behaviour. Lewis (2010) makes a similar argument, as do Roubini and Mihm (2010). They argue that executive compensation was very generous and truncated on the downside, so that if you made decisions that yielded high profits in the short run but caused harm in the long run, you were protected by your compensation package. Executives were given incentives to make decisions that could have disastrous consequences for their company, their employees and society at large, because they were insulated from their own risky decision-making. This is a classic moral hazard environment that was created by financial corporations and encouraged by government. This moral hazard environment extended to lower-level decision-makers, such as investment brokers and advisors, who were also protected from the costs of poor decisions by their compensation packages.

Rational consumers in the United States were also induced into making investments in housing based on low interest rates, such that individuals with little or no collateral were willing to take out mortgages in the belief that interest rates would remain low. Neither buyers nor sellers envisioned significant risks from the moral hazard institutional environment. According to Posner (2009, p. 104), the downside of the housing market was truncated, 'making [the buyer's and seller's] 'reckless' behaviour not only rational but also consistent with [their] being well informed about the risks'.

From this perspective, a misguided institutional environment is a more likely explanation of poor decision-making both from an individual and social perspective than is simple irrationality or even poor information. In this case, financial education cannot be expected to have much effect. You cannot educate people to behave differently if they are behaving as sensible individuals can be expected to behave in a world of bounded rationality. For example, you cannot teach people not to ride the tide, follow the herd, use their intuition, and take advantage of good deals when these are the best available options. Only after the fact can one argue that some of these heuristics reproduced 'bad' or sub-optimal decisions.

Given this perspective and analysis, key to poor decision-making from an individual and social backdrop, is a misguided institutional environment as opposed irrationality or even poor information. For example, Posner (2009, p. 111) concludes:

> In sum, rational maximization by businessmen and consumers, all pursuing their self-interest more or less intelligently within a framework of property rights and contract rights, can set the stage for an economic catastrophe. There is not need to bring cognitive quirks, emotional forces, or character flaws into the causal analysis. This is important both in simplifying analysis and in avoiding a search, likely to be futile, for means by which government can alter the mentality or character of businessmen and consumers.

Informational problems and errors in decision making

Even with correct incentives, informational problems can cause rational decision-makers to execute decisions that they would not otherwise engage in. Shiller (2008, 2009, 2010) emphasizes the significance of the informational environment to financial decision-making. Improvements to the quality of information, to access, and to understanding, through education can be expected to at least mitigate many of the poor financial decisions made in the past. However, role played by misleading information in decision making, all other things remaining the same, is particularly important. Education cannot easily address this issue.

For example, when assets receive a triple-A rating from respected rating agencies, consumers tend to trust this information and purchase what appears to be high-yielding, relatively low-risk assets. This is exactly what was happening in the global financial market before the 2008–09 financial crisis. Financial assets that were a mix of high-grade and low-grade assets (a mix referred to as toxic assets) were given a clean bill of health. Consumers who used asset ratings as one input into the investment decision-making process may have been misled into making high risk investments that they would not have made had more accurate ratings been provided by trusted rating agencies. Moreover, had consumers purchased fewer financial assets in a different information environment, the market for these assets would have been smaller, altering the dynamics of global financial asset markets.

One problem inherent in the rating of financial assets is that the rating agencies are private and self-regulating institutions in a highly uncompetitive market (at best an oligopolistic market). There exists a conflict of interest between the rating agencies and the corporations whose financial products are being rated. It is possible that decision making could be been improved with better, more accurate information and an improved understanding of the information at hand. But, as Shiller (2008, 2010) points out, past experience and the incentive environment suggest that such information is best provided within a regulatory framework, as is the case with food labels.

A similar type of scenario with regards to this type of information can be found in the mortgage market. It is not clear that purchasers of mortgages were made aware of the fine print relating to the structure of interest rates over the term of the mortgage in the American market. Many individuals do not read the fine print of financial documents or understand the complex language of the documents. Another common example of this is credit card arrangements, where interest rates can increase dramatically within a relatively short period after an individual signs up. Yet another example involving credit cards is the defaults established for increasing the maximum allowable expenditure. If the default is to increase the credit limit on demand, and consumers can be aware of this only after reading the details in fine print, they might be basing financial decisions on inadequate (imperfect) information.

The clear implication of these types of examples is that rational individuals can make choices that they will regret when faced with inadequate or false information. Improved financial decision-making can be achieved, therefore, when an impartial body, a government, for example, assures that consumers are provided with the information they require in a manner they can comprehend, together with the tools to better understand the financial information they are provided with. Under such a scenario, improved information yields improved financial literacy. Hence, institutional improvements and financial education go hand in hand towards improving the extent of financial literacy. And, it should be noted, providing quality assurance for the information and even for the defaults made available to consumers is a subset of consumer protection.

The trust heuristic

The trust heuristic is another non-conventional tool used by decision makers that is subject to critique by both the conventional and Kahneman–Tversky type perspectives as a form of irrational or biased behaviour. As with other fast and frugal heuristics, emotional and intuitive drivers affect the trust heuristic. But trust has a long tradition of being used by decision makers. In the absence of legal guarantees, it provides a second-best substitute. In a world of legal guarantees with bounded rationality, the trust heuristic saves on transaction costs by allowing for speedy, effective, and efficient decisions (Greif, 1989; Kohn, 2008; Landa, 1994, 2008).

Trust is the expectation that the other party to a transaction will deliver on promises made. This might be because the other party incorporates one's interests into her own. Also, of importance is a sense that reneging on a transaction would lead to economic consequences for the other party, either because of reputational harm or because of anticipated social or legal repercussions. But moral sentiments appear to be a key ingredient to trust relationships, with reputational, social, and legal variables adding strength to the mortar. Kohn (2008, pp. 38–39)) makes the following point about trust:

> ...cooperation may be initiated and sustained without trust. But once trust becomes possible it sustains interactions that would otherwise collapse, enhances the quality of cooperation, and threads the social fabric together. It is a prized sentiment whose absence is unthinkable in many contexts, and which is sought in contexts where reason might not find it to be strictly necessary. When our passions for a sentiment such as this run so high, our instincts are probably right. We value trust instinctively because it works for us, and has worked for our ancestors, in ways both familiar and beyond our grasp

Important factors affecting trust relationships are the signifiers of trustworthiness that act as proxies for specific and detailed information on the trustworthiness of individuals. Amongst these proxies are the ethnic, neighbourhood, religious and racial grouping with which one identifies. Many people believe they can trust those with whom they can more easily identify, those they think they know. This type of trust is enforced in an institutional environment where one has confidence that those breaking the bonds of trust will damage their reputations and result in legal and economic ramifications as well.

Ponzi schemes and the trust heuristic

An enlightening example of the trust heuristic in the world of financial decision-making, and rational failures, is the Bernard Madoff Ponzi scheme (LeBor, 2009). This American-based scheme, one of the most notorious in international financial history, had repercussions throughout the world. For over four decades the scheme defrauded clients of over US$40 billion. It was brought down in late 2008 when the global financial crisis led clients to attempt to cash in their assets beyond what Madoff's fund could sustain.

A Ponzi scheme pretends to provide legitimate (but high) returns on investment, whereas it actually provides these returns by paying out from the capital provided by new and existing clients. As long as there is enough new capital flowing into the Ponzi fund and there are no excess calls on current investments, the Ponzi scheme is sustainable, with the orchestrator of the scheme typically reaping significant economic returns. People invest in such schemes because they trust in their legitimacy, and more specifically in the legitimacy and integrity of those owning and managing the fund. The high rate of return promised (and delivered on occasion) is also important. One has the trust heuristic in play here, plus an economic incentive. Moreover, investors are not always aware that government does not guarantee their investments (at least their initial capital), as it does certain amounts of deposits held in banks. As a result, investors might engage in more risky behaviour than otherwise, believing that they are shifting the risk of their investment to government—another moral hazard dilemma.

Madoff was a well-established investor and player in American financial circles who had established a high level of trust in the international financial community. His fraudulent financial activities went undetected by the Securities and Exchange Commission, America's financial regulatory authority, in spite of early complaints laid against him and his investment house. Posner (2009), for example, argues that the lack of detection was a product of a weakened SEC and an increasingly deregulated environment in the financial market where the private sector was expected to appropriately self-regulate. Also, Madoff was trusted by the regulators who believed that investors were capable of self-regulation (this belief informed by the conventional economic wisdom). The fact that he passed the regulatory test earned Madoff an additional layer of trust by investors and provided some objective affirmation to the intuitive and emotive drivers underlying the trust heuristic. By all appearances, investors behaved rationally by investing in what they trusted to be a relatively low-risk, stable, and safe fund, yielding somewhat higher than average returns over the long term. But the trust that rational investors had placed in Madoff and in America's regulatory institutions was misplaced and eventually broken.

Madoff largely targeted members of the American Jewish community, investors small and large, sophisticated and unsophisticated, individual and corporate investors, not-for-profits and for-profits organizations. Madoff was highly active in the New York Jewish community and played an active role in charities, many of which invested in his Ponzi scheme. Given his focus on his ethnic and religious group, the SEC defines the Madoff fraud as an affinity fraud. He took advantage of the trust heuristic that people so often use in their decision-making process. Madoff earned the trust of his peers through his financial successes, which included his undetected Ponzi scheme of four decades standing.

Should prospective investors be taught not to use the trust heuristic even though it has been part and parcel of common and relatively successful decision-making practices for millennia, albeit contrary to the conventional neoclassical wisdom's benchmarks for best-practice decision-making? Would this avoid personal financial crises such as those caused by the Madoff Ponzi fraud? Would this keep consumers from investing in what they trusted to be highly-rated and relatively low risk financial paper?

The evolution of decision making makes it doubtful that this type of financial education would have had any effect. However, institutional change that provides consumers with vital and trustful information about financial assets they might want to purchase is another matter entirely (Shiller, 2008, 2009, 2010). So would an education providing consumers with a better understanding about the risks surrounding the purchase of different classes of financial assets. Related to this, investment advisors and brokers can be legislated to provide an easy-to-understand statement telling clients about the expected risks of investments and whether their proposed investments are underwritten by government. The latter is critically important, as it would clearly stipulate when individuals would have to bear the consequences of their risky behaviour on financial markets as opposed to transferring these costs to society at large. Finally, in extreme cases like that exemplified by the Madoff Ponzi scheme, regulatory frameworks need to be in place so that frauds can be more readily detected. As well, penalties for the architects of these frauds need to be severe and must be known and seen to be severe. Finally, with an appropriate level of financial literacy and regulation, there is a lesser probability that the bounds of trust would be broken, so the trust heuristic could be used in a more optimal or effective fashion.

Conclusion: Economic theory, financial literacy and public policy

Unlike the conventional economic wisdom, the modelling framework provided by behavioural economics suggests a role for financial education as well as for other types of external interventions to improve upon decision-making with respect to financial issues. The conventional wisdom assumes that individuals behave in a fashion consistent with calculating, deliberative, forward looking, non-emotive, non-intuitive, fully informed, and self-interested decision-making. Decisions are assumed to be optimal (or very close to it). In this world there can be no room for financial education to improve upon the decision-making process. Moreover, there is no room for institutional change to improve decision outcomes as it is assumed that institutions are optimal or at least decisions and choices made by individuals are consistent with an optimal institutional setting. Therefore, the conventional wisdom is highly pessimistic about financial education or improvements to the decision-making environment improving financial decision making and, thereby, related socio-economic outcomes.

Behavioural economics is not a unitary approach to economics and, therefore, does not suggest one approach to improving financial decision-making through education or other means. Different perspectives on behavioural economics yield different policy rules with regards to financial and financial literacy.

These points are summarized in Table 9.2. The Kahneman–Tversky perspective is more oriented towards policies that nudge or force individuals to change their behaviour in ways consistent with what experts consider to be ideal choices.

TABLE 9.2 Economic theory and public policy.

	Conventional economic theory	Behavioural economics: Kahneman–Tversky, heuristics and biases approach	Behavioural economics: Simon, bounded rationality-smart individuals approach
Savings/retirement planning	• Education (pessimistic on outcomes). Individuals are assumed to behave in the ideal fashion, although some recognize that some ignorance might exist and be corrected for.	• Education (pessimistic on outcomes). • Education can be used to change the decision-making processes and choices towards the conventional economic ideal. • Requires individuals overriding their hard-wired psychological dispositions. • Changing defaults for investing in pensions.	• Education (optimistic on outcomes). • Education provides the means for individuals to make intelligent choices based on their preferences, incentives and the information at hand. • Changing defaults for investing in pensions. • Transparency on the risks and returns of default pension funds. • Transparency on whether there is a lender of last resort.
Investing in financial assets	• Education (pessimistic on outcomes). Individuals are assumed to behave in the ideal fashion, although some recognize that some ignorance might exist and be corrected for.	• Education (pessimistic on outcomes). • Education can be used to change the decision-making processes and choices towards the conventional economic ideal. • Requires individuals overriding their hard-wired psychological dispositions.	• Education (optimistic on outcomes). • Education provides the means for individuals to make intelligent choices based on their preferences, incentives and the information at hand. • Transparency on the risks and returns of default pension funds. • Transparency on whether there is a lender of last resort • Reliable product labels for financial products.

Continued

TABLE 9.2 Economic theory and public policy—cont'd

	Conventional economic theory	Behavioural economics: Kahneman–Tversky, heuristics and biases approach	Behavioural economics: Simon, bounded rationality-smart individuals approach
Fraud and trust	• Education (pessimistic on outcomes). Individuals are assumed to behave in the ideal fashion, although some recognize that some ignorance might exist and be corrected for.	• Education (pessimistic on outcomes). • Education can be used to change the decision-making processes and choices towards the conventional economic ideal. • Requires individuals overriding their hard-wired psychological dispositions.	• Education (optimistic on outcomes). • Education provides the means for individuals to make intelligent choices based on their preferences, incentives and the information at hand. • Moral education to reduce fraud. • Improved transparency of financial transactions. • Well-resourced regulators to increase the probability of detecting financial fraud. • Severe financial penalties for those convicted of financial fraud so that marginal costs clearly outweigh marginal benefits.
Credit cards	• Education (pessimistic on outcomes). Individuals are assumed to behave in the ideal fashion, although some recognize that some ignorance might exist and be corrected for.	• Education (pessimistic on outcomes). • Education can be used to change the decision-making processes and choices towards the conventional economic ideal. • Requires individuals overriding their hard-wired psychological dispositions.	• Education (optimistic on outcomes). • Education provides the means for individuals to make intelligent choices based on their preferences, incentives and the information at hand. • Reliable product labels for financial products. • Easily identifiable and understandable contract clauses. • Interest rate policy should be easily understood by consumer. • Credit card policy changes should be easily recognized and understood by customers. • Defaults for credit limits should be to the advantage of the customers. • Key credit card terms and conditions should be verbally conveyed to consumers.

Financial education per se is not expected to have much effect in the face of the hardwiring of decision-making heuristics that lead to poor financial choices. The Simon-March, bounded rationality, approach is much more optimistic about the impact of financial education on choice behaviour. But the availability and access to relevant and quality information, how information and options are framed, and the incentive environment within which decision-making takes place are also important.

I would argue, based on the evidence, that public policy is best constructed on the foundations of the Simon-March, bounded rationality, approach to behavioural economics. There is much evidence to support the view that financial education positively affects decision making. A person more educated on financial matters, such as risk, rates of return, credit card payments structures, and household budgeting, makes better decisions, at least from the perspective of the decision maker. Education also incorporates learning-by-doing or experiential education. Moreover, educating individuals to become more literate in numeracy should reduce errors in decision making. Financial education in this case is not directed towards changing human behaviour, such as overcoming biases as defined by the conventional wisdom. Rather it is directed towards helping individuals who are boundedly rational to make better decisions—decisions informed by more specialized knowledge about financial issues, markets, and products. Following Shiller, one might argue that financial education should be subsidized when it has positive social effects, such as improving savings behaviour and reducing the chances that poor budgeting and investment decisions will be made. But improved decision-making requires much more than just improvements to financial education.

Policy interventions directed towards improving the quality and quantity of pertinent information are critically important. This includes introducing quality control measures with regards to this information. The 2008–09 financial crisis underscores the significance misleading information can have on investment behaviour. Echoing Shiller, agents and organizations marketing financial products, for example, should be obliged to clearly specify the risks and prospective returns involved in purchasing particular financial products. One might even go a step further and require the specification of the composition of financial products in terms of their components' risks and returns (for example, whether products that on average carry medium risk contain components that are very high risk). This is analogous to the requirements for nutrition and the content requirements for food labels. It should also be made clear whether the consumer bears the risk of the investment—whether government guarantees the value of the initial investment/purchase of the financial product. If individuals believe that government bears the risk, it will be rational for them to engage in riskier behaviour than they would otherwise. One way of partially fixing this problem is to oblige vendors of financial products to inform consumers/clients of the risk inherent in these products and even to require both parties to sign a document specifying that the conditions of risks are understood. Ceteris paribus, improvement to financial education, given poor and/or misleading information, is unlikely to have much positive impact on decision making. The expected positive effects of financial education on decision making is conditional upon the availability and easy (low cost) access to quality information.

It is also important to introduce baseline rules to assure that information is framed and presented in a manner easily understood by the consumer. This point is directly related to the importance of quality information. For example, it should be made clear and easily evident what the penalties are for late payments on credit cards, what the longer term rate of interest is, and whether the default for the card is to approve purchases even if they extend the cardholder beyond the contractually agreed credit limit. Another example relates to pension plans. Many behavioural economists recommend making investing in pension plans managed by the private sector, the default option to induce increased savings for retirement. Once investing in pensions becomes the default, employees tend to invest, using the default as a signal that such an investment is a good and safe one. For this reason, those setting the default should be obliged to specify the risks and prospective returns of such investments.

Once it is recognized that baseline rules for product information ought to be required, it becomes critical to define the level of financial literacy needed by the representative consumer and decision maker for whom these rules are constructed. Should the government consider the representative consumer to be an individual who is highly literate, or one who is just barely literate? I would argue that the representative consumer should be thought of as at the lower end of the scale since even the least financially literate individuals should be able to understand the financial information before them. It is these people who tend to make the most errors in financial decision-making. Increasing their level of financial literacy would provide these decision makers with the means with which to make the best use of the information at hand.

Finally, the Simon-March approach suggests that there is a need for interventions in the marketplace that will re-orient the incentive environment to ensure that individual investors bear the risks of their decisions. This is particularly important for key decision-makers in financial institutions. I do not mean to suggest that people should or can be educated not to value their own material well-being. Rather, investors can be obliged to consider the riskiness of their choices and not allowed to shift their risk onto other unsuspecting people. This would require government to intervene in setting up the structure of compensation packages for decision makers in financial institutions, a move which may be problematic for many policymakers. But given the importance of the financial sector and the possible repercussions of a failure in this sector for the economy at large—namely forced government bailouts (which transfers all risks to the government and thus to the general public)—the sensible alternative may be to impose minimal regulations that minimize the possibility that investors will make choices that are deemed to be too risky. Such policy has been most recently recommended, for example, by Posner (2009) and Roubini and Mihm (2010). As well, moral education is important for financial transactions insofar as there is a need to reduce the probability of fraudulent transactions. A more moral culture with more moral norms embedded in it, incentivize some individuals to engage in an increased level of moral behaviour. One can argue that moral education increases, at a minimum, the psychological costs of engaging in immoral behaviour in financial markets.

Behavioural economics also suggests that various types of experiments and surveys can be conducted to determine how consumers would behave under different sets of informational, educational (financial literacy), and institutional settings. One could also determine in this fashion differential behaviour amongst men and women, different ethnic, religious, and immigrant groups, as well as amongst individuals in different income and age cohorts and different occupations. One example of this would be to run experiments on how decision making is affected by the structure of the information provided. Variables should include complexity, location of key information, and font size. Another example would be to see how decision making is affected by altering the moral hazard environment for people at different levels of financial literacy. It would be equally important to clarify the relative role of defaults, information, clarity of information, and incentives in affected financial decision making. One might also examine the extent to which formal financial education instruments improve the quality of financial decision-making when information is misleading, overly complex or hidden, or when defaults are set contrary to the preferences of consumers.

Overall, behavioural economics open the door to the improvement in decision making through financial education. They also lend support to the possibility that other public policy initiatives can enhance financial literacy and thereby improve the quality of financial decision-making. The bounded rationality approach pays particular attention to how smart but non-neoclassical decision-makers are influenced by information and the incentive environment. Formal financial education courses and seminars are not as important here as are quantity, quality, and structure of information and its availability at low cost, as well as institutional parameters that affect financial decision-making. More formal education instruments are important with regards to enhancing the capacity of individuals to process and understand the information at hand. These educational capabilities are fundamentally important if one is to reduce the extent of financial illiteracy and the extent of x-inefficiency in the domain of financial decision making. Also, important is informal education, gaining experience in financial decision-making (learning-by-doing). But it is these factors combined, and not simply formal financial education, that can be expected have the most profound impact on financial literacy. A focus on formal education, neglecting the decision-making environment and experiential learning can be predicted to have limited effects on financial literacy related choices and outcomes.

References

Akerlof, G. A., & Shiller, R. J. (2009). *Animal spirits: How human psychology drives the economy, and why it matters for global capitalism*. Princeton: Princeton University Press.

Altman, M. (2006). What a difference an assumption makes: Effort discretion, economic theory, and public policy. In M. Altman (Ed.), *Handbook of contemporary behavioral economics: Foundations and developments* (pp. 125–164). New York: Armonk.

Altman, M. (2008). Behavioral economics, economic theory and public policy. *Australasian Journal of Economics Education*, 5(1 & 2), 1–55.

Altman, M. (2012). *Behavioral economics for dummies*. New York: Wiley.

Benartzi, S., & Thaler, R. H. (2007). Heuristics and biases in retirement savings behavior. *Journal of Economic Perspectives*, 21, 81–104.

Camerer, C., Issacharoff, S., Loewenstein, G., O'Donoghue, T., & Rabin, M. (2003). Regulation for conservatives: Behavioral economics and the case for 'Asymmetric Paternalism'. *University of Pennsylvania Law Review*, 1151, 1211–1254.

Damasio, A. (2006). *Descartes' error: Emotion, reason and the human brain*. London: Vantage.

de Meza, D., Irlenbusch, B., & Reyniers, D. (2008). *Financial capability: A behavioural economics perspective*. London: Financial Services Association.

Gigerenzer, G. (2007). *Gut feelings: The intelligence of the unconscious*. New York: Viking.

Greif, A. (1989). Reputation and coalitions in medieval trade: Evidence on the Maghribi traders. *Journal of Economic History*, 49, 857–882.

Hayek, F. A. (1948). *Individualism and the economic order*. Chicago: University of Chicago Press.

Kahneman, D. (2003). Maps of bounded rationality: Psychology for behavioral economics. *American Economic Review*, 93, 1449–1475.

Kahneman, D. (2011). *Thinking, fast and slow*. New York: Farrar, Straus and Giroux.

Keynes, J. M. (1936). *The general theory of employment interest and money*. London: Macmillan.

Kohn, M. (2008). *Trust: Self-interest and the common good*. Oxford: Oxford University Press.

Landa, J. T. (1994). *Trust, ethnicity, and identity: The new institutional economics of ethnic trading networks, contract law, and gift-exchange*. Ann Arbor: University of Michigan Press.

Landa, J. T. (2008). The bioeconomics of homogeneous middleman groups as adaptive units: Theory and empirical evidence viewed from a group selection framework. *Journal of Bioeconomics*, 10, 259–278.

LeBor, A. (2009). *The believers: How America fell for Bernard Madoff's $65 billion investment scam*. London: Weidenfeld and Nicolson.

Lewis, M. (2010). *The big short: Inside the doomsday machine*. New York: Allen Lane.

Lusardi, A., & Mitchell, O. S. (2014). The economic importance of financial literacy: Theory and evidence. *Journal of Economic Literature*, 52, 5–44.

March, J. G. (1978). Bounded rationality, ambiguity, and the engineering of choice. *Bell Journal of Economics*, 9, 587–608.

Munshaw, C. (2008). *Moving forward with financial literacy: Synthesis report on reaching higher: Canadian conference on financial literacy*. Ottawa: Financial Consumer Agency of Canada. Available at: http://www.fcac-acfc.gc.ca/eng/publications/surveystudy/reachhigherconf/pdf/reachhigher-eng.pdf.

Organisation for Economic Co-operation and Development. (2005). *Improving financial literacy: Analysis of issues and policies*. Paris: OECD.

Palmer, K. (2008). The financial literacy crisis: Ignorance lands Americans in debt. Is the solution more schooling or a simpler system? *US News and World Report, April 2*. Available at: http://money.usnews.com/money/personal-finance/articles/2008/04/02/financial-literacy-101_print.html.

Posner, R. A. (2009). *A failure of capitalism: The crisis of '08 and the descent into depression*. Cambridge and London: Harvard University Press.

Roubini, N., & Mihm, S. (2010). *Crisis economics: A crash course in the future of finance*. New York: Penguin.

Shefrin, H. (2002). *Beyond greed and fear: Understanding behavioral finance and the psychology of investing*. New York: Oxford University Press.

Shiller, R. J. (2001). *Irrational exuberance*. Princeton: Princeton University Press.

Shiller, R. J. (2008). Infectious exuberance: Financial bubbles are like epidemics—And we should treat them both the same way. *The Atlantic, June/July*. Available at: http://www.theatlantic.com/magazine/archive/2008/07/infectious-exuberance/6839/.

Shiller, R. J. (2009, January 17). How about a stimulus for financial advice? *New York Times*. Available at: http://www.nytimes.com/2009/01/18/business/economy/18view.html?_r=1.

Shiller, R. J. (2010). How nutritious are your investments? *Project Syndicate: A World of Ideas (web site)*. Available at: http://www.project-syndicate.org/commentary/shiller71/English.

Simon, H. A. (1987). Behavioral economics. In J. Eatwell, M. Millgate, & P. Newman (Eds.), *The new Palgrave: A dictionary of economics*. London: Macmillan.

Smith, V. L. (2003). Constructivist and ecological rationality in economics. *American Economic Review, 93*, 465–508.

Smith, V. L. (2005). Behavioral economics research and the foundations of economics. *Journal of Socio-Economics, 34*, 135–150.

Sugden, R. (2008). Why incoherent preferences do not justify paternalism. *Constitutional Political Economy, 19*, 226–248.

Sugden, R. (2009). On nudging: A review of nudge: Improving decisions about health, wealth and happiness by Richard H. Thaler and Cass R. Sunstein. *International Journal of the Economics of Business, 16*, 365–373.

Thaler, R. H., & Sunstein, C. (2003). Libertarian paternalism. *American Economic Review, 93*(2), 175–179.

Thaler, R. H., & Sunstein, C. (2008). *Nudge: Improving decisions about health, wealth, and happiness*. New Haven/London: Yale University Press.

Tversky, A., & Kahneman, D. (1974). Judgment under uncertainty: Heuristics and biases. *Science, 185*(4157), 1124–1131. New Series.

Tversky, A., & Kahneman, D. (1981). The framing of decisions and the psychology of choice. *Science, 211*(4481), 453–458.

Wärneryd, K.-E. (2001). *Stock-market psychology*. Cheltenham: Edward Elgar.

World Literacy Foundation. (2015). *The economic and social costs of financial illiteracy: A snapshot of illiteracy in a global context*. Available at: https://secureservercdn.net/160.153.137.20/4ac.996.myftpupload.com/wp-content/uploads/WLF-FINAL-ECONOMIC-REPORT.pdf.

World Literacy Foundation. (2018). *The economic and social costs of financial illiteracy*. Available at: https://worldliteracyfoundation.org/wp-content/uploads/2019/06/TheEconomicSocial-CostofIlliteracy-2.pdf.

Yoong, J. (2010). *Making financial education more effective: Lessons from behavioral economics*. PowerPoint presentation Rand Corporation Center for Financial and Economic Decision Making. Available at: http://www.oecd.org/dataoecd/47/62/45485586.pdf.

Chapter 10

How labour markets really work

Chapter outline

Introduction	245	Demand for labour and the		
What is behavioural labour		supply of effort	262	
economics	246	Efficiency wage and x-efficiency		
Modelling labour supply: A		theory	265	
standard rendering	247	Some labour market implications		
A behavioural model of labour		of generalized x-efficiency		
supply: A target approach	250	theory	269	
Non-labour market income and		Population growth with real		
labour supply	255	women	272	
Unemployment insurance and		Conclusion	274	
labour supply	257	References	275	
Non-economic variables and				
errors or biases in labour				
market decision-making	258			

Introduction

The focus of this chapter is decision-making in the labour market and how one's understanding of such important decisions effects policy as well as decisions by employees and employers. I elaborate on contributions of behavioural economics to modelling the supply and demand sides of the labour market, which is all about the decision-making by employees and potential employees and employers. I discuss some of the implications of this for analytical prediction, cause and effect analysis, and public policy. I pay special attention to the target theory of labour supply, where the supply of labour is a function of an individual's target income. In the standard model labour supply is product of the wage rate and income. I also discuss the implications of effort variability, which directly relates to the demand side of the labour market, affecting the marginal value product (productivity). In standard economics the supply of effort is assumed fixed, often at some maximum (see Chapters 3, 5, and 7).

Moreover, I discuss the theoretical and policy implications of modelling the reality of individuals having limited information processing capabilities and making decisions in a world of complex, costly and asymmetric information (often referred to as bounded rationality). Decisions are also affected by

Smart Economic Decision-Making in a Complex World. https://doi.org/10.1016/B978-0-12-811461-2.00010-9

how information is framed and by the institutional parameters within which decision are made (Chapters 1 and 7). Decisions are also affected by norms, social context, and past behaviour (path dependency). This can result in errors in labour market decisions, generating outcomes that are inefficient from both the individual's and society's perspective and can affect both the supply and demand side of the labour market. Errors in decision-making are inconsistent with the leading proponents of traditional economics, following upon the arguments of Alchian (1950) and Friedman (1953), that competitive markets will force efficiency. However, possible errors in decision-making are a focal point of contemporary behavioural economics and behavioural finance (Altman, 2005b; Akerlof & Shiller, 2009; Leibenstein, 1966; Shiller, 2000; Thaler & Sustein, 2008), especially given the pervasiveness of imperfect product markets. Behavioural economics attempts to explain such errors as well as resulting economic inefficiencies (Simon, 1987).

This speaks to the notion of the labour market as a social institution, promoted by Solow (1990), with deep roots in behavioural and institutional economics. This narrative enriches the standard demand and supply analysis of the labour market, with an enhanced economic toolbox by incorporating the importance of psychological, sociological, and institutional variables to decision-making, as they are in real-world labour markets.

What is behavioural labour economics

Following in the tradition of Hebert Simon, behavioural labour economics builds models based upon more realistic simplifying behavioural assumptions by integrating insights from psychology, sociology, and institutional analyses. These can be expected to generate more robust descriptions of labour market behaviour and more accurate analytical predictions and credible cause and effect analyses. More realistic modelling assumptions minimize the probability spurious correlations and convoluting correlation with causation by linking specific behavioural and institutional facts on the ground with predictions. Of course, this better helps us to understand the decision-making process.

Our modelling assumptions are based on the reality of the brain as a scarce resource, with limited processing capabilities (bounded rationality), imperfect and asymmetric information, heterogeneous decision-makers, transaction costs, the importance of social norms for decision-making, effort variability, and the importance of institutional parameters affecting the decision-making process, inclusive of bargaining-power. This enriches the price and income focus of traditional economics. Our model predicts that individual behaviour will often be inconsistent with the predictions of standard theory (Akerlof, 1982, 1984, 2002; Altman, 2005a, 2005b, 2006b, 2008; Berg, 2006; Gigerenzer, 2007; on complex information, see Hayek, 1945; Kahneman, 2011; March, 1978; Simon, 1955, 1978, 1979, 1987; Smith, 2003; Todd & Gigerenzer, 2003).

Behavioural labour is influenced by two different, but overlapping, approaches to behavioural economics. One approach, pioneered by Kahneman and

Tversky (1979), Kahneman (2003, 2011), and Tversky and Kahneman (1981), assumes that individuals tend to be error-prone and biased in decision-making because of how the brain is hardwired. This generates persistent sub-optimal outcomes from the individual's and society's welfare maximizing perspective. Such sub-optimal decisions need be corrected by the intervention of experts, often through the auspices of government (Babcock, Congdon, Katz, & Mullainathan, 2010; Thaler & Sustein, 2008).

In the alternative, bounded rationality approach pioneered by Simon (1955, 1978, 1979, 1987), individuals are not assumed to be hardwired to behave in a sub-optimal errors-prone and biased manner. Hence errors can often be corrected by improvements in the decision-making environment and through education. Moreover, individuals can deviate from standard economic decision-making norms, but this often results in superior economic outcomes (Altman, 2005a, 2005b; Gigerenzer, 2007).

Modelling labour supply: A standard rendering

A good entry point for introducing behavioural ideas into labour market theory is the standard labour-leisure model of labour supply. It hinges upon two behavioural assumptions: (1) leisure (non-market activities) is preferred to work and is modelled as a normal good whereby increases in real income increases the demand for leisure, thereby reducing market labour supply; (2) holding real income constant, making leisure more expensive, by increasing the real wage, increases market labour supply and lowering the real wage reduces it (Becker, 1965). It is implicitly assumed that individuals gain no positive utility from labour market activities. However, in reality, this is not the case (Frey & Stutzer, 2002; Helliwell & Huang, 2011; Jahoda, 1981; Sherman & Shavit, 2009). Actually, most people enjoy working. It is also assumed that individuals can afford not to work on the market. So, they can and will withdraw from the labour market if the wage rate is too low. Given these standard assumptions, the substitution effect predicts that as the price (wage rate) of leisure increases, market labour supply increases and therefore less leisure is consumed. But as the wage increases, income goes up, resulting in increasing the demand for leisure (income effect). The supply of labour is a product of the interaction of the substitution and income effects. Labour supply increases as wages increase—the labour supply curve is upward sloping—as long as the substitution effect dominates the income effect. But when the income effect dominates, this yields the 'classic' backward bending labour supply curve.

These points are illustrated in Fig. 10.1, by labour supply curve 1. At W*, market labour supply is zero—wages are simply too low to compensate prospective workers for sacrificing the good feelings generated from consuming leisure time. As wages increase, market labour supply goes up until wages rise to W2. Thereafter, the income effect dominates the substitution effect and market labour supply falls. All along the labour supply curve the individual is assumed

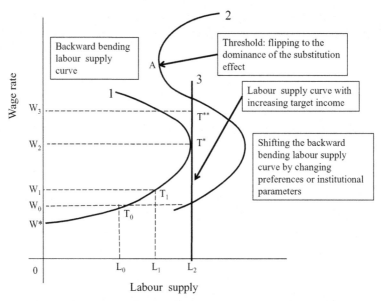

FIG. 10.1   The backward bending labour supply curve.

to be maximizing his or her utility, even if the individual is unemployed or is working 7 days week, 12 h per day.

What underlies (the micro-foundations) this type of labour supply curve is illustrated in Fig. 10.2. The nonlinear and convex to the origin indifference curve, presumes that income and non-labour time ('leisure') are substitutes. The individual increases labour supply from N_0N_1 to N_0N_2, given indifference curves U_0 and U_1, as the wage rate, the price of nonmarket time increases, from 1 to 2. Labour supply keeps on increasing as wages rise as long as the substitution effect outweighs the income effect. But when the wage rate diminishes, from 2 to 1, individuals substitute out of the market labour to nonmarket time and market labour supply falls as long as this substitution effect outweighs the income effect of falling real income.

Related to assumption (2), individuals will accept a wage offer only if their reservation wage—the minimal acceptable wage—is high enough. Policy, such as improvements to minimum wages, unemployment insurance and social welfare, that increase the reservation wage will reduce the percentage of wage offers accepted, increasing unemployment, whereas policy that reduces that reservation wage has the opposite effect. Changes in the reservation wage can also affect the supply of labour, by affecting the expected cost of leisure time. Increases to the reservation wage will reduce the supply of labour to the extent that individuals expect a higher wage rate to compensate them for sacrificing a unit of leisure (shifting the labour supply curve to the left). Moreover, increases in the reservation wage are predicted to increase the overall wage rates paid by

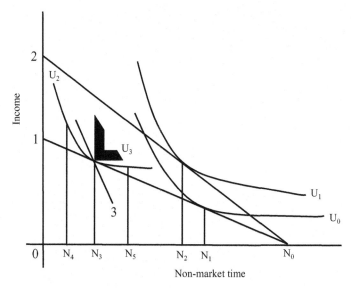

FIG. 10.2 Aspects of the standard model.

all firms irrespective of current wage levels, increasing average production costs and, thereby, increasing unemployment.

A critical problem with the standard model is that it fails to provide any reasonable predictions on the timing and direction of changes in labour supply. Rather, once one knows the shape of the labour supply curve, it is argued is that a particular change in the relationship between the substitution and income effect 'caused' a change in labour supply. By assumption, other possible causal variables, even those that are more plausible from a reality-based perspective are not ever brought into consideration (this is a serious omitted variable problem).

There is no empirical or theoretical basis to predict when, or the extent to which, there should be a change in the relationship between income and substitution effects such that labour supply increases and then diminishes, yielding an s-shaped labour supply curve (Fig. 10.1, supply curve 2). (For problems and issues with contemporary labour supply theory see, Altman, 2001; Pencavel, 1986; Prasch, 2000; Dessing, 2002; Sharif, 2000, and Chapters 5 and 7–11, this book).

In the real world, we have witnessed such s-shaped labour curves, wherein hours worked per week initially fell in currently developed economies, in the late nineteenth century, when workers often worked 6–7 days a week, often for more than 10 h a day, with little or no vacation time. More recently, in many of these economies, hours worked per week increased somewhat from lows of less than 40 h per week (Messenger, Lee, & McCann, 2007). What is required is a model that ex ante predicts labour market behaviour, generating analytical predictions using credible behavioural and institutional assumptions.

A behavioural model of labour supply: A target approach

In the target approach, real target income and target non-market activities are introduced into the modelling of market labour supply (see Altman, 2001; Camerer, Babcock, Lowenstein, & Thaler, 1997; Baxter, 1993; Kaufman, 1989, 1999, for more details). Labour supply decisions can be more robustly modelled here by making the simplifying assumption that individuals are most concerned with their target income and their target non-market activities. This is opposed to the standard focus on the relative price of leisure and the capacity of individuals to purchase more leisure time. The notion that target income can be important is not new, but has not had much impact on the standard labour supply literature.

One can write the target theory as market labour supply being a function of target market income, target nonmarket activities, nonmarket income, and the real wage rate (Altman, 2001). This argument can take the form of:

$$L^{SM} = F\left(TY, TNML, NMY, w\right)\ldots \tag{10.1}$$

TY is real target income, TNML is target nonmarket time, NMY is real nonmarket income, and w is the real wage rate. Market labour supply can be measured by hours supplied to the labour market. Given real target income, labour supply is given by the real wage rate, conditional upon target nonmarket time and real nonmarket income, or:

$$L^{SM} = \frac{TY - NMY}{W}, conditional\ upon\ TNML\ldots \tag{10.2}$$

Given TY, NMY, and W market labour supply is determined. It is important to note the importance of TNML, such as childcare and care of disabled loved-ones, for example, in determining TY. The higher the TNML, the lower the market labour supply. Such would be the case with single-parent female led households with no affordable childcare. On the other hand, artists or musicians who are happy (maximizing utility) at a low target income so that more time is devoted off-market to painting and music, will supply minimal labour to the labour market. Overall, ceteris paribus, one can model increasing target minimum nonmarket time as shifting the market labour supply curve to the left whilst reducing this target shifts the market labour supply curve to the right.

Real target income is defined inclusive of expenses required to earn a particular level of target real income, such as taxes, daycare, appropriate clothing, and transportation costs. Once target income is known, one can more accurately predict the price effect (the slope of the labour supply curve) of a change in wages. Moreover, ceteris paribus, changes in target income affects the extent to which changes in wages affect labour supply, since the ability to realize a given level of real target income is a product of real wages and hours worked.

For example, if real target income is met at a given real wage and number of hours worked, increasing real wages will reduce the supply of labour. Camerer et al.'s (1997) target model of labour supply focuses on taxi drivers where target income appears to be fixed, thus increasing wages reduces the labour supply. This model builds on very short run objective functions. See Farber (2005) for a critique of the Camerer et al. (1997). If real target income increases, on the other hand, the supply labour would increase at any given real wage to meet the increased target income. Moreover, if real target income exceeds what can be realized at the current real wage and a given (maximum) labour supply, increasing real wage can be expected to have no effect on labour supply. If real target income increases, labour supply would not fall in the face of increasing real wages if these higher wages, in combination with the existing level of market labour supply, are required to either approach or realize the higher level of target income.

There is evidence supportive of the hypothesis that target income increases over time resulting in a persistent and sometimes growing gap between actual real income of the individual or household and their real target income (Altman, 2001; Lebergott, 1993, p. 65). This could be a function of sellers promoting new products by creating new wants (Frank, 1985, 1999, 2005; Galbraith, 1958; George, 2001), the desire of individuals to maintain their income position in relation to their peers (Duesenberry, 1949; Easterlin, 2001; Leibenstein, 1950) and, the increasing material aspiration levels of individuals (Easterlin, 2001; Lebergott, 1993; Mack, 1956; March & Simon, 1968; Sanders, 2008; Shane & Loewenstein, 1999; Stutzer, 2004). If real target income did not increase over time in developed economies, most people there would not have to work very much at all. No more than 10–15 h work per week would be required to achieve the average income of early twentieth century Americans and no more than 10–15 min per week to reach the income levels of the Kapauku Papuans of the Pacific Islands (Altman, 2001; Lebergott, 1993, p. 65).

Hours worked have declined over the past-100 odd years in economies that are currently developed but not nearly as much as they should have if target real income had not increased. Moreover, hours of work tend to decline quite dramatically amongst developing low-income economies but only in a fashion consistent with increasing real income. And, amongst the developed wealthy economies there is little relationship between hours worked per week and increases in real wages (Messenger et al., 2007). The evidence tends to support the hypothesis that real target income increases over time.

The fact that real target income keeps increasing is critically important to understanding the evolution of market labour supply and to predicting future movements in market labour supply. Here we have an evidenced-based variable (unlike the substitution and income effects) that drives market labour supply. This allows for more substantive economic predictions and causal analyses.

A key point of the target approach is that the market supply of labour is driven by the wants and desires of individuals. This target income modelling of labour supply is based on Altman (2001). Here, substitution effects are often of little analytical consequence. Indeed, when market labour supply is fixed for target income reasons the individual's indifference curve for income and non-market time is L-shaped as with indifference curve U3 in Fig. 10.2—we have lexicographic indifference curves. Kaufman (1989), building upon Maslow (1954), argues that labour market choices are largely determined by the hierarchy of needs of the individual, which typically overwhelms any predicted substitution and income effects, often generating lexicographical or L-shaped indifference curves. As the wage rate changes from 1 to 3 or from 3 to 1, there is no change in the preferred amount of nonmarket activities and, therefore, in market labour supply. Individuals are not willing sacrifice real income to obtain more nonmarket activities. Labour supply changes here, not as a consequence of changes in the price of nonmarket or 'leisure' time (substitution effect), but as a function of changes in target income and whether an increase in the wage rate yields a real income that exceeds the current target income. If the latter occurs, there is a decrease in labour supply as a result of target income being surpassed at the higher real wage and the given amount of hours worked. Once one knows an individual's target income, one can predict market labour supply as the real wage rate changes. This is more consistent with the decision making process or workers and potential workers or employees.

The trade-off between market income and nonmarket activities is illustrated in Fig. 10.3. In the target income model, since the indifference curves are assumed to be L-shaped, the individual's market labour supply decision is based on target income, not income-'leisure' trade-offs in terms of substitution effects. As the wage rate increases, from 1 to 2, the individual can choose to maintain his or her prior supply of market labour (N_0N_1) and maximize income, at 0C. On the other hand, the individual can choose to maintain his or her prior supply of market labour (N_0N_1) and maximize income, at 0C. On the other hand, the individual can reduce market labour supply to N_0N_2, and increase income to 0B. In this case, BC of income is sacrificed in order to increase nonmarket activities from $0N_1$ to $0N_3$. These choices, based on an individual's target income, can all be utility maximizing and is given by the tangency of indifference curves U_1, U_2, and U_0, to their respective price lines.

In one plausible scenario, one begins a market labour supply narrative at very low real wages and a very high level of market labour supply, such as 60 h (a 10 h workday of 6 days) per week, not uncommon in the nineteenth century industrial world and prevalent in many developing economies today. Increasing nonmarket time as real wages increase eventually proves to be a higher order need than a further increase in real income (Cross, 1988). In Fig. 10.3, utility is maximized at a low level of nonmarket activities, such as 0N1, in an attempt to meet target income. Initial increases in real wages can be expected to have no effect on target nonmarket activities if target income has yet to be met. But as real wages increase further, the next step in the hierarchy of needs and wants would be to increase nonmarket time from its very low levels, maximizing utility at N3

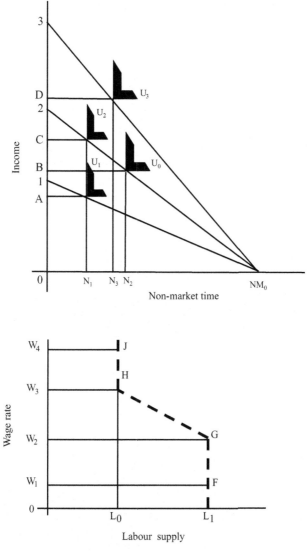

FIG. 10.3 (A) Income-non-market time trade-off. (B) Labour supply curve.

of nonmarket time. In this case, both nonmarket time and real income increases (to 0D from 0C). Once the need for more nonmarket time is met, it becomes possible to meet higher order needs as real wages increase, which can be either more nonmarket time or more market goods. If target real income increases whilst target nonmarket time is being met, further increases in real wages can be expected to have no effect on labour supply. In this scenario, utility can only be increased by increasing real income as wages rise. Increasing nonmarket time cannot compensate an individual for any reduction in income—the indifference curve is L-shaped. In this case the substitution effect is zero while the income effect depends on the time-specific ranking of market income and nonmarket time.

The resulting labour supply curve, FGHJ, mapped out from this indifference curve analysis, is illustrated in Fig. 10.3B. This is a long run market labour supply curve, where two independent variables are changing, both the wage rate and preferences for goods and services. At low levels of real income, the labour supply curve is perfectly inelastic, at 0L1, to changes in the real wage rate. There is a backward bend to the labour supply curve at point G, at wage rate W2. Thereafter, as the wage rate increases from W3, the labour supply curve is once again inelastic to increases in the real wage rate. This type of labour supply curve is consistent with the evidence across time and place (Messenger et al., 2007, p. 33). Based on the target theory, one would predict a drop in market labour supply only if target income no longer increases in pace with real wage growth.

This modelling of labour supply has not taken into consideration the utility that individuals obtain from market work (Frey & Stutzer, 2002; Helliwell & Huang, 2011; Jahoda, 1981; Sherman & Shavit, 2009). Quite rationally, the act of working and working with others, being part of a group, can make people feel better. This psychological variable, itself, can set a floor to market labour supply. Even if real target income is met, labour supply may not diminish if the given level of labour supply is utility maximizing in terms of the psychological kick the individual obtains from working. Any increase in the utility an individual obtains from market work can be modelled as an outward shift in the labour supply curve, such as from labour supply curve 1 to 2 in Fig. 10.1. However, if the work environment is nasty, this does not imply that an individual will reduce her or his supply of labour. This is especially the case when a given amount of market labour is required to meet the real target income of the individual. Still, one could predict that a poor work environment can, on the margin, in higher income societies, have the effect of shifting the labour supply curve inward to the left.

Another important psychological labour supply shift factor is the discouraged worker effect. An individual becomes discouraged if she loses confidence in her ability to find work and stops actively searching for work. This person drops out of the labour market even while still desiring market employment. This shifts the market labour supply curve to the left. Whilst increasing aggregate demand, invigorated animal spirits, improved job search mechanisms, reduce the discouraged workers' effect, shifts the economy-wide market labour supply curve outward to the right (on animal spirits, Akerlof & Shiller, 2009).

An important footnote to this target theory of labour supply is that individuals' ability to choose their preferred amount of labour supply, given the wage rate and their target income, is affected by the political-legal environment in which labour market decisions are made. Standard labour market theory assumes an institutional environment wherein individuals choose how much to work. But at one extreme, where free labour markets do not exist, such as with slavery or serfdom, individuals are not free to choose. Where free labour markets predominate, individuals legally own their labour power. Their market labour supply decisions are affected by institutional parameters such as labour unions and nonmarket income such as unemployment insurance and social security (social welfare payments). The target labour supply theory can incorporate various types of institutional parameters. For example, where labour has limited legal rights, labour supply can be constrained to the physiological maximum and the labour supply curve would be perfectly inelastic at this maximum supply, such as labour supply curve 3 in Fig. 10.1. Where more labour rights obtain, workers can choose to supply less labour as real wages increase, if this choice set maximizes their utility. Here, the slope of the market labour supply curve changes from being completely inelastic to somewhat elastic.

Labour market discrimination can also affect labour supply, shifting the economy-wide market labour supply curve to the left. If particular groups in society are precluded from labour market participation, members of these groups can't participate even if they are willing to work at prevailing wage rates. Their revealed preference for market work is stymied by institutional variables. Their absence from the labour market is not related to the substitution and income effects. Reducing labour market discrimination should shift the market labour supply curve to the right, as more individuals, women for example, choose to seek employment to meet their target income and to meet their psychological need to participate in the world of work. The extent of this shift can be in part determined by estimating the shortfall between actual real income and target income.

Non-labour market income and labour supply

Increasing nonmarket sources of income would not reduce labour force participation unless target income is met with the assistance of the nonmarket sources of income and market work has no positive effect on utility. This speaks to the potential impact of the introduction or increases in 'social welfare' payments or unemployment insurance on labour supply. The standard model predicts that such nonmarket increases in income (demogrants) will reduce labour supply whereas a decrease in such income will increase labour supply through the income effect, shifting the labour supply curve (Friedman, 1968; Mulligan, 2013). Such predictions pay no attention to individuals' target income, their target level of nonmarket time, their physical capacity to work, their hierarchy of wants, and the rules and regulations that dictate the terms under which individuals are entitled to demogrants (Altman, 2004a, 2004b). Also, no attention is paid to the utility gained from the act of engaging in market work (Sherman & Shavit, 2009). Such utility diminishes the impact that demogrants might otherwise have on labour supply. The traditional model's predictions need to be modified to incorporate these non-economic variables. In other words, one has to incorporate the reality of how individuals actually behave (make choices) in real world labour markets.

The target approach predicts that as long as target income is not met, ceteris paribus, labour supply should not be reduced with the introduction or increases in the level of social welfare. This is especially true if the individual gains utility from working on the labour market (Sherman & Shavit, 2009). In this case, social welfare would form a basis of economic support for individuals who prefer to work but are unable to obtain employment. The predicted impact of increases of social welfare on labour supply is much more complex than in the standard model, requiring information on target income and the utility of market work.

For work capable individuals, the target approach suggests that they might be on social welfare because they have a low target income (covered by social welfare), do not gain utility from working, have a higher order preference for nonmarket activities, or cannot find work. Behavioural economics would be open to the hypothesis that lack of job opportunities can result in individuals being on social welfare even though they prefer to work. Also, market work might also be discouraged, when jobs are available, if the tax rate on market work results in net income being greater if one does not accept available and otherwise acceptable job offers. This is an important institutional parameter requiring consideration. To increase labour supply here requires a change and/ or restructuring of the tax rate and more job opportunities; not the elimination of social welfare (Organisation for Economic Co-operation and Development, 2003; Starky, 2006).

Individuals who are not in the labour market for psychological reasons might not increase their labour force participation even if, as a consequence, they must suffer economic losses (their target income drops). The psychological cost of entering the labour market might outweigh possible benefits, especially if they have very negative views of labour market conditions. Reducing social welfare would, in this case, simply increase the level of economic deprivation amongst these individuals. Other means would be required to increase labour supply inclusive of overcoming individuals' biases and misinformation on the state of the labour market.

Overall, eliminating or reducing social welfare might increase labour supply, but realistically, not by much, given the small percentage of the population in most countries on social welfare. This increase in labour supply would have little to do with the income or substitution effects as specified in the standard model. What is critical to understanding labour market dynamics with regards to social welfare, from a behavioural perspective, is to better incorporate non-economic factors that underlie why individuals are outside of the labour market.

For example, the disabled who are not work capable can't work, so reducing social welfare simply increases these individuals' level of economic deprivation. Stay-at-home moms might be on welfare (low target income) so as to take care of their children, absent childcare facilities, for example. Reducing social welfare might force some of these individuals onto the labour market, shifting the labour supply curve outward and reducing the wage rate, thereby reducing the level of economic sustenance provided by the market (Solow, 2003). But this has nothing to do with traditional income effects. Rather, mothers are forced unto the labour market to meet minimal target incomes at the opportunity cost of taking care of their children. This can also have the long-term effect of reducing the supply of labour controlling for quality, by reducing the labour market capabilities of children. However, single mothers, can reduce target income as social welfare is cut, to take care of their children, increasing the economic deprivation within their household. In this case, any increase in labour supply predicted by the standard model would not take place or would be mitigated. Unless a vibrant labour market accompanies cuts to social welfare, the increased labour supply generated by such cuts, simply increases the number of unemployed and reduces the equilibrium wage. A key determinant of poverty and social welfare dependency is the absence or lack of work, hence the significance of vibrant labour markets (International Labour Organization (2010); Rice et al., 2013; Solow, 2003).

Unemployment insurance and labour supply

The above discussion is also pertinent to an understanding of unemployment insurance, which the standard model predicts should result in increasing unemployment. This increase is caused by attracting individuals into the labour market who intend to quit their new jobs to collect this benefit, by increasing the voluntary job search time of the unemployed workers already in the labour force, by inducing increasing quit rates of the currently employed so that they can search for better jobs, and by increasing the market wage thereby increasing the price of labour and reducing the competitiveness of the economy. Moreover, following upon the efficiency wage literature, unemployment insurance is expected to reduce the effort incentive effect of a given rate of unemployment (unemployment is viewed as a disciplinary devise to keep effort levels at higher levels) (see below on efficiency wages) (Altman, 2004a; Holmlund, 1998; Shapiro & Stiglitz, 1984). Having lower levels of support increases the penalty against workers who are not working enough.

The standard approach also assumes that the increased duration of short-term job search induced by unemployment insurance can have no positive effect on long term employment rates. It is further assumed that higher real wages necessarily or typically generate higher production costs and thereby higher rates of unemployment. Neither of these assumptions need hold (see Chapters 4 and 5). It is further assumed that the marginal worker maximizes utility or economic wellbeing at low levels of real income thus allowing unemployment insurance to serve as a utility maximizing 'wage of being unemployed'. Thus, some workers maximize their utility by getting themselves laid off so as to take advantage of this 'wage of being unemployed'.

The available empirical evidence provides no unambiguous support for the conventional proposition that unemployment insurance damages the economy (Altman, 2004a; Atkinson & Micklewright, 1991; Holmlund, 1998; Howell & Azizoglu, 2011; Howell & Rehm, 2009). For example, to the extent that unemployment increases search time and this produces a better match between job searcher and job, this can reduce job turnover and thereby reduce the long-term unemployment rate (Altman, 2004a). Also, since unemployment insurance is typically much less than market income, individuals won't quit their jobs to earn unemployment insurance unless their target income is relatively quite low and they attach little or no utility to market work. Moreover, most workers are not eligible for unemployment insurance if they simply quite their jobs. This institutional reality, critical to a behaviouralist analysis, often precludes unemployment insurance from actually directly causing an increase in the unemployment rate (Atkinson & Micklewright, 1991; Holmlund, 1998). Finally, one can't easily predict the extent to which unemployment insurance increases the market wage and the extent to which this increases costs and thereby unemployment. Efficiency wage theory and especially x-efficiency theory predicts different plausible outcomes wherein increasing wages have a positive effect on productivity that can offset any wage increases (see below).

It is critically important from both an analytical and public policy perspective to develop a theoretical framework that incorporates the empirics suggesting that unemployment insurance generates no long run negative economic effects. Introducing more realistic behavioural and institutional assumptions into one's modelling of unemployment insurance contributes to this task of developing and testing a variety of hypotheses relating unemployment insurance to labour supply and employment.

Non-economic variables and errors or biases in labour market decision-making

Labour supply can be affected by psychological variables such as inaccurate perceptions about labour market opportunities. Some behavioural economists define and interpret these as cognitive illusions (Babcock et al., 2010). This overlaps with the severely critiqued 'culture of poverty' literature wherein it is maintained that poverty persists because of the cultural (and related innate biases) of the poor (Gorski, 2008; Wilson, 1997). But these misperceptions can also be viewed as a product of poor or incorrect information sets, cognitive costs, loss or risk adverse behaviour in a world of uncertainty, peer effects, social capital, or psychological depression, all consistent with the Herbert Simon's perspective on behavioural economics (see also March, 1978). In this case, one has rational individuals whose choices might be improved (even from their own perspective or objective function) with improvements in their decision-making environment. Either way, introducing non-economic variables into the analytical mix allows one to better explain certain aspects behaviour and to suggest policy to improve labour market outcomes.

Of critical importance, is the now established fact that persistent involuntary unemployment causes depression and other mental health issues, including loss of self-esteem and loss of a sense of control amongst the unemployed. This also has negative, possibly long term, repercussions on the family of the unemployed. Moreover, long-term unemployment results in the depreciation in the human capital stock of the unemployed. This is one reason why the long-term unemployed tend to end up with jobs paying less than their former jobs. Long-term unemployment also reduces, on average, the long run capital stock of family members. Moreover, such unemployment sends negative signals to prospective employers resulting in the long-term unemployed being less likely to secure future employment than individuals who are short term unemployed. It appears that in a world of asymmetric information, employers use long-term unemployment as a signal for relatively poorer future performance and employability—a form of statistical discrimination. These variables cause a downward shift in the demand curve for labour.

Long-term unemployment also increases the probability of morbidity, reduces life expectancy, and increases the probability of family violence. The mental health effects of unemployment feed into the human capital side of the story, contributing to reducing human capital stock, which reduces the probability of get a job, which increases mental health problems, which reduces human capital stock. In addition, because of depression (related to this, loss of self-confidence), due to unemployment, there is a lower probability of job search amongst the long-term unemployed—this relates to the discouraged worker effect. Overall, long-term unemployment by reducing human capital stock per prospective employee reduces the employability of such individuals at any given real wage rate. For this reason, persistent long-term unemployment can have the effect of reducing the equilibrium rate of employment. This need not increase the official rate of unemployment if one is also increasing the number of discouraged workers sufficiently (Adams, 2012; Babcock et al., 2010; Darity & Goldsmith, 1996; Jahoda, 1981; Linn, Sandifer, & Stein, 1985; Paul & Moser, 2009; Stuckler & Basu, 2013; Zukin, 2009).

Applied economics is increasingly integrating these findings into its corpus. And many economists recommend that it is critically important to reduce long-term unemployment, not only for the mental anguish it causes the unemployed and their families, but also because of the serious deleterious effects it has on productivity. So, a big public policy question relates to how can one most effectively and efficiently reduce the long run unemployment rate by increasing employment given the importance of these particular non-economic variables.

With regards macroeconomic policy, behavioural economics places close attention to the importance of psychological variables, such as confidence and animal spirits, in moving the economy forward. It's not only about monetary and fiscal policy (Akerlof & Shiller, 2009). Rather it is about such policy recognizing the importance of psychological variables in determining the extent and timing of spending (see also, Chapter 8).

Behavioural economics also pays close attention to informational concerns, capital market imperfections, and uncertainty, affecting labour market behaviour. Unemployed workers can and do underestimate the probability of securing employment at preferred real wages rates and annual income. This can be a product of individuals suffering from a loss of confidence who then might become discouraged workers. This market failure, related to errors in decision-making, can be corrected by more direct intervention by job search agencies and client specific advisors who can provide individuals with more direct information on job prospects and facilitate the interview process. In this instance, the default is that the job search agency leads the job search process as opposed to the traditional default where the unemployed are left to take the initiative. The traditional default does not work effectively when workers are literally psyched out of the job search process and subject to imperfect and even misleading information. Workers may also not have the financial means to engage in effective job search—inadequate funds for transportation, presentable clothing, and childcare. This can be addressed by more direct intervention in the job search process, facilitating such individuals moving into the job market, to correct for market failure. In this case, the intervention increases the job search capabilities of the unemployment as opposed to building policy based on the conventional assumption that adequate capabilities are in place and the unemployed would rather engage in 'leisure' activities than find a job.

This approach does not assume that individuals are engaged in biased decision-making—an assumption made by many behavioural economists. Rather, 'real' variables generate correctable decision-making errors. Given these 'real' variables, changing the defaults affect decision-making in terms of how the new defaults provide better information, reduce uncertainty and transaction costs, and help compensate for under-confidence amongst the unemployed.

Moreover, behavioural economics, in the tradition of institutional economics pays close attention to components of long-run unemployment that are structural. Many unemployed will not find employment in jobs that require their former skill set because of the changing nature of the economy. To move forward in the job market, adequate job retraining is required as is accurate information on job opportunities and the necessary skills sets required for available jobs. In a world of asymmetric information and imperfect capital markets individuals may not have the capacity to invest in skill upgrading. In this case, either subsidized or public job retraining programs would be required to fix such a market failure.

But there is another approach to the causes of long-run unemployment embedded to the Kahneman–Tversky errors and biases approach to behavioural economics (for a survey of this see, Babcock et al., 2010). In this approach, individuals are assumed to suffer from a range of biases, such as present or status quo bias, loss aversion (losses weighted more heavily than gains), hyperbolic discounting (procrastination). This results in such individuals not knowing what's in their own best interest. As a result, the unemployed engage in inadequate job search and reject job offers that should be accepted given the objective labour market conditions. In this case, workers actually suffer from errors in decision-making based on an overconfidence bias. The unemployed set their reservation wage too high, based on the wages in their former jobs, which no longer reflects the objective reality of the labour market. The difference between their former wage and current and lower wage offers (the former wage is regarded as an anchor) are also treated as a loss of income by the unemployed. Given loss aversion, this type of framing of job offers incentivizes the unemployed to reject what are objectively optimal job offers. In summary, these various biases result in too many of the unemployed procrastinating in job search, not spending enough time searching for a job, and rejecting what are the best possible jobs offers. All this causes the rate of unemployment to be greater than it should otherwise be—what it would be in a de-biased world.

One solution to this type of biased decision-making is providing wage-loss insurance to the unemployed that would temporarily subsidize a worker's income when he or she accepts a relatively low-paying job. This reduces perceived income loss (as well as loss aversion) and therefore incentivizes individuals to increase their job search and increase the acceptance rate of relatively low paying job offers. It is also argued that framing wage loss insurance explicitly in the pay statement will help push wage expectations downwards towards an objectively given lower level. All of this would serve to reduce the long-run rate of unemployment by pro-actively dealing with the biased decision-making of the unemployed.

This errors and biases approach to long-run unemployment does not deny the importance of inaccurate information and information processing costs as possible causes of errors in decision-making. But the focus is on cognitive biases. The biased decisions of unemployed are an important cause of persistent unemployment. A key prior assumption here is that there exists a supply of jobs available to meet the demand for jobs given that price of labour is right—the real wage rate must be low enough. The demand side is not a problem. It is also assumed that there is no negative efficiency wage effect of dropping the wage rate, therefore, it is assumed that a lower wage rate *won't* cause such a drop in productivity that employing the lower wage, less efficient worker, becomes unprofitable (see Chapter 6).

In the bounded rationality approach to behavioural economics, where individuals are largely rational and smart, correcting information errors, more accurately framing information, providing less costly access to information, reducing job search costs, improving individual capabilities to engage in job search, job re-training, and addressing depression induced lack of confidence, is of greater importance to reducing long-run unemployment. From this perspective, correctable errors in decision-making and inadequate capabilities amongst the unemployed are thought to be the larger problem. This does not deny, however, the possibility of biases in decision-making. And, of course, given optimal conditions on the supply side, job offers must be available to the job searchers.

Otherwise, these individuals will remain unemployed irrespective of ideal supply side conditions that explicitly deal with decision-making problems related to cognitive, informational, and transaction costs issues.

Demand for labour and the supply of effort

Labour supply does not simply comprise of hours worked, although this is the point of focus of standard and even much of heterodox labour economics. Also of importance is the quality and quantity of effort supply per unit of employed labour. In other words, a given hour of work can be characterized by a wide range of effort inputs that, in turn, can have a very large effect on the quantity and quality of output. This effort dimension of labour supply is a critical point of focus of the behavioural economics (Akerlof, 1982, 1984, 2002; Akerlof, Dickens, & Perry, 1996, 2000; Akerlof & Yellen, 1986, 1988, 1990; Altman, 2005a, 2005b, 2006a; Bowles & Gintis, 1990; Frantz, 1997; Leibenstein, 1957, 1966, 1979; Solow, 1979, 1990). Variations in effort supply, in turn, are important determinants of the demand for labour, by affecting the marginal product of labour and therefore the marginal value product (see also Chapters 4, 5, and 7).

In the standard model, effort per hour worked is assumed fixed, invariant to any circumstance in which labour, management, or owners might find themselves. This assumes away the potential importance of effort as a critical component of labour supply. Introducing effort variability into the production function and the objective function of firm members allows one to better model how individuals might respond to a variety of incentive environments. Two critical areas of research incorporating effort variability fall under the nomenclature of efficiency wage and x-efficiency theory. Much of this literature assumes rational individuals who are smart, consistent, and goal oriented. But they are not necessarily motivated to maximize their effort inputs.

One should note that there is an abundance of evidence demonstrating that effort is a variable in the production function, (for a literature review see Altman, 2002; Frantz, 1997). It is also clear that effort varies with a variety of variables, inclusive of wages, other aspects of working conditions, relations with employers, and the known costs of shirking from 'maximum' effort inputs. Studies of firms across economies and over time strongly suggest that productivity varies across firms, controlling for traditional economic variables. An important determinant of such productivity differentials is variations in effort input per unit of labour. From these studies, it is clear that effort variability is significantly affected by managerial design, working conditions, and the extent of cooperation, trust, and fairness within the firm across agents, especially between and amongst agents and principles (Akerlof, 2002; Altman, 2002, 2006a; Bewley, 1999; Buchele & Christainsen, 1999; Gordon, 1998, Leibenstein, 1983; Levine & D'Andrea Tyson, 1990; Logue & Yates, 1999; McKersie & Klein, 1983; Pfeffer, 1995; Tomer, 1987; Winther & Marens, 1997).

Moreover, research in experimental economics, largely using classroom experiments, affirms what one finds in the real world. Experiments suggest that wages and effort inputs are highly and positively correlated. In some experiments, hypothetical workers reward hypothetical employers for paying higher wages by increasing effort and punish such employers for reducing wages by cutting effort input. This is referred to as reciprocal punishment. Thus, there is a cost involved in not paying employees what is perceived to be a fair wage (Ben-Ner & Putterman, 2009; Boyd, Gintis, Bowles, & Richerson, 2003; Fehr & Gachter, 2000, 2002; Henrich et al., 2001; Putterman, 2012; for a more critical perspective, see Rigdon, 2002). This experimental research is closely related to the Ultimatum Game experiments, pioneered by Güth, Schmittberger, and Schwarze (1982), where there is a proposer and responder. In this type of game, if the responder refuses the offer made by the proposer, then both parties end up with nothing. The standard economic prediction is that the rational proposer should offer next to nothing and the responder should accept the offer since something is better than nothing. However, from multiple such experiments, including some field experiments, offers that are below 30–40% of the proposer's allocation are rejected, even in one-shot games. Responders are willing to punish proposers, even at a cost to themselves, for what are deemed to be unfair offers. And, often proposers make fair offers from the get go. Subjects are not acting neoclassically rational. But they are rational, if fairness is part of their objective function or preferences. Some of this experimental literature is reviewed in Charness and Kuhn (2011, see also Falk and Fehr, 2003, for a more critical perspective, see Edwards, 2012, Levitt and List, 2008).

Some of the key implications of effort variability for labour supply are illustrated in Fig. 10.4. In the standard model, effort is invariant to differences in wage rates. It is fixed, such as at 0m, and is perfectly inelastic with respect to changes in the wage rate. It is typically assumed that 0m is a maximum in terms of both the quality and quantity of effort input. Once effort is assumed to be variable, one has an effort supply function, the form of which is an empirical question. In Fig. 10.4, there are three effort supply functions, illustrating diminishing returns, constant returns, and increasing returns subject to eventually diminishing returns. At a particular wage rate, the behavioural effort function converges to the standard one, where effort supply is maxed-out and is perfectly inelastic to further increases in the wage rate. In the behavioural model, for each hour worked, there can be a multiplicity of effort and, therefore, productivity levels as a function of the wage rate and, more generally, the level of working conditions and the state of industrial relations. Therefore, unlike in the standard model, the demand curve for labour cannot be derived independently of the wage rate and working conditions. As effort inputs change, by changing the marginal value product of labour, this shifts the demand curve for labour. Effort input becomes a demand-side shift parameter in the behavioural model (see also Chapters 4, 5, and 7).

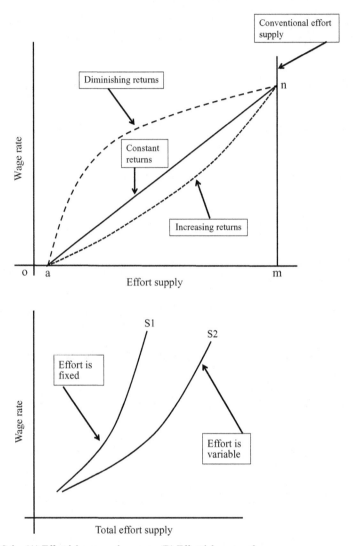

FIG. 10.4 (A) Effort labour supply curves. (B) Effort labour supply.

One can also derive an effort labour supply curve building on the standard labour supply curve, which relates wage rate to the supply of hours of labour. In this case, effort supply is given by hours supplied scaled by effort input per hour of labour supplied. This is illustrated in Fig. 10.4B. S1 assumes that effort input is inelastic to changes in wages. So, S1 is given by hours of labour supplied per wage rate scaled by a fixed amount of effort per hour supplied—this is standard assumption. S2 assumes that effort increases with wages. In this case, S2 pivots outward as wages increase. This assumes that workers work harder and smarter as wages increase—the behavioural assumption.

Efficiency wage and x-efficiency theory

Efficiency wage theory, originally formulated by Leibenstein (1957) to explain persistent unemployment in less development economies, specifies a unique profit-maximizing wage (the efficiency wage), yielding a unique profit maximizing level of effort input per unit of labour input. This was partially based on the argument that if wages were cut at low levels of nutrition, workers effort input would collapse, cutting into firm profits. Thus, rational decision-makers, maintain wages above their market-clearing rate, yielding persistent voluntary unemployment.

Akerlof's contemporary rendering of efficiency wage theory, makes the case for an above market-clearing unique efficiency wage, constructed by rational decision-makers, for social and psychological as opposed nutrition-related reasons. These include, social norms or fairness, reciprocity, moral sentiment, insider power, asymmetric information, and employers' fear of retaliation by employees for perceived unfair treatment (Akerlof, 2002; Akerlof et al., 1996, 2000; Akerlof & Shiller, 2009; Bewley, 1999).

Pioneered by Leibenstein (1966, 1979), x-efficiency theory offers a richer more nuanced modelling of effort variability, one that can be used to better explain issues such as involuntary unemployment as well as sub-optimal economic performance in terms of per capita output and unit costs and profitability. X-inefficiency is defined as output being less than it can potentially be given factor inputs and technology. This sub-optimal level of output is a function of the quantity and quality of effort inputted into the production process as compared to would be the case under best practice industrial relations. In terms of efficiency wage theory, a wage lower than the efficiency wage would yield x-inefficiency in production.

In the original specification of x-efficiency theory Leibenstein focuses on effort variability of management and owners. Ceteris paribus, reducing the quality and quantity of managerial effort makes the firm x-inefficient, increasing unit production costs by reducing firm productivity. This makes the firm less competitive, unless protected from competitive pressures through government support or through imperfect product markets. Or, such firms can survive if their competitors are equally x-inefficient (Simon, 1987, p. 223). Such reductions in firm productivity would also have the effect of reducing the firm's demand for labour shifting inward the firm's market demand curve. Firm decision-makers might very well be maximizing their utility by reducing their effort levels below some reasonable potential high (see also Chapters 4, 5, and 7).

One way of illustrating this particular take on labour supply is in terms of a very simple economy where labour is the only costed input (Altman, 2005a, 2005b).

$$AC = \frac{w}{\left(\dfrac{Q}{L}\right)}\dots \tag{10.3}$$

where AC is average cost, w is the wage rate and (Q/L) is the average product of labour, Q is total output, and L is labour input measured in terms of hours worked. If managerial effort input is reduced, firm productivity falls and this yields, ceteris paribus, higher average costs. Of course, increasing effort levels increases firm productivity, thereby reducing average costs. In a more complex model where labour is not the only input in the production function, the implications of varying effort inputs remain the same (see, for example, Altman, 2006a). But the latter case, increasing the wage rate increases average cost by less than the percentage increase in wages. So, for example, if labour comprises 50% of input costs, a 10% increase in wages only increases average cost by 5% (50% of 10%) as opposed to 10%. In this model, the competitively sustainable minimum effort levels are given by the extent to which x-inefficient firms are protected from competitive pressures.

One of the key predictions from this model is that more competitive markets yield, ceteris paribus, higher levels of x-efficiency. This would increase the demand for labour. Competitive pressures force firm decision-makers to increase their effort levels, even if this their preferred preference. This outcome would be an unstable equilibrium if decision-makers' preferences for lower effort levels remain stable. Therefore, if environmental constraints are relaxed, one would predict a reversion to lower levels of effort and higher levels of x-inefficiency. Another prediction flowing from this model is that firms invest in sheltering activity to preserve an institutional environment where they can choose lower levels of effort input thereby increasing their level of utility at the cost to the firm and society through higher average costs and lower levels of x-efficiency.

But x-efficiency theory speaks to a much broader spectrum of labour effort supply than simply the supply of managerial (or decision-makers') effort. Leibenstein (1982) introduces the multi-agent firm, where conflict and conflict resolution in the context of cultural and institutional variables (inclusive of power relationships across agents) play a key role in determining the levels of effort levels supplied across agents to the firm. Leibenstein regards the determinants of principle-agent related x-inefficiency as analogous to a potential Prisoner's Dilemma-type problem that can only be resolved by changing the industrial relations system—injecting trust, honesty, fairness, transparency, legal recourse to conflict resolution, and conventions into the system—so that agents make choices consistent with Golden Rule or maximum x-efficiency outcomes. Cooperation and trust across agents is the penultimate solution to maximizing the effort dimension of labour supply whilst minimizing various transaction costs related to effort monitoring (Leibenstein, 1979, 1982, pp. 92–94, 1983). The alternative, adversarial method of managing the firm, incentivizes agents to veer towards the low productivity solution (Nash equilibrium), to the firm-based Prisoners' Dilemma problem.

In a more generalized behavioural model of effort-related labour supply and x-efficiency (Altman, 1992, 2001, 2002), unlike in the efficiency wage literature, the wage rate is only one determinant of effort as part the overall system of industrial relations. X-efficiency is maximized given the appropriate mix and level of material and nonmaterial incentives, although material incentives are typically quite important. Increasing x-efficiency can be a product of voluntary cooperation across agents to maximize output and economic payoffs to workers and members of the firm hierarchy. Or it can be a product to shocks to the system such as increasing wages and improved working conditions or increased competitive pressures that force firm decision-makers as well as agents (workers) to revolve Prisoner Dilemma-type problems to remain competitive given the new binding constraints facing the firm.

Unlike with efficiency wage theory, with a unique equilibrium wage, this behavioural model allows for multiple equilibria with regards to the wage and the overall compensation package and work environment. There is a wide array of levels of labour compensation consistent with some unique unit cost of production. Average unit cost is inelastic with respect to changes in the level of x-efficiency if productivity increases just offset changes in the level labour compensation, inclusive of the costs related to changes in the work environment. Increasing wages, for example, need not increase unit cost, while cutting wages need not reduce unit cost. For this reason, changes in the rate of labour compensation need not affect the competitive position of the firm. More specifically, increasing the level of x-inefficiency need not make a firm less competitive, whilst reducing the level of x-inefficiency need not make a firm more competitive. More or less competition need not affect the level of x-inefficiency in this behavioural model, since changes in the level of x-inefficiency need not affect average cost. Cost minimizing firms, can choose from a relatively large set of wage rates (or more comprehensively, compensation packages and work environments), contingent on the preferences of firm decision-makers and the power relationships across agents. Therefore, in this model there is no unique efficiency wage that must be chosen by rational cost minimizing, profit maximizing decision-makers. This behavioural model provides an analytical framework that allows for the persistence of x-efficiency under different competitive environments as well for multiple equilibria in terms of levels of x-efficiency. In this model, product markets can even be perfectly competitive or at least contestable. Moreover, wages can vary across firms without there being any difference in average costs given a compensating variation in effort inputs and thereby in productivity.

This effort related labour supply modelling can help explain how and why firms and economies with different wage rates and working conditions can persist over time and how x-inefficient firms can persist over time. The survival of the fittest (or the most x-efficient) does not hold when changes in effort inputs compensate for changes in labour costs. Decision-makers can choose from a variety of utility maximizing combinations of x-inefficiency and wages and working conditions as all of these can be consistent with competitive average costs and profits. In terms of the demand for labour, when labour costs changes are just offset by changes in productivity, there would be no change in the demand for labour as wages change, since shifts in the demand curve just offset changes in labour compensation.

Some of these points are illustrated in Fig. 10.5. In the standard approach, given the assumptions being made about effort variability, any increase in wages or improvements to working conditions generates an increase in average cost. Any decrease in the value of these variables result in a drop average cost. This is given by ACW. The slope of this curve is determined by production function parameters. The efficiency wage story is illustrated by curve EW. There exists some unique wage, W1, that yields a unique minimum average cost at A, given by e1. Any wage that differs from the efficiency wage generates a higher average cost. No rational cost-minimizing firm would choose a wage that differs from the efficiency wage, in this case, W1. The more general behavioural (x-efficiency) narrative is illustrated by curve BM. As wages increase or fall in the a to e5 space, there are no changes to average cost. There exists some horizontal constant cost linearity to this particular average cost function. This is based on the assumptions being made with regards to the causal relationship between wages, overall working conditions, industrial relations, effort inputs, and productivity. After a certain point, effort increases with regard to increases in costs hits a wall of seriously diminishing returns and the behavioural cost curve reverts to the standard one wherein increases in wages and related costs generate increasing average costs. Output consistent with wage W3 would be consistent with the Golden Rule solution to the productivity problem. But at wage W0, for example, pie size is much smaller and is veering towards a Prisoner's Dilemma solution to the productivity problem. In the behavioural model, higher wages can also be predicted to incentivize technological change shifting the cost curve from BM to BMTC, allowing wages higher than W3 to be consistent with the competitive average cost of 0A (Altman, 2009).

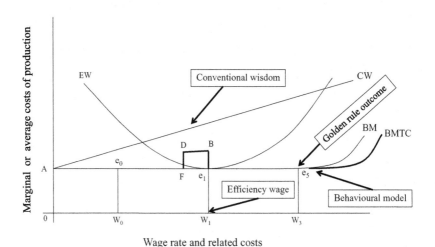

FIG. 10.5   Labour and production costs.

Further to the behavioural model, there are short terms costs involved in either increasing or decreasing the wage rate. This is given by FD or e1B. This is one reason that efficiency wage scholars find the nominal wage rate is sticky downward over the business cycle (Bewley, 1999). And since improving efficiency as wages increase involves short term costs, this can deter firms from engaging in higher wage-x-efficient strategies on their own (utility maximizing) volition, given trust levels and the uncertainty of future outcomes.

Some labour market implications of generalized x-efficiency theory

X-efficiency theory provides some insight into the observed effect of minimum wages and unions upon employment. The standard economics' prediction is that these variables will negatively affect the economy by reducing employment—making the marginal workers unemployable—and by making firms less competitive by increasing their average cost. To the extent that increasing wages, from minimum wage legislation or through collective bargaining, induces more effort and, thereby, productivity offsets to the increased labour costs, the predicted negative effects of minimum wages and unions need not transpire. The extent or size of the productivity offsets is an empirical question. In Fig. 10.5, increasing wages, up to a point (such as from W0 to W3), does not increase average cost and do not make firms less competitive.

In the standard model, increasing minimum wages (or even introducing minimum wages) or allowing unions to increase wages from some theoretical market clearing norm, causes employment to fall and labour supply to increase. In Fig. 10.6, the increase in the wage rate from W1 to WMWUN, yields an excess supply of labour, LEFL0. However, to the extent there is a x-efficiency effect

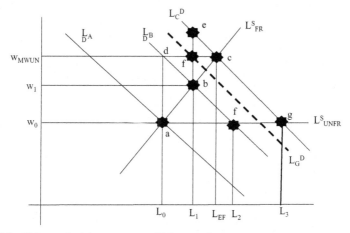

FIG. 10.6 Unions and minimum wages and labour markets.

of increasing the wage, the labour demand curve (based on marginal product curve) shifts outward from LBD to LGD or to LCD, for example. In the latter case, the labour market would clear at c, but at a higher level of employment. In the former case, there remains an excess supply of labour, only because one is assuming that more individuals are attracted onto the labour market by the increase in the wage rate. But the induced increased labour productivity restores employment to its prior level of L1. The extent to which the labour demand curve shifts outward is an empirical question. A similar argument can be made with respect to the impact of labour unions on the labour market. The evidence supports such a shift in the labour demand curve. (Card & Krueger, 1995; Doucouliagos & Stanley, 2009; Freeman & Medoff, 1984; Kaufman, 2010; Reich, Jacobs, & Dietz, 2014).

The flip side of this argument relates to the implications of wage cuts that might be a function of introducing rules and regulations that drive wages below the market-clearing wage in the context of standard supply and demand analyses (Altman, 2006a, 2006b). If such low wages can be maintained for institutional reasons, the standard model predicts that the supply of market labour falls and the demand for market labour increases along the respective supply and demand curves. But if this cut in wages has a negative impact on the effort supply per unit of labour, the demand curve for labour (based on marginal product curve) shifts inward, yielding a new but lower wage equilibrium, with less employment than when wages are higher. This point is illustrated in Fig. 10.6, with the initial labour market equilibrium at c; with demand LCD and labour supply LSFR. The wage rate drops to W0 for institutional reasons leading to an excess supply of labour (ag or L0L3). But the x-efficiency effect of the lower wage is to reduce effort inputs thereby reducing labour productivity, shifting the labour demand curve inward to LAD. And the market now clears at, a, at the lower wage W0 yielding employment L0.

This particular behavioural model of effort labour supply also casts some light on the efficiency wage theory of involuntary unemployment (Altman, 2006a, 2006b). Efficiency wage theory relies upon the assumption that there is a unique efficiency wage that yields an excess supply for labour—it is too high to clear the labour market (Akerlof, 2002; Akerlof et al., 1996, 2000; Bewley, 1999). But, to the extent that there is no unique efficiency wage, involuntary unemployment can be resolved from the supply side to the extent that relatively high wages are compensated for by relatively high levels of labour productivity and, therefore, higher levels of x-efficiency. Simply put, in the efficiency wage literature, there would be an efficiency wage given by WMWUN, for example, in Fig. 10.6. This wage rate is too high to clear the labour market at L1 and is, therefore, a supply side impediment to increasing employment. Cutting the wage to W1 wouldn't work since workers would reduce their effort inputs as a consequence, shifting the labour demand curve to the left, to LAD, keeping employment at its prior low level (see also Chapter 8).

This leads efficiency wage economists such as Akerlof and Fehr to posit that fairness considerations can generate excess levels of unemployment. One solution to this problem of the downward sticky real (and nominal) wage is to find a way of reducing the real wage whilst avoiding the predicted negative efficiency wage effect. This can occur if one assumes money illusion; that workers are quasi-rational and won't respond to mild inflation induced cuts to real wages (for transaction–cognitive costs reasons). In this case, the labour market clears at b at wage rate W1, along labour demand curve LBD. The labour demand curve does not shift inward, since effort inputs do not change as the real wage falls with mild inflation, for reasons of money illusion (Akerlof, 2002; Akerlof et al., 1996, 2000). This reintroduces the traditional long run Phillips Curve wherein there is a long run trade-off between inflation and unemployment—more inflation yields more employment and thereby lower rates of unemployment.

However, the behavioural-x-efficiency model suggests that money illusion is not required to restore full employment (Altman, 2006b). This is consistent with the vertical, inelastic, Philips Curve—there need not be a long run trade-off between inflation and unemployment (Friedman, 1968). Rather, if the higher wage WMWUN is associated with a higher level of x-efficiency such that the labour demand curve associated with this wage rate is LCD, the labour market clears at c and with LEF employment. If there is some linearity with regards to the wage-average cost relationship, then higher wages can yield the cost offsets necessary to allow the labour market to clear at the higher wage rates. Higher wages need not be the obstacle to 'full' employment suggested by standard economic theory and by the efficiency wage literature.

This point is further illustrated in Fig. 10.7. Assume that full employment is given by N2 and W2, in the standard model, given by marginal product of labour curve MP2. The market clears at e2. Efficiency wage theory assumes a market distorting efficiency wage of W1 and an equilibrium at e*. Employment is at N1, below full employment. Decreasing the wage to W2 is assumed to generate a reduction in effort inputs such that the marginal product curve shifts inward to MP3. In this case, decreasing the wage rate does not have the standard predicted effect of increasing employment. Only if workers are subject to money illusion will the marginal product curve be invariant to changes in the wage rate, allowing for full employment to be achieved by cutting real wages. But if increasing the wage rate from w2 to w1 yields a x-efficiency effect of shifting the marginal product curve upwards to MP1, full employment is obtained at N2 at the higher wage rate. The high wage x-efficiency full employment equilibrium is obtained at e1 (see also Chapter 8).

This is consistent with the evidence that across countries there is a positive relationship between wage rates and employment rates (Blanchflower & Oswald, 1995). There need not be a strict labour market constraint preventing the realization of full employment where the extent of x-efficiency is a function of the wages rate, working conditions, and system of industrial relations. Seeking means to increase productivity by increasing the extent of x-efficiency

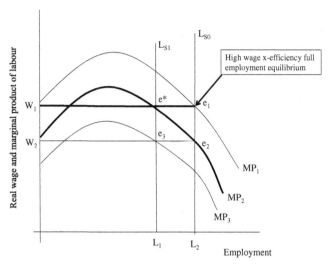

FIG. 10.7 Labour demand and marginal product.

and induced technological change is a plausible supply-side alternative to increase employment in contrast to the traditional focus on cutting real wages.

Population growth with real women

The standard economic approach to population growth is that men and women, together, decide on how many children to have. Or, men can be assumed to objectively represent the preferences of both men and women—men objectively represent household preferences. There is no conflict in preferences between men and woman. How many children a family decides to have is a product of the price or cost of having children and the quality of children the decision makers prefer to have. Prices and income and quality of product (children) determine decision making. This follows from the classic model developed by Becker (1976, 1981). But this type of model, ignores other factors that impact on the preferences of men and women and their ability (especially women) to realize their preferences.

The cost of having children is affected by the income women can earn on the labour market, when not pregnant and taking care of the kids. This represents the opportunity cost of having kids. Increase the opportunity cost, then one can predict a reduction in the preferred number of live children (this incorporates common knowledge on infant and child mortality. Therefore, increasing female employment opportunities and female wages should reduce the number of desired (live) children, as the costs of having children increases. And, moreover, it is assumed that individuals will tend to want higher quality children as they opt for fewer children. This further increases the costs of having children, further increasing the incentive to have fewer children. Within the cost model narrative, it is also noted that the cost contraceptives will affect the demand for live children. The lower the cost, the fewer the number of children desired (Easterlin, 1975).

Traditional economic factors are of importance. But on their own have difficulty in explaining the demographic changes taking place throughout the world. The world population growth rate is now (2019) around 1% per year. In the 1960s it was about 2% per annum. The 1960s represented a peak in the international populational growth rate and this rate has been declining continuously since. But from 1950 to the about 1990, world population doubled from about 2.5 to 5 billion. In the mid-nineteenth century the world's population stood at around 1.5 billion. Population growth was spectacular in the twentieth century not because women were having more and more children, but because given their target number of live children, death rates for children were collapsing. Eventually, birth rates dropped with the fall in death rates, dramatically reducing the rate of population growth.

But it does not appear that this demographic transition was a product of households simply engaging an economic-style cost-benefit analysis of having an additional child, though economic factors have played an important role. One of the missing pieces in the conventional approach is that it ignores the fact that men and women often have different preferences as to how many live children to have—how many children should one end up with. One difference in preferences relates to the fact that women are the ones having the child and raising the child. Women are the one's carrying the foetus to term and experiencing the pain of childbirth and also bearing the risk of dying at child birth—a major risk in the past but also currently ever present especially amongst women in less economically developed societies.

An alternative model (Altman, 1999) to better understand the choices people make with regards to the number children incorporates the reality the men and women tend to have different preferences, women tend to want fewer children than men (especially in less developed-high birth rate countries), and the power relationship between men and women and women and their families and peers are critically important. It can make a big difference if women have the power to actualize their preferences and also have ability to form their own 'true' preferences on the number of preferred preferences. These preferences are the preferences that women would have if they have access pertinent information related to contraception and child bearing, for example, and forming their preferences freely without coercion. Also significant is family planning education, especially for women. The evidence suggest that family planning education has little impact on men, but has a large impact of women's decision making, but only if women have the power to realize their preferences.

In this model, holding costs and income constant, one would predict that the number of live children (related to the number of preferred live children) will diminish when women are empowered in the decision making process, when they are free or freer to choose. Also, family planning education should negatively affect the number of live children given that women are free to choose.

Relatedly, providing women with capacity to form 'true' preferences will also have a negative effect on the number of live children, given appropriate education and the power to choose (Altman, 1999).

This model of how people make choices about the number of live children to target is actually a very good predictor of birth rates. In other words, even when the cost of having children is lower, one can expect birth rates to diminish when women have appropriate education, can form 'true' preferences and empowered to make choices about how many children to have. Women's empowerment also, eventually, affects the preferences of their husbands or partners. Assuming that choices are simply made with regards to costs and preferences for higher quality children is overly simplistic. Other factors are also fundamentally important to better understand choices generated particular birth rates and rates of population growth.

Conclusion

Behavioural models of labour markets are informed by how decision-making is affected by psychological, sociological, and institutional variables (on institutional variables, see Chapter 8, this book). A common concern of behavioural economists is that there are all too many empirical occurrences that are inconsistent with key elements of standard labour economic theory. As well, standard labour economics can't explain all too many labour market phenomenon. To better explain labour market behaviour and outcomes requires revisiting and revising some key simplifying modelling assumptions that are the mainstay of standard labour market theory.

In this chapter, I focus on three key areas where behavioural economics provides considerable theoretical insight. One area is the determinants of labour supply. This brings us to a discussion of a target theory of labour supply in contrast to the standard theory's focus on the income and substitution effects. Secondly, I pay critical attention to the fact that labour supply consists not only of time but effort as well. This contrasts with the standard view that effort inputs are fixed. Introducing effort variability impacts one's understanding of the demand side of the labour market through its impact on labour productivity. This affects one's understanding of employment levels and the effect of unions and minimum wages on employment and efficiency.

I also discuss the analytical and public policy insights that behavioural economics provide into what many behavioural economists refer to as errors and biases in decision-making that are said to produce inefficient labour market outcomes. In the standard modelling individuals are assumed to be calculating and omniscient, not subject to errors or biases in decision-making. Decisions are assumed to be optimal and not subject to regret.

Each school of behavioural economics, based on different methodological approaches to decision-making, proffers different solutions to correct for inefficient decision-making outcomes. If one assumes that individuals are fundamentally error-prone and biased then it becomes critical to de-bias decision-making. The alternative is to induce or force individuals to behave in a manner that's inconsistent with their preferences, but which is consistent with optimality and efficiency from the perspective of the expert.

If one assumes that individuals are largely rational and un-biased but sometimes do make error-prone decisions or decisions that are not optimal socially or even from the perspective of the decision-maker, the public policy focus is on changing the incentive and information environment and the capabilities of the decision-makers. This stands a good chance of inducing and facilitating choices that are more in line with individuals' own self-interest and that of society at large.

Both approaches to behavioural economics recognize and identify the gaps in the standard approaches to labour market modelling. Both approaches also have implications for understanding both the supply and demand sides of the labour market. Behavioural dimensions to decision-making, rational or not, affect our understanding of how much labour is supplied on the market as well as the determinants of labour productivity, which impacts on the demand side of the market. Behavioural economics thereby enriches the price and income–focused standard economic toolbox, generating alternative hypotheses to be tested and public policy designs to be evaluated. This is highly significant, given the importance of labour markets as determinants of the wealth of nations and the wellbeing of individuals.

References

Adams, S. (2012). *New study: Long-term unemployment viewed by hiring companies as worse than a criminal record.* Available at: Forbes Magazine http://www.forbes.com/sites/susan-adams/2012/09/18/new-study-long-term-unemployment-viewed-by-hiring-companies-as-worse-than-a-criminal-record/.

Akerlof, G. A. (1982). Labor contracts as partial gift exchange. *Quarterly Journal of Economics, 97*, 543–569.

Akerlof, G. A. (1984). Gift exchange and efficiency-wage theory: four views. *American Economic Review, Papers and Proceedings, 74*, 79–83.

Akerlof, G. A. (2002). Behavioral macroeconomics and macroeconomic behavior. *American Economic Review, 92*, 411–433.

Akerlof, G. A., Dickens, W. T., & Perry, G. L. (1996). The macroeconomics of low inflation. *Brookings Papers on Economic Activity, 1*, 1–59.

Akerlof, G. A., Dickens, W., & Perry, G. (2000). Near-rational wage and price setting and the long-run Phillips curve. *Brookings Papers on Economic Activity, 1*, 1–60.

Akerlof, G. A., & Shiller, R. J. (2009). *Animal spirits: How human psychology drives the economy, and why it matters for global capitalism.* Princeton: Princeton University Press.

Akerlof, G. A. & Yellen, J. L. (Eds.), (1986). *Efficiency wage models of the labour market.* Cambridge, England and New York: Cambridge University Press.

Akerlof, G. A., & Yellen, J. L. (1988). Fairness and unemployment. *American Economic Review, Papers and Proceedings, 78*, 44–49.

Akerlof, G. A., & Yellen, J. L. (1990). The fair wage hypothesis and unemployment. *Quarterly Journal of Economics, 105*, 255–283.

Alchian, A. A. (1950). Uncertainty, evolution and economic theory. *Journal of Political Economy*, *58*, 211–221.

Altman, M. (1992). The economics of exogenous increases in wage rates in a behavioral/X-efficiency model of the firm. *Review of Social Economy, 50*, 163–192.

Altman, M. (1999). A theory of population growth when women really count. *Kyklos, 52*, 27–43.

Altman, M. (2001). Preferences and labor supply: Casting some light into the black box of income – Leisure choice. *Journal of Socio-Economics, 31*, 199–219.

Altman, M. (2002). Economic theory, public policy and the challenge of innovative work practices. *Economic and Industrial Democracy: An International Journal, 23*, 271–290.

Altman, M. (2004a). Why unemployment insurance might not only be good for the soul, it might also be good for the economy. *Review for Social Economy, 62*, 517–541.

Altman, M. (2004b). The efficiency and employment enhancing effects of social welfare. In M. Oppenheimer & N. Mercuro (Eds.), *Law and economics: Alternative economic approaches to legal and regulatory issues* (pp. 257–285). Armong, New York: M.E. Sharpe Publishers.

Altman, M. (2005a). Behavioral economics, rational inefficiencies, fuzzy sets, and public policy. *Journal of Economic Issues, 34*, 683–706.

Altman, M. (2005b). Reconciling altruistic, moralistic, and ethical behavior with the rational economic agent and competitive markets. *Journal of Economic Psychology, 26*, 732–757.

Altman, M. (2006a). What a difference an assumption makes: Effort discretion, economic theory, and public policy. In M. Altman (Ed.), *Handbook of contemporary behavioral economics: Foundations and developments* (pp. 125–164). M.E. Sharpe: Armonk, New York.

Altman, M. (2006b). Involuntary unemployment, macroeconomic policy, and a behavioral model of the firm: Why high real wages need not cause high unemployment. *Research in Economics, 60*, 97–111.

Altman, M. (2008). Towards a theory of induced institutional change: Power, labor markets, and institutional change. In N. Mercuro & S. S. Batie (Eds.), *Alternative institutional structures* (pp. 300–329). London: Routledge.

Altman, M. (2009). A behavioral-institutional model of endogenous growth and induced technical change. *Journal of Economic Issues, 63*, 685–713.

Atkinson, A. B., & Micklewright, J. (1991). Unemployment compensation and labor market transitions. *Journal of Economic Literature, 29*, 1679–1727.

Babcock, L., Congdon, W. J., Katz, L. F., & Mullainathan, S. (2010). *Notes on behavioral economics and labor market policy*. Brookings Institute. http://www.brookings.edu/research/papers/2010/12/29-behavioral-econ-labor-market-policy (Accessed May 10, 2012).

Baxter, J. L. (1993). *Behavioural foundations of economics*. New York: St. Martin's Press.

Becker, G. S. (1965). A theory of the allocation of time. *Economic Journal, 75*, 493–517.

Becker, G. S. (1976). *The economic approach to human behavior*. Chicago and London: University of Chicago Press.

Becker, G. S. (1981). *A treatise on the family*. Cambridge, MA/London, England: Harvard University Press.

Ben-Ner, A., & Putterman, L. (2009). Trust, communication and contracts: An experiment. *Journal of Economic Behavior & Organization, 70*(1–2), 106–121.

Berg, N. (2006). Behavioral labor economics. In M. Altman (Ed.), *Handbook of contemporary behavioral economics* (pp. 457–478). New York: M.E. Sharpe.

Bewley, T. (1999). *Why wages don't fall during a recession*. Cambridge, MA: Harvard University Press.

Blanchflower, D. G., & Oswald, A. J. (1995). An introduction to the wage curve. *Journal of Economic Perspectives, 9*, 153–167.

Bowles, S., & Gintis, H. (1990, June). *Contested exchange: New microfoundations for the political economy of capitalism*. 165–222. Politics and Society.

Boyd, R., Gintis, H., Bowles, S., & Richerson, P. J. (2003). The evolution of altruistic punishment. *PNAS, 100*, 3531–3535.

Buchele, R., & Christainsen, J. (1999). Labor relations and productivity growth in advanced capitalist economies. *Review of Radical Political Economics, 31*, 87–110.

Camerer, C., Babcock, C., Lowenstein, G., & Thaler, R. (1997). Labor supply of New York cabdrivers: One day at a time. *Quarterly Journal of Economics, 112*, 407–441.

Card, D., & Krueger, A. B. (1995). *Myth and measurement: The new economics of the wage*. Princeton: Princeton University Press.

Charness, G., & Kuhn, P. (2011). *Lab labor: What can labor economists learn from the lab?* In Vol. 4 (Part A). *Handbook of Labor Economics* (pp. 229–330) San Diego: Elsevier Science.

Cross, G. (Ed.), (1988). *Worktime and industrialization: An international history*. Philadelphia: Temple University Press.

Darity, W., Jr., & Goldsmith, A. H. (1996). Unemployment, social psychology, and macroeconomics. *Journal of Economic Perspectives, 10*, 121–140.

Dessing, M. (2002). Labor supply, the family and poverty: The S-shaped labor supply curve. *Journal of Economic Behavior and Organization, 49*, 443–458.

Doucouliagos, C., & Stanley, T. D. (2009). Publication selection Bias in minimum-wage research? A meta-regression analysis. *British Journal of Industrial Relations, 47*, 406–428.

Duesenberry, J. S. (1949). *Income, saving and the theory of consumer behavior*. Cambridge, MA: Harvard University Press.

Easterlin, R. A. (1975). An economic framework for fertility analysis. *Studies in Family Planning, 6*, 54–63.

Easterlin, R. A. (2001). Income and happiness: Towards a unified theory. *Economic Journal, 111*, 465–484.

Edwards, P. (2012). Experimental economics and workplace behaviour: Bridges over troubled methodological waters? *Review of Socio-Economics, 10*, 293–315.

Falk, A., & Fehr, E. (2003). Why labour market experiments? *Labor Economics, 10*, 399–406.

Farber, H. S. (2005). Is tomorrow another day? The labor supply of New York City cabdrivers. *Journal of Political Economy, 113*, 46–82.

Fehr, E., & Gachter, S. (2000). Fairness and retaliation: The economics of reciprocity. *Journal of Economic Perspectives, 14*, 159–181.

Fehr, E., & Gachter, S. (2002). Altruistic punishment in humans. *Nature, 415*, 137–140.

Frank, R. (1985). *Choosing the right pond: Human behavior and the quest for status*. New York: Oxford University Press.

Frank, R. (1999). *Luxury fever why money fails to satisfy in an era of excess*. Princeton, NJ: Princeton University Press.

Frank, R. (2005). The mysterious disappearance of James Duesenberry. *New York Times*. Available at: http://www.nytimes.com/2005/06/09/business/09scene.html?_r=0.

Frantz, R. (1997). *X-efficiency theory: Evidence and applications* (2nd ed.). Boston/Dordrecht/London: Kluwer Academic Publishers.

Freeman, R. B., & Medoff, J. L. (1984). *What do unions do?*. New York: Basic Books.

Frey, B. S., & Stutzer, A. (2002). *Happiness and economics: How the economy and institutions affect human well-being*. Princeton, NJ: Princeton University Press.

Friedman, M. (1953). The methodology of positive economics. In M. Friedman (Ed.), *Essays in positive economics* (pp. 3–43). Chicago: University of Chicago Press.

Friedman, M. (1968). The role of monetary policy. *American Economic Review, 58*, 1–17.

Galbraith, J. K. (1958). *The affluent society*. New York: New American Library.

George, D. (2001). *Preference pollution: How markets create the desires we dislike*. Ann Arbor: University of Michigan Press.

Gigerenzer, G. (2007). *Gut feelings: The intelligence of the unconscious*. New York: Viking.

Gordon, D. M. (1998). Conflict and cooperation: An empirical glimpse of the imperatives of efficiency and redistribution. In S. Bowles & H. Gintis (Eds.), *Recasting egalitarianism: New rules for communities, states and markets* (pp. 181–207). London: Verso.

Gorski, P. (2008). Myth of the culture of poverty. *Poverty and Learning, 65*, 32–36.

Güth, W., Schmittberger, R., & Schwarze, B. (1982). An experimental analysis of ultimatum bargaining. *Journal of Economic Behavior and Organization, 3*, 367–388.

Hayek, F. A. (1945). The use of knowledge in society. *American Economic Review, 35*, 519–530.

Helliwell, J. F., & Huang, H. (2011). Well-being and trust in the workplace. *Journal of Happiness Studies, 12*, 747–767.

Henrich, J., Boyd, R., Bowles, S., Camerer, C., Fehr, E., Gintis, H., et al. (2001). In search of homo economicus: Behavioral experiments in 15 small-scale societies. *American Economic Review, Papers and Proceedings, 91*, 73–78.

Holmlund, B. (1998). Unemployment insurance in theory and practice. *Scandinavian Journal of Economics, 100*, 113–141.

Howell, D., & Azizoglu, B. (2011). *Unemployment benefits and work incentives: The US labor market in the great recession*. Political Economy Research Institute. Working paper no. 257.

Howell, D., & Rehm, M. (2009). Unemployment compensation and high European unemployment: A reassessment with new benefit indicators. *Oxford Review of Economic Policy, 25*, 60–93.

International Labour Organization. (2010). *World social security report 2010/11: Providing coverage in times of crisis and beyond*. Geneva: International Labour Organization.

Jahoda, M. (1981). Work, employment and unemployment: Values, theories and approaches in social research. *American Psychologist, 36*, 184–191.

Kahneman, D. (2003). Maps of bounded rationality: Psychology for behavioral economics. *American Economic Review, 93*, 1449–1475.

Kahneman, D. (2011). *Thinking fast and slow*. New York: Farrar, Strauss, Giroux.

Kahneman, D., & Tversky, A. (1979). Prospect theory: An analysis of decisions under risk. *Econometrica, 47*, 313–327.

Kaufman, B. E. (1989). Models of man in industrial relations research. *Industrial and Labor Relations Review, 43*, 72–88.

Kaufman, B. E. (1999). Expanding the behavioral foundations of labor economics. *Industrial and Labor Relations Review, 52*, 361–392.

Kaufman, B. E. (2010). Institutional economics and the minimum wage: Broadening the theoretical and policy debate. *Industrial and Labor Relations Review, 63*, 425–453.

Lebergott, S. (1993). *Pursuing happiness: American consumers in the twentieth century*. Princeton: Princeton University Press.

Leibenstein, H. (1950). Bandwagon, Snob, and Veblen effects in the theory of consumers' demand. *Quarterly Journal of Economics, 64*, 183–207.

Leibenstein, H. (1957). The theory of underemployment in densely populated backward areas. In H. Leibenstein (Ed.), *Economic backwardness and economic growth: Studies in the theory of economic development* (pp. 58–76). New York: John Wiley and Sons.

Leibenstein, H. (1966). Allocative efficiency vs. 'X-efficiency'. *American Economic Review, 56*, 392–415.

Leibenstein, H. (1979). A branch of economics is missing: Micro-micro theory. *Journal of Economic Literature, 17*, 477–502.

Leibenstein, H. (1982). The prisoner's dilemma in the invisible hand: An analysis of intrafirm productivity. *American Economic Review, 72,* 92–97.

Leibenstein, H. (1983). Property rights and X-efficiency: Comment. *American Economic Review, 83,* 831–842.

Levine, D. I., & D'Andrea Tyson, L. (1990). Participation, productivity, and the firm's environment. In A. S. Blinder (Ed.), *Paying for productivity: A look at the evidence* (pp. 183–237). Washington, DC: Brookings Institute.

Levitt, S. D., & List, J. A. (2008). Homo economicus evolves. *Science, 319,* 909–910.

Linn, M. W., Sandifer, R., & Stein, S. (1985). Effects of unemployment on mental and physical health American. *Journal of Public Health, 75,* 502–506.

Logue, J., & Yates, J. S. (1999). Worker ownership American style: Pluralism, participation and performance. *Economic and Industrial Democracy, 20*(2), 225–252.

Mack, R. P. (1956). Trends in American consumption and the aspiration to consume. *American Economic Review, 46,* 55–68.

March, J. G. (1978). Bounded rationality, ambiguity, and the engineering of choice. *Bell Journal of Economics, 9,* 587–608.

March, J. G., & Simon, H. A. (1968). *Organizations.* New York: John Wiley.

Maslow, A. H. (1954). *Motivation and personality.* New York: Harper and Row.

McKersie, R. B., & Klein, J. A. (1983). Productivity: The industrial relations connection. *National Productivity Review, 3,* 26–35.

Messenger, J. C., Lee, S., & McCann, D. (2007). *Working time around the world: Trends in working hours, Laws, and policies in a global comparative perspective.* New York: Routledge.

Mulligan, C. B. (2013). *The redistribution recession: How labor market distortions contracted the economy.* New York: Oxford University Press.

Organisation for Economic Co-operation and Development. (2003). Making work pay, making work possible. Chapter 3. In *OECD employment outlook 2003: Towards more and better jobs* (pp. 113–170). Available at: http://www.oecd.org/dataoecd/62/59/31775213.pdf.

Paul, K. I., & Moser, K. (2009). Unemployment impairs mental health: A meta analyses. *Journal of Vocational Behavior, 74,* 264–282.

Pencavel, J. H. (1986). Labor supply of men: A survey. In O. Ashenfelter & R. Laylard (Eds.), Vol. 1. *Handbook of labor economics* (pp. 3–102). Amsterdam: North Holland.

Pfeffer, J. (1995). Producing sustainable competitive advantage through the effective management of people. *The Academy of Management Executive, 9*(1), 55–69.

Prasch, R. E. (2000). Reassessing the labor supply curve. *Journal of Economic Issues, 34,* 679–692.

Putterman, L. (2012). *How much inequality is needed to support a strong economy?* Psychology Today. Available at: http://www.psychologytoday.com/node/100949. (Accessed 15 September 2012).

Reich, M., Jacobs, K., & Dietz, M. (Eds.), (2014). *When mandates work raising labor standards at the local level.* Berkeley, CA: University of California Press.

Rice, J. K., Wyche, K. F., Bowker-Turner, D., Bullock, H., Gamble, K., Lott, B., et al. (2013). *Making 'Welfare to Work' really work: Improving welfare reform for poor women, families and children.* American Psychological Association. Available at: http://www.apa.org/pi/women/programs/poverty/welfare-to-work.aspx.

Rigdon, M. L. (2002). Efficiency wages in an experimental labor market. *PNIS, 99,* 13348–13351.

Sanders, S. (2008). 'A pedagogical model of the relative income hypothesis.' Available at SSRN: http://ssrn.com/abstract=1262991 or https://doi.org/10.2139/ssrn.1262991.

Shane, F., & Loewenstein, G. (1999). Hedonic adaptation. In D. Kahneman, E. Diener, & N. Schwarz (Eds.), *Well being: The foundations of hedonic psychology* (pp. 302–329). Russell Sage Foundation: New York, NY.

Shapiro, C., & Stiglitz, J. E. (1984). Equilibrium unemployment as a worker discipline device. *American Economic Review, 74*, 433–444.

Sharif, M. (2000). Inverted 'S'—The complete neoclassical labour-supply function. *International Labour Review, 139*, 409–435.

Sherman, A., & Shavit, T. (2009). Welfare to work and work to welfare: The effect of the reference point: A theoretical and experimental study. *Economics Letters, 105*, 290–292.

Shiller, R. J. (2000). *Irrational exuberance*. Princeton: Princeton University Press.

Simon, H. A. (1955). A behavioral model of rational choice. *Quarterly Journal of Economics, 69*, 99–188.

Simon, H. A. (1978). Rationality as a process and as a product of thought. *American Economic Review, 70*, 1–16.

Simon, H. A. (1979). Rational decision making in business organizations. *American Economic Review, 69*, 493–513.

Simon, H. A. (1987). Behavioral economics. In J. Eatwell, M. Millgate, & P. Newman (Eds.), *The New Palgrave: A dictionary of economics* (pp. 266–267). London: Macmillan.

Smith, V. L. (2003). Constructivist and ecological rationality in economics. *American Economic Review, 93*, 465–508.

Solow, R. M. (1979). Another possible source of wage stickiness. *Journal of Macroeconomics, 1*, 79–82.

Solow, R. M. (1990). *The labor market as a social institution*. New York: Blackwell.

Solow, R. M. (2003). *Lessons learned from U.S. welfare reform*. Prisme: Cournot Centre for Economic Studies. Available at: http://www.centre-cournot.org/index.php/2003/11/26/lessons-learned-from-u-s-welfare-reform/#more-276/.

Starky, S. (2006). Scaling the welfare wall: Earned income tax credits. In *In Brief, PRB 05-98E*. Ottawa: Parliamentary Information and Research Service Library of Parliament.

Stuckler, D., & Basu, S. (2013). *The body economic: Why austerity kills*. London: Allen Lane.

Stutzer, A. (2004). The role of income aspirations in individual happiness. *Journal of Economic Behavior & Organization, 54*, 89–109.

Thaler, R. H., & Sustein, C. (2008). *Nudge: Improving decisions about health, wealth, and happiness*. New Haven/London: Yale University Press.

Todd, P. M., & Gigerenzer, G. (2003). Bounding rationality to the world. *Journal of Economic Psychology, 24*, 143–165.

Tomer, J. (1987). *Organizational capital—The path to higher productivity and well-being*. New York: Praeger Publishers.

Tversky, A., & Kahneman, D. (1981). The framing of decisions and the psychology of choice. *Science, 211*, 453–458.

Wilson, W. J. (1997). *When work disappears*. New York: Random House.

Winther, G., & Marens, R. (1997). Participatory democracy may go a long way: Comparative growth performance of employee ownership firms in New York and Washington states. *Economic and Industrial Democracy, 18*, 393–422.

Zukin, C. (2009). *The anguish of the unemployed*. Report, John J. Heldrich Center for Workforce Development, Rutgers, The State University of New Jersey. Available at: http://www.heldrich.rutgers.edu/sites/default/files/content/Heldrich_Work_Trends_.

Index

Note: Page numbers followed by *f* indicate figures and *t* indicate tables.

A

Average cost, 82–83, 109, 168, 172, 199–200, 265, 268

B

Bargaining power, 1, 88–89, 112, 181–182, 184, 199, 206–207, 246
Behavioural economics, 40–42, 46–48, 51
  assumptions matter and, 19–20
  conventional wisdom, 20–22, 34*f*
  Kahneman–Tversky approach
    choice behaviour, 219, 222–223
    financial asset prices, 228
    heuristics and biases approach, 237–238*t*
    individual decision-making, 219, 221
    investor behaviour, 227
    pension option, 225
  labour market decision-making, 246–247, 260
  Simon–March approach
    choice behaviour, 223
    institutional parameters, 218–219
    public policy, 239
    rational behaviour, 231
    rationality-smart individuals approach, 237–238*t*
Behavioural economists, 20–21, 39–41, 47, 71, 225, 227–228, 240, 258, 260
Bottom-up approach, 8, 10–11
  complexity in decision-making, 51–58
  superiority of, 55–56
Bounded rationality, 2, 4–6, 9–12, 14, 39–40, 51–52
  decision-making evolution, 20, 22–29
  freedom of choice, 116–117
  institutional and sociological factors, 26–27
  Simon–March approach
    bad investment decisions, 224
    choice behaviour, 223
    fast and frugal heuristics, 216–217
    financial education, 223, 236–239

high-risk savings plans, 225
individual decision-making, 213–214, 214–215*t*
institutional parameters, 218–219
institutions, 223, 231
interventions, in marketplace, 240–241
methodological terminology, 231
public policy, 239
rational behaviour, 216–217, 231
rational errors, 218
rationality-smart individuals approach, 237–238*t*
smart agents, 107, 120
x-inefficiencies/x-efficiencies, 116

C

Choice architecture, 32–33, 49, 118, 222
Choice behaviour, 19–24, 26, 29–30, 66*f*, 70, 149–150, 174–175, 219, 222–223
Choice x-efficiency, 115–116, 120, 136–137
Choice x-inefficiency, 116, 136–137, 142
Collateralized Debt Obligations (CDOs), 226
Competitive markets, 102, 139–140, 245–246, 266
Complexity, in decision-making, 17
  behavioural and institutional assumptions, 42–48
  bottom-up approach, 51–58
  ecological rationality and spontaneous order, 58–60, 63–67
  Hayek and behavioural economics, 40–42
  individualized norms for rationality, 51–58
  information complexity, 43
  institutional design, 60–63
  multiple equilibria, 63–67, 66*f*
  revisiting complexity and expert, 48–51
Conflicting preferences, 12, 35, 142, 163
Consumer choice, 80
Contemporary efficiency wage theory, 147–148, 159
Context-dependent rationality, 217
Conventional behavioural norms, 18, 21

Conventional economic theory, 40–41, 44, 47, 135–136
Corporate decision management, 112
Cost minimisation, 112
Cost offsets, 110–111

D

Darwinian process, 57, 62–64
Decision-making
  capabilities, 1–4, 10–12
  complexity in (*see* Complexity, in decision-making)
  environment, 1, 3–4, 6–8, 94, 99, 103–105, 112, 120–121, 125–126
  complex, 149–150
  evolution
    assumptions matter and behavioural economics, 19–20
    bounded rationality approach, 22–29
    conventional wisdom and behavioural economics, 20–22
    nudging *versus* constraints change, 32–33
    and redesign, 32–33
    satisficing and procedural rationality, 29–31
    x-efficiency theory and external benchmarks, 31–32
  financial literacy, socio-economic wellbeing
    bubbles and busts, animal spirits, 228–232
    informational problems and errors in, 232–233
  labour market (*see* Labour market decision-making)
  models, 9*f*
Demand management, 13, 190
Demand-side expansion, 189–190, 195–197

E

Ecological rationality, 41–42, 58–60, 63–67, 216–217
Efficiency wage theory, 150–156, 199, 201, 204–205, 258, 267
  labour market decision-making, 265–269
  Leibenstein's work on, 148
  origins of, 150–151
  revised, 156–163
  and x-efficiency theory, 265–269
Effort variability, 151–156, 198–199, 262–263
Error-prone, 19, 22, 28–29, 98, 106–107, 117
Errors and biases approach, 7, 10, 13–14, 47–49, 55, 57, 216–217, 219–222, 258–262
Externalities, 1, 3, 8–9, 13–14, 114

F

False preferences, 136–137, 140–142
Fast thinking, 2, 7–8, 10
Featherbedding, 155, 158–159
Financial advice, 224
Financial literacy, socio-economic wellbeing
  behavioural economics, 213, 215–216, 218, 222–224, 227
  conventional economic wisdom, 212–213, 214–215*t*, 215–216
  decision making
    bubbles and busts, animal spirits, 228–232
    informational problems and errors in, 232–233
  economic efficiency (x-efficiency), 212–213
  economic inefficiency (x-inefficiency), 212–213
  economic theory and public policy, 236–241, 237–238*t*
  education, 212, 222–224
  errors and biases and 'irrational' heuristics, 219–222
  fast and frugal decision-making and smart heuristics, 216–218
  financial illiteracy, economic losses, 212
  financial issues, 224
  incentives, 212
  institutional change and investment in, 212–213
  institutional parameters, 218–219
  investment, in financial assets, 227–228
  Kahneman–Tversky approach (*see* Kahneman–Tversky approach)
  pensions and saving, 224–226
  quality information, 212
  Simon–March approach (bounded rationality-smart decision maker) (*see* Simon-March approach)
  trust heuristic, 233–234
  voting behaviour, 212
Freedom of choice
  alternative model
    of preference formation, 132–134
    of welfare maximization, 136–141
  bounded rationality, 116–117
  choice x-inefficiency, 142
  conventional perspectives and critiques, 134–136
  rational inefficiency, 116–117
Free-market economics, 39–40, 68–69
Friedman's approach, 20, 76
Full employment, 161, 191–193, 202

G

Game theory, 177–178, 180–181
Generalized x-efficiency theory, 269–272
Golden Rule/maximum x-efficiency outcomes,
    266, 268

H

Hardwired-biased behaviour, 107, 117
Hayek's research
    behavioural and institutional assumptions,
        42–48
    complexity, in decision-making (*see*
        Complexity, in decision-making)
    emotions and intuition, 47–48
    implicit and explicit assumption, 41, 62–63
    top-down approach, 46, 56–58
Herd behaviour, 221
Heuristics and biases approach, 2, 4–10, 18,
    27, 44, 49, 118
Homo economicus, 48, 69, 79
Human behaviour models, 47
Humean fallacy, 95–96

I

Ideal preference index (IPI), 143
Individuals decision-making capabilities,
    20–21, 23, 25, 33–34, 94, 102, 104,
    116–117, 125–126
Information processing, 42–43, 114, 216–218,
    245–246, 261
Institutional design, 60–63, 131–133, 156
Intuitive thinking, 47
Involuntary employment
    behavioural model and, 198–206
    Keynes and demand side, 195–197
    Keynes and real wage rate, 191–195
Involuntary unemployment, 153, 158–159

K

Kahneman–Tversky approach, 21–22, 26, 106,
    148–149
    behavioural economics
        choice behaviour, 219, 222–223
        financial asset prices, 228
        heuristics and biases approach, 237–238*t*
        individual decision-making, 219, 221
        investor behaviour, 227
        pension option, 225
    decision-making
        choice irrationality, 219
        cognitive biases, 221

emotion and intuition, 219, 222–223
emotive variables, 230
systematic errors and biases, 213,
    214–215*t*
trust heuristic, 233–234
errors and biases, labour market
    decision-making, 260–261
heuristics, 221
irrationality, 229–230
neoclassical norms, 219
nudging, 228
prospect theory, 220
psychological variables, 218–219
rational behaviour, 222–223
slow and fast thinking narrative, 223

L

Labour market decision-making, 153, 194–195
    behavioural labour economics, 246–247, 260
    bounded rationality approach, 247, 261–262
    cognitive biases, 261
    demand for labour and supply of effort,
        262–264
    discrimination, 255
    economic deprivation, 256–257
    efficiency wage and x-efficiency theory,
        265–269
    generalized x-efficiency theory, 269–272
    Kahneman–Tversky errors and biases
        approach, 260–261
    labour supply
        behavioural model of, 250–255
        non-labour market income, 255–257
        standard labour-leisure model of, 247–249
        unemployment insurance, 257–258
    non-economic variables and errors/biases,
        258–262
    population growth, women, 272–274
    social welfare, 255–257
    sub-optimal errors-prone and biased
        decisions, 246–247
    target approach, 250–255
Labour supply
    labour market decision-making
        behavioural model of, 250–255
        non-labour market income, 255–257
        standard labour-leisure model of, 247–249
        unemployment insurance, 257–258
    maximum net revenue, 155
Leibenstein, Harvey, 110–111
    economic theory, 149–150
    modelling, 153, 155, 163, 173, 179–180
    optimal revenue, 153–155

Lexicographical/L-shaped indifference curves, 251–252
Life-cycle hypothesis, 224–225
Long run errors, 58
Long-term unemployment, 259, 261

M

Macroeconomic choices, 120–124
Macroeconomic policy, 123–124, 191, 204–207
Marginal product
  curves, 153–155
  labour
    demand, 154f, 162f
    and efficiency wages, 157f
    and increasing wages, 160f
Marginal product of labour (MPL) curve, 194–195
Market economy, 76, 139–140
Maximization-of-returns assumption, 95–96
Mean reversion hypothesis, 228
Meta-preferences, 135–136, 141
Microeconomic theory, 165
Minimum wages, 192–193, 203
Monetary/fiscal policy, 123
Money illusion, 123, 193–194, 199, 202–203, 205
Multiple equilibria, 63–67, 66f
  in consumption, 79–80
  economic entities, 80–81
  efficiency–inefficiency spectrum, 80–81
  formulation, 79
  historical and logical time, 87
  labour productivity, 83, 85–86
  production, 80–82
    scenarios, 86
    x-inefficiency and agency, 84–86
    x-inefficiency and managerial slack, 82–84
  rent seeking and x-efficiency, 87

N

Natural selection, 95–96
Negative externalities, 139
Neoclassical behavioural norms, 18, 21, 41–42
Neoclassical rationality, 2–4, 9–10, 148–149
New-Keynesian approach, 202–203
Non-cooperative solutions, 112
Non-labour costs, 200–201
Non-labour market income, 255–257
Normative theory, 117, 134

Norms, 23, 30, 32, 34, 148–149
1/N rule, 227–228
Nudging vs. constraints changes, 32–33
Null hypothesis, 22

O

Optimal behaviour, 31–32
Optimality, 3, 6–7, 9–10, 76, 274–275
Organizational capabilities, 115–117

P

Pareto-superior outcomes, 90
Phillips Curve, 271
Ponzi scheme, 234–236
Population growth, women, 272–274
Posner's perspective, 231
  emotive variables, 230
  incentive environment, 231
  institutional failure, 231
  telescoping thinking, 230
Power dynamics, 112
Power relationships, 93, 102, 116, 121–123, 126
Preference formation, 132–134, 137, 139–140, 140f
Price distortions, 150
Price mechanism, 43, 69
Price theory, 20–21, 26
Prisoner Dilemma (PD) model, 111–112, 266–268
Procedural rationality, 29–32, 51–52
Production possibility frontier (PPF), 68–69, 68f
Profit maximization, 24, 83, 112, 153, 157–158, 173
Psychology-based assumptions, 34f

Q

Quasi-rationality, 199, 202–203, 205

R

Rational choice behaviour, 94–95, 98–99, 106, 115–116
Rationality, 2–4, 94–99
  ecological rationality, 58–60
  inefficiency, 94–99, 114, 127f
    consumption inefficiencies, 115–120
    efficiency, and rationality, 99–102
    institutions, 99–102
    macroeconomic choices, 120–124

production inefficiency, 107–115
and rational behaviour, 120–124
types of, 102–107
satisficing and procedural, 29–31
social rationality, 101
types of, 102–107
Real wages, 151–156, 191–195
Reciprocal punishment, 263
Regret, 94, 103
Rent-seeking firms, 87, 114
Reservation wage, 248–249
Revealed preferences, 131–132, 136, 139–141
Revised efficiency wage theory, 156–163

S
Short run errors, 60
Simon-March approach
behavioural economics
choice behaviour, 223
institutional parameters, 218–219
public policy, 239
rational behaviour, 231
rationality-smart individuals approach, 237–238t
decision making
bad investment decisions, 224
financial education, 223, 236–239
institutions, 223, 231
interventions, in marketplace, 240–241
fast and frugal heuristics, 216–217
high-risk savings plans, 225
individual decision-making, 213–214, 214–215t
methodological terminology, 231
rational behaviours, 216–217
rational errors, 218
Slow thinking, 2, 7–8, 10
Smart agents, 3, 98–99, 107–110, 115, 120
Smart expert, 48–51
Social welfare, labour market decision-making, 255–257
Somatic marker hypothesis, 217

Spontaneous order
and ecological rationality, 58–60, 63–67
production possibility frontier (PPF) and, 68–69, 68f
utility and preferences, 67f
S-shaped labour supply curve, 249
Subjective expected utility (SEU) theory, 21–22, 51–52, 106
Sub-optimal decisions, 19, 25, 29, 31–32
Suboptimality, preferences and choices, 133
Suboptimal outcomes, 75–76
Substantive rationality, 53

T
Tacit information, 48, 50
Top-down approach, Hayek's research, 46, 56–58
True preferences, 97–98, 115–118, 134–135, 137–138

U
Ultimatum Game experiments, 263
Unemployment
insurance, 257–258
rate, 121–124
real wages and, 156
Unique equilibrium, 77, 80, 89–90

W
Wage flexibility, 190–191, 204
Welfare maximization choices, 136–141

X
X-efficiency theory, 31–32, 148, 163–177, 258, 265–269
Leibenstein's work on, 148
and rent seeking, 87
X-inefficiency theory
and agency, 84–86
and managerial slack, 82–84

Printed in the United States
By Bookmasters